Boundaries in Question

BOUNDARIES IN QUESTION

New Directions in International Relations

Edited by
John MacMillan and Andrew Linklater

PINTER
PUBLISHERS
LONDON & NEW YORK

Distributed in the United States
by St. Martin's Press

PINTER
An imprint of Cassell Publishers Limited
Wellington House, 125 Strand, London WC2R 0BB, England

First published in 1995

© The editors and contributors, 1995

Distributed exclusively in the USA by St. Martin's Press Inc.,
Room 400, 175 Fifth Avenue, New York, NY 10010, USA

British Library Cataloguing in Publication Data
A CIP catalogue record for this book is available from the British Library

ISBN   1 85567 265 0 (hb)
        1 85567 266 9 (pb)

Library of Congress Cataloging-in-Publication Data
A CIP catalog record for this book is available from the Library of Congress

Set in Monotype Ehrhardt by Ewan Smith
Printed and bound in Great Britain by Biddles Ltd,
Guildford and King's Lynn

Contents

Contributors

Simon Bromley is a lecturer in the Department of Politics at the University of Leeds.

Robin Brown is a lecturer in Political Communications in the Institute of Communications Studies at the University of Leeds.

Molly Cochran is a research student at the London School of Economics.

Richard Devetak is a research student and teaching assistant at Keele University.

Peter Doran is a research student at the Department of Politics and International Relations at the University of Kent at Canterbury.

Andrew Dorman, *Thomas Otte* and *Wyn Bowen* are research students at the Graduate School of International Studies, the University of Birmingham.

Rick Fawn is a research student at the London School of Economics and has taught International Relations and Central and East European Politics at Keele University and the LSE; he was editor of *Millennium: Journal of International Relations*.

Anne Guest is a research student in the Department of Politics at the University of Southampton.

Jill Krause is a lecturer in International Studies at Nottingham Trent University.

Kelley Lee is a lecturer in the Health Policy Unit at the London School of Hygiene and Tropical Medicine.

Andrew Linklater is a Professor of International Relations at Keele University.

John MacMillan is a lecturer in International Relations at Keele University.

Simon Mercado is a research student at Nottingham Trent University.

Robert O'Brien is a lecturer in International Relations in the School of English and American Studies at the University of Sussex.

Matthew Paterson is a lecturer in International Relations at Keele University.

Julian Saurin is a lecturer in International Relations in the School of African and Asian Studies at the University of Sussex.

Preface and acknowledgements

The majority of chapters in this volume were first presented at the 'New Directions in International Relations' conference held at Keele University on 23–24 September 1993. The conference was intended to provide a forum for those who had recently embarked upon an academic career or were at an advanced stage of postgraduate research. The objective was to meet one another in as informal an atmosphere as possible in order to gain a sense of how the field was developing.

The support and assistance of a number of people were invaluable in bringing the conference to fruition. Alex Danchev and Gillian Youngs provided encouragement from the outset; Maureen Groppe and Annette Owen provided valuable organizational assistance; and the Keele Department of Research Development and Business Affairs provided much appreciated financial support. Matthew Ball, Aishe Bhatti, Alan Collins, Michael Keaveney, Manisha Marwaha, Rahul Moodgal, Peter Newell and Thai Tan are to thank for ensuring the smooth running of the conference. Thanks go also to Christopher Brewin, Stuart Croft, Ranvir Kanwar, David Scrivener, Hidemi Suganami and Charlotte Thomson for chairing panels. Finally, the organizers would like to thank all those who participated in the conference for making it a worthwhile and enjoyable event (even if they do say so themselves!).

Abbreviations and acronyms

ACUNS	Academic Council of the UN
ARRC	Allied Command Europe Rapid Reaction Corps
CEFTA	Central European Free Trade Agreement
CFE	Conventional Forces in Europe
CIS	Commonwealth of Independent States
EC	European Community
ECOSOC	Economic and Social Council
FEP	foreign economic policy
FPA	foreign policy analysis
GATT	General Agreement on Tariffs and Trade
GEP	global environmental politics
GPE	global political economy
IDA	International Development Association
ILO	International Labour Organization
IMF	International Monetary Fund
IO	international organization
IPE	International Political Economy
IR	International Relations
LDC	less developed country
NAFTA	North American Free Trade Agreement
NATO	North Atlantic Treaty Organization
NGO	non-governmental organization
NIC	newly industrializing country
NIEO	New International Economic Order
NWO	New World Order
OECD	Organization for Economic Cooperation and Development
OMVS	Organisation pour la mise en valeur du fleuve Sénégal
OPEC	Organization of Petroleum Exporting Countries
START	Strategic Arms Reduction Talks
TNC	transnational corporation
UNCTAD	United Nations Conference on Trade and Development
UNDP	United Nations Development Programme
UNEP	United Nations Environment Programme
UNICEF	United Nations Children's Fund
UNGA	United Nations General Assembly
UNHCR	United Nations High Commissioner for Refugees
WHO	World Health Organization
WCED	World Commission on Environment and Development
WTO	World Trade Organization

Introduction: Boundaries in question[1]

Andrew Linklater and John MacMillan

EVOLUTION OF A DISCIPLINE

How cosy it was for students of International Relations in the 1960s, and how much easier for students throughout the 1970s and 1980s than it is now. Students in the 1960s could be quietly confident of mastering the discipline by understanding a small number of key texts centred on the writings of Carr, Claude, Herz, Morgenthau and Waltz. The debate between realism and idealism had apparently been resolved and a sense of the tragic uniqueness of international relations had been secured by the classic texts. A second debate emerged in the 1960s – the debate between science and traditionalism – though this hardly shook the discipline to its foundations and for many scholars life went on much as before (Bull, 1966). In this period, the discipline was crucially concerned with anarchy, the state and war, the foreign policy of the main powers, decolonization and modernization, and the role of international organizations. Engagement with other disciplines was rare. There was a firm consensus about the nature of the discipline, a small number of dissidents aside (Burton, 1972; Falk and Mendlovitz, 1966; Falk, 1987). Such clarity of focus meant that students were secure in the discipline. The basics mastered, students needed only to browse through the small number of dedicated journals to keep abreast of the field and to await the appearance of new works set within the dominant paradigms and concerned with the nature of the international system or the structure of international society. These could be found on the well-funded recent acquisitions shelf in the university library or on the shelf of a hospitable tutor with ample time to get to know each student by his or her first name.

Whether or not this caricature rings true, the discipline was more sharply focused in the 1960s than it has been in subsequent decades. Over the last twenty-five years its parameters have widened considerably and serious doubts have been raised about the value and legitimacy of a separate discipline of International Relations. Those writers who took issue with the dominant paradigms in the late 1960s and early 1970s aimed to enlarge a discipline which had been too narrowly defined by state-centric realism. The rise of foreign policy analysis in the United States, psychological approaches to decision-making and the study of transnational relations reflected this desire to enlarge the vision of International Relations by strengthening links with cognate fields.

This observation is also true of developments in the 1970s which explored the neighbouring field of international political economy in order to analyse growing international interdependence. As these perspectives began to make their mark upon the discipline, new questions began to be raised about the inherent conservatism of state-centric analysis, specifically in regard to the Third World and global inequality. The interest in dependency theory illustrated this widening intellectual focus, which encouraged a growing interest in sociology and normative political theory. The desire to create a different normative focus began to emerge and connections with approaches outside International Relations, as it had previously been defined, began to be made. By the end of the 1970s the discipline was firmly entrenched within the inter-paradigm debate which revolved around, although it was not entirely exhausted by, the famous trichotomy of realism, pluralism and structuralism (Smith et al., 1981).

Disquiet that the emerging agenda was in danger of becoming too diffuse was expressed in the light of these developments. Waltz's *Theory of International Politics* (1979) revamped the argument for a coherent discipline which was primarily concerned with the nature of anarchy and its implications. Liberal and radical perspectives (and many realist perspectives) were accused by Waltz of mistaking superficial and transient phenomena for the deep structure of the international system. Slightly more generous to the critics of realism, though equally keen to hold pluralism and structuralism in check, Holsti (1985) sought to protect realism from challenges from liberal and dependency perspectives.

But although the hegemony of neo-realism continued, most noticeably in the United States, these attempts to re-establish the boundaries of the discipline failed to produce any lasting consensus. Throughout the 1980s various challenges to realist orthodoxy emerged, tapping a vein which had earlier been ignored, namely Marxism and contemporary European social theory. Arguments about the poverty of neo-realism suggested a deep crisis in the discipline which found favour in many quarters and produced an attempted rebuttal from scholars committed to the traditional state-centric agenda (Ashley, 1984). The traditional agenda remains strong and important; however the proliferation of new and profound themes and perspectives engaging issues of inequality, the environment, identity and gender continues unabated. No single perspective about the nature of the discipline now commands a general consensus (see Rosenau, 1993), and evidence that a unifying overview is likely to appear is scarce. International Relations is less the dividing than the divided discipline in the 1990s.

RETHINKING BOUNDARIES

The traditional boundaries of the discipline were not carved out in isolation from features of the world 'out there'. Confidence in the nature of intellectual boundaries reflected an equal degree of confidence in the stability of the boundaries of the most influential sovereign states. Realism conveyed this sense of the security of political boundaries through the vocabulary of rational actors and monolithic units pursuing objectively ascertainable national interests within the constraints of anarchy. The process of state-building seemed more or less complete in the modern West, and no emergent challenge to state power was observed lurking in the wings. The process of state-building seemed troubled and incomplete in parts of the Third World but, at least for modernization theorists, powerful logics of nation-building held out the promise that Western history would become universal (Tilly, 1992). The growing impact of trans-national actors and processes did not pass unnoticed by traditional state-centric analysis, although invariably this impact was regarded as minor when compared with the politics of national security. Confidence in the tenacity of intellectual boundaries was anchored in confidence in the survival of the superpowers and their respective spheres of influence, combined with faith in the stabilizing consequences of nuclear bipolarity. In the late 1970s Waltz posed the question 'who is likely to be around 100 years from now – the United States, the Soviet Union, France, Egypt, Thailand, and Uganda? Or Ford, IBM, Shell, Unilever, and Massey-Ferguson?' Waltz answered that he 'would bet on the states, per-haps even on Uganda' (1979: 95). So much for predictions about the survival of the boundaries of apparently secure sovereign states.

The end of the post-war era has produced the familiar incantations that nothing fundamental has changed, and that the political conflicts with which Thucydides would have been familiar will survive, and may even be ex-acerbated, in the aftermath of the bipolar age (Mearsheimer, 1990). From the vantage point of the new approaches represented in this volume, these efforts to render the world familiar overlook some fundamental long-term patterns of change (Richardson, 1993). Few chapters in this volume doubt that states will be around a hundred years hence, but they strongly suggest that even the most powerful will be very different from sovereign states of old.

Drawing upon recent post-structuralist writing, Chapter 1 argues that the process of completing states is never finished and that political boundaries are more tenuous than traditional analysis has supposed. Chapter 2 explores normative questions which arise now that the sovereign state is threatened by the interlinked processes of globalization and political fragmentation. Chapter 3 stresses the impact of globalization upon the contemporary states system by describing the demise of 'the national project'; Chapter 4 draws attention to the processes of transporting culture into Central Europe; and Chapter 11 considers the implications of the dramatic rise of global environmental politics for Western conceptions of modernity.

The argument of these chapters is that the significance of conventional boundaries has been eroded by globalization and the burgeoning sub-national revolt. There is renewed support for the contention that many of the crucial actors in the world political system are not states but sub-national movements, transnational corporate interests, social movements and regional and universal international organizations. Of the latter, the United Nations is more inclined than it was in the Cold War age to breach sovereign boundaries to assist the victims of the failed or quasi-state (Jackson, 1990; Helman and Ratner 1992–93; Roberts, 1993; Halliday, 1994). However, the novel theme concerns processes rather than actors. Important economic, technological and cultural processes of global change clearly escape sovereign control and advance across national boundaries with astonishing speed and with remarkable ease. Communications technology and media coverage, integrated capital markets, the international division of labour and high levels of economic interdependence, modern instruments of intelligence and surveillance, the transmission of ideas and images (many of them Western or American) have blurred the divide between domestic and international politics.

The internationalization not only of elite culture but of mass culture in general is one of the major consequences of globalization. The outlines of a cosmopolitan culture are evident, as is the unmistakable revolt against Western ideas and ethnic fragmentation in Western and non-Western states alike, the latter being the most pronounced feature of the post-Cold War world (*Journal of Democracy*, October 1993). In some respects the politics of ethnicity may endeavour to reaffirm conventional political boundaries, but in other respects the ethnic revolt is the most important way in which these boundaries are being contested or redrawn. The idea that 'plus ça change, plus c'est la même chose', associated with some realist diagnoses of the post-Cold War world (Meirsheimer, 1990) needs to be balanced by the recognition that with the global revolution in technology and communications political boundaries are extraordinarily porous and offer low resistance to an assortment of external pressures and influences. Nevertheless, the shape of political boundaries over the next decade or so will depend heavily on the outcome of the interplay between the forces of globalization and fragmentation.

International Relations can no longer be regarded as the analysis of the relations between clearly and securely bounded sovereign states responding to the challenges of an immutable anarchy. The wasteland between states to which Michael Donelan (1978) referred is now pervaded with complex global economic and social linkages which suggest that Global Politics should replace International Relations. Whether or not this is a compelling move, it is clear that disciplinary boundaries have been thrown into confusion. Great uncertainty now exists not only about appropriate methodologies in the field but, more deeply, about whether or not International Relations possesses a clearly bounded intellectual domain or a distinctive subject matter.

What is clear is that the orthodox claim that international anarchy traps sovereign states in an unending struggle for power and security is a less insightful proposition than once seemed the case. Though the struggle for power and security is unlikely to be eliminated, important claims about the liberal zone of peace and the obsolescence of major war between Western industrialized societies have challenged the realist thesis that war is endemic within the international system. Orthodox conceptions of International Relations which stress the recurrent and repetitious no longer command the same respect. The realist claim that International Relations deals with an immutable realm for which no progressivist interpretation is possible is one that many scholars now reject on empirical grounds and oppose ethically because the discipline, so constructed, invites human beings to resign themselves to political circumstances which the critics believe can be transformed. This is the single most important transition within the discipline in recent years. It is interwoven with a massive literature on the growth of regional organizations and integration, the rise of the trading state, the existence of a security community amongst the Western industrialized societies and the absence of war between liberal states, which reinforces Wendt's (1992) astute observation that anarchy is what states make it.

Yet many of the chapters in this book (and especially Chapters 11, 12 and 14) would deny that their critique of realist and neo-realist images of immutability betrays a commitment to a progressivist account of international politics couched in the modernist discourse of the Enlightenment. They argue that many current global problems are inextricably connected with basic Enlightenment themes – for instance, that the human species has an unfettered right to subdue and transform nature. They add that the Western idea of progress has involved the devastation of the physical environment, acts of violence against allegedly inferior cultures and the systematic destruction of indigenous peoples.

The declining influence of realism is not accompanied by the return of some simplistic variant on early twentieth-century idealism. Many IR scholars deny that the state is capable of managing existing problems and of steering the human race towards a better moral condition, however defined. The growing sense that anarchy is what states make it is not coupled with any resounding confidence in the state's capacity to bring about profound and necessary political change. The contention that the state is an obstacle to peace and justice is not new. What is new is the peculiar conjunction whereby many authors deny that political boundaries are essentially fixed or that the context of anarchy is immune to significant change, yet simultaneously resist traditional theoretical and practical alternatives anchored in Western conceptions of nature, freedom, progress, the state and gender. The quest for an appropriate conceptual framework which rejects realism and neo-realism on empirical and normative grounds and searches for a critical standpoint which escapes traditional idealist confines is the primary task facing the discipline at the end of the Cold War age.

NARRATIVES OF CHANGE

The path beyond realism which recovers a critical standpoint involves reconsidering traditional accounts of the state. Two important ways in which the rise of the state has been narrated need rethinking: they are the progressivist and the geopolitical narratives. The progressivist narrative defends the state's place as a site for the realization of an ethical political community and stresses the state's role in realizing the principles of human equality and self-determination. According to progressivists such as Hegel, the state was valued because it enabled individuals to realize their freedom and provided citizens with membership of a cohesive, bounded community. Externally, it was expected that the state would recognize the equal rights of other states, at least within the ambit of Europe, so bringing an element of civilization to an otherwise violent international realm. The ability of the state to colonize non-European regions was cited as evidence of the superiority of the modern European state, indeed of the West as a whole. Yet the main progressivist narratives assumed that the modern European state would fulfil its mission in the non-European regions by providing the peoples there with access to the considerable spiritual and material achievements of Western civilization. Though at its peak in the nineteenth century, the progressivist narrative was reinforced during the twentieth century by the state's increased involvement in the area of social welfare, so adding social rights to the legal and political rights previously won by citizens.

In the early twentieth century confidence in the progressivist narrative began to be seriously challenged. The Marxist Left pointed to the rise of monopoly capital and the new imperialism. Liberals and the non-Marxist Left pointed to capital concentration, the perils of the nationalization of 'the social question' and the rise of jingoism and protectionism, each presaging greater failures to come. The Gladstonian faith that a concert of powers could take responsibility for international political management, and the conviction that international *laissez-faire* would promote the interests of peoples everywhere and encourage greater union, became increasingly difficult to maintain. The progressivist narrative began to envisage new models of economic and political organization, or new experiments in international cooperation, as remedies for the worsening condition. Writers at the end of the First World War argued that the balance of power should be replaced by collective security while international civil society should be managed by a complex web of global institutions. Writers at the end of the Second World War introduced the bolder suggestion that the state in Western Europe needed to share power and influence with a range of international authorities within a federal political structure. In response to the crisis of the early twentieth century, the progressivist narrative jettisoned an earlier assumption that the sovereign state was a sacrosanct form of political organization and imagined the state as a partner working with groups within civil society to realize international normative aspirations. The state was less highly esteemed in such accounts, but it was still regarded as a crucial engine of reform in international relations. Two major inter-continental wars and the rise of totalitarianism in the twentieth century dashed much of the confidence not only in the progressivist narrative but in the related supposition that the state could have a positive role in promoting international political change.

Whereas the progressivist interpretation focuses upon the state as an agent of reform, the geopolitical narrative focuses on the state as a power-container (Giddens, 1981). The literature on how the modern state originated and was able to accumulate political and military power demonstrates the importance of the geopolitical narrative. To illustrate, Mattingly (1962) argued that the modern state survived the turmoil of the fifteenth and sixteenth centuries by solving the problem of scale: by being neither too large nor too small to cope with the military challenges of the time. The state was small enough to be organized from a central administrative point but large enough to defend itself from external threats. Italian city states had been sufficiently compact to be centrally administered but proved to be too small to remain viable in military terms. The major sprawling empires were large enough for the purposes of conducting war but too large to be administered from a central point or to be viable economically. The territorial state turned out to be better adapted than the forms of political organization with which it was in competition. Uniquely adapted for the ordeal of war, the state survived the struggle for political dominance in Europe (Tilly, 1992). Modelski (1978) added that the state's solution to the problem of scale facilitated the creation of the great overseas empires. Secure in its boundaries, the state developed the military and bureaucratic apparatus that made the projection of imperial power possible. Those who wished to free themselves from the Western empires had to emulate the West by establishing their own sovereign boundaries to protect their economic and political interests. So did the state come to be exported to all parts of the world.

The geopolitical narrative stresses the state's accumulation of military and political power, its capacity to direct affairs within sovereign boundaries and its ability to project its power overseas. As the twentieth century has progressed many states have encountered new problems regarding scale. The state is no longer able to act autonomously in either the geopolitical or welfare domains. Neither de Gaulle nor Mitterrand was able to resist the power of international capital; both the British Labour and Conservative parties are ineluctably bound to the European Union; and President Clinton, despite his platform to the contrary, proceeded with Bush's planned NAFTA agreement once in office. Elsewhere, the ability of many states to determine their own economic policies is severely curtailed by the involvement of the IMF and the pressures to conform to neo-liberal orthodoxy. Citizenship means less when influential decisions are taken outside the sovereign state and beyond the reach of established national mechanisms for promoting democratic accountability and control (Held, 1993).

The state is too small to satisfy principles of democratic rule, and too small to pursue autonomous economic policies. The state has been most successful in marshalling arguments about its sovereign rights in the military domain, although there are powerful international norms in the post-Cold War era which help to limit unilateral military action and suggest that legitimate force is multilateral force. Just as the state is too small in some respects, so it is too large in others. The current challenge to the sovereign state occurs because of global processes and also because of the rise of identity politics within previously secure national boundaries. The emergence of sub-national groups within Europe, the rise of Islamicism around the Mediterranean basin and beyond and the actual and potential fracturing of sub-Saharan Africa along ethnic lines all contribute to a sense that the sovereign state no longer commands the authority and loyalty which it possessed or once claimed to possess. The ethnic revolt may often be initiated by particular groups with special interests (Gagnon, 1984); nevertheless, significant groups argue that their identities and interests are excluded from the dominant images of nation or community wielded by the state. Sub-national groups therefore look to new structures (including regional institutions such as the European Union) for recognition of their ethnic identity and satisfaction of their political interests.

Despite their different starting points, the progressivist and geopolitical narratives demonstrate how earlier claims about sovereign statehood need to be revised substantially in the light of worldwide processes of economic, technological, cultural and political change. Each narrative casts doubts on the claim that if the sovereign state did not exist, it would be necessary to invent it. The continued existence of sovereign states depends significantly upon the power of inertia, the ability of certain groups to reproduce structures of power and the lack of credible alternative visions of political organization. For a large number of reasons the state is no longer the authoritative or functional entity which it once was and which it has been for much of the brief history of International Relations. The changing nature of the modern state has profound implications for the future of the discipline.

TRANSFORMATION AND DECLINE OF A DISCIPLINE?

In the cosier world of the 1960s the student of International Relations was rarely called upon to reflect on the purposes of the discipline or its relationship with the other social sciences. The belief that the discipline was designed to promote peace or world government belonged to an earlier, more naïve age. The discipline was about describing the world without, it was argued, condoning dominant forms of behaviour. One of the major developments in recent years argues that the truth was rather different. The discipline was essentially problem-solving. It took the existing order for granted and asked how that order might be made to function more smoothly (Cox, 1981). The question of who was advantaged and disadvantaged by any given political order hardly arose. In the 1980s problem-solving approaches were challenged on the grounds that they produced knowledge which made it possible for a political order that favoured dominant interests to function more smoothly. However much traditionalists working with realist and neo-realist assumptions may have claimed to be engaged objectively with a reality 'out there', they performed (albeit unwittingly) the function of enabling the powerful to defend their interests and provided legitimacy for the international status quo.

The shift from methodology to epistemology and ontology is the most important respect in which the discipline has moved beyond the cosy world of the 1960s and the more comfortable world of the 1970s and early 1980s. The main impetus behind this shift stems from greater openness to developments outside International Relations, especially in the areas of social and political theory. In the early to mid-1980s (Cox, 1981; Ashley, 1984) students of International Relations imported from social theory a sophisticated challenge to the naïve empiricist view that a politically neutral or innocent interpretation of an external reality is possible. In this way questions of ontology and epistemology became central to the field. Students of International Relations became increasingly aware of the social and political purposes of knowledge, of the normative content which is intrinsic to all social inquiry and of the concomitant moral responsibilities of analysts of society and politics. Positivist methodologies were criticized (Chapter 8) not because empirical or 'problem-solving' work was thought to be without value, but because important normative questions about the principles by which political communities might live had been despatched to the margins of the discipline. The crucial point was that realism and neo-realism were specifically interested in understanding how bounded communities interacted with one another. Little attention was paid to the issue of how boundedness originated and developed, how the dominant constructions of nation and community had uneven levels of support from nominal members of the same nation and how the politics of contesting and redrawing political boundaries never comes to an end and never excludes the possibility of struggles to build new conceptions of community.

What some may regard as the horrifying consequence is that the student of International Relations now needs to be familiar with the main issues in the writings of Habermas, Foucault, Lyotard, Derrida and Rorty in addition to understanding the works of, *inter alia*, Carr, Keohane, Bull and Waltz. The key to recent developments in International Relations is that all forms of social analysis, International Relations included, raise important questions about the moral and cultural constitution of the observer. As with the observer, so with the observed. Moral and cultural assumptions are inherent in all social actions (Chapter 6). Such assumptions invariably reflect relations of power from which some actors benefit while others do not. What may be broadly described as the critical turn in International Relations (embracing not only Frankfurt School critical theory but postmodernism and feminism) highlights these dimensions of social and political life. Consequently, there is considerable interest in how images of ethnic identity, nation, national interests, community, state, international cooperation and global values help constitute power arrangements which favour some but disfavour others.

The inclusion of global values within this list is significant. Recent developments concerning epistemology have removed much of the stigma attached to idealist thought; however, new modes of thought reiterate the theme initially raised by E.H. Carr (1939) that liberal utopians failed to recognize that their normative aspirations were inextricably connected with relations of power and inequality. But unlike problem-solving theories such as neo-realism, critical theory has been concerned with producing knowledge about how structures and beliefs function to exclude or marginalize specific social groups, and with unmasking different axes of exclusion. What different authors describe as interpretive (Neufeld, 1993) or reflectivist thought (Keohane, 1988) is attuned not to making the existing order function more smoothly but to issues of critique and normative change. These modes of analysis reject structuralist approaches to international relations and systems-determinism, although they acknowledge the importance of structural constraints. They stress the role of human agents in fashioning the structures and practices of power and their actual or potential role in creating new arrangements which improve the circumstances of subordinate and marginal groups. The recent interest in epistemology and ontology, and in the moral and cultural underpinning of social and political structures, leads inexorably to a renewed emphasis on the central importance of questions of ethics in the study of International Relations (Thompson, 1992; Brown, 1992).

To make these points in a more concrete way, the critical turn takes issue with the assumption that International Relations is a discipline about states and for states. Critical analysis is concerned with producing a different kind of knowledge with an emancipatory interest or transformative intent (Chapters 5, 7, 8, 11, 12 and 14). The aim is not to establish new moral concepts to improve relations between existing nation-states but, in some cases, to take issue with the sovereign state as a legitimate mode of political organization (Chapter 12). Others (Chapters 8 and 9) suggest that considerations of the future role of the United Nations or reflections upon the management of water resources in West Africa need to reflect on all of the groups who gain and lose rather than concentrate on the effects upon the fiction of undifferentiated nation states. The moral considerations which are generated by the impact of global processes upon the complete range of human groups is different then from the moral considerations which are generated by reflecting upon the narrower realm of interaction between sovereign states.

Terms such as global environmental politics (Chapter 11) reflect this changing orientation, as does the idea of a global moral science articulated recently by Ken Booth (1994). The notion of Global Politics captures the shared fate of humanity in ways which International Relations fails to do; the former suggests a moral commitment to thinking about the human species and the planet in its entirety which International Relations does not foreground. Environmental degradation, nuclear safety, refugees, global warming, drugs, disease, population, international trade and investment, the issues of the new agenda (Halliday, 1991) invoke images of a global lifeboat rather than the billiard-ball model of old.

The emphasis on how political actors construct the political world and imagine its purposes, which has become fundamental to the field, is one reason why the insularity of the discipline has so rapidly come to an end. The trend towards inter-disciplinary and multi-disciplinary approaches is very pronounced in recent literature (Chapters 5 and 13). What characterizes International Relations at the present time is a strong sense of attempting to draw widely from different disciplines to understand the historical development of the system of states against the background of modernity, the relationship between this system and social and economic structures such as capitalism, hitherto regarded as the province of sociologists, economists and economic historians, and the prospects for fundamental global change (Chapters 13 and 14). The question which inevitably arises is whether the separate discipline of International Relations has a useful role to play within the social and political sciences. By ensuring that the study of war and relations between states occupied a prominent position within the academy, International Relations made an indispensable contribution to the social and political sciences. But if this realm is hard to separate from other realms, if it is an error to regard international politics as a domain apart (Waltz, 1979: 8), then the time may be ripe for moving away from International Relations to the more broadly conceived and normatively engaged discipline of Global Politics.

The notion of a bounded discipline which is separate from Politics, Sociology, Economics and Law, which presupposes the bounded nation state and concentrates on the relations between states, will not be readily abandoned. Realists and neo-realists are quick to stress the persistence of competition and conflict between political actors in the unique context of anarchy, as the literature on the international significance of the collapse of the Soviet Union has illustrated (Mearsheimer, 1990). Some might argue if not for confining International Relations to the study of political and military relations between states then for ensuring that this level of analysis remains at the core of the discipline. Alternative positions may be thought to run the risk of undermining intellectual distinctiveness and coherence.

Questions of coherence are fundamental, not least for those with the fascinating but increasingly challenging task of teaching International Relations. Restoring coherence by privileging the traditional heartland of the discipline would be a disastrous solution which puts antiquarianism in place of initiatives to develop closer intellectual ties with cognate disciplines. Large areas of research which tease out important points of convergence between International Relations and cognate fields have yet to be undertaken. Connections need to be made with the burgeoning literature in sociology dealing with the cultural and economic ramifications of globalization (Chapter 3). The compression of space is a crucial area of research in Geography. In historical sociology, the analysis of the rise and development of the modern state undertaken by Mann, Tilly and Giddens amongst others has yet to be integrated adequately within International Relations (Jarvis, 1989). Developments within International Law and Jurisprudence stand at the forefront of contemporary discussions about the future of the sovereign state. The notion of sovereign immunity is under pressure, with states being called as civil litigants in an increasing number of cases initiated by individuals and private corporations (Lawyers in Europe, 1994). The evolving international law of the rights of individuals and peoples (including indigenous peoples) aims to constrain the right of the state to act as a sovereign authority within the traditional sphere of domestic jurisdiction (Crawford, 1989). The literature on national minorities and, more specifically, on indigenous peoples refers to the need for new boundaries within states where cultural and political boundaries do not match (Kymlicka, 1989). Efforts to redefine security (see for example Buzan et al., 1990) in the light of economic, environmental and cultural threats involve similar patterns of convergence between previously discrete academic disciplines. The aim ought to be to deepen these intellectual connections rather than preserve the simplifying coherence of old.

THE STATE IN FUTURE NARRATIVES

For most of its history International Relations has focused upon the inter-actions between sovereign bounded communities. In recent times the sig-nificance of national boundaries has been eroded by various processes operating above and below national governments. Globalization and fragmentation are transforming the nature of political community across the world. The pro-gressivist and geopolitical narratives no longer provide compelling accounts of the role of the state. The state is under considerable pressure to reveal that it can continue to fulfil the aspirations of the progressivist narrative. One con-sequence of the global mobility of capital and the rise of the international division of labour is the pressure upon states to curtail welfare schemes and to restrict employment rights in order to remain globally competitive. Similar processes have reduced the state's effectiveness as a form of territorially concentrated power. References to the 'post-Westphalian era' or to 'post-international politics' abound, as do doubts about the adequacy of the state as a political community. Perhaps, then, the state should be less central to the field, as the 'world society' perspective observed two decades ago.

But those who favour the shift from International Relations to Global Politics would be mistaken if they moved the focus of the inquiry away from the state. The state retains various crucial monopolies: a monopoly of control of the instruments of violence and a virtual monopoly of the right of taxation, the European Union's 'own resources' aside. In many parts of the world, powerful social groups look to the state for protection against corporate capital-ism and for resistance to the spread of a universalizing Western ideology. Acquiring sovereignty remains the central aspiration of many groups involved in the struggle to revise post-colonial boundaries and post-war settlements. But the exceptional state will be the state which is the vehicle for a single national voice. One consequence of globalization is the rise of social groups which are strongly attracted by the culture of modernity and who oppose efforts to entrench or revitalize a traditional culture. Processes of fragmentation further disrupt the state's capacity to speak for a single national will within its boundaries. Recent evidence concerning intervention reveals that powerful states are subject to competing domestic influences regarding the value and legitimacy of military intervention in failed states (Chapter 10).

The argument for focusing much of the inquiry on the state is not simply a restatement of the realist theme that the state is the central actor in world politics. The crucial point is that despite the central importance of the concept of the state in the vocabulary of International Relations, the state awaits ad-equate analysis. It has been presented as a unitary actor responding to the pressures of anarchy (realism) or as the institutional site for competition between bureaucratic groups, societal forces and transnational actors (liberal-ism) or as the arena in which class interests compete for power and resources (Marxism). None of the main approaches to the state deals with the central issue raised earlier – which is that International Relations has concentrated on the interaction between bounded communities and has failed to analyse how boundaries were constituted in the first place and reconstituted subsequently. None deals directly with the construction of community – specifically with the state's role in determining who belongs to the community and how far it has obligations to those living in communities elsewhere. None deals, then, with the ways in which the boundaries of political communities come into being and change over time.

The combined importance of globalization and fragmentation underlines the seriousness of the omission. Realism sought to explain the survival and redrawing of boundaries by focusing upon the struggle for military power and the impact of inter-state war upon human society. But there is almost no analysis of how the members of a society understood the social bond which united them within a bounded community and separated them from the remainder of the world, and there are few resources in the realist approach for analysing the current challenge to political boundaries. The rationalist tradition recognized the significance of boundaries. Wight (1978: 25) argued that the emergence of the modern state involved the contraction of boundaries from empire to state and the expansion of boundaries from the feudal locality to central government. But the theme is underdeveloped in the rationalist tradition. However, a crucial issue to explore is whether the processes that Wight described are being reversed as many communities come under pressure to devolve power to subnational regions and transfer authority to transnational institutions.

The state should therefore stand at the centre of debates about how the global social and political system is changing. It should be central not because it continues to move to the rhythm of the progressivist narrative nor because it retains the role which the geopolitical narrative imputed to it, but because the conditions under which the state emerged as the primary form of political community appear to be in retreat. Whether or not this is an irreversible process is undoubtedly a moot point. Yet the changing character of modern political community has emerged as one of the central questions in contemporary social and political analysis. International Relations is one field of academic discourse which is uniquely placed to contribute to the analysis of political community, not least by forging new connections with cognate disciplines such as Economics, Geography, Sociology and Law.

One vision of the discipline envisages a field in which boundaries are located at the centre of the analysis and placed in question in keeping with the renewed normative emphasis in International Relations. The critical turn in International Relations has raised important questions about the state which received only passing attention in earlier periods. These are concerned with the interests the state privileges and excludes, the identities it supports or marginalizes and the moral choices it permits or discourages. The critical turn has taken issue with systems explanation and with the supposed immutability of the states system and highlighted the discretionary powers of the state, specifically its capacity to frustrate or promote not only the interests of those who live within its boundaries but the welfare of members of the human race more generally.

Globalization and fragmentation raise crucial moral questions about how, for example, the world community should help minority groups whose rights are violated by sovereign authorities, about the responsibility of the world community for preventing further disorder and for rebuilding order in failed states and about when an argument for sovereignty deserves respect since it protects the weak from external domination and when it should attract suspicion because it is a mask for the domestic abuse of power or a convenient way of ensuring that outsiders have no control over decisions that seriously affect them. Such questions invite a normatively engaged re-examination of traditional conceptions of sovereignty, community and citizenship (Linklater, 1993). The academic study of International Relations is therefore poised to overcome its peculiar separation from Political Theory and to play a leading role in envisaging principles of political life which might not simply improve the lives of citizens within the supposedly more malleable world of the state but ameliorate the condition of the weak within world society as a whole.

The crucial question of whether new forms of community and new principles of politics are emerging brings the discussion back to the sovereign state once more. Neither the progressivist nor the geopolitical account of the state sheds much light on this subject. The progressivist narrative either assumed that the state would realize the moral ends of modern societies unaided or collaborate with new international institutions to overcome its defects, but there are problems with each approach. The geopolitical narrative emphasized the military and administrative powers of the modern state. These powers have been reduced, but they are very far from exhausted. The upshot of this observation is that the sovereign state has powerful resources at its disposal which enable it to block alternative paths of development. Supported by sections of its citizenry who fear for the loss of national identity and political sovereignty, the state is well placed to obstruct the establishment of new organizational sites of power which share the responsibility for satisfying the needs of peoples everywhere.

The analysis of the state is crucial, because exercises in global reform need to thread their way through the modern state. Change has to pass through states although it may have originated elsewhere. The role of political groups within civil society, including an international civil society active in promoting human rights, and regional and international organizations, will be crucially important determinants of the cultural context in which states operate. Transnational or cosmopolitan democracy, themes developed in relation to Western Europe, can open up new channels of representation which simultaneously provide the recognition which sub-national groups demand and permit the development of transnational loyalties (Held, 1993; Linklater, 1993). The political theory of post-sovereign governance is in its infancy, but if democratic accountability has a role within transnational political theory then there is a strong case for representing international non-governmental agencies and social movements at the highest levels of international decision-making.

In this context there is an obligation on the part of the academic community to shape contemporary public debate. The critical turn in International Relations has increased the awareness of the relationship between knowledge and power, and pressed observers to reflect upon the political ramifications of modes of analysis. Responsibilities for disseminating academic debates and discussions about the options confronting political communities and about alternative paths of development arise in this context. Abridged versions of academic publications which are accessible to a wider, non-academic readership are as scarce as they are necessary. It is important that such publications are encouraged and valued positively in assessments of academic performance. The discipline is undergoing rapid transition from an essentially problem-solving approach to strategic interaction between existing bounded communities to a normatively engaged analysis of the history of bounded communities and the possibility of improved forms of political community. Concurrently, modern political systems face considerable uncertainty about the meaning and significance of national identity, citizenship and sovereignty, an uncertainty which is central to the current political malaise in the Western democracies. Trapped by short-term considerations, most of these political systems have been reluctant to initiate public debate about the aims and purposes of political community in the modern world. It is crucial that International Relations as an academic discipline continue to analyse the world of bounded communities; no less important is the obligation to play a far more prominent role in public debate.

NOTE

1. The authors would like to thank Alex Danchev, Rick Fawn, Matthew Paterson and Hidemi Suganami for their helpful comments on an earlier version of this introduction.

REFERENCES

Ashley, R.K., 1984, 'The Poverty of Neo-Realism', *International Organisation*, 38: 225–86.

Booth, K., 1994, 'Human Wrongs and International Relations', The John Vincent Memorial Lecture, Keele University, 1994.

Brown, C., 1992, *International Relations Theory: New Normative Approaches*, New York, Columbia University Press.

Bull, H., 1966, 'International Theory: The Case for a Classical Approach', *World Politics*, 18: 3.

Burton, J.W., 1972, *World Society*, Cambridge, Cambridge University Press.

Buzan, B., Kelstrup, M., Lemaitre, P., Tromer, E. and Weaver, O., 1990, *The European Security Order Recast*, London, Pinter.

Carr, E.H., 1939, *The Twenty Years' Crisis: 1919–1939*, London, Macmillan.

Cox, R., 1981, 'Social Forces, States and World Order: Beyond International Relations Theory', *Millennium*, 10: 2.

Crawford, J. (ed.), 1989, *The Rights of Peoples*, Oxford, Clarendon Press.

Donelan, M., 1978, 'The Political Theorists and International Relations', in M. Donelan (ed.), *The Reason of States*, London, Allen & Unwin.

Falk, R., 1987, 'The World Order Approach: Issues of Perspective, Academic Discipline and Political Commitment', in Falk, R., *The Promise of World Order*, London, Wheatsheaf.

Falk, R. and Mendlovitz, S.H. (eds), 1966, *The Strategy of World Order*, 4 vols, New York, World Law Fund.

Gagnon, V.P., 1994, 'Serbia's Road to War', *Journal of Democracy*, 5: 2.

Giddens, A., 1981, *A Contemporary Critique of Historical Materialism*, London, Macmillan.

Halliday, F., 1991, 'International Relations: Is There a New Agenda?', *Millennium*, 20: 57–72.

Halliday, F., 1994, 'The Gulf War 1990–91 and the Study of International Relations', *Review of International Studies*, 20: 2.

Held, D., 1993, 'Democracy: From City-States to a Cosmopolitan Order?', in D. Held (ed.), *Prospects for Democracy: North, South, East, West*, Oxford, Polity.

Helman, G.B. and Ratner S.R., 1992–93, 'Saving Failed States', *Foreign Policy*, 89: 3–20.

Holsti, K.J., 1985, *The Dividing Discipline*, Boston, Allen & Unwin.

Jackson, R.H., 1990, *Quasi-States: Sovereignty, International Relations and the Third World*, Cambridge, Cambridge University Press.

Jarvis, T., 1989, 'Society, State and Geopolitics: Challenges from Historical Sociology', *Review of International Studies*, 15: 281–92.

Journal of Democracy, 1993, Special Issue on 'The Challenge of Ethnic Conflict', 4: 4.

Keohane, R.O., 1988, 'International Insitututions: Two Approaches', *International Studies Quarterly*, 32: 379–96.

Kymlicka, W., 1989, *Liberalism, Community and Culture*, Oxford, Clarendon Press.

Lawyers in Europe, 1994, A conference on 'Sovereign Immunity: Foreign States as Civil Litigants' in association with The Centre for European Studies and The Research Centre for International Law, Cambridge University.

Linklater, A., 1993, 'Community, Citizenship and Global Politics', *Oxford International Review*, 4: 4–7.

Mattingly, G., 1962, *Renaissance Diplomacy*, London, Jonathan Cape.

Mearsheimer, J., 1990, 'Back to the Future: Instability in Europe after the Cold War', *International Security*, 15: 5–56.

Modelski, G., 1978, 'The Long-Cycle of Global Politics and the Nation-State', *Comparative Studies in Society and History*, 20: 214–35.

Neufeld, M., 1993, 'Interpretation and the "Science" of International Relations', *Review of International Studies*, 19: 1.

Richardson, J., 1993, 'The End of Geopolitics?' in R. Leaver and J.L. Richardson (eds), *Charting the Post-Cold War Order*, Boulder, CO, Westview.

Roberts, A., 1993, 'Humanitarian War: Military Intervention and Human Rights', *International Affairs*, 69: 3.

Rosenau, J.N. (ed.), 1993, *Global Voices*, Boulder, CO, Westview.

Smith, M., Little, R. and Shackleton, M. (eds), 1981, *Perspectives on World Politics*, London, Croom Helm.

Thompson, J., 1992, *Justice and World Order: A Philosophical Inquiry*, London, Routledge.

Tilly, C., 1992, *Coercion, Capital and European States, AD 990–1992*, Oxford, Blackwell.

Waltz, K.N., 1979, *Theory of International Politics*, New York, Random House.

Wendt, A., 1992, 'Anarchy is What States Make of it: The Social Construction of Power Politics', *International Organisation*, 46: 2.

Wight, M., 1978, *Power Politics*, London, Leicester University Press.

PART I
BOUNDARIES EXAMINED

1
Incomplete states: theories and practices of statecraft

Richard Devetak

This chapter surveys three prominent perspectives on the state in International Relations: neo-realism, critical international theory and post-structuralist international theory.[1] By drawing on the arguments of Machiavelli, Hegel and Derrida in addition to contemporary international theorists it seeks to offer one possible means of rethinking an aspect of the state that has recently been neglected: the question of how the state has been constituted. The argument advanced here is based on a claim which can be stated quite boldly: *there is statecraft, but there is no completed state.* Before establishing this claim, a few prefatory remarks on the theoretical position adopted here and its implications for statecraft will be made. These remarks will be followed by an examination of the three aforementioned perspectives with the intention of clarifying their ontological assumptions regarding the relationship between state and states system. It will be argued that the double gesture of deconstruction, which overturns and displaces this opposition, is crucial to the development of an adequate understanding of how the state is constituted and reconstituted.

SOLICITING THEORIES

In a passage meant to unsettle, Hegel tells us that 'the familiar, just because it is familiar, is not cognitively understood' (1977: 18). He continues that thought which relies on common sense 'never gets anywhere, and it knows not why' (1977: 18). For Hegel, if thought wants to 'get anywhere' it must defamiliarize the familiar. It must step back and estrange itself from the common sense of the 'unsophisticated heart' who adheres 'with trustful conviction to what is publicly accepted as true' (Hegel, 1967: 3). Theory inquires into how the all too familiar, common sense ideas were settled upon and the consequences that extend from them. A critical theory goes further: it submits these settled ideas or 'convictions' to critical scrutiny – in other words, it unsettles settled ideas.

Hegel's theoretical attitude was no doubt informed by the classical Greek notion of *theoria* as watching from a distance or from a position of exile or estrangement.[2] Derrida radicalizes this notion of theory as an unsettling posture of estrangement by developing a general mode of unsettling, or what he calls deconstruction. Though deconstruction defies definition, it can be understood as a strategy of interpretation and criticism directed at concepts which attempt closure or totalization. More importantly, it demonstrates how these attempts at closure (whether metaphysical or social) never succeed because there is always a remainder or 'supplement' that cannot be subsumed.[3] This remainder destabilizes the totality, hence Derrida's invocation of the notion of solicitation, which means to shake or agitate the totality (from the Latin *sollicitation*: *sollus* meaning 'entire', 'whole', and *citus* meaning 'to shake' or 'put in motion') (1978: 6). Deconstructive theory not only steps back from, but shakes and unsettles the whole edifice of common-sense notions, making them insecure in their most assured evidences (Derrida, 1974: 73). More precisely, perhaps, it shows how such apparently stable edifices are always in danger of being destabilized or undone by what they cannot secure, subsume or control.[4]

Deconstruction, as a theory of estrangement and solicitation, seeks to gain a certain exteriority from the whole edifice of common sense in order to criticize, unsettle and displace it. No edifice is natural, necessary or fixed; every edifice could be otherwise according to deconstruction.[5] It is this deconstructive approach which will be used here to question common-sense assumptions about the settledness of the state and states system. Before examining the three perspectives it may be helpful to make some preliminary observations about statecraft.

STATECRAFT: A PRELIMINARY INQUIRY

To claim that there is statecraft, but that no complete state exists, will no doubt conflict with the common-sense impression that states exist as fully present, complete political actors on the world stage. There may be some 'failing' or 'quasi-states' in the world, but they are the exception which prove the rule that the international system comprises a multiplicity of complete sovereign states.[6] It is this common-sense assumption which will be unsettled by deconstruction, for it will be argued that no state is complete and all states are struggling against failure.[7] Though this may seem an unusual argument it is not altogether unfamiliar. Thinkers such as Machiavelli and Hegel have made it clear that it is impossible to resolve once and for all the political production and reproduction of the state. The notion of statecraft as deployed here is intended to take this point seriously.

According to traditional understandings, statecraft refers to an activity undertaken by a state to achieve certain political, economic and military objectives in different milieu and under various constraints. The state is taken to be an already settled political entity and statecraft the activity undertaken by it. The revised notion of statecraft, however, focuses attention on the processes by which the state is constituted. It communicates with traditional understandings of statecraft associated with diplomacy and *raison d'état*, but is broadened to encompass the vast array of strategies, tactics, techniques, practices and policies which create the effect of a completed state. To clarify this notion of statecraft and its relation to the constitution of the state it is useful to reconsider the arguments of Machiavelli, who recognized the eternal political problem of constituting and reconstituting the state.

It is often stated that Machiavelli's primary concern was how to found a state. Equally important for Machiavelli, however, was the question of how to maintain, or keep a grip on, the state.[8] He recognized that political institutions were never established without danger, so their maintenance required great skill (*virtù*). Keeping a grip on the state required constant attention and vigilance, for, as he was fond of pointing out, in politics 'it is not possible to remove one inconvenience without another emerging' (*Discourses*: Bk. I, ch. 6). The revised notion of statecraft can be understood by analogy with this Machiavellian concern with maintenance: statecraft names the activity by which states are maintained and given form; it is the ongoing political struggle to prevent the founding of a state from becoming a foundering. So statecraft, as the constant maintenance of the state, does not so much bring about the completion of the state as constantly attempt to cancel inconveniences and threats to its maintenance. This revised notion of statecraft arises out of the encounter between Machiavelli and Derrida which suggests that the state is not complete before statecraft, but neither does statecraft complete the state. Unsettling inconveniences always remain, so further maintenance or statecraft always remains to be undertaken.[9] In sum, statecraft is a paradoxical notion, for it is a sign of the ceaseless activity of (re)constituting the state, and the impossibility of ever completing the state, once and for all, by closing it off (bounding it) in a unified totality. We turn now to consider how the constitution of the state and states system is handled in the three perspectives, beginning with neo-realism.

NEO-REALISM: 'OUTSIDE-IN' TURNED UPSIDE-DOWN

The currently dominant understanding of how states relate to the international system is to be found in neo-realist and neo-liberal institutionalist writings.[10] For these theorists, international theory is best to adopt systemic as opposed to reductionist theory. Reductionist theories assume that it is possible to comprehend the system by focusing on the units which comprise it. They are premissed on the supposition that explanations should begin with the internal attributes of the units. The line of causality runs from the unit to the system, or from the 'inside out' (Waltz, 1979: 63).

Systemic theories, on the other hand, insist that explanations located at the level of the unit will remain insufficient where structural forces are at work. For neo-realism and neo-liberalism, in order to account for regularity in International Relations it is necessary to refer to a notion of structure which operates at the level of the system. They seek to identify a level of causality that exists apart from the units, thereby uncovering a line of causality that runs from the system to the unit, or from the 'outside in'. In short, neo-realism believes that 'the keys to war and peace lie more in the structure of the international system than in the nature of the individual states' (Mearsheimer, 1990: 12).

So although Waltz might concede that neither structure nor units determine international outcomes (1979: 78), it is clear that structure figures as the strongest causal factor.[11] Indeed, according to neo-realism, this 'outside-in' approach alone makes it possible to account for the 'striking sameness' in state behaviour 'despite profound changes in the internal composition of states' (Waltz, 1993: 45). The primary concern of neo-realism is to explain the reasons for the functional likeness of states by looking to the international structure which constrains and disposes states to act 'within specified ranges' (Waltz, 1979: 68). It is at this point that Waltz makes the interesting assertion that, '[i]n systems theory, structure is a generative notion' (1979: 72). What Waltz means by this, however, is far from clear.

On the one hand Waltz wants to argue that structure is passive, and on the other hand he wants to argue that structure is active.[12] The former implies that the structure of international anarchy is important as a permissive condition; that '[w]ars occur because there is nothing to prevent them' (Waltz, 1959: 232). Structures in this sense 'are not causes in the sense meant by saying that A causes X and B causes Y' (Waltz, 1979: 74); this is because only agents within the structure act. Structure does not determine outcomes, but *allows* them. On the other hand, Waltz perceives structure to be causal. This implies that rather than being merely passive, structure acts 'as *a force that shapes and shoves* the units' (Waltz, 1990: 34; emphasis added). Mearsheimer concurs, arguing that '[c]onflict is common among states because *the international system creates powerful incentives for aggression*' (1990: 12, emphasis added). Though it is clear that anarchy, at a minimum, 'designates a set of constraining conditions' (Waltz, 1979: 73), there is some degree of uncertainty as to why Waltz calls structure generative. The following section seeks to clarify what Waltz means when he says generative structure.

Neo-realist structuralism: generative or causal?

To come to grips with structure Waltz asks: 'What is the principle by which the parts [of the international system] are arranged?' (1979: 81). Of the two possibilities he identifies, there is little question in Waltz's mind about what the fundamental ordering principle in international politics is: anarchy rather than hierarchy distinguishes international politics.

At the domestic level politics is organized according to principles of centralization and hierarchy. It is the realm of authority, administration and law where the government arrogates to itself the sole right to use force. The use of force in domestic politics is said to be the *ultima ratio*. By contrast, international politics remain (dis)organized by principles of decentralization and anarchy. Politics here, so it is argued, occurs in the absence of government and is witness to the incessant struggle for power. 'In the absence of a supreme authority, there is then constant possibility that conflicts will be settled by force' (Waltz, 1959: 188). It is not the use or non-use of force in itself which distinguishes the two levels, but the different principles of organization for managing force at each level (Waltz, 1979: 103). Waltz makes his point manifestly clear when he says that '[t]he essential structural quality of the system is anarchy – the absence of a central monopoly of legitimate force' (Waltz, 1989: 42). In short, the difference between the two realms turns on the presence or absence of sovereignty.[13]

Anarchy is taken to be the ontological condition in which states find themselves. Within this condition there is no higher legitimate authority or power that can impose rules or effectively prohibit the use of force (Waltz, 1959: 205). In the absence of sovereignty self-help necessarily becomes the principle of action because states alone are responsible for protecting their own interests (Waltz, 1979: 111). In their constant attempt to ensure their own survival and security, states generate anarchy in much the same way that the self-interested acts and interactions of firms 'spontaneously' generate an economic market (Waltz, 1979: 89–92). The upshot of this is that '[i]nternational structure emerges from the interaction of states and *then* constrains them' (1990: 29, emphasis added). Waltz regards self-interested states as *prior* to structure, as if the structure was merely derived from the prior interaction of states in a vacuum. Structure is taken to be subsequent to the units; conceived as an after-effect which is dependent upon the prior existence of states. It is through the interaction or 'coaction' of these pre-constituted states that the structure of the international system is established (Waltz, 1979: 88–93).

It is clear, then, that for neo-realism, a 'generative' notion of structure really means causality. The structure cannot be generative, because it is only generated through the 'coaction' of pre-existent states. The structure of anarchy does not generate the states or states system, rather, it generates constraints on the given states-as-actors. Because neo-realism offers a 'theory of the conditioning effects of the state system itself' (Waltz, 1959: 231), it is compelled to conceive of structure as 'a set of constraining conditions' (Waltz, 1979: 73), rather than generative. It provides an auto-generative explanation where internal forces alone continually reproduce the system. The system is abstracted from other social systems and treated as a closed circuit, with endogenous means of reproduction.

There is little evidence here of a generative notion of structure. Instead we are provided with a causal notion; structure is generated, not generative. In confining its attention to the causal force of structure, neo-realism cannot address ontological issues such as the constitution of the state and states system. If that is the task, then the state-centric approach of neo-realism provides no means of inquiring into how this state comes into being in the first place.

Neo-realist totalizations

As Ashley has observed, neo-realism takes the state to be ontologically prior to the states system (1984: 240). As a result, it understands the international structure to be an external joining of given, already completed, fully formed states-as-actors. Despite the stated intention to elaborate a generative notion of structure, which would inquire into the constitution of the state and states system, it has been demonstrated on several occasions that neo-realism is constrained in doing so by its ontological assumptions (Ruggie, 1983, 1989 and 1993; Wendt, 1987 and 1992; Ashley, 1984). Neo-realism 'never gets anywhere' with its notion of generative structure because it fails to question the familiar, common-sense impression that the state is a fully present and complete actor before it interacts.

As a consequence, the neo-realist understanding of structure not only remains blind to the '*continual* process of producing and reproducing state actors' (Wendt and Duvall, 1989: 69 n.12, original emphasis), it also ignores the mutually constitutive, or 'co-determined' nature of the state and states system (Wendt, 1987: 360). The identity and nature of both states and the states system are held to be fixed and self-enclosed, according to neo-realism. It assumes that it is possible to begin from the point of view of a given unit whose boundaries and identity can be defined from the start in a politically neutral way. Consequently, it effaces the ongoing political production of states.

It is clear, then, that neo-realism subscribes to totalizing conceptions of the state and states system. It views the state as an already complete, fully formed, unitary whole, which subsequently enters into interaction with other like totalities. In so doing, states establish a structure which then constrains them to act in particular ways. This structure is thought to be the exclusive product of state interaction. By conceiving the states system as completely closed in on itself, without any internal relations to other social systems, neo-realism also results in a totalizing view of the system. In sum, neo-realism rests on a closed circuit comprising a multiplicity of bounded, unitary states inside a bounded, totalized system.

Although neo-realism begins by advocating an 'outside-in' approach, it ends up delivering an 'inside-out' approach. It could be argued that while it does retain an 'outside-in' causality, its ontology turns the hierarchy upside-down, reverting to an 'inside-out' approach which posits the prior existence of the unit/state without accounting for its constitution at all. With this in mind we turn to critical international theory and its handling of the state and states system.

CRITICAL INTERNATIONAL THEORY[14]

Critical international theory has sought to unsettle this closed circuit of neo-realism in at least two ways: first, by demonstrating that the states system is not a totality closed in on itself, and second, by showing that the state is not a pre-existent, unitary totality. For critical international theory the scope must be broadened so that the states system is placed in a wider social context. It refuses to abstract the states system from this context, arguing instead that it helps to constitute the states system. The states system is but one of many international systems, and to understand how it is constituted it is necessary to work from the 'outside in'. That is, an understanding of how the 'inside' (the states system) is constituted must begin with the 'outside' (the wider social context). Similarly, the state must also be understood as dialectically constituted by wider forces than the states system alone. Critical international theory thereby seeks to unsettle the neo-realist totalizations by broadening the notion of 'outside'. This makes it possible for critical international theory to contribute to a genuinely generative notion of structure which neo-realism failed to deliver.

Unsettling neo-realist totalizations

Critical international theory accepts the neo-realist claim that an adequate understanding of the modern state must comprehend the dynamics and structures of war and international conflict, but denies that such an understanding can be acquired by abstracting the states system from its wider social and economic milieu. The state and states system may have been forged on the 'anvil of war', but wider and deeper social forces contribute to the war imperative than neo-realism's causal approach can illuminate. This necessitates a move to a broader problematique which integrates insights from Marxism, and historical sociology as well as traditional international relations theory (Linklater, 1990a).

In order to understand the forces which condition and generate international relations, critical international theory eschews explanations based on a single, endogenous logic, preferring instead explanations based on a recognition of multiple logics. For critical international theory, it is wrong to treat international outcomes as simply the product of systemic reproduction because there are other structures and processes that help to shape the states system, but lie outside it.[15] It is crucial that it be located in relation to the social, economic, moral and cultural conditions which make it possible. The upshot of this is that the states system is constituted through the intersection of multiple systems; it is not auto-generative and cannot be accounted for in isolation from these other systems.

In further contrast to neo-realism, which emphasizes 'a unitary state reacting to geopolitical pressures exclusive of other forces' (Jarvis, 1989: 281), critical international theory endeavours to understand how modern states are simultaneously located in the domains of the states system, the society of states, class structure and the capitalist world economy (Linklater, 1990a: 120). It is alert to the multiplicity of domestic and international social forces which the state is open to, and which help constitute it.[16]

The state denotes not simply a 'national-territorial totality' (Halliday, 1987: 217), but also 'a specific set of coercive and administrative institutions' (Halliday, 1987: 218). It is built upon social power as well as territory, and consequently is produced by social forces which extend beyond the sovereign territorial confines (Mann, 1986b: 132). It is for this reason that the state is not to be conceived as 'an unproblematic, unitary totality' (Mann, 1986a: 2).[17] The institutionalization of boundaries gives the appearance of unity, but the infrastructural power that erects them is constantly outflanked by social and historical dynamics. As a result, the boundaries should be understood as temporary and provisional supports rather than 'present and invariable' structures (Mann, 1986a: 13). The social and historical forces behind, and constitutive of, the state mean that it is not reducible to an abstract, ahistorical, unitary totality. The upshot of critical international theory is that the historically produced state and states system must be located in an evolving social context. They must be conceived as constantly open to, and threatened by, historically contingent social forces.

Comprehending this evolving social context creates difficulties for neo-realism. By holding fast to its totalizing circuit, neo-realism myopically focuses on the 'striking sameness' in history to the exclusion of historical change. The shift from the medieval to the modern international system, which is perhaps the most fundamental transformation in international politics, passes entirely undetected by neo-realism (Ruggie, 1983).

Sovereignty as principle of separability

As we shall see, the striking political transformation that marks this transition cannot be comprehended or accounted for within neo-realist explanations. The defenders of neo-realism deny the existence of structural change at the international level, emphasizing instead the continuity of the 'deep' structure of anarchy.[18] The question is whether the shift from the medieval to modern system was a *change of system* or *change within the same system*. At stake is the question of whether there was a change in the ordering principles by which the system is arranged. In addition, there is the more general question of whether the totalizing circuit tendered by neo-realism is in fact the most useful explanatory approach to understand the state in relation to the system, or whether it is an example of what Vico called a 'conceit of scholars' such that they fix upon a particular feature of history and assume it to be universal and timeless (Cox, 1981: 133).

Regarding the eclipse of the medieval system, Giddens remarks that the 'best single expression of the fact that a new type of state system had come into being' is the recognition by each state of 'the spheres of legitimate autonomy of others' (1985: 85). States were cognizant of the new rules and expectations that were emerging. Fundamental to this new system was the concept of sovereignty. Prior to the advent of sovereignty, there existed no clear constitutive principle or criterion by which to determine the basis of legitimacy and entry into the international society of a political unit (Bull, 1977: 29).[19] Not until the 'newly emerged territorial states defined their essence, their very being, by the *possession* of territory and the *exclusion* of others' (Ruggie, 1989: 23, original emphasis) did the international system acquire its new 'ordering principle'. Through this double gesture of self-possession and exclusion, political space was monopolized by a single legitimate authority, and the international system acquired a new ordering principle which structured relations between the constitutive units. Sovereignty forcefully marked the boundary between inside and outside, thereby transcending the fuzziness endemic to the medieval system, and simultaneously providing 'an ordering principle for what is "internal" to states and what is "external" to them' (Giddens, 1985: 281).

The social recognition of this new propriety transformed the context in which relations between these units took place. Indeed, it is only with the institutionalization of sovereignty as a structural attribute of the system that borders could clearly demarcate internal and external political spaces.[20] Prior to the advent of sovereignty it was 'unusual for the administrative power of the state apparatus to coincide with defined territorial boundaries' (Giddens, 1985: 49). This shift from the medieval system of overlapping frontiers to the modern system of precise borders was largely a result of higher levels of internal and external surveillance (diplomacy and espionage) made possible by advances in administrative power.[21] To simplify, these advances had their origins in the development of industrial capitalism, instruments of violence and the military. But how did these advances congeal (across Europe) into the system of sovereign states?

The problem, as Waltz has correctly informed us, is: '*how to conceive of an order without an orderer and of organizational effects where formal organization is lacking*' (Waltz, 1979: 89, emphasis added). In other words, how can the concept of sovereignty be institutionalized as a constitutive principle of the international system when there is no sovereignty to impose it? International order does not spontaneously result from self-interest as Waltz presumes, nor from a supra-Leviathan, 'but from concurrent, voluntary observance of certain rules of mutual conduct in each state's pursuit of its own interests' (Poggi, 1978: 88).[22] To provide an adequate understanding of how order is produced without an overarching orderer, the micro-economic theory that Waltz employs must be eschewed and replaced with an approach that focuses on the intersubjective generation of constitutive principles.

The exclusion of the intersubjective realm by neo-realism disallows it from comprehending the shift from the medieval to modern international system or from arriving at a generative notion of structure. Integral to this shift was the concept of sovereignty, which could only be claimed if it was acknowledged by other states. State sovereignty is an intersubjective property (Giddens, 1985: 281–2). States are always already intersubjectively constituted; it is a condition of their existence. Such an argument can be found in Hegel who argued that a 'state is as little an actual individual without relations to other states as an individual is actually a person without *rapport* with other persons' (1967: §331). It is only through this rapport with, and 'recognition by other states' (Hegel, 1967: §331), that states come to have actual existence as sovereign states. A state's condition of possibility is its relation to other states. The modern concept of sovereignty as understood by Ruggie needs to be amended by Hegel's point: sovereignty does indeed involve the possession of territory and the exclusion of others, but only in so far as this is intersubjectively recognized by other claimants. The upshot of these reflections on the state is that 'before the state is an actor, it is already [in] a social relation', as Rosenberg claims (1990: 251).

As Hegel points out, sovereign statehood as a constitutive principle derives from the system. Principles of individuation, or 'principles of separability', as Ruggie calls them (1983), are not internally generated by the state-as-actor, but derive from the level of the system. There is no individuation prior to the system, prior to others, or without intersubjectivity. The state-as-actor is not fully formed or complete prior to interaction; it only takes on the appearance of completion in interaction. States and the states system are the product of a reflexively monitored system which mutually constitutes the states and states system. This suggests that the closed circuit of neo-realism which conceives of the state as an already completed political entity prior to the system is inadequate. We turn now to the post-structuralist account of 'the state as an historically constituted and constantly reconstituted form of political life' (Walker, 1993: 46).

POST-STRUCTURALISM AND THE STATE

To understand how states take on the appearance of an already completed political entity it is necessary to begin, as Waltz does, from the 'outside' and work 'in'. The 'outside' (system), however, can no longer be understood as simply the structurally fixed, spontaneous product of co-acting states, nor simply as a 'constraining condition'. Rather, it is a condition of possibility of states and, in a sense, precedes states.

Critical international theory has gone some way toward demonstrating the inadequacy of conceiving either the state or states system as closed totalities. It has begun to unsettle the neo-realist circuit by showing that they cannot be understood in isolation from other actors, social forces and systems. By focusing on intersubjectivity it has also hinted at the constitutive priority of the outside over the inside, thereby overturning the neo-realist conception. In the following section, we continue with Derrida's invitation 'to speculate upon the power of exteriority as constitutive of interiority' (1974: 313), by giving further consideration to Hegel's reflections on international relations. The final section, however, displaces the very opposition between inside and outside altogether and focuses instead on what generates the inside and outside: statecraft. Overturning the opposition (privileging what was thought to be secondary) is only a moment in the overall deconstruction. The moment of displacement that accompanies the overturning leads to a release from the opposition's conceptual hold.

States of negation and negativity

It has already been noted that Hegel locates the state in intersubjectivity. For Hegel, this is absolutely essential to the constitution of the state. A structural trait of the state is its relation to the outside, its 'rapport' with other states. Hegel insists that 'the state is an individual, and *individuality essentially implies negation*' (Hegel, 1967: §324[A], emphasis added). States necessarily stand in relation to a multiplicity of other states and this is a condition of their individuality or subjectivity (Hegel, 1967: §329). This negative relation lies at the heart of the state's existence. As expressed by Hegel:

This negative relation of the state to itself is embodied in the world as the relation of one state to another and as if the negative were something external. In the world of existence, therefore, this negative relation has the shape of a happening and an entanglement with chance events coming from without. But in fact *this negative relation is that moment in the state which is most supremely its own* (Hegel, 1967: §323, emphasis added).

Hegel says that it *appears* as if the state's relation to other states was merely contingent, accidental, or secondary, *as if* the state does not require relations to other states. Hegel's point, however, is that the negative relation is not a contingent or secondary feature, but a necessary and primary trait of the state; something 'supremely its own' and internal to its constitution. Negation does not indicate something 'external', but something 'internal', something upon which the state necessarily depends; something intrinsic to its being. In other words, the 'outside' is a condition of possibility of the 'inside'; it is intrinsic to the inside, and constitutes an integral part of its structure. The state contains a constitutive trace of the outside. To put Hegel's point about negation in more contemporary (post-structuralist) language, the self-identity of a state rests on a prior difference from other states. That is, individuation requires negation or separability; indeed, negation is a condition of possibility of individuation (Bennington, 1994: 250).

One thing needs to be made clear before continuing: for Hegel, individuation is neither 'innocent' nor complete. Rather, it is an ongoing process in which violent confrontation is a constant possibility. It is this ongoing process of negation, which Hegel calls negativity, which requires some clarification. For our purposes it should be enough to recall that negativity, as the 'movement of becoming' or 'principle of motion in history' (1977: 21), designates a conflictual process for Hegel. The power-house of negativity pushes history forward through a series of struggles and conflicts. History is as much a 'slaughter-bench' (1956: 21) as the progressive unfolding of freedom. The violence intrinsic to negativity holds important implications not only for how we conceive of history, but also for how we conceive of subjects in history. For Hegel, negativity constitutes the subject, but the subject is always 'in process/on trial' (*en procès*), as Kristeva says (1984: 111). Its existence is never safely secured or complete, but is always in danger of being destabilized by the forces that give rise to the apparent unity of the subject. For Hegel, what appears to be a settled or 'inert' subject or state of affairs is in fact a tense holding together of contending forces (1977: 87). There is a 'solicitation' or 'play of forces' which produce the binding effect on the subject. Hegel's main point is that subjects are never static, but are temporary, transient productions held together in a rather fragile manner by these forces.[23] So when Hegel talks of the 'outside' (intersubjectivity and rapport between states) as being constitutive of states, four things must be kept in mind: first, that the 'outside' is a prior condition of the 'inside', second, that the constitution of 'inside' and 'outside' is not free of violence, third, that the process is dynamic and ongoing, and fourth, as a consequence of these, that the constitution of the state remains incomplete.

Through Hegel, therefore, it is possible to recover Waltz's 'outside-in' approach and apply it to questions of ontology. In contrast to Waltz's resort to an 'inside-out' ontology, however, Hegel conceives of an 'outside-in' ontology where the system (intersubjectivity) is a prior condition of the unit/state which is always in process and incomplete.

To summarize: we have arrived, then, at the inversion of the ontological privileging of the state over anarchy, inside over outside, unit over system. Critical international theory overturned these hierarchical oppositions by demonstrating how, in a certain sense, the 'outside' is constitutive of the 'inside'. But it is clear from Hegel's reflections that we cannot stop here. Simply overturning the opposition would be to remain on the very same conceptual terrain, it would be to fall back within the limits of that opposition. To effect the deconstruction it is necessary to displace as well as overturn the opposition; for the apparently clear opposition between inside and outside is neither clear nor an opposition, as each depends on, is internally related to, and already harbours, the other. As expressed by Derrida, the 'outside bears with the inside a relationship that is, as usual, anything but simple exteriority' (Derrida, 1974: 35). There is, as Hegel has shown, an intrinsic relation between inside and outside, state and system. The task then is to analyse what it is that produces this difference or opposition; to identify what it is that precedes, and makes possible, both the inside and the outside, sovereignty and anarchy, unit and system. One approach to this issue is to foreground those historical practices which constitute the conditions of possibility in which these oppositions are established; that is, to foreground the historical practices that mark boundaries.

Statecraft: the inscription of boundaries

The opposition between inside and outside, sovereignty and anarchy, state and system, implies a prior boundary. It is boundaries which separate inside and outside, thereby constituting their opposition. Neither the inside nor the outside, sovereignty or anarchy, is fixed and permanently delimited, as the domain ascribed to each is not given in advance of the political inscription of boundaries. In short, political space is never simply 'present', but only takes effect after boundaries have inscribed and demarcated different domains.

More specifically, boundaries function to divide an interior, singular, sovereign space from an exterior, pluralistic, anarchical space (Walker, 1990). This 'traditional gambit of defining and unifying national identity through the alienation of others' gives rise, as Der Derian says, to the apparent permanence and intractability of the anarchy problematique (1992: 94). It makes it appear as though the inside and outside were pre-political, already given domains. Inherent in such a view is the supposition that the political begins with the fully formed state's attempts to negotiate, and survive in, the international anarchy, to the exclusion of the constitution of the state itself. For post-structuralism, however, the political begins with the practices that inscribe and administer the boundary which establishes space for political institutions. The political is not inaugurated after political space appears demarcated, but is inherent in the very acts of demarcation, that is, statecraft.

Statecraft is a 'practice of differentiation' which relentlessly attempts to separate, enframe or totalize a political space (Ashley, 1989a: 259). It is a practice operating at the borders, and marking those borders to produce the effect of the state as bounded and complete (Ashley, 1988: 101). Statecraft embodies the interminable attempt to constitute or frame the state's identity against difference, its inside against the outside, its sovereignty against anarchy.

Statecraft, in short, names the various practices and activities which produce the effect of a completed state by inscribing boundaries which constitute an inside and outside. The division of political space between sovereignty and anarchy does not exist prior to the inscription of a boundary. This implies that the state does not exist apart from statecraft; that it is only through statecraft that the state comes into existence, for it is only through statecraft that space is divided. Statecraft is a 'boundary-producing political performance' (Campbell, 1992: 69) central to the production and reproduction of the state and, by default, the anarchical system beyond sovereign space. It is, as Ashley explains, concerned with 'the never completed story of *the geopolitical domestication of global political space*' (Ashley, 1987: 423, original emphasis). The constitution of state sovereignty depends, therefore, on the vigilant displacement and transference of anarchy through statecraft. Importantly, as Ashley points out, this attempt to constitute domestic political space is a 'never completed story'.

Statecraft produces the state by the implementation and operationalization of an ensemble of practices and policies, both domestic and foreign. It is the mutually supportive relationship between these that combines to produce the effect of the state by instituting its various arms, apparatuses and spaces. As Foucault has documented so well, the performance of surveillance and intelligence operations internally is as attentive and vigilant as that which is maintained externally (Foucault, 1977 and 1991). His analysis of governmentality provides insight into the ways in which states organize practices of discipline and exclusion to effect the unity and homogeneity of the state. This suggests that the state is to be seen as an effect of both disciplinary practices which seek to normalize and homogenize a population, giving it a sense of internal unity, and exclusionary practices which seek to guarantee the security of this domestic society by differentiating it from, and securing it against, a threatening outside. The security discourse which is facilitated by statecraft depends on the complementary containment of 'threats', 'others', 'foreigners', etc., at both internal and external levels simultaneously. The overall effect is that the ensemble of practices referred to as statecraft continuously resecure the state by remaking the border.

In this formulation, the state is performatively constituted, and has no identity apart from the ceaseless performance of the ensemble of spatial and temporal enframing practices (Campbell, 1992: 8–9). It is through the constant administration and implementation of governmentality and foreign policy that statecraft produces the state by ordering and maintaining (in Machiavelli's sense) political borders and spaces. Its presence is an effect created by constant state-*crafting*, an effect constituted through the regular enactment of various acts of enframing and exclusion.

32 *Richard Devetak*

In no way is the state to be understood as simply present, as it is constantly in the process of being constituted or 'carried through', as Arendt might say. It is never settled or permanently closed off, sutured, sealed or completed. It is for this reason that Campbell asserts that foreign policy should not be understood simply as 'the external orientation of a pre-established state' (1992: 47). Foreign policy, as a form of statecraft, is a practice that gives shape to states, not something to which states resort *after* their full, completed constitution. Statecraft does not merely function to preserve an already given and complete state, but names the activity which creates the effect of the state. The implication of this is that statecraft constitutes the state in whose name it operates. 'Practices of statecraft do not radiate out from, and in the rational service of, centers of politics already made whose boundaries are already given' (Ashley, 1988: 101). Rather, statecraft makes possible the appearance of states as being already complete, self-present actors. The upshot of this is that statecraft is not something subsequent, or secondary to the state, but something 'supremely its own', something fundamental to its constitution. Perhaps the common view of the state preceding statecraft needs to be overturned, for in a certain (paradoxical) sense, statecraft precedes the state by making it possible.

This post-structuralist understanding leads to an interpretation of the state as an effect produced by the ceaseless work carried out in the service of a 'yet-to-be-completed' state identity. The state, therefore, is to be understood 'as an historically emergent and always contested product of multiple practices' (Ashley, 1987: 410). It is not a fixed, pre-given, once-and-for-all creation, but an ongoing political accomplishment (Wendt, 1992: 413). As Campbell points out, 'states are never finished as entities', they are necessarily 'always in a process of becoming' (1992: 11). Statecraft is employed here to capture this notion of the state as eternally 'becoming-state'; constantly struggling to maintain itself. Statecraft is the sign of the structural (that is, essential) impossibility of imposing closure over political space by finally marking the permanent presence or end of the state. As both Machiavelli and Hegel pointed out, the state is always in the process of being constituted and never arrives at a final moment of completion. The notion of the state as a unified totality breaks apart because incompletion is a structural trait of the state; there is negativity at the heart of the state. This is but another way of saying that there is statecraft, but there is no completed state.

CONCLUSIONS

The neo-realist supposition that the state exists prior to the system, or prior to the inscription of boundaries which make the demarcation of inside and outside possible, is not adequate to the task of comprehending the generative structure at play in international relations. In order to offer a generative notion of international structure it is necessary to inquire into the prior constitution of both the state and states system. This leads us to consider the constitutive role of boundaries and their inscription through statecraft, for states and the states system are both constituted through boundary-making.

The inscription of boundaries, however, is a ceaseless activity; so statecraft, which is the name for this activity, must also be ceaseless. Hence the conclusion that although there are no complete states, the maintenance work of statecraft continues.

The normative issue, which has not been broached here but which remains as an unsettling, supplementary question, is whether and how statecraft can be 'otherwise'. There are at least two dimensions to this: first, whether there can be a different statecraft which constitutes something other than the sovereign state, and second, whether statecraft can accept responsibility for both internal and external 'others'. If boundaries and totalities are neither complete nor fixed, it would appear that the idea of the *sovereign* state is rather tenuous. Alternative forms of state and statecraft might arise which are no longer sovereign or based on sovereignty. Perhaps the challenges from both above and below the level of the sovereign state are opening new possibilities for a state-craft which is not predicated on sovereignty and the exclusion of otherness, but allows a space for the 'other' to respond: an ethically 'responsible' statecraft will need to find ways of responding to demands for justice which are not accommodated by the system of sovereign states.[24] Indeed, an analysis might begin by acknowledging that moral obligations have never been completely totalized by sovereign states (Linklater, 1990b), which necessarily leads us to reflect once again on questions of community and the legitimacy of 'familiar' moral boundaries.[25] The task would be to inquire into the ways that the present mode of statecraft, in its continual struggle to exclude alternatives, may be giving way to an ethically 'responsible' statecraft. Such a statecraft, which is beyond sovereignty, is still to come.

NOTES

1. I am grateful to Hidemi Suganami, John MacMillan and Andrew Linklater for the extensive comments and advice they offered. It goes without saying, of course, that they are not responsible for the 'incompleteness' of the arguments advanced.
2. See the epigraph which heads Ashley and Walker's introduction to the special issue of *International Studies Quarterly* where Kristeva asks: 'how can we avoid sinking into the mire of common sense, if not by becoming a stranger to one's own country, language, sex and identity?' (1990: 259). For further discussion of the classical Greek notion of theory see Lobkowicz (1967: ch. 1).
3. For Derrida's discussion of the 'dangerous supplement' see *Of Grammatology* (part II, ch. 2). This, along with the opening chapter of the book, perhaps offers a useful place to begin reading Derrida.
4. There is a massive, and still growing, literature on deconstruction. Apart from Derrida's own work, very useful discussions can be found in Hart (1989: chs 4 and 5), Gasché (1986: chs 8 and 9), and Bennington (1994: parts 1 and 3 especially). Bennington (1994: chs 13 and 14) in particular broaches the sorts of political and international issues addressed here.
5. Although ethical issues will not be directly confronted here, it should not be assumed that deconstruction avoids or refuses discussion of ethics. Although deconstruction does not offer blue-prints for the future it maintains a critical

posture by pointing out how historically and politically contingent our social institutions are. It is particularly concerned with questions of 'alterity', that is, thinking about *other* possibilities in the present, and responsibility towards the *other*. See Derrida (1978: ch. 4), Critchley (1992) and Bernstein (1991: ch. 6) especially. Discussions of ethics and international relations from similar perspectives can be found in Walker (1993) and Ashley and Walker (1990: 389–95).

6. The notion of 'failing' states is to be found in Helman and Ratner (1992–3), that of 'quasi-states' in Jackson (1990).

7. A necessary corollary of this is that the system is never complete either, a claim which cannot be defended or developed here.

8. The Italian verbs which Machiavelli frequently used in reference to the state (*lo stato*) are *tenere* and *mantenere*, which mean respectively: to hold/grip, and to keep a hold/grip. See also the analyses by Walker (1993: ch. 2) and Honig (1991: 108–11) which offer comparable readings of Machiavelli.

9. A similar view of the state is to be found in the political philosophy of Hannah Arendt. Her understanding of political action draws upon the two Greek verbs *archein* ('to begin, to lead, and finally to rule') and *prattein* ('to carry something through') (1961: 165). All political institutions are predicated on political action which not only founds but maintains or carries them through. This leads to a view of the state as utterly dependent upon further acts to keep it in existence (1961: 153). For further discussion see Honig (1991).

10. Neo-realism refers to the work of Waltz, Grieco, Krasner and Fischer. Though it would require a separate chapter to argue the case that neo-liberals such as Keohane (1984) depend on essentially the same ontology as neo-realism, Wendt (1989) and Kratochwil and Ruggie (1986) begin the case.

11. It will be remembered that system comprises interacting units and structure in neo-realism (Waltz, 1979: 79). For an extended analysis and revision of these terms see Buzan, Jones and Little (1993). Discussion of 'successive causal depth levels', and the distinction between deep and shallow structure is to be found in Ruggie (1983: 266), Buzan (1989: 164) and Buzan, Jones and Little (1993: 37ff).

12. Hollis and Smith suggest that there has been a shift in Waltz from a 'strict structuralist account' to a 'softer notion of structure' (1990: 105) which gives greater causal weight to units. Waltz's concessive remarks on the US as 'better than most nations' on 'external as well as internal grounds' (1991: 670) also appear to vindicate their suggestion. It should be remembered, however, that Waltz was providing a 'foreign policy perspective' there rather than a theory of international politics. For his not altogether convincing rationale behind this distinction see Waltz (1979: 121–2 and 1986: 340).

13. Examples of this defining feature of the neo-realist ground are numerous. Consider James's claim that, 'the most fundamental characteristic of the international scene is the absence of an overarching authority' (1986: 5); and Oye's assertion that, 'Nations dwell in perpetual anarchy, for no central authority imposes limits on the pursuit of sovereign interests' (1985: 1). There is no question for neo-realists that anarchy is the 'first principle' which defines and organizes the international system (Waltz, 1979: 89). Waltz even dismisses the possibility that mixed orders such as 'mature anarchy' might exist (1979: 114). It appears beyond question that, '[a]narchy is', as Wight asserts, 'the characteristic that distinguishes international politics from ordinary politics' (Wight, 1986: 102). That is, anarchy becomes the first principle, origin or ground (*archè*) of neo-realist theory. The immutably anarchic condition is taken to be the natural point of departure for any inquiry into

international relations. Ashley refers to this defining moment of the neo-realist discourse as the *anarchy problematique*. According to Ashley, 'the anarchic international system ... becomes a foundational presence in its own right. It becomes the fixed external reality' (1989b: 287). Ironically, anarchy (an-*archè*) becomes the *archè*, the centre, the beginning and the end of neo-realist analysis. It is held to be the constant, essential presence of the international system and any study of international relations is obliged to begin by assuming anarchy as the permanent ordering principle which shapes international relations. Of course, the intention of this chapter is to show that this *archè* is in fact dependent on an anterior assumption (an unacknowledged *archè*) of the complete and bounded state.

14. By critical international theory is meant the work of Cox (1981 and 1987) and Linklater (1990a, 1992a, 1992b, 1994) in particular, but also Hoffman (1986). Linklater (1990b) and Ashley (1981) provide a normative basis upon which critical international theory builds.

15. In contrast to neo-realism, which privileges the states system, and Marxism, which finds strategic competition reducible to the world economy, critical international theory finds no fixed or determining relation between the states system and the capitalist world economy (Linklater, 1990a: ch.6). In his later work Linklater has elaborated an approach which analyses the dialectical relations between technical-instrumental, strategic, and moral-practical rationalization processes (1994). This means that the states system must be located in a wider social context which would necessarily include international society as well.

16. An indispensible source for critical international theory in this regard is the historical sociology literature. The work of Mann, Hall, Tilly and Giddens, amongst others, has provided an important means of integrating Marxian and Weberian themes into understandings of the state and states system. See Linklater (1990a), Jarvis (1989) and Rosenberg (1990), for further elaboration.

17. Mann was, of course, referring to societies in making this statement. However, it seems reasonable to extend it to the state, for it too is 'constituted of multiple overlapping and intersecting sociospatial networks of power' (1986a: 1). The opening pages of *The Sources of Social Power: Vol 1* make it abundantly clear that Mann considers the notion of totality to be less than useful in social inquiry; presumably the state as totality must also be jettisoned.

18. In his defence of neo-realism, Fischer denies that the emergence of the modern international system entailed any change in the behaviour of states or the deep structure of anarchy. His point is that a shift does occur at the level of discourse from one of 'communal norms' (1992: 434), to the 'discursive principle of sovereignty' (Fischer, 1992: 430), but that no such shift is discernible at the level of practice. According to Fischer, 'feudal actors ultimately disregarded their communal discourse and engaged in power politics in the manner of modern states' (Fischer, 1990: 443). Fischer seems to miss the point of critical international theory here. He assumes that critical international theory is bemoaning the shift into the modern international states system and its corollary of sovereignty, however, there is no such sentimentalizing of the medieval system in critical international theory. Critical international theory is concerned with explaining and understanding the shift in constitutive principles. See Ruggie (1983, 1989 and 1993) who provides the most useful analysis of this shift.

19. As Bull points out, the idea of an international order consisting 'principally or exclusively of a single kind of political entity called "states" could not take shape' until the concept of sovereignty was institutionalized (1977: 29). See Ruggie (1993)

for an excellent survey of the political, material, social and conceptual changes
which made possible the emergence of the modern states system.

20. Giddens distinguishes between frontiers and borders. In the medieval system,
frontiers marked areas on the 'peripheral regions' of political units in which 'the
political authority of the centre is diffuse or thinly spread' (1985: 50). In the
modern international system, borders represented 'nothing other than lines drawn
to demarcate states' sovereignty' (Giddens, 1985: 51). See also Ruggie (1993: 150).

21. The consolidation of sovereignty 'was partly achieved through centralization of
methods of law enforcement' (Giddens, 1985: 151). By this Giddens suggests that
internal pacification and the exclusion of outsiders is predicated on the organization
of the means of violence; in short, sovereignty is intrinsically linked to violence.
Giddens' analysis is influenced here by Foucault's analyses of discipline and
governmentality. Poggi also refers to the concern with policing in the absolutist
states: 'a prime concern of absolutist rule was exactly the authoritative regulation
and promotion of the private preoccupation of individuals' (1978: 78). See also
Tilly's argument about state formation resulting from a mixture of war-making,
state-making (subjugating internal rivals), protection (of friends), and extraction of
finance (1985: 181-6).

22. The work of the English school (or rationalism) provides a rich resource regarding
the dissemination and cultivation of international norms and rules. In its
examination of the constitutive systemic principles which generate the international
system, it demonstrates that diplomatic and international political culture function
to impose criteria which determine the actors and shape their actions. Apprehension
of these constitutive or ordering principles is only possible if something like an
'international social consciousness', as Wight called it, is presupposed (1966: 97). A
discussion of the rationalist contribution to critical international theory can be
found in Linklater (1990a: 15-21, 1992a). Other recent redeployments of rationalism
include Wendt and Duvall (1989), and Der Derian (1987).

23. This discussion draws from Hegel's discussion of 'Force and the understanding'
(1977: 79-103). See also Hegel's famous discussion of the struggle between 'lord'
and 'bondsman' (1977: 111–19). This reading of Hegel draws heavily from Kojève's
influential interpretation, see Descombes (1980: ch.1), Kristeva (1984: part II), and
Roberts (1988: 68ff) for similar readings of Hegel.

24. Derrida invokes the notion of 'responsibility' as the 'right of response' in his
reflections on European identity/culture (1992a: 105). In connection with this see
also his reflections on justice (Derrida, 1992b).

25. Reflections on community, exclusion and otherness can be found in Linklater
(1990b, 1992b and 1993) and Walker (1993). Linklater (1992a and 1993) explores
the notion of 'good international citizenship', which might also be taken as an
alternative form of statecraft.

REFERENCES

Arendt, H., 1961, *Between Past and Future: Six Exercises in Political Thought*, London,
Faber and Faber.

Ashley, R.K., 1981, 'Political Realism and Human Interests', *International Studies Quarterly*, 25 (2): 204–36.

Ashley, R.K., 1984, 'The Poverty of Neorealism', *International Organization*, 38 (2),
Spring: 225–86.

Ashley, R.K., 1987, 'The Geopolitics of Geopolitical Space: Toward a Critical Social Theory of International Politics', *Alternatives*, 7: 403–34.

Ashley, R.K., 1988, 'Geopolitics, Supplementary, Criticism: A Reply to Professors Roy and Walker', *Alternatives*, 8: 88–102.

Ashley, R.K., 1989a, 'Imposing International Purpose: Notes on a Problematic of Governance', in Czempiel, E.-O. and Rosenau, J. (eds), *Global Changes and Theoretical Challenges: Approaches to World Politics for the 1990s*, Lexington, Lexington Books: 251–90.

Ashley, R.K., 1989b, 'Living on Border Lines: Man, Poststructuralism, and War', in Der Derian, J. and Shapiro, M.J. (eds), *International/Intertextual Relations*, Lexington, Lexington Books: 259–321.

Ashley, R.K. and Walker, R.B.J., 1990, 'Reading Dissidence/Writing the Discipline: Crisis and the Question of Sovereignty in International Studies', *International Studies Quarterly*, 34 (3), September: 367–416.

Bennington, G., 1994, *Legislations: The Politics of Deconstruction*, London, Verso.

Bernstein, R., 1991, *The New Constellation: The Ethical-Political Horizons of Modernity/Postmodernity*, Cambridge, Polity Press.

Bull, H., 1977, *The Anarchical Society: A Study of Order in World Politics*, London, Macmillan.

Buzan, B., Jones, C. and Little, R., 1993, *The Logic of Anarchy: Neorealism to Structural Realism*, New York, Columbia University Press.

Campbell, D., 1992, *Writing Security: United States Foreign Policy and the Politics of Identity*, Minneapolis, University of Minnesota Press.

Cox, R.W., 1981, 'Social Forces, States and World Orders: Beyond International Relations Theory', *Millennium*, 10 (2): 126–55.

Cox, R.W., 1987, *Production, Power, and World Order: Social Forces in the Making of History*, New York, Columbia University Press.

Der Derian, J., 1987, *On Diplomacy: A Genealogy of Western Estrangement*, Oxford, Basil Blackwell.

Der Derian, J., 1992, *Antidiplomacy: Spies, Terror, Speed, and War*, Oxford, Basil Blackwell.

Derrida, J., 1974, *Of Grammatology* (trans. Gayatri Chakravorty Spivak), Baltimore, MD, Johns Hopkins University Press.

Derrida, J., 1978, *Writing and Difference* (trans. Alan Bass), Henley, Routledge and Kegan Paul.

Derrida, J., 1992a, *The Other Heading: Reflections on Today's Europe* (trans. P.-A. Brault and M. Naas), Bloomington, Indiana University Press.

Derrida, J., 1992b, 'Force of Law: The "Mystical Foundation of Authority"', in D. Cornell, M. Rosenfeld and D. Carlson (eds), *Deconstruction and the Possibility of Justice*, New York, Routledge.

Descombes, V., 1980, *Modern French Philosophy* (trans. L. Scott-Fox and J.M. Harding), Cambridge, Cambridge University Press.

Fischer, M., 1992, 'Feudal Europe, 800–1300: Communal Discourse and Conflictual Practices', *International Organization*, 46 (2), Spring: 427–66.

Foucault, M., 1977, *Discipline and Punish: The Birth of the Prison* (trans. A. Sheridan), Middlesex, Penguin.

Foucault, M., 1991, 'Governmentality', in G. Burchell, C. Gordon and P. Miller (eds), *The Foucault Effect: Studies in Governmentality*, Hertfordshire, England, Harvester Wheatsheaf.

Gasché, R., 1986, *The Tain of the Mirror: Derrida and the Philosophy of Reflection*, Cambridge, MA, Harvard University Press.

Halliday, F., 1987, 'State and Society in International Relations: A Second Agenda', *Millennium*, 16 (2), Summer: 215–29.

Hart, K., 1989, *Trespass of the Sign: Deconstruction, Theology and Philosophy*, Cambridge, Cambridge University Press.

Hegel, G.W.F., 1956, *Philosophy of History* (trans. J. Sibree), New York, Dover Press.

Hegel, G.W.F., 1967, *Philosophy of Right* (trans. T.M. Knox), Oxford, Oxford University Press.

Hegel, G.W.F., 1977, *Phenomenology of Spirit* (trans. A.V. Miller), Oxford, Oxford University Press.

Helman, G. and Ratner, S., 1992-3, 'Saving Failed States', *Foreign Policy*, 89, Winter: 3–20.

Hoffman, M., 1987, 'Critical Theory and the Inter-Paradigm Debate', *American Political Science Review*, 16 (2), Summer: 231–49.

Hollis, M. and Smith, S., 1990, *Explaining and Understanding International Relations*, Oxford, Clarendon Press.

Honig, B., 1991, 'Declarations of Independence: Arendt and Derrida on the Problem of Founding a Republic', *American Political Science Review*, 85 (1), March: 84–113.

Jackson, R., 1990, *Quasi-States: Sovereignty, International Relations, and the Third World*, Cambridge, Cambridge University Press.

James, A., 1986, *Sovereign Statehood: the Basis of International Society*, London, Allen & Unwin.

Jarvis, A., 1989, 'Societies, States and Geopolitics: challenges from Historical Sociology', *Review of International Studies*, 15: 281–93.

Keohane, R.O., 1984, *After Hegemony: Cooperation and Discord in the World Political Economy*, Princeton, NJ, Princeton University Press.

Kratochwil, F. and Ruggie, J. G., 1986, 'International Organization: a State of the Art on an Art of the State,' *International Organization*, 40 (4): 753–75.

Kristeva, J., 1984, *Revolution in Poetic Language* (trans. M. Waller), New York, Columbia University Press.

Linklater, A., 1990a, *Beyond Realism and Marxism: Critical Theory and International Relations*, London, Macmillan.

Linklater, A., 1990b, *Men and Citizens in the Theory of International Relations*, 2nd edn, London, Macmillan.

Linklater, A., 1992a, 'What is a Good International Citizen', in Keal, P. (ed), *Ethics and Foreign Policy*, Canberra, Allen & Unwin.

Linklater, A., 1992b, 'The Question of the Next Stage in International Relations Theory: A Critical-Theoretical Point of View,' *Millennium*, 21 (1), Spring.

Linklater, A., 1993, 'Community, Citizenship and Global Politics', *Oxford International Review*, 5 (1), Winter: 6–9.

Linklater, A., 1994, 'Rationalisation Processes and International History: Critical Theory, Post-structuralism and International Relations', in N. Rengger and M. Hoffman (eds), *Beyond the Inter-Paradigm Debate: Critical Theory and International Relations* (forthcoming), Brighton, Sussex, Wheatsheaf.

Machiavelli, N., 1970, *The Discourses* (trans. L.J. Walker), Harmondsworth, Penguin Books.

Mann, M., 1986a, *The Sources of Social Power: Volume 1, A History of Power from the Beginning to A.D. 1760*, Cambridge, Cambridge University Press.

Mann, M., 1986b, 'The Autonomous Power of the State: Its Origins, Mechanisms and Results,' in J. Hall (ed.), *States in History*, Oxford, Basil Blackwell.

Mearsheimer, J., 1990, 'Back to the Future: Instability in Europe After the Cold War', *International Security*, 15 (1), Summer: 5–56.

Oye, K., 1985, 'Explaining Cooperation Under Anarchy: Hypotheses and Strategies', *World Politics*, 38 (1): 1–24.

Poggi, G, 1978, *The Development of the Modern State: a Sociological Introduction*, Stanford, CA, Stanford University Press.

Roberts, J., 1988, *German Philosophy: An Introduction*, Cambridge, Polity Press.

Rosenberg, J., 1990, 'A Non-Realist Theory of Sovereignty?: Giddens' *The Nation-State and Violence*', *Millennium*, 19 (2): 249–59.

Ruggie, J.G., 1983, 'Continuity and Transformation in the World Polity: Toward a Neo-Realist Synthesis', *World Politics*, 35 (2), January: 261–85.

Ruggie, J.G., 1989, 'International Structure and International Transformation: Space, Time, and Method', in Czempiel, E.-O. and Rosenau, J. (eds), *Global Changes and Theoretical Challenges: Approaches to World Politics for the 1990's*, Lexington, Lexington Books: 21–35

Ruggie, J.G., 1993, 'Territoriality and Beyond: Problematizing Modernity in International Relations', *International Organization*, 47 (1): 139–74.

Tilly, C., 1985, 'War Making and State Making as Organized Crime,' in P. Evans et. al. (eds), *Bringing the State Back In*, Cambridge, Cambridge University Press.

Walker, R.B.J., 1990, 'Sovereignty, Identity, Community: Reflections on the Horizons of Contemporary Political Practice', in R.B.J. Walker and S. Mendlovitz (eds), *Contending Sovereignties*, Boulder, CO, Lynne Reinner: 159–85.

Walker, R.B.J., 1993, *Inside/Outside: International Relations as Political Theory*, Cambridge, Cambridge University Press.

Waltz, K., 1959, *Man, the State and War: A Theoretical Analysis*, New York, Columbia University Press.

Waltz, K., 1979, *Theory of International Politics*, New York, Random House.

Waltz, K., 1989, 'The Origins of War in Neorealist Theory', in Rotberg, R.I. and Rabb, T.K. (eds), *The Origins and Prevention of Major Wars*, Cambridge, Cambridge University Press.

Waltz, K., 1990, 'Realist Thought and Neorealist Theory', *Journal of International Relations*, 44 (1): 21–37.

Waltz, K., 1991, 'America as a Model for the World? A Foreign Policy Perspective', *PS: Political Science and Politics*, December: 667–70.

Waltz, K., 1993, 'The Emerging Structure of International Politics', *International Security*, 18 (2), Fall: 44–79.

Wendt, A., 1987, 'The Agent-Structure Problem in International Relations Theory', *International Organization*, 41 (3), Summer: 335–70.

Wendt, A., 1992, 'Anarchy is What States Make of it: the Social Construction of Power Politics', *International Organization*, 46 (2), Spring: 392–425.

Wendt, A. and Duvall, R., 1989, 'Institutions and International Order', in Czempiel, E.-O. and Rosenau, J. (eds), *Global Changes and Theoretical Challenges: Approaches to World Politics for the 1990's*, Lexington, Lexington Books: 51–73.

Wight, M., 1966, 'Western Values in International Relations,' in Butterfield, H. and Wight, M. (eds), *Diplomatic Investigations*: 89–131.

Wight, M., 1986, *Power Politics*, 2nd edn, Harmondsworth, Penguin Books.

2
Cosmopolitanism and communitarianism in a post-Cold War world

Molly Cochran

Since 1989, the global order has experienced significant changes. The end of the Cold War has loosened two opposing forces, integration and fragmentation, releasing many practical difficulties for an emergent global order. This chapter argues that the normative questions generated by these practical difficulties suggest the need for a re-examination of the focus of international theory. The first section examines the features of this post-Cold War world and the practical problems it presents for sovereign states in particular. The second examines why the changes in a new global order require a shift in our theoretical approach to international relations. The third section argues that the recent debate between cosmopolitans and communitarians provides a helpful point of departure for addressing the fundamental questions of the new global order.

THE POST-COLD WAR WORLD

The events that have signalled the emergence of a new global order are numerous, namely the fall of communist regimes in Eastern Europe and the former Soviet Union, the unification of Germany, collapse of the Warsaw Pact, the 1990 CFE treaty, START I and II; a revitalized if not altogether clearly defined role for the United Nations in Iraq, Somalia, Yugoslavia and Rwanda; and the beginnings of the end to white minority rule in South Africa. This period has been marked by the most broadly significant and rapid change that has taken place since 1945. In this changed landscape, the ethical as well as the political language of the Cold War must be called into question.

With the collapse of the Soviet Union withers the previous bipolar international system. Nor is it likely to experience a rebirth, given that the Commonwealth of Independent States (CIS) remains an association with no real shape or purpose, and the economic tailspin from decades of communist over-centralization has left lifeless the renewal of a Greater Russia. So what are we left with structurally? Multipolarity is a misnomer as it connotes a time in the nineteenth century when five great powers, for the most part equal, balanced power among themselves. No such analogous situation exists today. Although the United States is the world's one military stalwart and has served as captain of a world police force under United Nations sponsorship, there is no sign of an emerging unipolar arrangement. Power is more complex, as the fall of the USSR clearly demonstrates. Discussion of world political structure in terms of polarity has broken down.

The breakup of the Cold War stalemate changes the dimensions of security. As Gaddis points out, 'one can no longer plausibly point to a single source of danger, as one could throughout most of that conflict ... the end of the Cold War, therefore, brings not an end to threats, but rather a diffusion of them' (Gaddis: 1991, 113). And what is the source of this multiplicity of threats? Simply put, the ground is shifting. The artificial anchor of international relations, state sovereignty, is losing its hold. As Rosenau expresses it, we are moving into 'post-international politics' (1992: 13). States are more permeable; their sovereignty is disintegrating under the strains of two forces, the rise of ethnic/national pressures below the level of the state and the increasingly significant expanding transnational linkages above.

Clearly, tumult in international politics is nothing new or unique, yet the forces of integration and fragmentation are a profound new source of disorder. While the traditional notion of balance is still relevant, it now has a changed meaning – we seek balanced transition as these forces play themselves out.

Gaddis outlines these forces by pointing towards integration in communications, ideas, economics and security. Of the communications revolution, one could argue that the media pictures of camps in the former Yugoslavia and the emaciated figures of human beings in Somalia were, in large measure, the source of renewed outcry and international effort towards these crises. Communications have led to the spread and integration of ideas. Evidence rests in the force of liberal democratic ideas which toppled authoritarian regimes in Eastern Europe. Of economic integration, this means that no state can sustain itself in isolation for very long. Transnational actors thus have increasing influence upon states and their economies. Of security, although it is true that states still rely on their own forces for security, the effect of this creeping integration in ideas, communications and economics, as well as the shared security dilemmas represented in the transition to a new global order, is a realization that a renewed attempt at collective security could be advantageous. Thus the United Nations is at the centre of current security debates.

Integrationist trends are challenged by forces of fragmentation. Three such forces discussed by Gaddis are nationalism, religion and economics. The collapse of the Cold War structures unleashed ethnic nationalism as a primary source of international insecurity. In the new states of the former USSR, former Yugoslavia, former Czechoslovakia, Spain, Belgium, Canada, Sudan, Ethiopia and Rwanda, to name but some, borders and sovereign governments as we knew or know them cannot be taken for granted. Religion, particularly the rise of Islam, is a source of fragmentation. Currents within Islam have sought to set themselves apart as a force in opposition to Western hegemony. Gaddis points to Beirut as a picture of what the world could resemble if such forces predominate. Although economics is noted in the section on integrationist tendencies, it also encourages fragmentation in the form of protectionism. The Uruguay round of GATT nearly ground to a halt at the conclusion of

1992 over agriculture subsidies. Gaddis's list does fail in one important respect. In his discussion of economic fragmentation he fails to mention the glaring inequalities between rich and poor states, which threaten world order. Although seemingly not as immediate a threat as ethnic nationalism, the demands for a just global distribution of wealth represents another source of international fragmentation.

At least one significant change from the Cold War world is clearly evident. The bipolar world structure has seemingly crumbled overnight. Yet changes in the nature of power, state sovereignty and the emergence of integrationary forces or ethnic nationalism are not necessarily new. World society approaches and the pluralist paradigm developed in international theory two decades ago in an attempt to understand and account for the effect of such changes in international relations. Thus one could certainly argue that these aspects of multidimensional power structures, porous states and integrationist and nationalist forces are really nothing new. These *features* may not be new, but in the vacuum left by the collapse of Cold War structures, the forces of integration and fragmentation have realized an unprecedented intensity.

The collapse of what Gaddis aptly terms the Cold War 'crisis management regime' leaves us with no signposts for decision-making in the face of several practical difficulties which these opposing forces present. Faced with this level of fragmentation in world politics, how do we decide whether and when the international community should grant recognition to the many ethnic minorities clamouring for status as autonomous states? What are the requirements of sovereignty – economic self-sufficiency, a monopoly on the legitimate use of violence, or something more constitutive regarding its relation to the individual? How many new states can international society peacefully absorb? Is there or should there be a limit? The timeliness of recognition is also an issue, as the war in former Yugoslavia demonstrates. The international recognition of the independence of Slovenia and Croatia at an early stage in the Yugoslav conflict only served to exacerbate ethnic tensions, extending hostilities.

Regarding the present level of integration, does integration require us to think again about the constitutive unit of contemporary international relations, the sovereign state? Questions about changes in the role of the state raise a host of related issues about the bounds of state authority, the nature and locus of justice, and what entitlements individuals and states legitimately hold. If the state is experiencing multi-level infringments, does this limit the state in effectively fulfilling its role as regards its citizens, and if so how and to what extent? Whose responsibility is it to fill in the gap, if it is anyone's? For example, with no effective government in Rwanda, does the international community have any obligations towards the Rwandan people? If so, what is the extent of these obligations and to whom are they owed – to all Rwandans, or just to certain parties?

These questions inevitably accompany the forces of integration and fragmentation identified above. For reasons of both integration and fragmentation, we must be clear on the requirements of sovereign statehood and the responsibilities of not just states but other international actors as well. To this end, philosophical evaluation of fundamental political concepts and values is required.

THE NEW GLOBAL ORDER: THE NEED FOR A NEW THEORETICAL APPROACH

Joseph Nye notes that shortly after the 1991 Gulf War 'the flow of White House words about a new world order slowed to a trickle' (1992: 83). When the Gulf War sands settled, the size of the task left at hand was daunting: Saddam remained, as ever the tiger who would not change his stripes; the Kurds, encouraged by the West to overthrow Saddam, then desperately needed the West's protection and pressed for the Kurdish state promised in First World War settlements; former Soviet republics were asking for international recognition and economic assistance; and Yugoslavia, ripped apart by civil war, left constituent republics also asking for international recognition and support. With these pressures Bush could not continue rhetoric at the pre-war level, describing the new world order as:

> an order in which no nation must surrender one iota of its own sovereignty; an order characterized by the rule of law rather than the resort to force; the cooperative settlement of disputes, rather than anarchy and bloodshed, and an unstinting belief in human rights (Kissinger, 1991).

The complexities of this statement reflect the conflicting norms regarded as 'settled' within international relations.[1] Norms and laws in international relations facilitate a conception of international society, a society in the Bullian sense that promotes order and cooperation among international actors (Bull, 1977). Yet contradictory principles within this set of norms pull at one another, which in turn perpetuates tensions within international society. These norms require thought and discussion in order to avoid normative confusion and enable the pressing questions of the new global order to be addressed.

How can the society of states and its conventional principles of state sovereignty and non-intervention be preserved while at the same time maintaining a norm of human rights? The right to self-determination written into the United Nations Charter to protect its member states has evolved to safeguard minorities within states, potentially sanctioning secession.[2] As each state is sovereign, the equality of states is also assumed within international norms, yet only five states sit permanently, with veto power, on the Security Council of the United Nations. And without equality, force may remain a seductive recourse for international actors. There is an understated hierarchy among 'settled norms' to counterbalance these tensions; none the less questions must be asked. Are these norms as they exist justifiable? If so, how do you choose among or prioritize them?

At the crux of these dilemmas lies a philosophical question: what are the freedoms/obligations of individuals by nature of their humanity versus the freedoms/obligations by nature of their citizenship of a state? Andrew Linklater (1990) writes that this 'problem of the relationship between men and citizens' is a 'very significant part of the history of modern international thought'. Do individuals within a state have any obligations to individuals living outside the state? Do states have obligations to anyone else but their citizenry? What is the moral standing of states? Clearly, answers to these questions are pivotal to the tensions apparent in the norms of the international system, tensions exacerbated by the practical difficulties faced in the forces of integration and fragmentation at work today.

In order to evaluate whether certain norms are justifiable, or decide how to prioritize them, moral philosophizing cannot be avoided. This presents a problem. Political theory, our strongest link to these moral philosophical questions, has long suffered under the weight of Martin Wight's 'Why is There No International Theory?', an essay that burns the bridge between political theory and international theory.[3] Wight writes that political theory is speculation about the state and international theory is 'imagined' speculation about the relation of states. Never the twain shall meet as, unlike domestic politics, international politics is 'less susceptible to progressivist interpretations' (Butterfield and Wight, 1966: 26). The work of Brown, Frost and Linklater serves to rebuild the connecting bridge between political and international theory. Although each labels that bridge differently – Linklater makes a case for international political theory, Brown writes about international relations theory, Frost elaborates a normative theory of international relations – they all work to get us to the same place, a recognition that international theory benefits from an understanding of itself as an extension of the project of political theory beyond the confines of the state. This is a project better equipped to ask the necessary questions outlined above.

As Chris Brown's book is the latest addition to such a project, I choose to focus on his construction of the international political theory bridge here.[4] Brown answers Wight by pointing to a definitional problem. In defining political theory as speculation about the state, Wight sidetracks himself into placing international and political theory on dual, but separate, tracks. Brown argues this definition is 'highly contentious'. True, political theory is more than consideration of the state and relations within. It also evaluates societal value structures. As Brown writes, Plato was primarily concerned with justice, not the state of which he had no experience. As the picture painted in the last section demonstrates, a normative value such as justice has just as much relevance to the international system today, but why did Wight not see it that way? Brown answers:

> It can be seen that the sorts of limits accepted by Wight were characteristic of the age: it can also be seen that modern work which transcends these limits is also characteristic of *its* age (1992: 7).

It is the argument of this chapter that the emerging global order suggests a need for the development of normative theory in International Relations. The seeds for this development are evident in the transition of Hedley Bull's thought. In an early essay by Bull, also in the *Diplomatic Investigations* collection, Bull has similar doubts to Wight regarding morality in international relations, arguing that Grotius is premature to set laws substantiating his moral vision 'over the facts' (Butterfield and Wight, 1966: 73). The facts are clearly different today. As Brown points out, '"real-world" events' such as the Six Days War, the Vietnam War and the call for a New International Economic Order have led to the practical realization that morals are not above the facts of international relations. Hedley Bull's last writings evolved with recognition of the new facts.

Never one to deny the relevance of moral questions to international relations, Bull none the less writes with an element of moral scepticism, particularly in *The Anarchical Society*.[5] In this work, Bull sets up a dichotomy between order and justice, privileging order. In his 1984 Hagey Lectures Bull moves beyond this dichotomy, arguing that international society's failure to accommodate Third World demands for justice indeed threatens international society. To preserve international society, order must be reconciled with justice, building upon the existing conception of a 'world common good' with as wide a consensus as possible in the interest not of states, but of 'the human species maintaining itself'.[6] If this 'traditional', as he called himself, English School theorist came to recognize moral theory as a fact in international society, then perhaps a shift in international theory from discussion of realist, rationalist or revolutionist paradigms towards international political theory is a plausible alternative better to study the new global order.

The recent writings of two foreign policy analysis writers, Charles Kegley and James Rosenau, speak to the importance of normative values in the post-Cold War world. Rosenau writes that the forces of integration and fragmentation creating the new global order will force choices with huge moral implications, and he offers grounds to be optimistic about the creation of new normative standards that will guide international relations (1992: 16). Kegley also writes that the search for a moral vision is necessary:

> we would be mistaken to endorse a purely instrumental pragmatism that evaluates alternative courses of action exclusively by 'rational' cost benefit analysis of their relative merit. An ethical consensus *is* needed more than ever to promote justice and security in a new world order that is not really new, and certainly not orderly (1992: 24).

Having examined the need for a normative theory of international relations, we must now look at the task outlined by international political theory. Chris Brown writes that 'the aim is to show how things "hang together"', but this definition of the task is somewhat lacking. If in continuum with political theory, international political theory should do more than see 'how things "hang together"'. D.D. Raphael writes that there are two aspects to political philosophy: the critical evaluation of beliefs and the clarification of concepts (1970: 8–20). The critical evaluation of beliefs is an attempt to move from *doxa* to *sophia*, from mere opinion to wisdom or knowledge, seeking a hierarchy of values to guide thought and action. This means putting commonly accepted beliefs under rational scrutiny, pursuing grounds for their justification. The clarification of concepts in large measure works to serve the evaluation of

beliefs. It attempts to chip away at what Gallie has labelled 'essentially contested concepts' such as equality, justice and democracy in order to understand
what we mean by these terms.

Thus political theory does not simply explore established values and what
we understand by them. It is normative, asking the 'should' and 'ought' questions of which values or standards generate a better polity. In discussing the
confusion surrounding normative theory, Brown acknowledges there are two
activities involved in such theory – the setting of standards and the study of
how standards are set – but the tone of his discussion is repentant, stating that
normative theorists have 'no right to prescribe'. Brown is unwilling to offer
normative grounds for value preference or suggestions for improvement within
the international system. Perhaps that is not the task of his book. None the
less, Brown, like Wight, is left with a definitional problem. His definition of
international political theory limits him in regard to pursuing the traditional
role of political theory, the critical evaluation of beliefs.

The clarification of debates and processes of standard-setting, while bene-
ficial, is not enough. The questions thrust upon us by this new global order
require that we draw some conclusions regarding what constitutes a good global
order. Thus Linklater's notion of political theory as 'articulating the principles
of a more perfect political order' is better suited to the task (1990: 3). I want
to define the aim of international political theory as evaluating the processes of
value consensus toward an improved world order. Understood in this way,
international political theory is useful not just in examining how the difficult
choices of a new global order are arrived at, but in critically evaluating criteria
which may shape that order.

COSMOPOLITANS AND COMMUNITARIANS

The remainder of this chapter aims to demonstrate how international political theory as defined above can help us address the questions left at the end
of the first section. As the state experiences multi-level infringements on its
sovereignty, what becomes of its role? What is the proper relationship between
individuals and states? Are states no more than privileged power practices or
should they, like individuals, be the subject of justice? Before us are moral
ends that do not square easily: the advancement of human rights and individual
freedoms, regard for community/state autonomy and integrity, and a fair distribution of resources and goods. Choices among these ends have become all
the more pressing under the force of integrationary and fragmentary oppositions at work in the international system today.

The cosmopolitan/communitarian debate recently outlined by Brown and
Janna Thompson provides an excellent framework for dealing with the above
issues (Brown, 1992; Thompson, 1992). Herein rests the appropriateness of
international political theory, as the two ethical positions – cosmopolitanism
and communitarianism – address the value assumptions at the base of the
choices we face in a new global order. At stake within the debate are three
issues: (1) a conception of the person and what constitutes the good life for

the individual; (2) the question of the moral standing of states, whether states promote or impede the living of a good life by individuals; and (3) universalism versus particularism, whether there exists an external standpoint by which moral judgements can be made across cultures.

Regarding a conception of the person, two cosmopolitans, Charles Beitz and Thomas Pogge, hold that individuals have moral personality, that is, individuals are free and equal moral persons capable of a sense of justice, and of forming and revising a conception of the good (Beitz, 1979 and 1983 and Pogge, 1989). This person is a pre-social individual who chooses his or her own attributes, unencumbered by social attachments. For the communitarian, such an understanding of the person is untenable as the individual is socially embedded. Janna Thompson and Mervyn Frost understand the individual to be constituted by the social matrices in which one is participant.[7] The moral ends of cosmopolitan individuals are empty, as they have no grounding in the shared understandings of communities. Moral personality is not a feature of persons we can take as given. Instead, the autonomy it suggests requires development within a social context.

From these two conceptions of the person follow dissenting views regarding the moral standing of states. To the cosmopolitan, states have no normative relevance. Beitz acknowledges that the existence of states is a fact of world politics, but holds that the autonomy of states cannot be maintained in the face of complex interdependence. Autonomy is something we confer upon states, a mistake which results from 'reading "states" for "persons"' (1979: 76). Unlike persons, states are not morally relevant. For the cosmopolitan, the primary source of value rests not in institutions that compartmentalize humanity, but in humanity itself. Communitarians, on the other hand, do regard states as morally relevant. As Thompson writes, a case for the morality of states can be made if a state 'protects, enhances or makes possible the national life that people value' (1992: 177). The state is an ethical forum where duties are made possible, where the socially constituted individual can realize himself or herself fully. As Frost writes, 'citizenship of a good state is not an option for a free person, but it is rather a precondition for the existence of a free person' (1986: 174–5). Both recognize that not all states fulfil this role, but that their potential to do so must be explored and encouraged.

The universalism versus particularism question asks whether there are any independent criteria for moral judgements. The cosmopolitan recognizes in each individual a capacity to form and follow a conception of the good, yet sees no rational means for arbitrating among those goods when they come into public, political conflict. Avoiding an appeal to religious or metaphysical foundations, the cosmopolitan posits a detached standpoint in order to transcend the particularism of plural goods. Beitz and Pogge borrow John Rawls's notion of an original position, extending its scope to a global original position between individuals under a veil of ignorance. In this way a consensus on international distributive justice can be reached procedurally by all, allowing the universal claims that a cosmopolitan concern for the entitlements of humankind wants to make. For communitarians, values, ends, goods fostered within the state, constitute a tradition. Social tradition within the state is the framework that founds and enables the ethical discourse in which social judgements are possible. Thus the search for independent criteria is not an issue within states; it is a problem between states, as the world is not a single community whose social tradition shapes or constitutes individuals.

The framework provided by cosmopolitanism and communitarianism facilitates an understanding of the values at stake in a new global order, but Brown and Thompson agree that in the end we are led to what seems to be an impasse. Indeed, Brown says 'in the last resort the extent to which communitarian as opposed to cosmopolitan thought is convincing seems to depend more on the "gut" feelings of individual authors than on processes of reasoned argument' (1992: 75). It remains a question for this debate whether the above issues can be reconciled or whether they are incommensurable. While Brown is unwilling to draw conclusions, Thompson suggests that the impasse can be avoided. One indicator of this possibility is seen if we compare notes with an older cousin, the liberal/communitarian debate in political theory.

This debate has featured prominently in political theory for twenty years, prompted by the publication of John Rawls's *A Theory of Justice* in 1971. Although the morality of states is not an issue in this debate, a conception of the person and the question of universalism versus particularism are significant issues that it shares with cosmopolitans and communitarians.[8] In recent years it appears that a substantial part of the debate has ebbed. Rawls has written numerous articles, revised and collected in *Political Liberalism* (1993), which in the opinion not only of his critics, but also of those sympathetic to his earlier work, significantly alters his theory of justice. The extent to which Rawls has been swayed by the communitarian position is a matter of debate, but his later work does exhibit more expressly communitarian concerns (Kukathas and Petit, 1990; Mulhall and Swift, 1992; Bellamy, 1992). As Charles Beitz, Thomas Pogge and Janna Thompson all draw upon Rawls's work to internationalize distributive justice, the movement in Rawls's thought has repercussions for the cosmopolitan/communitarian debate as well. A closer examination of these three writers' positions on the issues of a conception of the person, the moral standing of states and universalism versus particularism leads to the suggestion that the poles of the debate are narrowing.

A CONCEPT OF THE PERSON

The conception of the person offered by these writers ranges from a Kantian notion of moral personality to a Hegelian understanding of individuals as socially constituted. In response to his critics, Beitz acknowledges in 'Cosmopolitan Ideals and National Sentiment' (1983) that international interdependence is not at a level that can sustain his argument for a global cooperative venture. None the less, he still wants to maintain that membership of an original position should be global. Leaning upon a Kantian conception of moral personality, he writes that the criterion of membership is a capacity for justice and an ability to form a conception of the good. As all humans have these capacities whether they are members of cooperative schemes or not, membership of the original position should be global. Thus Beitz fixes this concept of the person as an Archimedean point from which a consensus on justice can be universalized.

Pogge, on the other hand, only implicitly endorses this notion of moral personality (1989). In using a Rawlsian framework, extending Rawls's idea of a domestic overlapping consensus to the international level, Pogge endorses the notion of a person as a free and equal moral being. The value of an overlapping consensus rests in its public justifiability, that it is agreed to by all, which in turn is linked to respect for this conception of the person as free and equal. The problem is, if anyone objects to this liberal conception of the person, saying his or her own conception of the good is compromised by this public liberal notion, the consensus falls apart. In considering such a challenge, Pogge does not choose to justify why we should accept the conception of the person implicit in his work. In defence, he falls back upon the notion of reasonable disagreement, that there are bound to be issues of contention without resolution which we must bear with tolerance.

Thompson's concern with Rawls's starting point is that it yields a conception of justice which cannot adequately explain why individuals regard it as important to be committed to their nation. In contrast, she begins with a concept of persons as socially organized. Yet like Rawls, Thompson is interested in the possibility of political consensus in plural societies. Beyond the notion of an overlapping consensus, she develops a notion of overlapping, interlocking communities to found an international distributive justice which can account for an individual's loyalty to community.

These different representations of themes in Rawls's work illuminate an interesting shift. That is, the Archimedean point Beitz wants to establish in a concept of the person as a fixed point for a global theory of justice is not taken up by the theorists who write subsequently. Unlike Beitz, Pogge is unwilling explicitly to defend this conception of the person, and Thompson abandons it altogether.

THE MORALITY OF STATES

On the question of the moral standing of states, Beitz is clearly the harshest critic of the three of the value conferred upon state sovereignty. None the less, in *Political Theory and International Relations* he vacillates as to whether states or individuals should be the subject of justice. He offers a two-phase argument, first accepting the self-sufficiency of states to make a case for international distributive justice, then challenging the sufficiency of states to argue for a global difference principle. His appeal to moral personality in 'Cosmopolitan Ideals and National Sentiment' finally settles upon the individual as the proper subject of justice, but his charge regarding the moral irrelevance of states appears to have relented. In responding to his critics he chooses to rely upon a conception of the person rather than to step up the attack against the moral inadequacy of states. In the end, as Brown (1972: 177) writes, Beitz compromises his case against prioritizing sovereign statehood by conceding that there are good reasons for supporting patriotic sentiments.

Pogge's position on the morality of states is unclear. He writes that an international original position should begin with individuals, not with states as Rawls suggests. He comes to this conclusion not through considered arguments regarding the moral inadequacy of states, but from the position that Rawls 'would be begging a crucial question, provided we allow that justice may *fail to require* the states system in its present form' (1989: 258, original emphasis). Yet when discussing the value of international pluralism he writes that its 'widespread acceptance' would allow that 'value clusters with their coordinate national forms of regime, are morally accepted and permanently protected' (1989: 231). Pogge accuses governments and statesmen, not the state itself, of being morally repugnant. One can only infer that Pogge wants to leave open the possibility that the state system might not be integral to the development of international justice.

As mentioned above, Thompson believes that the case for the morality of states can be made by stressing its role in fostering and protecting the social commitments valued by individuals. She writes that not all states fulfil this role, but that if the social basis for national unity exists, we should invest in the state's potential. Yet not all nations or states are worthy of value. Thompson also recognizes Beitz's concern for the impediments autonomous states represent to global justice, their status leaving us seemingly incapable of addressing duties beyond borders.[9]

Considering Beitz's acknowledgement of good reasons for patriotic sentiment, Pogge's reluctance to denigrate the state form, and Thompson's awareness of the nurturing role states can play for valued associations, all three authors demonstrate an openness to accept the value of states.

UNIVERSALISM VERSUS PARTICULARISM

Finally, on the issue of universalism versus particularism, this argument turns to the Archimedean points invoked by these writers. Despite Rawls's (1987) acknowledgement of moral personality being particular to the social and historical conditions of liberal democratic society, Beitz has not offered a rejoinder to his position maintaining a concept of the person as a universal fixed point from which a conception of justice is to be evaluated. Pogge also posits an Archimedean point. His is located not in a concept of the person, but in an overlapping consensus. Such a consensus on values provides 'institutional fixed points that stand above ordinary negotiation ... immune to shifts in power and interests' (1989: 228). In Thompson's amendment of an overlapping consensus, the idea of interlocking communities, she does not invoke such a fixed point. Instead she writes that it is one of her premises that there is 'no metaphysical measuring stick, no "original position" which we can use can determine what conception of justice we ought to accept' (1992: 177). As Thompson finds the ethical life of the community to be the best guide, and does not regard the world as one community, she holds a particularist line. Nonetheless, her intention is a theory of justice universal in scope.

What separates Beitz and Pogge from Thompson on the issue of universalism versus particularism is a question of method. Each is concerned with the problem of how we can reach consensus on a conception of justice in a world of plural societies. Also, each shares a reluctance to appeal to foundations in his/her theorization of international justice. Where they differ is on method, on how to sidestep foundations, yet state something positive with grounds in plural societies. Beitz and Pogge assume that they can find grounds through acknowledgement of certain fixed points, reasonable and agreed to by all, serving as a stable standard of judgement. For Thompson, such a method leads to a conception of justice incapable of explaining the value of the social attachments that differentiate persons.

Thompson contends that her theory of interlocking communities can accommodate cosmopolitans and communitarians alike. Her theory of international justice is like a 'grab-bag' of sorts, containing the concerns of Kant, Herder, Hegel, Rawls and Beitz, from which she picks and chooses. Although the argument as it stands in her book is not altogether convincing, it points to an interesting opening. Aside from the dispute on method, the poles of opposition within the debate appear to be yielding. Rawls and Pogge have moved away from a strong argument regarding a conception of the moral person as universal. And despite the starting points of Rawls, Beitz and Pogge, they do acknowledge the importance of individuals' social connectedness. Regarding the morality of states, an openness to the issue is indicated among cosmopolitans, and the more communitarian position of Thompson acknowledges cosmopolitan concerns for the privileging of citizens within borders as unjust. Shifts in the cosmopolitan position are not surprising against the background of movements in Rawls's work. Theorists have noted a decidedly Hegelian flavour in the later work of Rawls as his starting point has moved to an examination of values located in current social practices (Kukathas and Petit, 1990; Galston, 1982).

Granted, the dispute on method stands. For this reason, it should be noted that the poles of debate may have narrowed but they have not collapsed. However, most important for international theory's purpose of addressing the issues raised by a new global order is that the cosmopolitan/communitarian debate has at its centre the problem of adjudicating values and their scope. This kind of normative analysis is required by the pressing demands outlined in the first section of this chapter. True, the problem of finding criteria of social judgement will always be with us, but cosmopolitans and communitarians are asking the questions the post-Cold War world needs to address. Also, the movement on issues within the debate is encouraging, indicating the possibility of extending moral commitments, if theory and practice are indeed intertwined.

NOTES

1. For discussion of a settled body of norms in International Relations, see Frost, 1986: 120–28.
2. For an account of this evolution and supporting General Assembly resolutions see Buchheit, 1978.

3. In addition to Wight's essay in Butterfield and Wight, 1966: 17–34, other factors contributing to the dearth of political theory or philosophy in the study of International Relations are discussed in Frost's account of the positive bias: (1986 9–37), and in Chris Brown's discussion of the dominance of meta-ethics over moral philosophy in the first half of this century (1992: 82–103).

4. I prefer to use the label international political theory as it most clearly expresses the condition of international theory as an extension of political theory. To the uninitiated, international relations theory may still read as an assumption of international theory being a discipline unto itself.

5. John Vincent's essay, 'Order in International Politics', in Miller and Vincent, 1990: 38–64, discusses Bull's moral scepticism.

6. Bull, 1984: 14. In true Bull fashion, he writes (p. 7) that 'the attempt to apply the concept of justice to distribution of military power, indeed, demonstrates the limitations of justice as an objective in human affairs'. The lecture is riddled with moral scepticism in several places. None the less, he contends that the sense of a world common good which incorporates justice and an end-state principle for meeting the basic needs of all individuals exists.

7. It should be noted that neither Janna Thompson nor Mervyn Frost labels her/himself as a communitarian, although the positions they take are characteristic of the communitarian position as outlined by Brown, 1992. In fact, both see themselves as offering a resolution between the two positions. See Thompson, 1992 and Frost, 1993.

8, Rawls is not concerned whether justice is a matter for states as well as individuals. None the less, from a conception of the person, a position on the morality of states is implicit. The cosmopolitans and communitarians have worked to make these positions explicit.

9. Thompson (1992: 179–83) goes on to consider the relation between nations and states, concluding that a closed state is not compatible with an open nation whose duties do extend beyond borders.

REFERENCES

Beitz, C., 1979, *Political Theory and International Relations*, Princeton, NJ, Princeton University Press.

Beitz, C., 1983, 'Cosmopolitan Ideals and National Sentiment', *Journal of Philosophy*, 80: 591–601.

Bellamy, R., 1992, *Liberalism and Modern Society*, Cambridge, Polity Press.

Brown, C., 1992, *International Relations Theory: New Normative Approaches*, New York, Columbia University Press.

Buchheit, L., 1978, *Secession: The Legitimacy of Self-Determination*, New Haven, Yale University Press.

Bull, H., 1977, *The Anarchical Society*, London, Macmillan.

Bull, H., 1984, *Justice in International Relations: The Hagey Lectures*, Waterloo, University of Waterloo Press.

Butterfield, H. and Wight, M., 1966, *Diplomatic Investigations*, Cambridge, MA, Harvard University Press.

Frost, M., 1986, *Towards a Normative Theory of International Relations*, Cambridge, Cambridge University Press.

Frost, M., 1993, 'Towards a Resolution of the Debate Between Liberals and Communitarians', paper presented at the British International Studies Association Conference, Warwick, 16 December: 1–17.

Gaddis, J.L., 1991, 'Toward the Post-Cold War World', *Foreign Affairs*, 70: 102–23.

Galston, W., 1982, 'Moral Personality and Liberal Theory: John Rawls's Dewey Lectures', *Political Theory*, 10: 492–519.

Kegley, C., 1992, 'The New Global Order: the Power of Principle in a Pluralistic World', *Ethics and International Affairs*, 6: 21–40.

Kissinger, H., 1991, 'Which Key to Global Order?', *Los Angeles Times*, 1 December: M1.

Kukathis, C. and Petit, P., 1990, *Rawls: A Theory of Justice and its Critics*, Cambridge, Polity.

Linklater, A., 1990, *Men and Citizens in the Theory of International Relations*, London, Macmillan.

Miller, D. and Vincent, J., 1990, *Order and Violence: Hedley Bull and International Relations*, Oxford, Clarendon Press.

Mulhall, S. and Swift, A., 1992, *Liberals and Communitarians*, Oxford, Blackwell.

Nye, J., 1992, 'What New World Order?', *Foreign Affairs*, 71: 83–96.

Pogge, T., 1989, *Realizing Rawls*, Ithaca, NY, Cornell University Press.

Raphael, D.D., 1970, *Problems of Political Philosophy*, London, Macmillan.

Rawls, J., 1971, *A Theory of Justice*, Cambridge, MA, Belknap Press of Harvard University Press.

Rawls, J., 1987, 'The Idea of an Overlapping Consensus', *Oxford Journal of Legal Studies*, 7: 1–25.

Rawls, J., 1993, *Political Liberalism*, New York, Columbia University Press.

Rosenau, J., 1992, 'Normative Challenges in a Turbulent World', *Ethics and International Affairs*, 6: 1–19.

Thompson, Janna, 1992, *Justice and World Order: A Philosophical Inquiry*, London, Routledge.

3
Globalization and the end of the national project

Robin Brown

INTRODUCTION

In 1926 the Fabian Society sponsored a series of lectures on 'The Shrinking World: Dangers and Possibilities' (Toynbee, 1948: 97). In 1960 Edmund Carpenter and Marshall McLuhan coined an enduring phrase when they observed that '[p]ostliterate man's electronic media contract the world to a village or tribe where everything happens to everyone at the same time ... Television gives this quality of simultaneity to events in the global village' (Carpenter and McLuhan, 1960: xi). The idea that the world is getting smaller is one of the central beliefs of the twentieth century, yet it is an idea that has been more frequently asserted than examined. However, there are signs that this is changing. The idea of 'globalization' is attracting growing attention in the social sciences and is infiltrating the language of business and politics, even if sceptics are already emerging (Ferguson, 1992; Hirst and Thompson, 1992).

In this chapter I want to argue that the concept of globalization has a twofold contribution to make to the study of International Relations. First, at a theoretical level, globalization places the changing nature of space and territory at the centre of our concerns. Given that the central actor in International Relations, the state, is defined in terms of territory, the neglect of 'space' as a category is a major blind spot (Ruggie, 1993: 174). Second, drawing on ideas of globalization, including those developed in other disciplines, helps to illuminate the problems faced by contemporary states from Canada to China. In particular, there is a growing gap between the practice of politics in an integrated world and the categories used to analyse that practice.

In the first section I explore what is meant by globalization. I then go on to examine the development of the states system in this context. The third section looks at some of the work on globalization done in the fields of economics, management, sociology, geography and communications. In the final section I return to the implications of globalization for International Relations.

DEFINING GLOBALIZATION

I want to begin by examining Roland Robertson's definition of globalization as 'the compression of the world and the intensification of consciousness of the world as a whole' (1992: 8). Although abstract, this definition raises three issues.

The first of these is that globalization is a process rather than an end state. Like Immanuel Wallerstein, Robertson sees the compression of the world as a long-term process reaching back to the early voyages of European explorers. The contemporary era, with its mass tourism and communications satellites, represents an acceleration and deepening rather than something totally new. The term globalization does not automatically imply that globalization is good or bad or that it indicates the victory of Western liberalism or that globalization has the same effects everywhere. These are questions for debate and investigation. The likelihood is that some people will benefit from the process of global integration more than others.

The second issue implied by the definition is the divergence between what the structures of integration look like from a global perspective and from a local perspective. Social institutions come under the pressures of globalization, while patterns of thought and meaning fail to come to terms with the fact. Coming to terms with globalization is as likely to involve rejection, for instance nationalist reactions, as acceptance.[1] Everyday life may be shaped by the functioning of the global economy without the affected individuals being aware of it. At the same time events that from New York look like the triumph of liberal values may look from Teheran like the imperialist machinations of the Great Satan. People may not be conscious of globalization, and even if they are they will respond to it differently. Globalization should not be read as creating a uniform response.

The third aspect is that what is being compressed is space. All human activities take place somewhere. The compression of space implies that individuals and communities which have been separate or only loosely connected are pulled together. The multiplicity of human social organizations are forced into closer contact and find themselves dependent on each other. Contact breeds change and conflict. New social and cultural forms emerge. The world's economic system becomes more interdependent and people and ideas move around the world in greater numbers, propelled by what geographers term 'space adjusting technologies' (Brunn and Leinbach, 1991) of communication and transport. As communication becomes more reliable, forms of organization shift to take this reality into account. These developments simultaneously aid a movement towards homogenization. Different places become more alike; architecture, food, TV, clothes, values become more similar.

'Global' is a spatial term rather than a political one like 'state'. The discourse of 'globalization' argues for seeing the world as a single place, albeit one with a complex and diverse social system. An understanding of this system requires the ability to make sense of a world of simultaneous diversity, as Kristin Ross argues following Feuerbach: 'time ... excludes and subordinates where space tolerates and coordinates' (Harvey, 1993: 5, also Harvey, 1989). Edward Soja has argued forcibly that modern social theory has tended to focus on time, in particular historical change, and to ignore the importance of *where* things happen (Soja, 1989).

This spatial logic is emphasized by Giddens (1990). Globalization implies a pattern of society where social relationships are conducted across great distances. Actions and relationships reach across space to shape social life. For each place these relations pose the risk of destruction or pollution beyond direct control.

Globalization does not abolish difference or power, but it does change the context of politics. The corollary of the compression of space is the expansion of the horizon of political action. New possibilities, values, allies, enemies become open to individuals and groups, and the world becomes a bigger place containing more possibilities. For instance, a transnational movement emerges to save the habitat of Amazonian Indians. The global media network carries the message and under international pressure legislation is passed to protect the endangered region. The irony is that some of the Indians then discover that they can make a lot of money out of the natural resources that their newly protected land can provide (*The Economist*, 1993d).

GLOBALIZATION AND THE STATES SYSTEM

In this section I want to suggest that the tendency to oppose the state to growing interdependence is a mistake that grows out of the realist tendency to treat the state as an unproblematic and fixed category. The state is a key element within processes of globalization rather than something opposed to them.

It is the globalization of the state that has done more than anything else to create the modern world. This has both linked the world into a universal network of governance and standardized the form of political life. The basis for this claim becomes clearer if we examine the development of the states system in a historical perspective.

The territorial state developed in early modern Europe essentially as a system of political control. Rulers sought to protect their hold on power against challengers from the areas that they claimed to rule and from outside. The need to mobilize armed force led to the development of administrative bureau-cracies, tax collection, roads, mapping and attempts to stimulate commerce to generate more income for the state (Mann, 1986; Porter, 1994).

The process by which the modern state emerged can profitably be seen in spatial terms. Kings attempted to extend the area over which they could exert effective control even within their nominal territories. This not only secured against threats but also allowed the more extensive exploitation of local re-sources. However, local identities and feudal rights were well entrenched and deployed against the centralizing efforts of kings (Greengrass, 1991). Transport networks were poorly developed. There were numerous local dialects. The means of integrating these kingdoms were few, and weak local administration translated into weakness in international conflict, as France found in its eighteenth-century struggles with Britain (Mann, 1993: 171–2, 179–80).

The states of the early modern era were not nation states as we would understand them. Ideas of national identity originated among those associated with, or who benefited from, the enterprises of the state machinery. These states were nation states only to the extent that these élites were the nation

(Mann, 1986; Anderson, 1991; Greenfeld, 1993). The 'masses' played little part in politics and their attitudes counted for little. The state was a distant and alien force. These entities, although states in that they were sovereign and possessed increasingly well-defined borders, differed from today's states in that they performed a limited range of functions and had relatively little impact on the life of ordinary people.

The nineteenth and twentieth centuries saw change in the nature of the relationship between state and people. The Industrial Revolution created a mobilizable mass population and pushed politics in the direction of national-ism (Gellner, 1983). Nationalism and other demands for a more democratic political order shattered multinational empires in Europe. These movements led to a search for ways to bind the working classes to the state. The means used included ritual, ideology, the provision of services and a welfare state (Hobsbawm and Ranger; 1983, Porter, 1994, ch. 5). Simultaneously, railways, the electric telegraph and mass circulation newspapers provided spatial in-tegration of the nation state. This encouraged the development of a pattern of politics in the developed countries where the state and its abilities to exercise control and redistribute resources were central to political practice (Cerny, 1990, ch. 2). The aim was to bind all elements of society to the state.

This is an image of politics that we tend to take for granted. In the twentieth century the ideal at the heart of politics has been, and for many continues to be, a nation state incorporating a homogenous nation, a common culture, a distinct economy subject to democratic control existing within distinct and secure boundaries. This image of the world emerges from a nationalist con-ception, and it is an ideal that few states can live up to.

Even in classic models of the nation state, such as France, the convergence of ideal and reality is more recent than many might expect. Eugene Weber's (1977) analysis of rural France suggests that national sentiment only became universal with the experience of the First World War. The tensions within Italy or a reunited Germany should not be surprising given the short time that they have existed within their current borders.

The nation state outside Europe is an even more recent development. With few exceptions, the world was brought under the territorial control of the European states and their offshoots during the nineteenth century. The Euro-pean colonial system constructed proto-states over most of the world's surface. These possessed, in embryonic form, the administrative institutions of the European states but lacked sovereignty.

Again with few exceptions, independence was won and accepted on the basis of the existing colonial territories. This implied the mutual recognition of colonial territories as, for example, was built into the charter of the Organ-ization of African Unity. The leaders of newly independent states sought to strengthen their own position (Krasner, 1985). They sought to achieve the orientation of social life towards the state, to make people feel that they were part of this imagined community. While this process was at the heart of the national project (Anderson, 1991; Bayart, 1993), the ability to realize it varied widely, depending on the history of the territory and the ability of the state to

provide resources or exercise effective control. This led to the situation identified by Jackson and Rosberg that states existed as juridical entities within the
states system but lacked effective institutions (Jackson and Rosberg, 1982).
State and nation-building have been central to world politics over the last fifty
years, but the consolidation of effective states is not a foregone conclusion.

Once we begin to regard the nation state as a historical construction rather
than a natural object, it becomes clear that the political community of the
nation state is an ideal and that its achievement depends more on the 'state'
than the 'nation'. Even in the classic nation states the identification with the
state is a product of the policies and institutions of the state itself operating
over a long period. The ability of states to achieve this end depended on their
access to resources and the ability to defeat those who oppose these processes
of state-building.

If the pressures of economic and cultural change reduce the ability of the
state to shape society and economy, then patterns of political community will
shift just as they have in the past. If individuals and groups supported, or at
least did not actively oppose the state, because of a mix of coercion, material
benefits and ideological persuasion, can we assume that if the ability of the
state in general, or particular states, declines they will continue to behave in
this way? At this point let us turn to the dynamics of economic and cultural
change.

THE GLOBAL ECONOMY

The challenge of contemporary international political economy is, in broad
terms, the coexistence of a territorially based political system with an economic
system that is increasingly global in scope. Since 1945 there has been a movement from distinct national economies towards a single global economy. This
is implicitly admitted even by critics of globalization (Hirst and Thompson,
1992). International trade and investment have consistently grown faster than
national economies. This growth has lead to an accelerating degree of economic
interdependence (Hirst and Thompson, 1992). These developments have had
effects both on the organization of firms and industries and on the workings of
national economic policies.

Peter Dicken distinguishes between the internationalization of economic
activity and globalization; the former represents a geographical spread of economic activity, while the latter represents a qualitative shift whereby functional
integration of economic activity is achieved. Production is organized on the
basis that functions such as design, finance, manufacturing, distribution and
advertising may all be located in different countries but the company operates
as a single whole (Dicken, 1992).

The decline of barriers, both legal and informational, to international trade
and investment creates a situation in which firms find themselves in competition with firms whose home is on the other side of the world. In the past
competition may have occurred between firms situated in a small location, a
single country or a region, but now, firms seek out markets anywhere on the

planet. Transport costs and lack of information no longer protect producers in other countries. Firms can identify potential markets and attempt to penetrate them (Porter, 1986; Stopford and Strange, 1991, ch. 3).

In an industry where the nature of the product makes it feasible firms have no alternative but to accept the challenge of global competition unless they can rely on political or geographical protection. They must seek to optimize their production strategy, for instance by locating activities where tasks can be achieved most cheaply, and by attempts to expand the scope of their operations so that the ever increasing research and development costs can be spread over more sales. These considerations led to the search for 'global strategies', 'global brands' and 'global management'. Despite this the new buzzword is 'global localization': marketing a product that is basically the same in a way that is specifically adapted to local conditions, ensuring that the company appears to be at home everywhere (Ohmae, 1990: 115).

Only a few companies can aspire to being everywhere. Most operate in a small range of countries and have a distinct home country. Most foreign investment takes place in just a few countries. During the mid-1980s 75 per cent of foreign direct investment took place in the developed market economies (Dicken, 1992: 5) But increasingly the world is seen as a single space. Recent doubts about the feasibility of global strategies have been aimed at whether this is the best way of coping with global competition, not at the fact.[2]

The global mobility of firms spurred on by global competition forces states to compete with each other in an attempt to attract investment and employment. For firms the incentives offered to them by governments become part of the calculation of where to invest (Stopford and Strange, 1991, ch. 4; Dicken, 1992, ch. 4). The attachment of firms to particular countries becomes nominal, so that it is quite likely that an American wishing to buy to improve the trade balance should buy a Honda rather than a Pontiac (Reich, 1992: 134).

These developments are subjecting 'powerful states' to problems that have confronted Third World states. Indeed, it is claimed that the international economy is becoming 'post-imperialist'. The kind of structured exploitative relationship posited by dependency theory has been superseded by a more complex organization of capitalism in which the location of particular functions within the world economy is no longer rigidly divided into core/First World and periphery/Third World pairings. The core can be in the periphery, and vice versa (Cox, 1987: 328).

Economic globalization reaches its ultimate position in finance, where Richard O'Brien can point to the incipient 'end of geography'.[3] The deregulation of financial markets and the development of communications technologies have led to a tremendous growth in financial flows: the flow of funds around the world is now forty times greater than that required to fund trade and direct investment (Frieden, 1991: 428; Myerson, 1992). Finance can be regarded as one of the central elements in the globalization of production. Easy access to capital is essential to fund the operations of multinationals. This is not to say that money can go anywhere, but in a situation of global competition access to cheap capital can become a source of competitive advantage. Recent examples of this are the pressures from Korean firms for a further deregulation of their operations to allow them easier access to overseas financial markets, and the moves of Daimler Benz to obtain a stock exchange listing in New York (Webb, 1992; Mitchener, 1993; *The Economist*, 1993c). Capital movements have also been an autonomous element in global politics. Capital can flow around the world seeking the maximum return and fundamentally affect the ability of states to manage their economies.[4] The world's combined foreign currency reserves are no larger than one day's trading volume on the markets and the ability of states to defend their currencies against the markets is steadily reduced (Myerson, 1992, Goldstein et al., 1993).

The restructuring of the economy has generated large secondary effects. The changing spatial organization of the world is striking; for instance the rapid development of new industrial centres in East Asia and the decline of old-established industries in the Western countries. The changing pattern of the world economy has also stimulated changing patterns of employment, for instance the role of women in Third World industrialization (Dicken, 1992: 424–6; Rothstein and Blim, 1992). The restructuring of the global economy threatens the patterns of labour relations that developed under Fordism (Lash and Urry, 1987). These processes of economic restructuring stimulate large-scale population movements (Castles and Miller, 1993).

Potentially the welfare state is left with the problem of securing the prosperity of its people without any real control over the economy. The problem is exacerbated by the increasing role of knowledge-based tasks in the economies of the more developed countries, with the kind of well-paid low-skill jobs that characterized the Fordist regime of mass production either disappearing or being relocated in countries where the cost of labour is lower (Reich, 1991, pt. III). The shift to a more open economy creates problems for the state both at the macro-economic level of financial openness and at the micro-economic level of multinational corporation.

TOWARDS THE GLOBAL VILLAGE?

Within the discipline of International Relations culture is a concept that is often obscured. For realism, the objective, universal categories of political interest and power make culture peripheral. Others take the idea more seriously. For instance, to what extent does the notion of international society depend on shared European values and to what extent does the creation of a global states system with members from many cultural origins pose a threat to orderly international relations (Bull and Watson, 1984, pt. IV)? This is a debate that has been reopened by Samuel Huntington with his claim that civilizations are the ultimate units of social life and that with the end of communism world politics will increasingly be dominated by conflict along the fault lines between civilizations (Huntington, 1993).

In a period of rapid political change culture can, in embodying a sense of identity, assume increased significance both for individuals in the real world and for analysts. Despite this the kind of position taken by Huntington, where culture is seen as something primeval and unchanging and which determines politics, is not widely accepted. Culture changes. Increasingly it changes because of external influences. The political implications of these changes have not been fully explored.

In an era of globalization, where ideas and images can flow around the world in seconds, the power to control meaning slips away from the state. The 'legitimacy' of rulers is intimately tied to patterns of meaning; as David Hume observed, 'the governors having nothing to support them but opinion' (1987: 32).[5] Changing patterns of culture may have immense if indirect political effects (Weber, 1968, ch. 3; Collins, 1986). At one level would-be yuppies walking through the streets of Shanghai or the popularity of heavy metal bands in South-East Asia may seem trivial but they point to possible cultural impacts that may, in time, feed back into the political system, which in turn invests great efforts in cultivating the symbols of legitimacy.[6]

Defined as shared patterns of meaning, 'culture' is a universal aspect of social existence (Schroeder, 1993: 6; Geertz, 1973: 5). The space defined by the modern state contains many different cultures, of which some are widely shared, others less so (Hannerz, 1992). National and local cultures coexist with networks of meaning reaching out over much larger areas. In an era of advanced communications these networks reach out across space so that people within them share many meanings with others located thousands of miles away. The rapidity and ease of communication allows, in embryo at least, a global civil society where political and economic structures are matched by a broader set of relationships (Lipschutz, 1992). These developments pose a challenge to the attempt by states to create a coherent national culture.

The challenges to 'national culture' are reinforced by the development of global mass media. If the state is the political organ of the nation and the nation is defined by its culture, then erosion of culture represents a threat to national autonomy. While this is an argument that has been put forward by Third World states it has resurfaced in the arguments in the Uruguay round of GATT on the threat to European culture and civilization posed by *Jurassic Park* (Tomlinson, 1991; Reeves, 1993; Buchan, 1993; see also Chapter 4 in this volume). In this debate 'culture' stands for national culture.

Beyond this there is more fundamental debate about the relationship of cultural and social change on a global scale. Is globalization producing a homogeneous global culture? Are individuals becoming more alike and distinctive cultures disappearing? This position is implied within the liberal perspective implicit in some International Relations literature and in modernization theory. The processes of modernization produce a complex society in which the world is disenchanted and reason embodied in science creates common patterns of thought, consumption politics and values (Sztompka, 1993, ch.5; Von Laue, 1987; Knutsen, 1992: 226–8, 235, 237; Fukuyama, 1992). If cultural difference is disappearing, what will the end result be? One position is that a world culture will simply be Western culture writ large. An alternative view is that a common culture will emerge but it will be a hybrid combination of cultural elements, what Stuart Hall (1992) calls the 'global postmodern'.

This view breaks with the simple cultural imperialism position which assumes that cultural flow is in a single direction. Instead it posits a situation characterized by a multiplicity of flows in which it is impossible to assert that Western culture in general, or American culture in particular, will come to dominate others. It is just as likely that elements of Western culture will be replaced by others (Tomlinson, 1991: 175). Large-scale processes of social change affect both First World and Third World social forms: economic restructuring; the migration of large numbers of people from the South to the North; the growing access to travel and media. These bring new values and practices into play, challenging simple images of coherent homogeneous 'national cultures' (Hall, 1992: 309–10).

However, the consequences of these cultural flows are not passively accepted. The blurring of distinct spatial boundaries can have the effect of reinforcing particular identities. The compression of space through communication and travel has the effect of bringing cultures into close contact and creating a perception of threat which leads to a need to assert distinctiveness. From this perspective, a central cultural consequence of globalization is the redefinition of identities (Robertson, 1992: 98–9). Individuals and groups must decide where they fit in, and in forming or reasserting identities differences are emphasized. Religious fundamentalism, nationalist movements or other manifestations of exclusivist identity politics are symptoms of the reshaping of the world's social system (Hall, 1992: 311–14).

Threats to existing cultures and identities bring counter-movements into play asserting the value of the pure culture and attempting to defend threatened values. Such reactions can take numerous forms, from religious fundamentalism in the United States, Israel and the Islamic World to fascist politics in Europe or local media movements in Australia (Robertson, 1992; Beyer, 1994; Dowmunt, 1993). The political significance of these movements varies, as does our evaluation of them. At the same time we see definite attempts to use culture to create a hegemonic position, for instance in Turkey's efforts to use satellite TV to strengthen its influence in Central Asia (Harden, 1992).

The idea of a universal global culture is simplistic but we can see the diffusion and acceptance of many practices, ideas and values, from rock music to human rights. Increasingly ideas and images flow across territorial borders and it becomes increasingly difficult for states to police them effectively. One cannot draw any general conclusions, but where national cultures are under construction the shock of globalization does nothing to make the task easier.

GLOBALIZATION AND WORLD POLITICS

We live in an era where the world's social system is becoming more tightly integrated. Economic and social and cultural flows increase, but the dominant paradigm of politics is territorial. Patterns of politics are tied to certain areas of the world. There is an apparent disjuncture between the scale of political organization and the scale of emerging social organization. Making sense of these unfolding changes implies a significant change in the way in which we think about change. The processes of integration identified here are changing the frame of reference for actors, and creating new organizational possibilities. These changes mean that the simple division of world politics into 'international' and 'domestic' has to be abandoned. This is not only a response to contemporary events but an acceptance that the image of the world as neatly divided into nation states was only tenable for small portions of the world for small stretches of history.

If many IR theorists see the world as fundamentally composed of billiard balls slamming into each other, many in other fields are quite happy working on the insides of those billiard balls. The basic units of analysis in sociology, economics or political science presuppose the existence of territorially bounded states (Giddens, 1985: 17; Mann, 1986: 13–17; Wallerstein, 1991: 64–6). Because of the assumption that national societies could be studied in isolation research in the social sciences took on a national or comparative form (Robertson, 1992: 16, 52). Indeed, as Robertson argues, it was this separation of inside and outside that provided the basis for the development of International Relations as a discipline. Within much of social science the unproblematic status of the state is taken for granted, and with it the split between 'inside' and 'outside' as a paradigm for organizing the world's affairs.

Kenneth Waltz (1993) has recently suggested that change in world politics begins at the unit level, inside the state. In contrast, the globalization perspective suggests that many major changes that affect the international system are not actually 'domestic' but products of broader cross-border processes. Phenomena like the spread of environmental values, demands for democracy and ideas of economic liberalization may be manifested in national contexts, but it is difficult to explain them solely by reference to the inter-state system or purely indigenous sources. It seems that today's characteristic issues are ones that are neither simply 'international' nor 'domestic' – liberalization, democratization, ethnic conflict and the disintegration of state-structures. At the same time globalization gives a clearer focus on the sources of change in the inter-state system and its origins in 'domestic' society. In a historical perspective it is clear that 'domestic' societies have been shaped by external processes (Wolf, 1982; Gourevitch, 1978; Scholte, 1993).

The state remains at the heart of world politics. However, conceptually we need to modify our understanding of state from 'state as country', that is assuming that 'state' incorporates everything within the legal territory, to 'state as organization'. The capabilities of states are variable and by no means to be taken for granted. The state has many instruments with which to shape social existence, regulations, police, taxes and redistribution of resources, but for many states effective implementation of policy is impossible and policy itself is constrained (Cerny, 1990). The image of the world implied by the 'national project' is that it is natural that social life should be oriented on the state. The paradox is that steps taken by states to ensure their success, for instance economic liberalization, may have the effect of weakening the ability of the state to shape the orientation of social life.

Although the state is not disappearing, many existing states are suffering fragmentation. Due to war, ethnic fragmentation and changed economic circumstances, from Western Europe to Bosnia, China, Eritrea, Somalia, Canada and the former Soviet Union, the decay of statehood is a problem. This is not to say that states in the sense of territorial and sovereign entities are disappearing, but that the boundaries and coherence of existing states are being challenged. The state as an administrative organization is proving unable to integrate the social entities that exist within its territory into a coherent whole.

Increasingly the definition of political community imposed by particular states is being challenged and alternative definitions – regional, ethnic or religious – are being proposed. Our discussion in the previous section has suggested why this is not a random event but a response to the pressures generated by economic and cultural globalization. The end result has been an increase in the demand for separate statehood and a weakening of the forces that maintain state structures. The argument of the Northern League in Italy is an illuminating one. Put crudely, it asks the question: why should the rich north subsidize the poor south? The nationalist has an easy answer: because we are all Italians. Two questions might be raised in response: why is it necessary for all Italians to live in the same state? Who counts as a 'real' Italian? Although the fragmentation of Yugoslavia and the Soviet Union demonstrate that the appeal of the national project has not waned, it does demonstrate that the feasibility of many existing states can be questioned.

Recent discussions of regional government are suggestive of the problems that can confront the contemporary state. If a state is composed of several regions, each of which has distinct forms of economic activity, is it likely that a single state policy will benefit all of them? It might be sensible to treat the territory of the state as several regions, which should have their own governments with powers to manage economic growth.[7] The logic of such considerations is the weakening of the centralized state and the devolution of more power to the regions. If regional governments are effective then local inhabitants may see them as more important than national governments and see their 'local' identity as more important than their 'national' identity. There are reports of provincial governments in the People's Republic of China imposing restrictions on the movements of goods from other provinces. It was the removal of such restrictions in Europe that helped to develop the notion of modern states as a single space (Segal, 1994; Greengrass, 1991). The corollary of the fragmentation of the state is the assumption of support from the multilateral institutions of the states system (Brown, forthcoming).

Globalization is changing the context in which states operate, yet much social science reinforces and is in turn reinforced by the power of the national project in political life. The 'national project' insinuates itself into academic and political discourse. While the world is full of states, there are few that can meet this aspiration, yet it is often implicitly assumed that these cases are the standard by which all others should be judged. From John Major to Slobodan Milosovic, much of contemporary world politics is driven by the tension between aspiration and the demands and possibilities open to states faced with a global economy or the realities of ethnic heterogeneity.

If we view the development of the states system in a historical process then we gain a clearer perspective on today's world. The states system has not always existed, and where it has states have constantly evolved. Powerful forces are producing another mutation in the form of political authority and with it the issues, interests and means of coping that lie at the centre of world politics. Some of these pressures point towards the decentralization and fragmentation of existing states. On the other hand the globalization of social life creates pressures for the creation of new forms of governance (e.g. Nadelmann, 1993). The pressures that have been discussed here affect different states in different ways. The conclusion that follows is that the states system needs to placed at the centre of International Relations but as an object of study, not as an assumption. As Clausewitz observed, the proper starting point for theory is practice.

NOTES

1. The variety of responses is made clear both in Robertson, 1992 and Beyer, 1994.
2. For a summary of recent thinking on multinational firms see *The Economist*, 1993a and *The Economist*, 1993b.
3. (O'Brien, 1992) but for a sceptical commentary see (Malkin, 1992).
4. See Frieden, 1991; Cerny, 1993; McKenzie and Lee, 1990; Norman, 1993.
5. See also the views of Max Weber (Weber, 1968, ch. 3; Collins, 1986).
6. On the relationship between governments and rock bands see Wong, 1993; on changing styles of clothing in China see Menkes, 1993.
7. On the arguments for regionalism see Harvie, 1994; also Ohmae, 1993 and Goldsborough, 1993.

REFERENCES

Anderson, B., 1991, *Imagined Communities: Reflections on the Origins and Spread of Nationalism*, London, Verso.

Ashley, R., 1988, 'Untying the Sovereign State: A Double Reading of the Anarchy Problematique', *Millennium*, 17: 227–62.

Bayart, J.-F., 1993, *The State in Africa: The Politics of the Belly*, trans. Mary Harper, London, Longman.

Beyer, P., 1994, *Religion and Globalization*, London, Sage.

Bird, J. et al. (eds), 1993, *Mapping the Futures: Local Cultures and Global Change*, London, Routledge.

Brown, R., forthcoming, *Globalization and the State*, Cambridge, Polity

Brunn, S. and Leinbach, T. (eds), 1991, *Collapsing Space and Time: Geographic Aspects of Communication and Information*, London, HarperCollins.

Buchan, D., 1993, 'Plea to Defend Europe's Cultural Identity', *Financial Times*, 29 September: 3.

Bull, H. and Watson, A. (eds), 1984, *The Expansion of International Society*, Oxford, Clarendon.

Carpenter, E. and McLuhan, M. (eds), 1960, *Explorations in Communication*, Boston, MA, Beacon.

Castles, S. and Miller, M., 1993, *The Age of Migration: International Population Movements in the Modern World*, Basingstoke, Macmillan.

Cerny, P., 1990, *The Changing Architecture of Politics: Structure, Agency and the Future of the State*, London, Sage.

Cerny, P., (ed.), 1993, *Finance and World Politics*, Aldershot, Edward Elgar.

Collins, R., 1986, *Weberian Sociological Theory*, Cambridge, Cambridge University Press.

Cox, R., 1987, *Production, Power and World Order: Social Forces in the Making of the Modern World*, New York, Columbia University Press.

Dicken, P., 1992, *Global Shift: The Internationalization of Economic Activity*, second edn, London, Peter Chapman.

Dowmunt, T. (ed.), 1993, *Channels of Resistance: Global Television and Local Empowerment*, London, BFI/Channel 4.

The Economist, 1993a, 'The Global Firm: RIP', 6 February: 85.

The Economist, 1993b, 'Everybody's Favourite Monsters: A Survey of Multinational Corporations', 27 March.

The Economist, 1993c, 'Daimler Plays Ball', 27 March: 106.

The Economist, 1993d, 'The Savage Can Also be Ignoble', 12 June: 76.

Ferguson, M., 1992, 'The Mythology about Globalization', *European Journal of Communication*, 7: 69–93.

Frieden, J., 1991, 'Invested Interests: The Politics of National Economic Policies in a World of Global Finance', *International Organization*, 45: 425–51.

Fukuyama, F., 1992, *The End of History and the Last Man*, London, Hamish Hamilton.

Geertz, C., 1973, *The Interpretation of Cultures*, New York, Basic Books.

Gellner, E., 1983, *Nations and Nationalism*, Oxford, Blackwell.

Giddens, A., 1985, *The Nation-State and Violence*, Cambridge, Polity.

Giddens, A., 1990, *The Consequences of Modernity*, Cambridge, Polity.

Goldsborough, J., 1993, 'The Foreign Policy of California', *Foreign Affairs*, 72: 88–97.

Goldstein, M. et al., 1993, *International Capital Markets, Pt. I: Exchange Rate Management and International Capital Flows*, Washington, DC, IMF.

Gourevitch, P., 1978, 'The Second Image Reversed: The International Sources of Domestic Change', *International Organization*, 32: 881–912.

Greenfeld, L., 1993, *Nationalism: Five Roads to Modernity*, Cambridge, MA, Harvard University Press.

Greengrass, M., 1991, *Conquest and Coalescence: The Shaping of the State in Early Modern Europe*, London, Edward Arnold.

Hall, S, 1992, 'The Question of Cultural Identity', in Hall, S. et al. (eds), *Modernity and its Futures*, Cambridge, Polity.

Hall, S. et al. (eds), 1992, *Modernity and its Futures*, Cambridge, Polity.

Hannerz, U., 1992, *Cultural Complexity: Studies in the Social Organization of Meaning*, New York, Columbia University Press.

Harden, B., 1992, 'Ankara's War for Central Asia: Waged at the Hearth, On TV', *International Herald Tribune*, 24 March: 5.

Harvey, D., 1989, *The Condition of Postmodernity*, Oxford, Blackwell.

Harvey, D., 1993, 'From Space to Place and Back Again: Reflections on the Condition of Postmodernity', in Bird, J. et al. (eds), *Mapping the Futures: Local Cultures and Global Change*, London, Routledge.

Harvie, C., 1994, *The Rise of Regional Europe*, London, Routledge.

Hirst, P. and Thompson, G., 1992, 'The Problem of "Globalization": International Economic Relations, National Economic Management and the Formation of Trading Blocs', *Economy and Society*, 21: 357–93.

Hobsbawm, E. and Ranger, T. (eds), 1983, *The Invention of Tradition*, Cambridge, Cambridge University Press.

Hume, David, 1987, *Essays: Moral, Political and Literary*, Indianapolis, IN, Liberty Classics.

Huntington, S., 1993, 'The Clash of Civilizations', *Foreign Affairs*, 72: 22–49.

Jackson, R., and Rosberg, C., 1982, 'Why Africa's Weak States Persist: The Juridical and Empirical in Statehood', *World Politics*, 35: 1–24.

Krasner, S., 1985, *Structural Conflict: The Third World Against Global Liberalism*, Berkeley, CA, University of California Press.

Knutsen, T., 1992, *A History of International Relations Theory*, Manchester, Manchester University Press.

Lash, S. and Urry, J., 1987, *The End of Organized Capitalism*, Cambridge, Polity.

von Laue, T., 1987, *The World Revolution of Westernization: The Twentieth Century in Global Perspective*, New York, Oxford.

Lipschutz, R., 1992, 'Reconstructing World Politics: The Emergence of Global Civil Society', *Millennium*, 21: 389–420.

McKenzie, R. and Lee, D., 1990, *Quicksilver Capital*, New York, Free Press.

Malkin, L., 1992, 'Financial Borders Prove Difficult to Tear Down', *International Herald Tribune*, 28 March: 7–8.

Mann, M., 1986, *The Sources of Social Power: Volume I, A History of Power from the Beginning to A.D. 1760*, Cambridge, Cambridge University Press.

Mann, M., 1993, *The Sources of Social Power: Volume II, The Rise of Classes and Nation-States, 1760–1914*, Cambridge, Cambridge University Press.

Menkes, S., 1993, 'Yuppie Shanghai Shows an Old Flair', *International Herald Tribune*, 25 May: 1, 15.

Mitchener, B., 1993, 'Wall Street Breakthrough with a German Twist', *International Herald Tribune*, 25 March: 1, 12.

Myerson, A., 1992, 'Traders Overwhelm Central Banks: Volume of Transactions Out-paces Government Reserves', *International Herald Tribune*, 28 September: 1, 11.

Nadelmann, E., 1993, *Cops Across Borders: The Internationalization of US Criminal Law Enforcement*, University Park, PA, Penn State University Press.

Norman, P., 1993, 'Pension Funds Can Rock the Financial Markets', *Financial Times*, 4 May: 23.

O'Brien, R., 1992, *Global Financial Integration: The End of Geography*, London, Routledge/RIIA.

Ohmae, K., 1990, *The Borderless World: Power and Strategy in the Interlinked Economy*, London, Fontana.

Ohmae, K., 1993, 'The Rise of the Region State', *Foreign Affairs*, 72: 76–87.

Porter, M. (ed.), 1986, *Competition in Global Industries*, Cambridge, MA, Harvard Business School Press.

Porter, B., 1994, *War and the Rise of the State: The Military Foundations of Modern Politics*, New York, Free Press.

Reeves, G., 1993, *Communication and the 'Third World'*, London, Routledge.

Reich, R., 1991, *The Work of Nations: Preparing Ourselves for 21st Century Capitalism*, London, Simon and Schuster.

Rieff, D., 1992, *Los Angeles: Capital of the Third World*, London, Jonathan Cape.

Robertson, R., 1992, *Globalization: Social Theory and Global Culture*, London, Sage.

Rosenau, J. and Czempiel, E.-O. (eds), 1992, *Governance without Government: Order and Change in World Politics*, Cambridge, Cambridge University Press.

Rothstein, F. and Blim, M. (eds), 1992, *Anthropology and the Global Factory: Studies of the New Industrialization in the Late Twentieth Century*, New York, Bergin and Garvey.

Ruggie, J., 1993, 'Territoriality and Beyond: Problematizing Modernity in International Relations', *International Organization*, 47: 139–74.

Sadler, D., 1992, *The Global Region: Production, State Policy and Uneven Development*, Oxford, Pergamon.

Scholte, J., 1993, *International Relations of Social Change*, Milton Keynes, Open University Press.

Schroeder, Ralph, 1993, *Max Weber and the Sociology of Culture*, London, Sage.

Segal, G., 1994, *China Changes Shape: Regionalism and Foreign Policy*, Adelphi Papers 287, London, Brassey's/IISS.

Soja, E., 1989, *Postmodern Geographies: The Reassertion of Space in Critical Social Theory*, London, Verso.

Stopford, J. and Strange, S., 1991, *Rival States, Rival Firms: Competition for World Market Shares*, Cambridge, Cambridge University Press/BISA.

Sztompka, P, 1993, *The Sociology of Social Change*, Oxford, Blackwell.

Tomlinson, J., 1991, *Cultural Imperialism: A Critical Introduction*, London, Pinter.

Toynbee, A., 1948, *Civilization on Trial*, Oxford, Oxford University Press.

Wallerstein, I, 1991, *Unthinking Social Science: The Limits of Nineteenth Century Paradigms*, Cambridge, Polity.

Waltz, K., 1993, 'The Emerging Structure of World Politics', *International Security*, 18: 44–79.

Webb, S., 1992, 'Korean Companies Press for Foreign Funds', *Financial Times*, 27 October: 22.

Weber, E., 1977, *Peasants Into Frenchmen: The Modernization of Rural France, 1870–1914*, London, Chatto and Windus.

Weber, M., 1968, *Economy and Society: An Outline of Interpretive Sociology*, Berkeley, CA, University of California Press.

Wolf, E., 1982, *Europe and the Peoples without History*, Berkeley, CA, University of California Press.

Wong, K., 1993, 'Metallic Gleam', *The Wire*, 110: 18–21.

4
Central Europe since the revolutions of 1989: states, economies and culture in a time of flux

Rick Fawn

The enterprising son of a Czech, Roumanian or Serb peasant entered a town, learnt a German art and spoke German to his fellow shopkeepers; his children despised their father's peasant dialect, and his grandchildren, safely arrived in state jobs, forgot that they had ever been anything but Germans and town-dwellers (A.J.P. Taylor, *The Habsburg Monarchy*, describing the assimilation of minorities in the eighteenth- and nineteenth-century Austrian empire).

Czech playwright and President Václav Havel recently commented: 'For the first time in history, the planet we inhabit is encompassed by a single global civilization' (Havel, 1994). The Central and East European revolutions of 1989 were inspired in part by the desire to join and recreate the defining elements of that global civilization – liberal democracy and market economics – and in turn also allowed Havel, among many, to assert that such principles constituted an unprecedented global civilization.

In order to recreate domestically the constituent elements of this global civilization in Central Europe, the dissidents who became political leaders after the 1989 revolutions had by definition to open their societies to foreign influences. The capital-starved economies of Central Europe[1] had no choice but to turn to foreign capital and trade to resuscitate their economies. Foreign assistance was requested in the social and political realm for the running of elections, the establishment of norms in media reporting, and the revamping of education. But in seeking these foreign influences, the post-Communist leaderships were forced to sacrifice other elements of their vision for society.

Central Europe was pulled into an orbit of non-Western traditions after the Second World War. Consequently, the region was both severed from its natural socio-economic and political conditions and had an alien system imposed upon it. Communist Czechoslovakia, even more than Hungary and Poland, was isolated from Western influence (e.g. Musil, 1992: 177), and Czechoslovaks were also deeply concerned with the fate of their culture under Soviet domination. Whereas the Poles, for example, 'fear far less for the survival of their national culture than others elsewhere in Eastern Europe' (Croan, 1989: 188), the Czechoslovaks saw their culture under communism as 'besieged', 'a catastrophe', and undergoing 'a massacre' (e.g. Heneka et al., 1985). Being heavily industrialized, post-communist Czechoslovakia needed foreign capital for its economic tranformation, and its leadership decided firmly in favour of the market economy, rejecting any adaptation of socialism (e.g. Havel, 1992: 60–79). The transition to the market economy also meant that the post-communist government withdrew state support for indigenous culture (see Hájek, 1994, for the consequences). Thus, after the 1989 revolution, Czechoslovakia changed rapidly from a position of relative isolation from foreign cultural and economic influences to one of extensive exposure while also stripping itself of state mechanisms to limit those influences.

The efforts by both the post-communist leadership of Central Europe and various Western countries to use state instruments to reintegrate the region into what might be called 'global' practices provides an opportunity to study the interaction between the states system, the market and culture (see Chapter 3). This chapter will look first at how sub- and supranational forces confound the conception of Central Europe that dissidents had advanced.[2] Then, by focusing in particular on Czechoslovakia, the chapter considers the economic and cultural activities of five major states in turn. These are: the Soviet Union and independent Russia, the United States, Britain, France and Germany. The objective will be to establish what these states have sought to achieve and how successfully. That will be contrasted with the impact of non-state actors emanating from those countries. How the impact on Czechoslovak society of these actors has differed from the apparent expectation of the post-communist philosopher-leadership will then be considered. Finally, based on this case study, the chapter offers some preliminary conclusions on the relationships between, on the one hand, foreign social groups, institutions and states with, on the other, domestic socio-economic and cultural transformation. Before turning to the economic and cultural questions inherent in the post-communist transformation, the chapter considers the efforts to develop a Central European identity.

SUPRANATIONALISM?

A key element in the design of independent thinkers for Central Europe was supranationalism, even if the discussion of the meaning of Central Europe did not usually turn specifically to region-building (e.g. Neumann, 1993: 350). The Czechs were among the most vociferous advocates. As Tony Judt has written, 'it is the Czechs, more than most, who have opened up for debate the original wisdom of destroying the multinational state, and their sense certainly is that it is Czechoslovakia ... that has suffered the most from events since 1918' (1990: 47). It will be remembered that, albeit for political reasons, the founding father of the Czechoslovak state, Tomáš G. Masaryk, had favoured until the outbreak of the Great War the preservation of the Austro-Hungarian empire and the nineteenth-century Czech nationalist historian František Palacký wrote that if such an entity did not exist then it would have had to be created.

Havel appears nostalgic about the multinational nature of the Austro-

Hungarian empire, perhaps sharing the view of many contemporary Western observers who credit the empire with having created or at least permitted a level of ethnic tolerance which produced great and positive cultural fervour. It is not surprising that the Central European dissidents aspired to supra-nationalism in the region. For all the restrictions on freedom of movement inherent in the Soviet bloc, Central European dissidents had mutual respect for one another and aspired to work together. Havel's seminal 'Power of the Powerless' was written to mark the start of cooperation between Czecho-slovakia's Charter 77 and Poland's KOR. Polish and Czech dissidents would hike up their respective sides of the mountains between the two countries to hold meetings (Havel, 1989: 126). Leading Polish dissident Adam Michnik praised the work of Havel, and Hungary's George Konrád drew heavily on the Czech and Polish experiences (Garton Ash, 1986: 165); the three men eventu-ally met in Prague in 1990 as old friends. Konrád even considered cooperation among Central European independent thinkers as a step toward the con-struction of 'global culture' (Konrád, 1984: 210).

Discussions among Central European independent intellectuals about the identity of their region have generally omitted ominous characteristics of the interwar period (Eisfeld, 1993: 43). Supranationalism in practice, however, has been impaired by the resurgence of these 'old' problems. Initial expectations that right-wing extremism would become a major challenge to the political transition in Central Europe have not been fully realized (see the conclusions of RFE/RL, 1994: 50–71). The numerous instances of anti-Semitism and racist attacks such as those by skinheads on Vietnamese guestworkers and Romanies (or Gypsies) can be seen either as a backlash to the Westernizing influences of the market economy which has created a new class of dispossessed, or as the expression of long-suppressed feelings now liberated by Western norms of liberal democracy. Reaction to economic liberalization is attributed to the re-election in Poland and Hungary, as elsewhere, of former communists (e.g. Oltay, 1994). In Czechoslovakia, differences between the rapidly marketizing Czech lands and interventionist Slovakia over integration into the world market eco-nomy contributed heavily to the demise of the Federation (Martin, 1991; Wolchik, 1994: 166–7).

The challenges presented to Central European supranationalism by the economic and political forces of globalization likely compound indigenous feelings. One need only talk with young people in the region to confirm that the reality of a new generation of tolerance of each other is far from the original aspirations of the post-Communist philosopher-statesmen. The caution of Slovak independent intellectual Miroslav Kusý, written shortly before the 1989 revolutions, remains relevant:

> So far, no spontaneous grassroots process of integration has happened since the war (in any sense comparable with the West European integration process) and each of us secretly hopes that it never will in the near future. Our mutual national antagonisms are still sufficiently alive as to push us in the opposite direction. Your average Slovak still finds the idea of a closer territorial union with Hungary unthinkable. Czechs and

Poles are hardly going to form a community with the Germans, but then nor are the Czechs and Slovaks with the Poles, for that matter (1989: 92).

Havel acknowledged (March 1994) that 'Many dangerous conflicts in the world today can be explained by the simple fact that the closer we are to each other, the more we notice our differences'.

These problems notwithstanding, Havel in particular has energetically pursued the establishment of an institutional basis for regional cooperation. Following from his addresses to the Polish and Hungarian parliaments in early 1990, the Bratislava process came into being, now referred to as the Visegrád Group. While the three – and then four – countries have cooperated on various matters, especially defence, economics and lobbying for membership in coveted West European organizations, the group is limited in its efforts by the danger of success. Were they to achieve a fully functioning free-trade zone or a regional military organization, these countries could exempt Western Europe of the exigency of admitting them to the EC or NATO.

In the security realm, NATO's fear that Central European membership would alarm Russia is well known in the Partnership for Peace talks. A Central European Free Trade Agreement (CEFTA) has come into effect, making for tariff-free trade among the partners, but achieving no more than the Europe Agreements of December 1991 would have required independent of locally sponsored Visegrád cooperation. In addition, Czech Prime Minister Václav Klaus reiterated that such cooperation cannot be allowed to inhibit the chances of his country entering the European Union (Klaus, 1994). The strictly functional nature of Visegrád collaboration has been demonstrated by the lack of trilateral military agreements among the countries in order to prevent making the appearance of a military bloc.

It is impossible to measure the extent to which the embryo of a Central European ethos might result from private philanthropic organizations such as the Soros Foundation's Central European University which, with the assistance of national governments, brings together students and academics from the region. But it might have a greater chance to overcome regional animosities, if not lay the foundation for a supranational identity, than the regional diplomacy of Central European states. CEFTA and the lack of meaningful multilateral political-security architecture ensures that the institutions which could help to create a Central European supranationalism are absent.

MARKET ECONOMICS AND CIVIL SOCIETY: IMPORTING FOREIGN INFLUENCES

As mentioned already, the post-communist Central European leaderships wanted to reconstruct market economies and liberal democracy in their countries. They required foreign assistance to achieve these goals, but opening the floodgates meant losing elements these intellectuals apparently wanted retained and permitting those which they might well have sought to exclude.

Before considering the transmission of foreign influences into post-1989 Czechoslovakia, some caveats are in order. Culture is generally an elusive term, defying quantification. It is also not exactly obvious what the dissidents wanted in terms of 'culture'. Prolific and coherent on numerous subjects, on culture Havel warned against interpreting his views. In his 1984 'Six Asides about Culture' on the fate of Czechoslovak culture under communism, he offered 'polemical and marginal comments' and cautioned that '[i]f anyone chooses to derive something from them for the future, that will be his business and on his head be it' (1984: 124).

As a further caveat, this chapter does not presume that the countries studied herein are the only major actors in Central Europe. And in dividing the following discussion into the activities of countries and, within that, the activities of state organs and non-state actors (as elaborated below), this chapter of course does not maintain that such distinctions can be cleanly entertained. For example: some of the first teachers of English as a second language in Czechoslovakia were Austrian; Britain and the US have cooperated on some of their cultural programmes; and the impetus that brought tens of thousands of private Americans to live in Czechoslovakia began not so much in the US as in Canada. Cognizant that achievements in a state's trade and cultural policies towards another society are impossible to judge either in absolute or relative terms, this section seeks to outline broadly how foreign influences have come into the region and with what consequences, before it turns to some conclusions on the interaction of states, the economy and culture in post-communist Central Europe. This section begins with Soviet and Russian cultural influence in the wake of the 1989 revolutions.

The Soviet Union and Russia

In his 1983 article 'Un occident kidnappé – ou la tragédie de l'Europe central', published in translation in a 1984 edition of the *New York Review of Books* with the more innocuous title 'The Tragedy of Central Europe' (1984), Kundera spurned Russian influence as anathema not only to Central Europe but to all of European tradition, warning that the fate of Central Europe was the fate of all of Europe. So extreme is his dismissal of Russian culture as European that Kundera rejects even those products accepted as international culture, notably the works of Dostoevsky.

For all his repute in the West, Kundera may be rare among Central European intellectuals for his outright rejection of the appropriateness of Russian culture to the region. Josef Brodsky has mauled Kundera's view as entirely mistaken (1986: 477–83). While Konrád claimed that Hungarians could learn nothing from visiting the Soviet Union, one of the few places to which they could travel (1984: 76), Michnik cautioned against being anti-Russian (Croan, 1989: 194). Melvin Croan maintains that '[c]ritical intellectuals [in Central Europe] may get some gratification from intertwining their specific cultural disdain for Russia with the general popular animus against the Soviet Union as a political system' (Croan, 1989: 193). At the same time, however, he observes that Polish author Czeslaw Milosz favoured inclusion of Russian culture in Central Europe once 'Russian art and literature again recover their spontaneity' (cited in Croan, 1989: 194). In Czechoslovakia there have been calls for the creation, hitherto absent in spite of Masaryk's legacy of having been the foremost expert on Russia in his age, of an institute to study the Soviet Union (e.g. *Lidové noviny*, 25 September 1990). Havel says his writing has been influenced by Chekhov (Havel, 1985: 237), and as Czechoslovak President, Havel stated his belief that Russian culture has a place in Czechoslovak society (*Lidové noviny*, 3 March 1990). The Czechoslovak–Soviet Treaty of Good Neighbourliness included plans to augment bilateral scientific, cultural and educational cooperation (Obrman, 1991: 3).

The popular response, not surprisingly, differs greatly from the official one. While the Soviet-made cartoon series 'Počkej zajíci', featuring the fumbling [Soviet male?] wolf attempting to eliminate the benign [Czechoslovak female?] hare continued on Czechoslovak television, enrolment in Russian language classes, once universally obligatory, has dropped to negligible levels.[3] The Novosti information centre closed (*Pravda*, 1991) and the once ubiquitous sale of Russian music and literature has ceased. If that is not enough to signal the demise of Russian culture in Central Europe, official Russian sponsorship of its culture in Czechoslovakia came to a dramatic if inglorious end. What Russia's official news agency TASS called the last objective source on Russian culture in Czechoslovakia, Moscow's cultural centre in Prague, was blockaded on the first anniversary of the 'democratic' August coup by 'the hefty lads' of a security service for falling into arrears on its rent (ITAR-TASS, 1992). As much as Central European dissidents might have disliked the Soviet system, they were intent at least on preventing anti-Russian sentiments and even on keeping some Russian cultural influence in the region. But Russia lacked the means in Czechoslovakia's market economy to maintain a modicum of official cultural presence, or to counteract popular contempt.

The Soviet/Russian case suggests that if a country does not offer benefits, let alone is viewed as a colonizer more socio-economically primitive than the colonized, then no amount of intention on the part of that state or its recipient government will ensure interest in its culture. Countries attractive to the post-communist Central European states and societies alike were those that provided the example and means to recreate liberal democracy and economics. Foremost among these were the English-speaking nations.

The United States

The Czechoslovak philosopher-leadership seemed particularly intent on English-speaking influences generally, and American specifically. Havel, not surprisingly, used his state powers towards this end. During his official visit to Washington in February 1990, which included an address to a joint session of the United States Congress, he asked the US to provide Czechoslovakia not with funds, but with instruction in economics and management, and education in political science for the running of elections and instruction in the English language. The Czechoslovak ambassador to the US named English language instruction an area of education 'where we are in need of handouts and gifts, and very badly so' (cited in Kramer, 1990). Requesting such aid, rather than direct financial assistance or trade concessions, was condemned in private by senior Czechoslovak officials as impractical and even stupid, although Czechoslovaks expected that most favoured nation status, the start of negotiations for which coincided with Havel's visit, would certainly be forthcoming (e.g. *Lidová demokracie*, 1990).[4]

If Havel was appealing for American government assistance, the official cultural response appears to have been small. On 7 February 1990, in a well-crafted speech at Prague's Charles University, US Secretary of State James Baker pledged official American activities in the form of increased cultural and educational exchanges, the opening of US Information Agency centres in Prague and Bratislava, and a Peace Corps language programme (Baker, 1990: 2). But, according to the Czechoslovak press, a total of only 200 Peace Corps volunteers were sent to Czechoslovakia, a country of 15.5 million. Twenty-five came at first, arriving ten months after Havel's visit to Washington, with the remainder scheduled to arrive only in 1991 (*Lidové noviny*, 14 November 1990). Havel also asked that the broadcasts of Congress-funded Radio Free Europe and Voice of America continue to supplement the domestic media (RFE, 1990: 58). These state activities notwithstanding, the United States Information Service, the government agency responsible for dissemination of American culture abroad, favours private initiatives, and the response has in fact been largely that.

The American presence in Central Europe, and in Czechoslovakia in particular, leads to two broad distinctions of how cultural influences can be transmitted across borders. The first is cultural diplomacy, conducted by governments or government agencies. This takes the form of direct government funding for cultural and educational projects, but also includes agencies which might be independent of their government but whose objectives remain the same and who work with that government. The British Council, the US Peace Corps or Germany's Goethe Institute fall into this category. By contrast, the second category is cultural relations, where government involvement is indirect or absent. These include private exchanges, tourism and mass culture and the results of business activity (adapted from Mitchell, 1986).

In examining the propagation of English and English language culture – by state or non-state actors – it is important to remember that English has a momentum and an inherent attractiveness. Half of the world's scientific publications are in English; English is an official language in thirty-four countries and the chosen international language of a further twenty-four (Arnold, 1979: 47). Interdependence, as one writer contends, perhaps facetiously, 'would be complete when all foreigners sensibly learned some English' (Seers, 1983: 10).

Turning, then, to American cultural diplomacy, from the 1950s the US government acknowledged the value of cultural diplomacy to its multifaceted struggle in the Cold War. But while the US expected increased communication among peoples to garner increased understanding, this has often become much more a one-way process, with little regard to the impediments of reciprocity (Rosenberg, 1982: 203 and 217).

This problem seems to be replicated in post-communist Central Europe, where American mass culture, rather than cultural diplomacy, is leading to a potential backlash, and possibly a rejection of the American values that were so very welcome immediately following the 1989 revolutions. While other English-speaking expatriates have certainly resided in post-communist Czechoslovakia, none have had the population or the eminence or, perhaps most significant, such high expectations held of them by Czechoslovaks as the Americans. Czechoslovaks expected that freedom corresponded to their image of Americans. That familiar image, described here by an émigré academic, is of a people 'who never have to deny themselves anything ... They live in an enchanted land free of all mundane cares, a land where wishing makes it so. Most of all, they live in a land which is totally dedicated to the unlimited expansion of individual material influence' (Kohák, 1992: 209).

However much Americans would protest this image, Czechoslovaks feel that their revolution failed to yield American-style opulence while ironically, simultaneously, providing exactly that to American expatriates in Czechoslovakia. These Americans, according to the BBC, have totalled as many as 50,000 in Prague alone (BBC, 1993). They have constructed their own community, leading an apparently carefree lifestyle sustained by networks inaccessible to the Czechoslovaks who ostensibly host them. US diplomats acknowledge that Americans reside technically as tourists and work illegally as English teachers (Wheatly, 1992), thereby avoiding taxation. Some of the Americans have succeeded in attaining positions as advisers to republic and federal government ministers, part of a trend that one American expatriate equated to the New York fashion of keeping a Filipino maid (Wheatly, 1992). They refer to Czechoslovakia as the land of milk, honey, work opportunities and cheap beer. Many of these same admit having no work at home and refer to Prague as their 'second-chance city', while believing that future Hemingways and Fitzgeralds will trace their steps (Procházka, 1991).

By contrast, even though they have the prospect of an excellent economic recovery, one propelled not least by foreign tourist spending, the Czechoslovaks have suffered a decline in their standard of living after the end of communism. For all the popularity of the American 'invaders' (BBC, 1993), some Czechoslovaks are heard to say, as did this one to *The Times*:

> At the beginning of the revolution we were flattered to see all these people from the States. It was like if you have a party, you want the smartest people to come. But every day there are more of them. They don't seem to know how to fix the economy any more than we. Czechoslovak people are now starting not to like all these advisers that the politicians have. We have already been ruled by powerful people from another country (Wheatly, 1992).

The unofficial American presence is contributing to the development of post-communist Czechoslovak society. Instances of English diction are occurring in the Czech language; the population has been introduced to Chicago-style deep-pan pizza, American dance and theatre and evangelical movements and the laundromat (although economic conditions have, if only initially, ensured that only expatriates frequent the latter). Globally pervasive American mass culture in its powerful form of film has dominated other foreign culture entering post-communist Czechoslovakia, with three-quarters of films being American. But all of this is not without disfavour. In film, for example, the Czechoslovak Association of Applied Graphics planned an 'anti-Oscar' award for vulgarity to the American Academy of Motion Picture Arts and Sciences 'for parasitism, lack of taste, and the primitivism of American film posters forced on Czecho-slovak filmgoers' (RFE, 1991: 26).

While Czechoslovakia has been receiving not only large amounts of Ameri-can mass culture but also representatives of that society, the Czechoslovak enjoyment of those fruits might well be said to be soured. This sentiment will certainly be exacerbated if Czechoslovaks do not feel immediate and meaningful improvements in their personal wealth as a result of the use of the genuine Bohemia by Americans who failed to be Bohemians at home.

Britain

Both the British state and society have had a base from which to expand their cultural activities. While the radio broadcasts of US government-sup-ported Radio Free Europe and Radio Liberty and West Germany's Deutsche Welle were jammed by the Eastern bloc regimes, BBC Russian-language broad-casts were unjammed in January 1987. The BBC was widely regarded as being more reputable than other Western state media agencies to the extent that some felt that Soviet authorities made a distinction between the BBC and other foreign media (*Guardian*, 1987). Czechs listened to the BBC, perhaps trusting it more than other sources. In terms of popular culture, where the rock scene in relatively liberal socialist Yugoslavia was both American and British (Ramet, 1988: 400), British influence seems particularly strong in Czechoslovakia. In so far as they represent British culture and not merely English-speaking culture, the Beatles are routinely mentioned first if not solely among rock groups (e.g. Gzowski, 1992: 23, 75 and 78), and the music of 'Yesterday', although not its inappropriate lyrics, is often played as a Czech groom puts the ring on his bride's finger.

The British government has attributed importance to exporting its culture and sees a connection between culture and trade. British emeritus diplomat Anthony Parsons writes that: 'If you are thoroughly familiar with someone else's language and literature, if you know and love his country, its cities, its arts, its people, you will be instinctively disposed, all other things being equal or nearly equal, to buy goods from him rather than from a less well known and well-liked source' (1984/5: 6). On his July 1990 visit to Czechoslovakia, British Foreign Secretary Douglas Hurd appeared to echo these words, de-claring that Britain aimed 'to replace Russian with English as the main foreign language in Central Europe.' (ČTK, 1990).

To this end, one would expect British cultural diplomacy to be active in Central Europe. The British Council's spacious facilities in Prague are now, not in the least symbolically, on the former premises of the East German

Cultural Centre. While the British government pledged in 1990 to spend £5 million per annum for five years on English-language teaching in Central and Eastern Europe, with £1.3 million designated for Czechoslovakia (Tytler, 1992), Britain was the slowest of the major language states to become active in the region. Bill Jefferson, the British Council director in Czechoslovakia, who only arrived in Prague in September 1990, said: 'As usual Britain responded less rapidly than anybody else.' The British Council defends its tardiness by saying that it could thereby provide what Czechoslovaks actually desired (Tytler, 1992). The British can also claim success in that, as with RFE and VOA, Havel requested that the BBC continue broadcasting (RFE, 1990: 58), and British universities have received a plurality, but not a majority, of Central and East European students funded by the European Community to study in EC countries (e.g. Claveloux, 1991).

None the less, Czechoslovaks and Britons feel that the British presence – both cultural and especially as regards business – is small. Czechoslovak citizens and officials have often been quoted as missing British investment in the country (*Financial Times*, 23 July 1990; *Guardian*, 1991), and some British businesspeople operating there have commented: 'It's a question of contact and language and so far the British have been pretty useless' (Harris, 1991). Even if the British Council claims that, despite its late start in Central Europe, 'We are now well ahead of the French, Germans and the Americans' (quoted in Harris, 1991), the British government cannot be pleased that Czech textbooks of English have adopted American spelling and grammar. If Britain does indeed see a mutually reinforcing link between cultural diplomacy and trade, it has lost ground to other states. France may be in a similar position.

France

Like Britain, France had a cultural base in Central Europe on which to build after 1989. Its culture was exemplified by interwar Central Europe. For Poland's Milosz, 'much of Europeaness was bound up with the cultural eradiation of Paris, something which has almost died away and, by implication, has not been replaced by a functional equivalent' (Schöpflin, 1989: 21). In interwar Czechoslovakia, the poetry of France 'became the touchstone of Czech literati' (Scruton, 1986), and French literature was the most popular of translated works (Korbel, 1977: 67).

The French government has undertaken an extensive state-initiated cultural programme in Central Europe, part of its perennial project to advance French culture worldwide (Mitchell, 1986). French cultural diplomacy is active in post-communist Czechoslovakia. The French Embassy alone contributed to Prague's important October 1990 Peoples to Peoples Conference, and the French ministers responsible for language and culture deliver lectures on topics like Victor Hugo (*Lidové noviny*, 18 and 25 October 1990). Private French initiatives have been successful in Czechoslovakia, particularly in the nuclear power and automotive sectors, and they include the first major private radio station in the country, featuring bilingual broadcasts and contemporary French music. But even the French ambassador concedes that French cultural relations with Czechoslovakia far outstrip business relations (*Lidové noviny*, 24 August 1990).

For all its official cultural efforts, observers wrote even before the 1989 revolution that 'it is hard for the French and others to match the German drive, not just in trade but in things cultural, such as university staff exchanges, art exhibitions, literary symposiums and the like' (*The Economist*, 1989). The 1989 revolution could be seen as a blow to the French language: communist-bloc countries used French, in addition to Russian, as an alternative diplomatic language. Whereas Czechoslovak passports until 1989 contained details in Russian and French, the post-communist Czechoslovak government, like others, replaced French in its passports with English, and included all UN languages for particulars. Remarkably, it also included German, a non-UN language. It is on the strength and attractiveness of Germany that the next section focuses.

Germany

Like Britain and France, Germany has a state programme designed to advance its language and culture in post-communist Central Europe. The same process of using state organs to create a non-state civil society that led to the American influx of American 'Bohemians' is also responsible for encouraging foreign investment. This leads to a final apparent element of the Central European intellectuals' conception of 'Central Europe': the place of Germans therein.

Germany and German minorities have had an immense role to play in Central Europe, and the duality of their role as modernizers and hegemon is complex. An interwar conception of 'Central Europe', advanced in particular by Masaryk 'was conceived not only without Germany but against it' (Rupnik, 1990: 241). The extent to which similar thinking was entertained by contemporary Central European intellectuals is not precise, but several indications exist of a Central Europe without Germany.

To begin with, the Central European dissident debate on the question of Central Europe 'is generally remarkable for its omission of Germany and "the German question"' as much as there was an acknowledgement that the re-unification of Germany was the precursor to ending the geopolitical division of Europe. Similarly, the West German discussion was 'remarkable for the relatively small part played by these East European visions and aspirations' (Garton Ash, 1991). Even though much solidarity and cooperation existed among Czechoslovak, Hungarian and Polish dissidents, Czech-born Jacques Rupnik cites a Polish dissident newspaper as stating that 'the natural representative of the interests of East German citizens is the German Federal Republic' – in other words, he clarifies, 'a Central Europe without Germans' (Rupnik, 1990: 253–4). To these ends, for example, Polish dissidents excluded the possibility of cooperation with the East German opposition.

It is not clear to what extent the post-communist Czechoslovak leadership shared the view of limiting German involvement in 'Central Europe', and Havel himself sought to elevate his knowledge of German to that of his English

(Havel, 1985, *passim*), but as the post-communist leaderships explicitly desired the creation of a market economy, then no agent willing to trade or invest could be declined. Thus the Czechoslovak state surrendered whatever control it might have had over other influences that market liberalization brought. Private economic influences will be returned to presently, but first it is important to note that well before 1989 the West German state developed a deliberate plan to sow a 'whole fabric of ties' with Central and Eastern Europe, of which the cultural were but one thread (Garton Ash, 1990: 11).

This policy was expanded after the 1989 revolutions, when, more broadly, Kohl undertook to have German 'elevated' in the EC and the CSCE (Tomforde, 1992). In 1992, the German Foreign Ministry dedicated an unprecedented DM35.4 million (£12.2 million) for the 'spreading of the German language abroad' (Tomforde, 1992). The bulk of German-language learners have always been in Eastern Europe (Arnold, 1979: 50; Szabo, 1993) and this money need not, unlike in the case of Britain or France, be spread thinly across several continents. To leave no doubt as to German policy, the director of Germany's short-wave radio station Deutsche Welle explained that a 'media and cultural offensive' had been initiated for Central and Eastern Europe (*Washington Post*, 16 February 1992).

The influence that Germany might be said to have in Central Europe results not so much from state activities as from other, non-state sources. Even German cultural officials concede that Germany does not have the resources, despite quadrupling its foreign language instruction budget since 1989, to conduct its Germanizing mission. As anecdotal evidence, a diplomat from an English-speaking country commented that German teachers of German had come to him for teaching materials. Germany's prime role is the integration of the East German *Länder* while minimizing disruption to its economy (interview with German official, July 1992; Szabo, 1993: 41).

Instead of state-sponsored activities, German presence in Central Europe has been the result of private business. The extent of that presence will be briefly described and the consequences then considered. Of all foreign investment entering Czechoslovakia between the end of 1989 and early 1992, when foreign investment decreased, 80 per cent has been German (*Christian Science Monitor*, 1992).[5] Czechoslovak trade with Germany increased both relatively and absolutely by several times that of Czechoslovakia's next-largest Western trading partner.[6] And whatever reaction the Czechoslovaks might have to German economic influence might be only heightened by Austrian business activities, because 'the "German Problem" from the Czech perspective has always meant "Austro-German"' (Hauner, 1993).

Total Czechoslovak exports in 1991 to Britain, France the US and Japan *combined* were approximately one-fifth of those to Austria and Germany and one-quarter of imports.[7] It is of little consequence that German analysts respond that German trade with Central European countries forms a small share of Germany's total foreign trade, using spurious terminology such as 'peanuts by American standards' (Eisfeld, 1993: 44). None of these apologies or justifications change the consequences for a recipient country like Czechoslovakia, the next issue to be examined.

Consequences

To a capable population aware of its previous relative wealth but current poverty, a language will be attractive for the potential wealth it offers. With German and Austrian business being so pivotal for Central Europe, it is not surprising that German is now the most popular second language in schools, with slightly more than 50 per cent of students studying it (*Lidové noviny*, 23 April 1990; Szabo, 1993: 53; Tomforde, 1992); and although English remains popular at universities, German continues to gain ground even there. Czechs who now work for German companies have said that their employers pay for German language instruction. While they have not been coaxed into studying German, and they note that the German management often has good knowledge of English, they also agree that in order to be promoted, they need German. Czechoslovakia's ambassador to the United States, Rita Klimová, warned that German and Austrian influence will predominate 'if all the manuals are in German and the foreign language teaching is in German' (Kramer, 1990).

German financial prowess impinges on Czech national sensibilities, with German companies acquiring control over ticket sales to Czech castles like Karlštejn, described as a national inheritance. The residents of the historic south Bohemian town of Český Krumlov say that the buildings of their town can only be saved by foreign purchase, and this, they add, is being done largely by Germans (BBC, 1994). The pull of financial opportunities that materialize – be they by foreigners in the country or outside – has resulted in cultural consequences: the *Financial Times*, for example, reported a growing fear that after 1989 Czechoslovakia 'will suffer the same drain of music talent to foreign parts as in the eighteenth and nineteenth centuries' (Clark, 1991), a time corresponding to the height of Habsburg assimilation (see quotation at the beginning of this chapter; Taylor, 1948: 24–5). That drain is to German-speaking countries: 'The Czech Philharmonic Orchestra, the country's premier ensemble, recently lost two key employees to well-paid jobs in Germany. The most promising young singers ... have signed contracts in Vienna, Stuttgart or other German-language theatres' (Clark, 1991). Majority control of Czechoslovakia's chief recording enterprise Editia Supraphon, 'and with it the decisive control of nearly all Czech musical production', was sold to a foreign company (*Prague Post*, 1993).

Fearing a backlash, German companies now controlling Czechoslovak enterprises have become more sagacious, earlier than American companies,[8] assuaging national feelings by retaining original Czech company names or by making indigenous managers prominent. Despite these measures, a poll of Czechs conducted at the end of 1992 found that 80 per cent felt German 'business had too large a stake in Czechoslovakia' (Szabo, 1993). Even the élite newspaper *Lidové noviny* demonstrated concern over German financial influence. Its political cartoons showed Kohl driving a Mercedes with jaws that tore into the Czech lands and a highway sign, in the shape of Czechoslovakia, with the German advertisement 'Tschechoslowakei Zimmer Frei' (*Lidové noviny*, 31 January 1992, 16 October 1990).

The Czechoslovak government replied to criticism by Britain, France and the US of the German economic preponderance by declaring that those states should invest more in Czechoslovakia. But more vigorous Western investment is not enough to counter the explanation by Czechoslovak Prime Minister Marián Čalfa that one of his reasons for favouring Volkswagen's bid for Škoda over that of Renault-Volvo, by far the biggest foreign investment in the former communist world, was that 'the Germans are our neighbours' (*Financial Times*, 26 October 1990).

It is certainly possible that 'The traditional Central European view of Germany as modernizer has predominated over the fear of German hegemony, and the German social market economics and stable brand of federalism have become the model for East Europeans' (Szabo, 1993: 37–8). But even if the German model were to serve only as a model for post-communist Central Europe, repercussions could not be avoided.

While private Germans, like Americans, are collectively characterized by and detested for their abusive behaviour in Czechoslovakia,[9] at least German interests provide extensive welfare. American mass culture and its expatriate population spread American values and English language but the direct benefit to the welfare of the Czechoslovaks has been slow, if not questionable, especially in view of the high expectations. National cultures will inevitably be influenced by the nations that can provide work and welfare. As such, German investment becomes synonymous with influence. But in conditions where that influence becomes disproportionately great the results for a nation and its culture can be unwanted. As the Czechoslovak ambassador to the United States warned shortly after the 1989 revolutions: 'My feeling is that the German-speaking parts of Europe, including Austria, will succeed where the Hapsburgs, Hitler and Bismarck were unsuccessful – in Germanizing Central and Eastern Europe by purely peaceful and laudable methods of market economic development' (Kramer, 1990).

CONCLUSION

To paraphrase Kundera, while political regimes are ephemeral, the frontiers of civilizations are traced by centuries. Even in the short time since the 1989 revolutions, the contours of foreign cultural influence in post-communist Central Europe are already being forged. The efforts to create a regional identity and, domestically, civil society and a market economy by using state instruments has resulted in consequences which were probably unintended by the philosopher-leadership.

In regional relations, where the state instruments of diplomacy were applied, sub-national and supra-regional concerns have thus far limited the process of identity-building. In addition, globalizing influences have provoked or, at the

least, permitted expressions of xenophobia and racism as well as the fragmentation of domestic political unity in all Central European countries save perhaps
the Czech Republic. And the breakup of the Czechoslovak federation, an act
perceived as destablizing regional stability, resulted not so much from Slovak
nationalism as much as from the pressures of accommodating to the Western
economic system.

Based on the criteria used in this chapter, the effectiveness of state activity
in the form of cultural diplomacy appears to be limited. The Soviet Union
had such an extensive programme of state-sponsored culture that it created
animosity. Britain and France attach importance to cultural diplomacy but
could be said to have suffered setbacks in post-1989 Czechoslovakia. And while
Germany has what is probably the most overt cultural and linguistic 'campaign'
for this region, by its own admission, it cannot employ it fully. By contrast to
these four, the US appears to accent private initiative.

In so far as the Central European states seek economic and political
modernization, this leads to the importation of non-state influences. And it is
non-state influences, more than any state's foreign cultural policy, that will
determine the influence of one foreign culture over another. In post-communist
Czechoslovakia, this was being decided largely by two conduits of culture:
thousands of American expatriates, and German capital. Significantly, to the
extent that the latter provides welfare, it has tackled, if not offset, the universal
appeal of American mass culture and encouraged 'Germanization'. It appears
that the result of the short-term aim of recreating civil society and bringing
Central Europe into global civilization is that the form and content of cultural
and regional relations is apparently what the dissident leadership did not want.

NOTES

1. The geographic and cultural boundaries of Central Europe are not defined; instead,
   the debate over their limitations is itself part of the debate of the notion 'Central
   Europe'. For simplicity, and in accordance with general post-1989 geopolitical
   terminology, Central Europe is used here to denote Poland, Hungary, Czechoslovakia
   and its post-1992 successors the Czech Republic and Slovakia. For an introduction
   to the cultural and philosophical debate on the meaning of 'Central Europe', see
   Schöpflin and Wood, 1989; for references to the geographic terms of East Central
   Europe, see Wandycz, 1992: 12–17.
2. For a comparative analysis of Central European visions by a leading independent
   thinker from each of Hungary, Poland and Czechoslovakia, see Garton Ash, 1986.
3. As early as spring 1990 only 5.5 per cent of those pursuing foreign languages studied
   Russian (*Lidové noviny*, 23 April 1990). This figure is almost certainly inflated, as
   many students had to study Russian for lack of alternatives (Gzowski, 1992: 8).
4. While Havel said before his visit to the United States that 'I expect some significant
   economic help', he added the qualification that any aid had to be 'on the basis of
   equality, and not on the basis of somebody big and rich giving presents to somebody
   small and poor'. He also said he expected 'moral support for the processes taking
   place in Czechoslovakia' (*International Herald Tribune*, 1990).
5. While US foreign investment in the Czech Republic in 1993 accounted for 55 per
   cent of all foreign investment, and combined Austrian and German totalled only 19

per cent, foreign investment in 1993 was half of the 1992 level (*Business Central Europe*, 1994: 38).

6. Trade with former socialist countries was still substantial for all Central European countries, but steadily diminished.

7. Compare the figures as given below:

		1989	1990	1991
Germany	Exports	17,964	27,639	80,659
	Imports	19,931	31,734	59,630
Austria	Exports	9,938	12,717	18,631
	Imports	11,830	23,124	23,329
United Kingdom	Exports	4,396	5,521	6,143
	Imports	4,731	6,862	6,182
France	Exports	3,936	5,662	7,847
	Imports	3,350	4,203	6,830
United States	Exports	1,413	1,639	3,195
	Imports	813	1,368	5,427
Japan	Exports	1,343	1,592	2,057
	Imports	1,113	1,144	3,571

All figures in millions of Czechoslovak crowns
Source: EIU, 1993: 32.

8. American companies in the Czech Republic and Slovakia have begun 'Czech-ification' of their employees (*Prague Post*, 1994a).

9. Such as this anecdotal evidence by a Czech journalist: 'Noisy, fat Germans ... holler on the trams and stumble around the streets drunk on beer that comes cheaply for them ... All in all even those Czechs whose livelihood depends on tourism have to ask themselves if they are getting more than they bargained for' (*Prague Post*, 1994b).

REFERENCES

In addition to the sources below, some of the material used in this chapter comes from interviews conducted with foreign and local officials and private individuals, the assistance of whom is greatly appreciated.

Arnold, Hans, 1979, *Foreign Cultural Policy: A Survey From a German Point of View*, trans. Keith Hamnett, Tübingen and Basle, Horst Erdmann Verlag and London, Oswald Wolff.

Baker, James, Speech to Charles University, 7 February 1990, United States Information Service, US Embassy (London).

BBC, 1993, Radio 4, 9 January.

BBC, 1994, Radio 4, 4 January.

Brodsky, Josef, 1986, 'Why Milan Kundera is Wrong About Dostoevsky', *Cross Currents*, 5: 477–83.

Business Central Europe, 1994, April.

Christian Science Monitor, 1992, 28 February–5 March.

Clark, Andrew 1991, 'Czech Music After the Revolution – Prague is Paying the Price for Years of Artistic Stagnation', *Financial Times*, 23 February.

Claveloux, Denise, 1991, 'Students Soak Up Western Culture With New Grants', *European*, 18 January.

Croan, Melvin, 1989, 'Lands In-between: The Politics of Cultural Identity in Contemporary Eastern Europe,' *Eastern European Politics and Societies*, 3 (2): 176–97.

ČTK, 1990, 23 July, in *Summary of World Broadcasts*, 25 July 1990.

The Economist, 1989, 29 April.

Economist Intelligence Unit, 1994, *Country Report: Czech Republic and Slovakia. 1st Quarter 1994*, London.

Economist Intelligence Unit, 1993, *Country Profile: Czech Republic and Slovakia*, London.

Eisfeld, Rainer, 1993, 'Mitteleuropa in Historical and Contemporary Perspective', *German Politics and Society*, 28: 39–52.

Garton Ash, Timothy Garton, 1990, 'Mitteleuropa?', in Graubard (ed.): 1–21.

Garton Ash, Timothy Garton, 1986, 'Does Central Europe Exist?', in *The Use of Adversity: Essays on the Fate of Central Europe*, Cambridge, Granta, 1989: 161–91.

Graubard, Stephen (ed.), 1991, *Eastern Europe ... Central Europe ... Europe*, Boulder, CO, Westview Press.

Guardian, 1991, 25 January.

Guardian, 1987, 6 February.

Gzowski, Alison, 1992, *Facing Freedom: The Children of Eastern Europe*, Toronto, Viking.

Hájek, Igor, 1994, 'Czech Culture in the Cauldron', *Europe-Asia Studies*, 46 (1): 127–42.

Harris, Francis, 1991, 'Blank Czech on Offer for British Business', *Sunday Telegraph*, 22 September.

Hauner, Milan, 1993, 'The Introduction of German Studies in the Czech Republic: a "Denkschrift"', *German History*, 11 (3).

Havel, Václav, 1984, 'Six Asides About Culture', in Jan Vladislav (ed.), *Living in Truth*, London and Boston, Faber & Faber, 1986: 123–35.

Havel, Václav, 1985, *Dopisy Olze*, Toronto, Sixty-Eight Publishers, Corp.

Havel, Václav, 1989, *Dálkový Výslech (Rozhovor s Karlem Hvížďalou)*, Prague, Melantrich.

Havel, Václav, 1992, *Summer Meditations on Politics, Morality and Civility in a Time of Transition*, London and Boston, Faber & Faber.

Havel, Václav, 1994, 'Theatre Can Help Achieve Peace Among Mankind', *Toronto Star*, 26 March

Heneka, A., Frantisek Janouh, Vilem Precan and Jan Vladislav (eds), 1985, *A Besieged Culture: Czechoslovakia Ten Years After Helsinki*, Stockholm and Vienna, The Charta 77 Foundation and International Helsinki Federation for Human Rights.

International Herald Tribune, 1990, 13–14 January.

ITAR-TASS World Service, 1992, 'Russian Cultural Centre in Prague "Blockaded" in Dispute [of] Ownership', 21 August, in *Summary of World Broadcasts*, 24 August 1992.

Judt, Tony, 1990, 'The Rediscovery of Central Europe', in Graubard (ed.): 23–58.

Klaus, Václav, 1994, 'The Radical Transformation of Czech Society and Its European Context', Speech to the Royal Institute of International Affairs, 7 March.

Kohák, Erazim, 'Ashes, Ashes ... Central Europe after Forty Years', *Dædalus* 121(2): 197–215.

Konrád, George, 1984, *Antipolitics*, London, Quartet Books.

Korbel, Josef, 1977, *Twentieth-century Czechoslovakia: The Meanings of Its History*, New York, Columbia University Press.

Kramer, Gene, 1990, 'US Urged to Help Czechoslovakia Avoid "Germanization"', *Associated Press*, 20 February.

Kundera, Milan, 1984, 'The Tragedy of Central Europe', *New York Review of Books*, 26 April: 33–8.

Kusý, Miroslav, 1989, 'We, Central-European East Europeans', in Schöpflin and Wood (eds): 91–6.

Lidová demokracie, 1990, 23 February.

Lidové noviny, 1992, 31 January; 1990, 3 March; 23 April; 24 August; 25 September; 16 October; 18 October; 25 October; 14 November.

Martin, Peter, 1991, 'Economic Reforms and Slovakia', RFE, *Report on Eastern Europe*, 5 July.

Mitchell, J.M., 1986, *International Cultural Relations*, London, Allen & Unwin.

Musil, Jiří, 1992 'Czechoslovakia in the Middle of Transition', *Dædalus*, 121(2): 175–95.

Neumann, Iver B., 1993, 'Russia as Central Europe's Constituting Other', *Eastern European Politics and Society*, 7(2): 349–69.

Obrman, Jan, 1991, 'Treaty Signed with the Soviet Union', RFE, *Report on Eastern Europe*, 1 November.

Oltay, Edith, 1994, 'Former Communists Win First Round of Hungarian Elections', *RFE/RL Research Report*, 27 May: 1–5.

Parsons, Anthony, 1984/5, 'Vultures and Philistines: British Attitudes to Culture and Cultural Diplomacy', *International Affairs*, 61(1).

Pravda (Bratislava), 1991, 31 December.

Procházka, Zdeněk, 1991, 'Hej Hou, Hej Hou, Yankeeové Jdou', *Mladý svět*, XXXIV: 25.

Prague Post, 1994a, 6–12 April; 1994b, 13–19 April; 1993, 12–18 May.

Ramet, Pedro, 1988, 'The Rock Scene in Yugoslavia', *Eastern European Politics and Society*, 2(2): 396–410.

RFE, 1991, *Report on Eastern Europe*, 1 November.

RFE, 1990, *Report on Eastern Europe*, 13 July.

RFE/RL, 1994, 'The Politics of Intolerance: East Central Europe', *RFE/RL Research Report*, 22 April: 50–71.

Rosenberg, Emily, 1982, *Spreading the American Dream: American Economic and Cultural Expansion, 1890–1945*, New York, Hill & Wang.

Rupnik, Jacques, 1990, 'Central Europe or Mitteleuropa?', in Graubard (ed.): 233–65.

Schöpflin, George, 1989, 'Central Europe: Definitions Old and New', in Schöpflin and Wood (eds): 7–29.

Schöpflin, George and Wood, Nancy (eds), 1989, *In Search of Central Europe*, Cambridge, Polity.

Scruton, Roger, 1986, 'Lament for a Poet Patriot. Obituary of Jaroslav Seifert', *The Times*, 28 January.

Seers, Dudley, 1983, *The Political Economy of Nationalism*, Oxford, Oxford University Press.

Szabo, Stephen F., 1993, 'The New Germany and Central European Security', in John R. Lampe and Daniel N. Nelson (eds), *East European Security Reconsidered*, Baltimore, MD, Johns Hopkins University Press: 35–54.

Taylor, A.J.P., 1948, *The Habsburg Monarchy, 1809–1918*, London, Hamish Hamilton.

Tomforde, Anna, 1992, 'Germans Demand Linguistic Equality Despite Fury of "Mad English"', *Guardian*, 6 February.

Tytler, David, 1992, 'Spreading the Word in Eastern Europe', *The Times*, 27 July.

Wandycz, Piotr S., 1992, *The Price of Freedom: A History of East Central Europe from the Middle Ages to the Present*, London and New York, Routledge.

Wheatley, Keith, 1992, 'Overpaid, Oversexed and All Over Prague', *The Times*, 11 April.

Wolchik, Sharon L., 1994, 'The Politics of Ethnicity in Post-Communist Czechoslovakia', *East European Politics and Societies*, 8(1): 153–88.

PART II
BOUNDARIES CONTESTED

5
International political economy and International Relations: apprentice or teacher?[1]

Robert O'Brien

The past two decades have seen the field of international political economy develop into a major sub-discipline in the subject of International Relations. There has been an explosion in the number of courses available and the variety of textbooks on the market. Publishers such as Cambridge, Cornell, Edward Elgar and Macmillan have dedicated IPE series. Both the British International Studies Association and the International Studies Association have IPE sub-sections and 1994 saw the launching of a new journal devoted to IPE, the *Review of International Political Economy*. In the context of mainstream International Relations, the growth of interest in IPE is a new direction in the field. Yet IPE is an extremely diverse area, and some approaches may be more fruitful than others. This chapter offers some thoughts about the development of the field and its possibilities in the future.

A survey of the field of international political economy (IPE) could utilize a number of different typologies. At its most crude, relevant work only would be listed (Gayle, Denemark and Styles, 1991). A more sophisticated approach would be to group work by three competing ideologies (Gilpin, 1975, 1987) or perspectives (Gill and Law, 1988). Liberal, Realist and Marxist thought (or how these authors view them) could be outlined, compared, contrasted and evaluated. Alternatively, IPE could be divided into traditions which highlight different methods of enquiry. An American-led 'scientific' versus a British-led traditional approach (Tooze, 1985) could echo previous controversies about the merits of empiricism. IPE could also be divided along divisions that are seen in the social sciences generally – positivist, interpretative, post-modern, feminist. This would be a rather unbalanced division, with most of the work in the first category.

This chapter examines the field by exposing and exploring another division – labelled the traditional and inclusive approaches. The traditional approach identifies international political economy as a range of economic issues areas having important political effects or subject to political pressures. It is traditional in the sense that it flows from dominant International Relations traditions and seeks to identify IPE as a sub-discipline or subject of that tradition. Those who view IPE as a sub-discipline can themselves use two different methodologies. The first draws upon the traditional IR disciplines of politics and history to reveal the politics of what are otherwise seen as economic subjects. This could be called the politics of international economics. Alternatively, scholars try to explain IPE issues such as trade conflicts or monetary relations through the application of micro-economic theory. Here, the subject can vary, but the method remains the same. International political economy issues, similar to other IR issues (e.g. arms races) and other social sciences are investigated through the application of models such as public choice theory. This could be termed the economics of international politics. However, the division between these groups is not clear-cut because many from the first group use micro-economic assumptions in their analysis.

The other approach is to view IPE as a methodology that identifies the interaction of economic and political domains as the central phenomena in international relations. The methodology can then be applied to numerous issue areas. This chapter labels it 'inclusive' because its adherents try to open up and include new areas for investigation and it threatens to outgrow the traditional boundaries of IR. An alternative and more threatening label would be 'expansionist'. It gathers an eclectic group of scholars working on a wide range of issues from diverse perspectives. This approach has limited support in Britain and Canada. In the United States it is even more marginalized because IPE as subject approach dominates in either the public choice or traditional IR form. A significant contribution to this approach or perhaps an element in dialogue with it is that of feminist theory or gender analysis.

The presence of two discernible views of the nature of IPE – as IR sub-discipline or encompassing methodology – raises a number of questions for teaching, research and practice. Academics teaching IPE courses grapple with such questions as: what is the relevant scope of the subject, should it be confined to issues such as trade, money and development or can it be extended to include the environment, migration and militarization? If the broader approach is used, how can it possibly be included in a single course? In both teaching and research one must consider whether the standard IR epistemological and ontological assumptions can be applied to IPE subjects or whether these need to be reviewed and challenged. IPE is viewed both as a sub-discipline of traditional IR and as an attempt to transcend old boundaries by creating an umbrella field incorporating traditional IR, economics and politics. Which is the preferable path and what are the implications for the study of International Relations and its practice? This chapter provides initial responses to these issues.

The chapter is divided into three sections. The first reports on the present state of international political economy in the international relations traditions as it is taught in British universities. The second reviews a number of the leading texts and approaches, considering the state of the divide between traditional and inclusive views. The third section speculates on the growth of the inclusive approach and the directions in which it might lead. The chapter argues in favour of an inclusive approach to IPE.

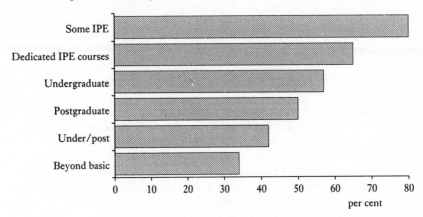

Figure 5.1 Percentage of universities teaching IPE

IPE IN BRITAIN

A survey of thirty-one British university International Relations and Politics departments was undertaken in August 1993 to determine how much international political economy was being taught and what form it was taking. Twenty-six (83 per cent) eventually returned useful information by 1 December 1993.[2] Since IR is studied in a number of different departments and is not taught at all universities, the survey may have passed over some departments. The list of universities was compiled by determining which departments offered at least one course in IR by checking the *Which Universities Guide 1993*. A copy of the survey and a list of universities approached are shown in Appendices 5a and 5b at the end of this chapter. The survey asked respondents if they offered IPE courses, what those courses were and which texts were recommended as essential reading for students. Two additional questions asking whether public choice and feminist theories were examined or used in teaching IPE were included. The results were as follows:

Of the twenty-six returns, twelve or 46 per cent laid claim to studying IR as a separate discipline. Twenty-one (80 per cent) of the respondents offer IPE material to their students in some form. Four departments (15 per cent) offer IPE issues only as components of other courses such as an introduction to IR, European integration or peace studies. Seventeen (65 per cent) offer dedicated IPE courses at the undergraduate and/or postgraduate level. Five universities (19 per cent) have separate streams or specialization in IPE.[3] Fifteen universities (57 per cent) offer IPE at the undergraduate level and 13 (50 per cent) at the graduate level. Eleven universities (42 per cent) have both under and graduate IPE courses, four (15 per cent) at the undergraduate level only and two (7 per cent) at the graduate level only. This information is summarized in Figure 5.1.

The survey was also able to gather some information about what is being taught in IPE courses. Of the fifteen introductory courses, twelve (80 per cent) focused on issues such as trade, investment, monetary affairs, development and world order. Three other introductory courses (20 per cent) also explicitly look at gender and security/militarization issues. It could be argued that the other introductory courses dealt with security under broad sections such as hegemonic stability theory, but the lack of gender consideration seems less contestable.

Nine universities (34 per cent) of the twenty-six offer courses beyond the introductory level. Two-thirds of these universities offered courses dealing with aspects of European integration. Courses in international business were offered by three universities. At least two different universities offered courses in the subjects of international trade; international finance; gender; development, foreign aid; East Asia; world systems; and Pax Americana/US Foreign Policy. There were a wide variety of courses that were offered only at one university. These included: environment, multinational corporations; international (business) law, the state and IPE; IPE theories; international relations of social change; politics of international economic organizations; imperialism, Africa, Middle East, world order; natural resources, ocean politics and economic diplomacy.

The questions about public choice and gender reveal that neither of these areas is prevalent in UK universities. Two respondents were unable to reply to this question. Of the nineteen that did answer, no respondent indicated that public choice was used frequently, ten declared occasionally, seven rarely and two added the answer never. For gender or feminist analysis the responses were: one frequently; six occasionally and twelve rarely.

Twenty of the respondents were able to provide information about the major texts they recommended to their students. The two leading texts were Robert Gilpin's *Political Economy of International Relations* and Stephen Gill and David Law's *Global Political Economy*. Both books were cited by eleven, or 55 per cent, of the universities. Not far behind were Joan Spero's *Politics of International Economic Relations* and Susan Strange's *States and Markets*. These texts were used by ten, or half, of the universities. Other books mentioned included: Blake and Walters, *Politics of Global Economic Relations* five (20 per cent); Craig Murphy and Roger Tooze, *New International Political Economy* three (15 per cent); Robert Cox, *Production, Power and World Order* two (10 per cent); Peter Dicken, *Global Shift* two (10 per cent). One reader was also frequently cited – Jeffry Frieden and David Lake's *International Political Economy* seven (35 per cent). A number of other books were recommended only at one university and have not been included because they tend to reflect a particular specialization or idiosyncrasy.

In the following sections of the chapter, basic texts will be divided into two categories – traditional and inclusive. The traditional texts are those of Spero and Gilpin, while Strange, Gill and Law are part of the inclusive set. Of the twenty responses the traditional set was most represented, with eighteen (90 per cent) using either Gilpin or Spero. Five of those (25 per cent) did not recommend the main inclusive books (Gill and Law or Strange) as primary texts. The inclusive texts were recommended by fourteen of twenty (70 per

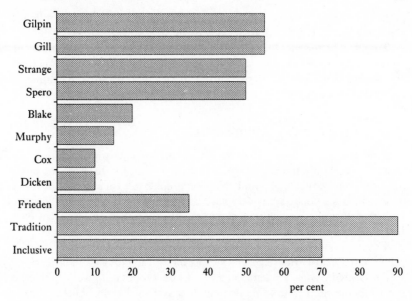

Figure 5.2 Percentage of courses using major texts

cent). Two of those (10 per cent) did not use Gilpin or Spero. Twelve of twenty (60 per cent) recommended a mixture of traditional and inclusive texts by referring to Gilpin/Spero as well as Gill and Law/Strange.

The data compiled by this question have some shortcomings. The first is that some departments which teach IR or IPE may have been overlooked. If this is so, the number should be quite small and not affect the overall sense of the figures. The second is that respondents tended to give curt replies and may have passed over some of their own courses or relevant information. In one or two cases, the information was compiled by someone who did not actually teach the relevant courses. The third drawback stems from the nature of classification involved in responding to the survey. For example, some may view and teach a European integration course as part of the political economy tradition, while others would not. Similarly, the question of gender analysis in introductory courses is difficult to quantify. The approach of the survey was to conclude that it was not used unless there was specific reference to it in the respondent's survey. It is possible that a course could use gender as a primary concept without actually having it appear in an outline or as a separate lecture/ seminar topic. Despite these drawbacks, conclusions can be drawn from the survey.

The major conclusion is that IPE seems firmly established in the majority of institutions teaching IR in Britain. Almost all do some political economy, even if it is only as part of a broader course. Two-thirds offer courses dedicated to IPE issues or approaches, and over a third offer courses allowing specialization beyond the introductory level. Most of these specialized courses are in trade, investment or world order issues. European integration also appears as a popular option. It would appear that IPE is a thriving sub-discipline of IR alongside more traditional areas such as foreign policy analysis.

To get a better idea of what is being taught and the implications of this approach one needs to move a little deeper by examining some of the texts and approaches that were mentioned in the survey. The rest of the chapter moves on to this task.

THE TRADITIONAL APPROACH

This and the following section review major texts presently used in IPE courses. The books under examination were written for different purposes and have different projects in mind. No single book can adequately address every issue. Since the books are widely used as core IPE texts, they will be examined with regard to the picture they present of the discipline and its relationship to International Relations.

The revival of IPE in leading politics or IR departments in the United States and Great Britain can be traced back to the late 1960s and early 1970s. In the United States, academic and practitioner's interests were spurred on by the strains in the Bretton Woods monetary system, Nixon Shock, OPEC price rises and disillusionment caused by the Vietnam war.

Robert Keohane's work in IPE has been at the forefront of this movement since the early 1970s and has been influential in shaping views of the subject matter. Collaborating with Joseph Nye, Keohane identified a separate sphere in international relations characterized by interdependence and transnational links. Reacting against realist obsession with the state, power, and conflict, they developed a contrasting ideal type of international system labelled 'complex interdependence' (Keohane and Nye, 1977). A situation of complex interdependence was marked by multiple channels of international relations rather than simply state-to-state relations, an absence of hierarchy among issues rather than the dominance of military security and a lack of effectiveness of military force. In such an environment international institutions were capable of playing a major role in political bargaining, information provision and the formation of international coalitions.

There are a number of things to be noted about Keohane's interdependence approach. The first is the focus on international organizations and regimes. It highlights the possibility of cooperation and stresses the importance of principles, norms, rules and decision-making procedures. Institutions and regimes are advocated as a means to lessen anarchy and facilitate cooperation in the international system.

The second aspect of note is that the approach is meant to stand alongside traditional realist analysis as a supplement rather than a replacement. Interdependence applies to particular issue areas and tempers the realist elements of eternal conflict. In *After Hegemony* (Keohane, 1984) the focus is on trade, finance and oil. Although Keohane would probably argue for the crucial importance of these issue areas, it appears that interdependence applies to issues of 'low politics' while 'high politics' issues are ceded to realist assumptions.

The third aspect is the continuing focus on the position of the United States in the world. The enquiry is undertaken to determine how the American government can deal with the rising tide of interdependence. How can the United States further its interest in an environment where its power is reduced? Keohane's answer is that it should make greater use of international institutions, strengthen regimes and seek allies in the world community. The regimes in place should be maintained without too much thought to their replacement or to radical overhaul. Interdependence and regimes can and should be used to the benefit of the United States.

Surprisingly for this author, no respondents put any of Keohane's books down as standard texts. This is probably because his work does not take a textbook form, but focuses on particular concepts such as regimes or the role of international institutions. However, his work does appear in the reading lists some respondents sent along with their surveys. Students are being directed to the standard work on interdependence, but not as textbook reading.

Joan Edelman Spero's many editions of *The Politics of International Economic Relations* has been a central text in the study of IPE. For a number of years it dominated the field and has only recently been challenged by the Gill and Law, Gilpin and Strange texts. Spero chooses to explore how international politics shapes international economics rather than how international economics might shape international politics or how they might influence each or be part of a single system. The text is further divided into parts examining three sub-systems – the Western, the North-South and the East-West. While acknowledging that the separation is artificial, Spero believes that the systems are characterized by different modes of management (interdependence, dependence, independence) and have different political problems and processes. The focus in each section is on trade, monetary and investment issues and how the complex relationships can be managed.

Spero notes that with the strength of liberalism in the nineteenth century the study of political economy became separated into politics and economics. Because of changes in the 1970s (Bretton Woods collapse, inflation, OPEC) such a separation was no longer feasible if theory and analysis were to stay in touch with reality (Spero, 1990: 3). In this view politics and economics might or might not be related depending upon the historical position of Great Britain and the United States. Such a view is revealing because it emphasizes two key elements of the text. The first is a fixation with management of the system from the perspective of the strongest state actor. Asking how the system can be managed rules out consideration of systemic change. The system is accepted as it is, and the task on hand is to tinker with the present arrangement to make it run more smoothly. As Robert Cox (1981) might point out, such a management approach is problem-solving with the intention of system preservation, and stifles critical thought about system transformation.

The second is the neglect of the role of ideology in influencing the perception of the international or global political economy. A different view would argue that economics and politics were not separated in the post-war period, but only appeared to be separated to serve satisfied interests. It is only when the international economic system begins to impose upon American interests that the link between economics and politics is rediscovered.

Robert Gilpin's work in IPE has followed a realist logic and has been explicitly formulated as a rejoinder to the interdependence themes of Keohane and Nye (Gilpin, 1987: xi). Over half of the British universities teaching IPE use this text. Gilpin's chosen themes have been the decline of American hegemony (power, dominance), politics influencing economic relations and economic forces altering political relations. A later issue of importance has been the rise of Japan and growth of a rival power base in the Pacific. Gilpin's IPE textbook, *The Political Economy of International Relations*, has three substantive elements. The first considers theoretical issues, the second issue areas (finance, trade, investment) and the third speculates on the nature of future world order.

Gilpin's form of analysis fits neatly into the traditional IR discipline for two primary reasons. The first is his focus on the state as the most important actor and its independence of other forces and actors. Such a position is not surprising, given his explicit attempts to revive realist views of international relations. He wants to reproach liberal writers for their minimization of the state and to prompt fellow realists to take note of economic issues. The welfare of the state, particularly the American state, is at the centre of Gilpin's work. The power relations between states are examined in the context of 'economic' issues and problems. The central problem to be addressed is declining American state power.

Second, although there is an attempt to focus on the interaction between political and economic factors, this is not done completely. Politics might affect economics and economics might affect politics, but there is not a sense that they are in a circular, reinforcing relationship. Politics remains dominant and as such, IPE fits easily into the study of politics and traditional International Relations.

IPE as the economics of politics

A sub-section of the mainstream view of IPE is the utilization of liberal economic analysis to understand international political economic events. This is not confined to IPE, but is found in other IR literature as well. For example, Kenneth Waltz (1979) built his case for structural realism by drawing upon micro-economic theory. Robert Keohane also draws upon such models. For example, Part II of *After Hegemony* concentrates on the theory of rational choice and its relationship to international regimes. Both authors make assumptions similar to that of micro-economics, although Keohane modifies them considerably. The basic assumption of such an approach is that states are rational, unitary actors operating in an anarchic world.

Although Waltz and Keohane draw upon rationality assumptions, they shy away from the use of mathematics to advance their arguments. Others do not. Michael Nicholson (1989) has made the case for understanding international relations through the use of formal theories. By formal theories he means the representation of reality through symbols. His work and that of numerous other formal theorists has been in the area of conflict analysis. Most IR theorists and students will be familiar with game theory constructions such as prisoner's dilemma and chicken.

Although micro-economic approaches in IPE have had some resonance, a new contender in the field is public choice theory. Widely used in many aspects of American political science such as electoral behaviour and theories of federalism, it also has its advocates in IPE. It is the economic application of economic models in the area of the political or public arena (Caporaso and Levine, 1992: 133–43). As outlined by Bruno Frey (1984) public choice methodology has three major features: it takes the individual as the basic unit of analysis, it explains the individual's behaviour by focusing on changes in the constraints in the environment (preferences are assumed to be constant) and the analysis must be rigorous, that is subject to econometric or politicometric testing. The assumption of the individual as the basis of analysis is difficult to maintain in International Relations, but it does allow for criticism of those treating the state as a single actor through game theory. For example, Frey (1988) adopts this tactic in criticism of Keohane's use of game theory. Very little use is made of public choice theory in teaching IPE in British IR courses. No survey respondents indicated that they used it frequently or as their primary method. The situation is most likely very different in American universities and British economics departments.

The picture that emerges from what I have chosen to label a traditionalist approach is that of IPE as a sub-discipline of International Relations. Most departments use traditional texts and a sizeable minority (33 per cent) use them exclusively. The focus remains, even in the interdependence version, on the policy of states, particularly the American state. IPE fits easily into existing departments by establishing a course that examines specific issues such as trade, finance and investment not covered by other courses. Established practice can be expanded by examining formerly neglected issues. Although the scope of International Relations is slightly enlarged, it fits smoothly into strict boundaries. The limits are set by the focus upon issues of major importance to governments (Strange, 1991: 34) and the American government in particular. While not a major problem for a US foreign policy course, such a focus is highly misleading as the basis for the study of international political economy.

Why is an American state-centric approach misleading? The United States remains the most powerful state and its decisions continue to affect millions around the world. It would be mistaken to argue that the American state is unimportant. However, to say that it is important is not the same as saying that the concerns of other state actors should be neglected. The Chinese, Brazilian, Indian and Indonesian states preside over millions of people equally concerned with important issues. Although the states in these countries may not have as much global power as the United States, their task is even more urgent since so many of their citizens are victims of poverty. IPE as the study of 'What should the American state do?' glosses over issues of vital concern to the majority of the earth's population.

There is a British variation to equating the future of a particular state with the discipline of international political economy. If a university offers a course beyond an introduction to IPE, it is most likely to cover the issue of European integration. In some cases the study of IPE is only composed of the study of Europe. IPE is confined to problems of European integration or Europe and the world.

It is not just the focus on the *American* (or European) state that causes problems but the focus on the state itself. State élites often do not reflect or embody the concerns of their citizens. State agendas are often not citizen agendas. Popular reaction to the Maastricht Treaty is an example of these divisions in advanced capitalist countries. To indicate that particular concerns are in the domain of citizens rather than states does not justify their exclusion from study, research and teaching. Which state espouses feminism in the global political economy? How many green states are present in the international system? For activity and movement in these areas we must look in other places, most likely social movements and non-governmental organizations. Yet a traditional approach does not suffice if these concerns are to be taken seriously.

INCLUSIVE APPROACH

This section sketches out another way of viewing both the discipline of IPE and the world itself. The inclusive approach is marked by a number of characteristics. Scholars are far more willing to examine actors other than states in their analysis. Concerns spread wider than the issues of trade, investment and monetary relations. While not ignoring those issues, attention is paid to other aspects such as militarization, development, gender and ecology. The inclusive approach tends to view IPE as a broad interdisciplinary undertaking rather than as a sub-discipline of politics.

In ontological terms, the focus is not simply the state system. Depending on the particular scholar, it is usually the global political economy. Primary divisions are along gender, class, firm as well as state lines. Relations across state boundaries in their many forms, rather than the affairs of state are the subject of investigation. Many scholars are cautious or opposed to positivist methods to verify or establish truth. Contrary to public choice advocates, the evidence of an econometric model would be held in doubt.

One of the early advocates of a political economy approach in the 1960s was Susan Strange. She was urging IR scholars to pay more attention to international economics and international political economy as a central part of their activities before today's undergraduates were born (Strange, 1970). Her textbook *States and Markets* attempts to integrate the study of international politics and economics through a focus on the structures of security, production, finance and knowledge. The goal is to 'synthesize politics and economics by means of structural analysis of the effects of states – or more properly any kind of political authority – on markets and, conversely, of market forces on states' (1988: 13–14).

An interesting aspect of the book is the attempt to broaden what is usually understood to be IPE. By adding knowledge and security to the more familiar areas of production and finance attention is turned to other issues. For example, the importance of trade is relegated to a secondary position while welfare and transport arrangements are brought into view. The knowledge structure highlights both technology and ideas as sources of power and influence. The security structures seem to be an attempt to integrate traditional International Relations work on the questions of war and peace and the state. Importantly, the relationship between structures in each area is a subject of investigation as much as the structures themselves. The four structures make up a single whole and continuously influence each other.

The first hint of a more inclusive approach to the study of IPE in Stephen Gill and David Law's *The Global Political Economy* is the title itself. The focus is on global rather than international (interstate) relations. The interaction of states is of concern, but so is that of other organizations and groupings such as corporations and class. Moreover, the concern is to discuss the welfare of people as opposed to particular states' power. Similar to Gilpin's book, sections focus on perspectives, issue areas (trade, monetary, investment, oil), north-south, east-west, and prospects for the future. Unlike Gilpin there is a discussion of militarism, transnational class interests, ecological elements, and alternative visions of world order.

The chapter on militarism is indicative of an approach that examines the reciprocal or dialectical relationship between economic and political domains. Rivalry between states is seen to be partially driven by powerful bureaucratic/economic interests. The economic necessity of exporting arms to achieve economies of scale, mercantilist protection of strategic industries and trade-off between arms expenditure and other forms of investment are examined. In this analysis economic factors become relevant to traditional security issues.

The Gill and Law work also differs from other texts in that it is explicitly not concerned with supporting dominant American state interests in the international political economy. An attempt is made to open up the research agenda to groups not sharing the liberal transnationalist or mercantilist visions of world order.

Feminism

Another element of this move to expand international political economy and international relations is the work of feminist scholars. They bring forth their own insight into international issues by drawing upon feminist scholarship in numerous disciplines (see Chapter 7). Particular strong contributions have been made in the area of women and development by scholars stressing the need to consider gender in development planning. Feminists point out that here are a whole set of international relationships that have been ignored by traditional International Relations, but are of vital importance to millions of people. For example, Cynthia Enloe (1989: 2) highlights the experiences of 'the women tourist, the Jamaican chambermaid, Carmen Miranda, the American housewife, the British soldier and the Belize prostitute' to shed light on significant, but neglected, international relations.

The feminist argument is not simply that these relationships are important or affect many people, but that patriarchy is a crucial element of the present system. Enloe's (1989) first chapter is titled 'Gender Makes the World Go Round'. The implication is that if gender relations were modified, the world would go round in a different manner. Gender analysis comes to International Relations from outside the discipline, drawing upon scholarship from feminist work in many disciplines. It promises (threatens?) to redefine standard notions of rationality, security and power (Tickner, 1991). If there is a single message from this work it is that the first step is to acknowledge the importance of gender and become sensitive to its role. For some, the present task is simply to unmask previous assumptions and draw attention to issues evaded by mainstream approaches (Sylvester, 1990).

IMPLICATIONS OF AN INCLUSIVE APPROACH

Although the inclusive approach offers many new areas for research, its attempt to incorporate the mainstream IR issue of war and peace or security issues remains disappointing and underdeveloped. A nod is made in the direction of military affairs, but the effort seems half-hearted at best. The subject of militarization or arms spending is often covered, but strategic thought bypassed. It is not clear where traditional IR studies and knowledge fit in the inclusive approach. One of the problems may be that space and time prevent an adequate treatment of such issues in a textbook. Yet this is a problem with all textbooks, and can be readily used as an excuse for more traditional views ignoring issues deemed vital by inclusive views.

Inclusive approaches may try to refine security to include elements other than just safety from the violence of rival militaries. Tickner (1991: 203), for example, suggests 'the absence of violence, whether it be military, economic or sexual'. There may be common ground here with some traditional IR approaches, as security is being redefined as a result of the end of the Cold War. Suddenly, environmental questions can count as security issues as well. This is a developing area and it is difficult to judge whether the inclusive approach will make progress in this field.

The inclusive camp is heterogeneous and contains some sharp divisions. Neither of the major texts in this category deals with gender issues or seems sensitive to them. Feminist analysis may share some interest in this approach, but remains estranged from it. Similarly, while Strange's structural approach and desire to examine firms' activities opens the subject up, it does not share the counter-hegemonic vision of the Gramscian (Gill et al.) group. There may be a desire to challenge widely held assumptions, but not to overturn the system. Another area that has been left out of this study and the inclusive group in general is that of ecologist thought. Ecology is considered in Gill and Law, but a radical perspective based on sustainable or limited development has yet to make its way into the field (see Chapters 11 and 12 in this volume).

More than half (60 per cent) of UK universities responding to this survey use one of the inclusive books as primary texts for their IR international political economy courses. While Gill and Law, and Strange to a lesser extent, have emerged as challengers to the traditional approach, the feminist perspective remains on the side lines. No text that could be classified as feminist was recommended as essential reading. If it is correct that there is an inclusive approach to IPE which has gained ground in UK universities over the past decade, what are the implications of this development for teaching, research and practice?

Teaching

Susan Strange has moved on from exploring four structures of the global economy to championing consideration of the role of the firm in International Relations (Stopford and Strange, 1991). The implications for teaching International Relations are immense. Strange suggests that students studying IR and IPE take courses not only on financial history and institutions, but also on international business history and practices (Strange, 1991: 48). In comparison to American undergraduates, British students study a narrow range of courses and would benefit from a broader education. The reorganization of courses, departments and degrees would be a more difficult task.

To accept the inclusive approach would be to broaden the subject matter of International Relations from inter-state relations, as cherished by some (James, 1989) to relations across borders. International Relations and IPE would have to be truly interdisciplinary. It would no longer be the preserve of politics departments; the disciplinary doors would have to be opened to philosophers, sociologists, economists, lawyers, historians, anthropologists, etc. They would not be invited in just for the occasional seminar, but to actively research and teach in the field. In this way IR and IPE could become an umbrella discipline for the social sciences that takes the global dimension seriously.

The optimum solution is straightforward, but controversial and extremely difficult to implement because it involves a massive reorganization of disciplinary boundaries. Taking relations across state boundaries as the starting point and globalization as the primary process, schools/departments/programmes of global or international political economy could be established. The goal would be to devise a programme giving a holistic account of the world we inhabit. In addition IPE students would be required to develop a knowledge of business studies, economics, gender studies, history, law, political theory, conflict analysis and inter-state relations before moving on to specializations in any of these areas.

Such an approach gores many oxen and is subject to criticism that the programme would lack intellectual coherence. Indeed, in my own university (where IR has a proud and distinct tradition as a separate subject group) there seems to be unending pressure to merge it with the politics group. International Relations is still viewed as politics at the international level. Although expanding the purview of IPE faces immense institutional barriers, it would provide the intellectual coherence and context that the present separation and exclusion of disciplines does not.

Such reorganization of university departments seems unlikely. In the face of immobility, the alternative is for IPE specialists to broaden their own courses, initiate new courses and build cooperative links with scholars in other disciplines who realize that their own work is also affected by the global dimension of modern human organization.

Research

An inclusive approach to IPE and IR, by definition, opens up the research agenda. Research into issues such as the role of women in the global political economy, the role of underprivileged groups, alternative development strategies, transnational social movements, business organization, migration and democratization become possible and acceptable. Of course, research into those issues is presently taking place, but, with the exception of business organization in business schools, they remain on the margin. An inclusive research agenda would suggest that they are not marginal, but are a vital part of understanding the global political economy and improving welfare. Not only will 'new' topics be investigated, but research will have to be collaborative across disciplines because of the vast amount of material to be covered. The potential to learn from other disciplines in a sustained manner seems great.

Practice

One reason why people embark upon a poorly paid (financially) teaching career is the desire to help others to learn and acquire knowledge. Contrary to some of our more instrumental students' intentions that the things they are taught will last only long enough to get past their final exams, some elements will influence their lives and behaviour. Having students study and think about new areas will modify their behaviour, sometimes in unpredictable ways. An increase in the inclusive view of IPE will contribute to a change in global practice in the longer term. Ideas do not strictly define practice, but they do influence the world. Indeed, unlike the natural sciences, the act of theorizing and studying about politics or IPE practice has the potential to change it (Taylor, 1983).

Many of the scholars working in the inclusive field are aware of the need to change the way people think before change can take place in the way people live. Two examples are particularly striking. The first is the work undertaken by Stephen Gill and others in the Gramscian school. Their intention is to promote a research agenda sympathetic to non-dominant concerns which would provide the intellectual basis for a counter-hegemonic bloc (Gill, 1993: 1–18). The opening up of IPE is seen as a prelude to long-term change in the functioning of the global political economy itself. As a first step, students are encouraged to think about the world in a manner different from that of the traditional approach.

Similarly, feminist scholars are explicit about the purpose of their work. One of the goals of highlighting women's experiences is to demonstrate that 'the world is something that has been made; therefore, it can be remade' (Enloe, 1989: 17). The world is not something simply to be observed from a distance; it should also be changed. In this case the change sought is an end to patriarchy and gender inequality.

Advocates of expanding the discipline need not subscribe to either the feminist or historical materialist project; they need simply share a concern for those groups presently excluded from power and privilege. Yet judgement about expansion cannot skirt the ideological issue if one believes that how we think about the world will affect how we behave and how, eventually, the world will operate. To choose to expand the subject is a choice for including formerly neglected issues and voices which will lead to a shift in economic and political power in the long run. The direction and impact of the shift is not knowable, but change in practice will result from a change in outlook.

CONCLUSION

The study of IPE in International Relations and Politics departments is thriving in British universities. The majority of respondents to this survey indicated that they undertook such study, and a number stated that plans for expansion were under way. However, this growth raises some questions about the relationship between IPE, International Relations and the social sciences. By adopting what this chapter has termed a traditional approach, IPE can be contained within the discipline of International Relations as inter-state relations. Particular issue areas such as trade, investment and finance can be studied with regard to their political effects or the influence of political factors upon those areas.

There is another trend, which is to define IPE as a more inclusive approach to trans-border relations. This does not fit as comfortably into present academic structures. The insistence on applying the dynamic of authority/market interaction to many spheres of social life, and emphasis upon global structural influences, set this apart from the traditional approach. The tendency is to roam over numerous issue areas with little regard for established boundaries. As has been suggested in the previous section, the use of IPE as a broad ranging methodology as opposed to a subject area opens new and fruitful avenues for teaching, research and practice. For those interested in genuinely new directions in International Relations, the inclusive global political economy approach offers a rich opportunity.

APPENDIX 5A: INTERNATIONAL POLITICAL ECONOMY SURVEY, AUGUST 1993

This survey is part of a small research project examining the state of British International Political Economy (IPE) and its relationship with the field of International Relations. I am particularly interested in getting a picture of the degree to which International Relations programmes contain an IPE component and what subject matter is addressed in that component.

Institution:
Name of respondent:

1) Is International Relations studied as a separate discipline at your institution?

        Yes [ ]   No [ ]

   If no, in which department are you located? (politics, history ...)

2) Does your institution offer any International Political Economy courses at the undergraduate level?

        Yes [ ]   No [ ]

3) Does your institution offer any IPE at the post-graduate level?

        Yes [ ]   No [ ]

4) Do you offer separate degrees, sections or streams in IPE?

        Yes [ ]   No [ ]

5) To what extent is public choice theory used in your IPE courses?

            Frequently [ ]   Occasionally [ ]   Rarely [ ]

6) To what extent is feminist or gender theory used in your IPE courses?

            Frequently [ ]   Occasionally [ ]   Rarely [ ]

7) Please list the titles and years of any IPE courses offered by your department.

8) For any introductory IPE (undergraduate or post-graduate) course, please attach an outline of the subject matter covered. A list of weekly topics would be sufficient.

9) Please list the principal texts or collection of readings recommended to students in your introductory IPE course(s).

Thankyou very much for your assistance. Please return the survey as soon as possible to:

Dr Robert O'Brien, School of English and American Studies
University of Sussex, Falmer, Brighton, BN1 9QN

APPENDIX 5B: UNIVERSITIES SURVEYED

University of Aberdeen	Lancaster University
Queen's University of Belfast	University of Leeds
UCW Aberystwyth	University of Leicester
Bradford University	London School of Economics
University of Birmingham	University of Reading
Cambridge University	Nottingham Trent University
Coventry University	University of Newcastle upon Tyne
University of Durham	Oxford University
University of Dundee	University of Sheffield
University of Essex	University of Southampton
University of Exeter	Staffordshire University
Glasgow University	University of Sussex
University of Hull	University of St. Andrews
University of Kent	Warwick University
King's College	University of York
Keele University	

NOTES

1. This chapter was originally presented to the Keele University 'New Directions' conference, while an updated version was given to the British International Studies Association meeting in Warwick in December 1993. Although there still may be points of disagreement my thanks for comments go to the editors of this volume, and to Stephen Gill, John MacLean, Tim Sinclair and Susan Strange.
2. The author's thanks go out to all those who responded to the survey.
3. The universities are: Birmingham, Hull, LSE, Newcastle and Warwick.

REFERENCES

Caporaso, James A. and David P. Levine, 1992, *Theories of Political Economy*. Cambridge, Cambridge University Press.

Cox, Robert W., 1981, 'Social Forces, States and World Order: Beyond International Relations Theory', in Robert Keohane, ed., 1986, *Neorealism and its Critics*, New York, Columbia University Press: 204–54.

Cox, Robert W., 1987, *Production, Power and World Order*, New York, Columbia University Press.

Dicken, Peter, 1992, *Global Shift: The Internationalisation of Economic Activity*, 2nd edn, London, Paul Chapman.

Enloe, Cynthia, 1989, *Bananas, Beaches and Bases: Making Feminist Sence of International Relations*, London, Pandora.

Frey, Bruno S., 1984, 'The Public Choice View of International Political Economy', *International Organization*, 38(1): 199–233.

Frey, Bruno S., 1988, 'Perspective', *The Political Economy of International Cooperation*, New York, Croom Helm: 51–7.

Gayle, Dennis J., Robert A. Denemark and Kendall W. Styles, 1991, 'International Political Economy: Evolution and Prospects', *International Studies Notes*, 16(3): 64–8.

Gill, Stephen and David Law, 1988, *The Global Political Economy*, Baltimore, MD, Johns Hopkins University Press.

Gill, Stephen (ed.), 1993, *Gramsci, Historical Materialism and International Relations*, Cambridge, Cambridge University Press.

Gilpin, Robert, 1975, *U.S. Power and the Multinational Corporation*, New York, Basic Books.

Gilpin, Robert, 1987, *The Political Economy of International Relations*, Princeton, NJ, Princeton University Press.

Grant, Rebecca and Kathleen Newland, (eds), 1991, *Gender and International Relations*, Buckingham, Open University Press.

James, Alan, 1989, 'The Realism of Realism: The State and the Study of International Relations', *Review of International Studies*, 15: 215–29.

Keohane, Robert O., 1984, *After Hegemony*, Princeton, NJ, Princeton University Press.

Keohane, Robert O. and Joseph Nye, 1977, *Power and Interdependence: World Politics in Transition*, Boston, Little Brown.

Nicholson, Michael, 1989, *Formal Theories in International Relations*, Cambridge, Cambridge University Press.

Spero, Joan, 1990, *Politics of International Economic Relations*, London, Unwin Hyman.

Stopford, John and Susan Strange, 1991, *Rival States, Rival Firms*, Cambridge, Cambridge University Press.

Strange, Susan, 1971, *Sterling and British Policy*, London, Oxford University Press.

Strange, Susan, 1988, *States and Markets*, London, Pinter.

Sylvester, Christine, 1990, 'The Emperor's Theories and Transformations: Looking at the Field Through Feminist Lenses', *Transformations in the Global Political Economy*, Christine Sylvester and Dennis C. Pirages, ed., London, Macmillan: 230–53.

Taylor, Charles, 1983, 'Political Theory and Practice', *Social Theory and Political Practice*, ed. Christopher Lloyd, Oxford, Clarendon Press: 61–85.

Tickner, J. Ann, 1991, 'On the Fringes of the World Economy: A Feminist Perspective', *The New Political Economy*, ed. Craig Murphy and Roger Tooze, Boulder, CO, Lynne Rienner: 191–206.

Tooze, Roger, 1985, 'International Political Economy', *International Relations British and American Perspectives*, ed. Steve Smith, London: Basil Blackwell: 108–25.

Walters, R.S. and D.H. Blake, 1992, *The Politics of Global Economic Relations*, Englewood Cliffs, Prentice Hall.

Waltz, Kenneth, 1979, *Theory of International Politics*, Reading, MA, Addison-Wesley.

6

Towards a new understanding of international trade policies: ideas, institutions and the political economy of foreign economic policy

Simon Mercado

INTRODUCTION

A quick survey of 1990s media news bulletins quickly highlights how trade issues have become central to 'high' questions of security and power, with no clearer recent example of this than the much reported international tensions over the Uruguay Round of GATT world trade talks. When Peter Sutherland, Secretary-General of the GATT, described the conclusion of these negotiations in Geneva in mid-December 1993 as 'a defining moment of world history', he underscored not only the gains of freer trade and the establishment of a multilateral World Trade Organization (WTO), but also the centrality of a sustainable trading order to the maintenance of the wider international equilibrium. One may justly seek to remember here how trade wars deepened the degeneration of the 1930s.

Understanding international trade policies: old task, new directions

In the modern world, trade policies have a substantial impact on the operation of the world's political system and on the nature and functioning of the international economy. They not only effect business and diplomacy, but are indissolubly linked to our collective welfare and security. As such, there can be no stonger rationale for the constant improvement of our understanding of trade behaviour and of the trade policy process. As Odell and Willett (1990: 1) remind us, 'better knowledge about these processes is of obvious practicable importance both to those affected by changes in trade policies and to those recommending policy strategies.'

This is in no sense a new task, and the pluriformity of existing work on foreign economic policy (FEP) formulation has a long historical pedigree. At present, however, the field is marked by a disparate and fragmented knowledge of trade politics and the formulation of trade policies, within which many analytical frameworks are narrowly conceived and fail to render any deep understanding. This reality and the simple immaturity of this divided field of inquiry demands 'new direction' and initiative in order to realize progress and improvement in our understandings of international trade policies. This chapter signposts three necessary future directions in the study of the political economy of foreign economic policy.

First, it is argued that a process of 'intellectual bridging' between separate established analytical frameworks must be accomplished, which crosses schisms between 'competing' political economy analyses.[1] A case is made for an eclectic use of theory in a domain of complex choices in complex environments, encompassing an interchange of ideas from IPE and the existing study of foreign economic policy, with those contextualized in comparative political analysis, foreign policy analysis (FPA) and public policy theory.

Second, the chapter stresses the particular importance of domestic-level variables in trade policy formulation for the optimal development of the above objective. Individual and unit-level analyses are subsumed in this chapter under the encompassing term of 'domestic-centred' frameworks. In developing the relationship between ideas, values and domestic institutions, and in placing a new primacy (in the analytical sense) on the processes and contexts of their interaction in the understanding of trade policy choices, a move is made away from ascendant economistic, structural and micro-political explanations of trade policy formulation. This marks a contribution to a new direction in FPE with arguments allied to recent examples of integrative domestic-centred analytical frameworks in other IR and public policy-related contexts.[2]

Equally, it is argued here that one 'new direction' must be to broaden the scope of empirical enquiry in such positive political economy analysis. The established literature is overwhelmingly centred on US commercial policy and must be moved towards a fuller range of nation states, including developing economies, and beyond the traditional state policy-maker in order to augment the small number of studies of the political economy of EC commercial policy.[3] Some effort is made here to consider the influences on trade policy in the latter case, where the supranational exercise and management of international commercial policy both challenges our concepts in this field and suggests the key role of ideas, values and institutions in the formulation of international trade policy.

THE STUDY OF FOREIGN POLICY-MAKING: WHY POLITICAL ECONOMY?

If we ask 'why does protectionism appear?' or 'why is a particular foreign economic policy adopted?', we cannot find an accurate answer in the assumptions of traditional free-trade theory alone, or indeed in the terms of much current economic literature on trade behaviour. A more satisfactory explanation is to be found among the actors and processes in the political system and in questions about its processes and context, which require an understanding of social, political and economic considerations. Political economy explanation is characterized by such a study of the international level through explicit attention to both political and economic conditions and their interaction, and is therefore a necessary approach to the understanding of the trade policy process, its dynamics, environments and outputs.[4]

The growth of this form of inquiry and methodology is itself a consequence of the exposed deficiencies and limitations (in the descriptive sense) of the liberal economic orthodoxy underpinning international trade theory and the bulk of relevant economic analysis.[5] For many political scientists, the grave dissonance between contemporary commercial realities on the one hand, and the assumptions and expectations of trade theory on the other, is the product of the false assumptions, idealized conditions and absent explicit political analysis that characterize liberal trade theory as rooted in the Ricardian model of comparative advantages and in the Heckscher-Ohlin theorem.[6] Even the revision of that orthodoxy by product cycle and intra-industry trade models, and more profoundly by the strategic trade policy theorists of the 1980s, has not overcome the need for a stronger conception of international trade and an enabling of explicit political analysis. Where economists have responded to this need, in the form of international public choice or endogenous trade theory (Magee and Young, 1987; and Baldwin, 1985), narrow economic analysis clearly gives way to political-economic explanation, if to a flawed endogenous treatment of social and political factors.

This is not to say, however, that the insights given by economic analysis into the effects of alternative trade policies and into the economic impacts of trade policies on various interest groups should be disregarded, for they represent an important resource for a more complex analysis of political economy. In postulating that action is rational and efficiency-driven, trade theory reminds us at least of one set of considerations confronting the policy-maker. Equally, where liberal premises are more seriously relaxed, as in the strategic trade policy literature, insight is gained into the forces of strategic calculation and high-rent seeking behind policy selection.[7]

This is not enough, however, to explain the political economy of trade policies; equally, broader macro-market explanations of protectionist demands and trade barriers (Ray, 1981; Gallorati, 1985; Takasc, 1981; Grilli, 1983) also have only a limited value *vis-à-vis* the theory of the political economy of trade. Macro-economic hypotheses confirm that macro-economic conditions significantly influence the demand for trade barriers, with sectoral imbalances, declining trade balances and pressures of exchange and interest rate movements[8] all contributing to demands for protectionism. They also highlight the fact that protectionist sentiment often rises with the downside of the macro-economic cycle,[9] and attention to the degree of concentration, multinationalization and export market reliance in industries helps explain why some organize to lobby and others do not. Yet, as with trade theory, the absent or underdeveloped political analysis and the generally specific and narrow concentrations of these macro-economic models (e.g. corporate preferences and inter-industry patterns of protection) leave them some distance from meeting the more complicated task of building a theory of foreign economic policy formulation.

The conclusion is clear, despite the utility of these insights: an understanding of trade politics and commercial policy formulation ultimately requires a political economy explanation that carefully and explicitly addresses social, institutional, ideological and power variables and dynamics. This need not exclude economic variables or overlook the many useful elements of such economic analysis, but it clearly involves an explicit attention and focus beyond the limited reach of such analysis. It is worth remembering after all, that economics does not hold the explanation of government behaviour to be its central task.[10]

POLITICAL ECONOMY EXPLANATIONS: LEVELS AND DICHOTOMIES

Political economy explanations, however, are themselves diverse, identifying a wide range of political and social variables at a range of levels of analysis, the choice of which is the key methodological issue. While analysts of foreign economic policy are generally in agreement that both international and domestic factors are fundamental to explanation, most analyses afford an analytical primacy to either the system, unit or individual level. Approaches working at the same level or intersection of levels continue to emphasize different variables and policy influences, preventing the establishment of any single body of widely accepted theory.[11]

International-level analysis

International- or 'systems-' level analysis, as observed in International Relations, works effectively from the 'outside in' and involves focus upon the sovereign state as the basic unit of study, with the state treated as a rational and unitary actor.[12] Theoretical propositions are derived from the interrelationships among states for whom opportunities are afforded and constraints imposed by their power as units in an 'anarchic' international system (Ikenberry et al., 1988: 3).

In the study of foreign economic policy, analyses pitched at this level emphasize the international forces determining state action and apply international realist fundamentals. Krasner's (1976) power theory, for example, claims that foreign economic policy will be set primarily to increase economic and competitive power in accordance with state priorities and the pursuit of the 'national interest'. Affirming a link between national security and economic interest, it broadly argues that a nation's trade policy will reflect its foreign policy. Elsewhere the *'realpolitik'* approach has especially emphasized the security externalities of trade, that is the influential role played by security concerns in the determination of national trade policies (e.g. Gowa, 1989).

However, foremost amongst international approaches to the study of foreign economic policy is 'hegemonic stability theory'. The hegemonic stability theorists, including Kindleberger (1973) and Gilpin (1975), start with the basic argument that a state's position in the international economy decisively shapes its foreign economic policy. The characteristic argument is that nations with preponderant power hold an interest in pursuing liberal trade and that, in the long term, policy will always reflect the international configuration of power. Dominant or hegemonic states have the power to create and maintain liberal regimes, and will do so until faced with a diminished capacity to absorb the costs of imposing order on the international economic system.

This argument, most seriously advanced as a theory of British hegemony in the nineteenth century and of US hegemony in the mid-twentieth century, has been left wanting in the sense of several empirical anomalies[13] and has been refined in a fashion underscoring the limits of the core theory. Keohane and Nye (1977) have made the argument issue-specific, suggesting that it is only when a hegemon loses relative power on a specific issue that it abandons its support for the existing regime, and Krasner (1976 and 1982) has developed the notion of lags between altered interests and policy, explained by the existence of a constraining trade regime. Critics such as Goldstein (1986), however, powerfully argue that such refinements of the core model and regime theories are little more than 'a descriptive addition' to a form of structural analysis that is inherently flawed. For Goldstein, hegemony arguments cannot explain internal tensions between free, fair and redistributive principles in contemporary US policy, and are unable to explain satisfactorily the lack of a sharp break in trade policy comparable to that in monetary management.

Many of the limitations and weaknesses of hegemonic stability theory are those of international-level analysis more generally. Attention is directed to the international constraints and systemic pressures driving unitary state actors, and, though useful in explanations of patterns of state interaction over time and the role of security considerations, this approach does not explain why particular policy outcomes emerge within a universe of possible outcomes. Its 'black box' treatment of the policy-making process means that there is no theory of the domestic political process,[14] and this extends to a marginalization of the important role of ideas and values. It should be remembered that the international realm is peopled by human beings who, 'given their immediate or vicarious humanity', will, in their individual and representative capacities, 'be influenced by their calculations, hopes, purposes, beliefs, anxieties, fears, and all the other elements of the human condition' (James, 1993: 284).

In short, international or *realpolitik* approaches may have value in the study of the international political economy, but even if we recall Waltz's clarification that states have room for manoeuvre under international pressures (1986: 122–3), they remain inherently limited. Such approaches provide only a simplified perception of state behaviour in individual cases and cannot explain the complex domestic-level factors motivating behaviour, or the variety of actors and mechanisms of the foreign policy-making process. What is demanded is a theory of the domestic determinants of foreign economic policy which can more powerfully (if less parsimoniously) confront a realm where individuality, cognition, volition and human interaction are so fundamental to outcomes; and where individual units of analysis are variably shaped by alternative historical experience, by individual socio-economic factors, domestic structures and political dynamics.

Existing behavioural and cognitive approaches go some way to meeting this demand, exhibiting a lesser if varying emphasis on the international sources of behaviour, and crucially focusing on the structures, actors and processes of the foreign policy-making process at and below the unit level. Here there is a basic dichotomy in analysis between what has been characterized as 'state-' and 'society-' centred analysis (Ikenberry, Lake and Mastanduno, 1988), and an important if often marginalized contribution by scholars stressing the role of ideas, values and beliefs in policy. As the subsequent analysis will make clear, divisions are not always clear-cut.[15]

Society-centred analysis

Society-centred analysis moves the focus away from international constraints and opportunities to the importance of domestic politics in shaping outcomes, thus relaxing the assumption of the unitary state actor. Beginning with societal preferences, these approaches trace policies to the demands placed on government by private groups and sectors and to the relationship between social forces and coalitions and the polity. Two general perspectives can be identified here.

A distinctive society-centred perspective attempts to explain government behaviour and responsiveness to societal pressures in terms of the organized social coalitions that underpin political administrations (Gourevitch, 1986). Policy is seen as constructed so as to meet the terms of the said coalitions, in the face of which the government has little or no autonomy, and for which it chooses 'satisficing' policies. Government receptivity to private interests is dependent upon changes in coalitions and the composition and interests of a coalition at a given time. The basic argument is that: 'there seem to be no characteristics of associations of state structures that can stand independently of social factors in explaining policy outputs' (Gourevitch, 1986: 20).

The second distinct perspective, and a more widely adopted approach, is that of interest group politics, a micro-political approach to societal interests and their political effects extending from Schattsneider's (1935) seminal analysis of the Smoot-Hawley Tariff Act. Relaxing the assumption that nation states are unitary actors, interest-group studies emphasize the varied interests of particular private industries in shaping trade policies. The recent development of this approach has been led by academics advancing public choice and endogenous trade theories of protection. Analysts such as Baldwin (1985), Pincus (1977), Lavergne (1983) and Magee and Young (1987) have been associated with the extension of the study of pressure-group activity to show how broad social and corporate groups are often driven by market conditions and how a political market for protection functions.

If a 'political market' for protection is established, politicians, as rational utility maximizers themselves, will have a self-interest in satisfying the protectionist sentiments of organized private interests (albeit under institutional constraints) in their quest for the 'rents' of votes and revenue.

These assumptions effectively create a problematic notion that trade policies lie outside the control of policy-makers. Whilst a balance of domestic political forces is captured here, the policy-maker is seen as an auctioneer in a product market balancing supply and demand (Magee and Young, 1987: 145), as a register for sectoral pressures. The policy-maker's own preferences are seen to impart no long-term direction to policy as he mediates between interest groups. Further, the assumption of individuals as rational utility maximizers with given preferences and interests arguably underscores the extent to which individuals' responses to their situations (individuals within an institutional and intellectual environment) may not be governed by objective and autonomous self-calculated interest. In Gourevitch's approach too, the definition of interests is economistic, with little sense of how the 'extraeconomic privileges the economic' (Kesselman, 1992: 654).

As cognitive FEP analysis has illustrated, interests not only affect ideas, but ideas, belief systems and perceptions shape the interpretation of 'interests' and underlie policy choices (Odell, 1982; Goldstein, 1986). Equally, to a large extent, institutionalized authority structures are 'conditioning', shaping definitions of interest and sometimes behaviour (Odell, 1990). Trade and other regulatory policies depend in part on inherited institutional structures which have the power to shape preferences and to constrain their pursuit, and which are far from mere conduits for either international or societal pressures.

Analysis associated with a concentration on societal preferences and demands has now countered some of these problems, with far greater attention being paid to the role of belief systems in the determination of interests (Marks and McCarthur, 1990). And work by Milner (1988) provides a theory not only of protectionist demands and societal preferences, but also of how those demands actually function in the policy-making process. In her eclectic model, in which international market and domestic macro-economic variables are also formally incorporated, Milner stresses the permeability of fragmented state structures (in the US and France in the 1970s) to corporate liberal interests in a decade of adverse economic conditions.

State-centred analysis

The contention that the state matters, which is central to much of the critique of society-centred approaches, does not however in itself yield a single approach to the state. The 'statist' assertions of Krasner (1978), Katzenstein (1978) and Mastanduno (1988), are themselves quite varied, and are clearly distinctive from more directly 'institutionalist' approaches evidenced in the work of Pastor (1980), Hall (1986), Goldstein (1986, 1988 and 1989) and Ikenberry (1988). Again divisions are not clear-cut, but a central differentiation extends out of the basic conceptualization of the state.

The former 'statist' approaches move forward from state-centric international realism to analyse how politicians and state officials, under international and internal constraints, may be prominent figures in the shaping of policy outcomes. They are seen as playing a crucial role in the interpretation of international and societally generated pressures or imperatives and in the definition of the 'national interest'. Krasner (1978) suggests, for example, that high-level government officials are uniquely charged with protecting and promoting broad national security interests and are thus led to develop autonomous preferences and favour particular regimes for broader reasons than narrow economic interest alone (Ikenberry et al., 1988: 10). This is evidenced, he argues, in the defence by top decision-makers against protectionist interest groups represented in Congress over a key forty-year cycle of American trade policy. Though highlighting the constraining effects of US official preference divisions over post-war East–West trade, Mastanduno builds a similar argument in contending that if trade issues are judged to be of direct national security significance, then state officials are likely to enjoy even greater authority

However, another variant of this analysis Katzenstein's 'domestic structures' approach, suggests that the capacity of state decision-makers and executive officials to resist private-interest pressure, and to exert state leadership along the lines of their autonomous preference sets, differs in different state 'types'. This capacity is lessened in examples of 'weak states' (e.g. the United States), where the domestic structure is de-centralized and where government officials may be more constrained by private demands and by greater difficulties in acting purposefully. But in many cases (especially in stronger domestic structures such as those of France and Japan), purposive goal-driven executive officials are less accountable to legislatures and interest groups and have a greater range of policy instruments to direct policy in accordance with their calculation of the national interest (Ikenberry et al., 1988: 10).

Though concentration falls upon the goal-oriented behaviour of state politicians and officials here, this analysis does encompass the view that institutions have a major effect on the process of domestic politics and that institutional structure influences foreign economic policy. Yet in contrast to institutionalist variants, the focus begins with the goal-driven behaviour of state officials and the relationship between their preferences and international and societal forces.

Such analysis is a clear improvement on primarily systems-level study in that it realizes a linkage between international and domestic forces, but it is inherently limited in a number of important respects. The strong state argument central to Katzenstein's 'domestic structures' variant is in some sense challenged by the studies of Samuels (1987) and Nowell (1983), providing empirical evidence of cases in so-called strong states where politicians have reversed the judgements of state officials and blocked their power to shape outcomes. Milner (1988), whose ideas have been previously considered here, has also shown how private interests can permeate even 'strong' states such as France.

Not far removed from this, analysts emphasizing the social or socioeconomic roots of policy argue that the autonomy of actors from societal demands is exaggerated in these approaches, that the national interest 'is not a blank slate upon which the international system writes at will; [that] it is internally determined by the socio-economic evolution of the nation in question' (Frieden 1988: 88). These arguments, from what is on its own an equally flawed perspective, do underscore the problematic conceptions of interest and autonomy in these approaches. Odell (1982: 47–8) and Ikenberry, Lake and Mastanduno (1988: 11) also make the important point that however useful the weak state/strong state concept is in explaining policy differences between states, it is limited when the subject is the behaviour of one. And the intellectual, institutional and ideological basis of interests may also be emphasized to support Frieden's cited argument that with officials calculating the national interest, the slate is not blank and has internal socio-economic determinations.

Equally, while these approaches open up the black box of the state and centralize the role of state officialdom and bureaucracy, they do not fully account for the complex 'bureaucratics' of trade policy-making. In other words, the concentration on the relationship between executive official and state structure, and on the goal-purposive behaviour of the former, does not equate with an understanding of the role of bureaucracy and bureaucratic politics in commercial policy-making and negotiations. The bureaucratic machinery can, for example, limit the choices of policy-makers (information, processing issues, etc.) and, significantly for trade issues, specialist or expert bureaucrats, officials and lawyers may operate at some distance from the immediate control of chief executives, as in specialized negotiations within tranches of the GATT negotiations. We have learnt too of internal 'bureaucratic politics' (Allison and Halperin, 1974). In most successful trading powers, such as the US, Japan, Korea, Germany and the wider European Union (EU), trade policy structure is fragmented and broad policies and strategies are influenced by the push and pull of competing bureaucracies or sub-units. These are not necessarily integrated or conditioned by mutual interests or goals, and those who have amassed autonomy, political influence and measured authority (e.g. the European Commission and MITI in Japan) are effectively 'institutional actors' in the trade policy process.

These limits to the statist approach and the importance of the bureaucratic layer in policy development and negotiation establish a case for a fuller institutional approach to the understanding of trade policies. This can emphasize the role of executive officials and of bureaucratic entities and politics, *and* provide a wider view of the organizational structure within which officials and politicians play out their roles. The important role of bureaucracy in policy development, when identified, often relates fundamentally to the complex relationship between bureaucratic groupings in committees and institutions within the wide organizational setting. The policy-making system in the European Union, for example, is clearly 'bureaucratic' (Ostry, 1990; Patterson, 1983), but that bureaucratic quality is one of a complex multi-levelled decision-making process entailing multiple institutions and committees.

The institutionalist approach is premised on a conception of the state as an organizational structure consisting of institutions of government and sets of rules and laws.[16] Here the focus is on the relationship between institutions and their embedded values, on the constraining effect institutions have upon state officials, and on the relationship between institutional structure and international and societal pressures. Exhibiting several variants as applied to foreign economic and industrial policy-making, it is premissed on a number of basic assumptions.

Institutions and rules affect the distribution of the power of political actors and help to mould political preferences and interests. Institutions thus have structural characteristics which establish them as more than simple reflections of social forces and as more than mere conduits for the transference of societal or international forces into policy.

These approaches also generally make the assumption that policy-making takes place in an institutional setting constituted by structures that have emerged in an episodic fashion and are the product of particular historical developments. Much institutional analysis centres on moments of institutional shift. The view is that 'institutional structures, once established, are difficult to change even when underlying social forces continue to evolve' (Ikenberry, 1988: 223). Institutions are defended and preserved by their functionaries and representatives, who frequently seek to preserve their missions. This extends in many analyses to the argument that particular ideas or ideologies are embedded in an institution at its foundation and continue to affect policy even if the thrust of that ideology is countered by contradictory ideas elsewhere in the institutional setting (Goldstein, 1986, 1988 and 1989).

Several empirical studies have generated a persuasive case for a central examination of organizational structure and the balance of power between institutions and their constraining roles. Going further than the importance awarded to institutional constraints in the domestic structures approach of Katzenstein (1978), investigation of US foreign economic policy by Goldstein (1986, 1988 and 1989), Pastor (1980) and Destler (1986) has established the central role of domestic institutional structure in policy formulation, especially in commercial policy.

Destler (1986), for example, has shown how the protectionist tide of US industrial and trade policy legislation since the early 1980s must be understood not merely as a response to economic pressures but also as a product of the eroded effectiveness of relevant government institutions to 'resist protectionism'. For him the American trade crisis of the 1980s is a 'political story' emphasizing the histories of relevant institutions, notably the opening up of Congress to pressure from import-impacted industries and the increased political burden of the executive branch.

Goldstein's studies of US trade policy and protection have also demonstrated how, in the US experience of trade policy, contradictory beliefs in free, fair and redistributive principles have been embedded in a decentralized state structure of multiple game-playing institutions and bureaucratic organizations. She argues that despite the mercantilist pressures generated by a relative economic decline since the late 1960s, the US has remained broadly if imperfectly committed to free trade principles. This is explained primarily by the fact that a liberal set of beliefs has been dominant in the state's organizational complex and has remained the predominant encased ideal. Understanding US trade and import policy must thus begin with the institutional structures of the trade policy system and the balance of power within that setting.

Work from this perspective, then, has highlighted the point that political institutions should not be peripheralized in explanations of foreign economic policy formulation. The perspective persuasively suggests that political institutions are more than simple mirrors of social forces or conduits for international pressures, and demonstrates how state structures and complex institutionalized relations influence the way that actors perceive interests and the capacities of government officials to carry out policy. A closed institutionalist approach has important limitations of its own, however, not least in a limited capacity to tell us what *is* as opposed to what *is not* possible for states (Ikenberry, 1988; Odell, 1990), and in a tendency to exaggerate the autonomy of state structure from a social basis. It is therefore of fundamental importance that, as in the considered work of Goldstein and Destler, an institutionalist approach must be broadly based to give the role of ideas, beliefs and values due prominence.

Here, then, we broach a theoretical argument and research agenda rooted in an open institutionalist approach that amalgamates cognitive analysis and the political power of ideas. Substance will be given to the heralded 'cognitive' perspective in FEP analysis in the following section.

TOWARDS A COMPLETE THEORY OF POLICY FORMULATION: IDEAS, VALUES, INSTITUTIONS AND THE BENEFITS OF EXCHANGE

Elements of the institutionalist literature, as has been argued, treat the political power and role of ideas as a central variable in the explanation of foreign economic and, more precisely, trade policy outcomes. We have noted, for example, Goldstein's particular emphasis on the ideological underpinning of state institutions, and the permeation of ideas in the organizational structure in Destler's analysis. These studies are supported in their emphasis on institutions and the role of ideas by Hall's (1986) analysis of industrial policy-making in Britain and France. This combines attention to the institutional labyrinths of policy-making in modern industrial states with an assertion of the importance of labour and class interest, as well as of the great weight of ideas in economic policy-making.

Other elements of varied domestic politics literature also identify, albeit often in a loose or *ad hoc* manner, the fact that 'ideas' are influential elements in the situation and interpretations of policy-makers. Amongst the public choice theorists, for example, Baldwin (1985) recognizes that in the wide range of behaviour patterns observable in the trade policy arena, the official pursuit of public policy goals follows not simply self-interested calculation, but also values and perceptions.

In summary, then, much of the domestic determinants of foreign policy literature (most powerfully of the broadly institutionalist variant) treats the political power of ideas as an important part of the policy process. As competitive ideology or values in the policy-making environment, as encased or embedded in domestic institutional structure, and/or as an innovative force at times of institutional change or crisis; ideas and values are seen to count.

While pointing to the benefits of such integrative analysis, and to a synergy of institutional and cognitive elements in a multi-variate approach to FEP, how then do we further support such a framework as a necessary and valuable direction in the development of a theory of the political economy of trade policy? First, we may be better sensitized to the political power and role of ideas in FEP formulation by deeper consideration of the cognitive perspective in IPE. Second, we may highlight the illuminative and instructive work in fields outside FEP where such a synergy has been reached. And third, we may observe, in support of the prior comments on US commercial policy, the fundamental role of the interplay of ideas and domestic structures in the development of EU international trade policy.

The political economy of foreign economic policy: a cognitive view

Odell (1990: 149), himself a central contributor to this perspective, perhaps best describes the essential premiss of the cognitive view, that: 'political behaviour is partly a function of leaders' and publics' values, policy beliefs, and ideologies, and that differences and changes in these ideas will shift policies accordingly.' In its broadest sense it encompasses the base of consensual knowledge or economic culture that contextualizes and legitimates policy-making on external economic and trade concerns, and makes the important assumption that policy ideas (which are not reducible to material interests) can have a substantive effect upon policy content. The dominant figures here, if Goldstein is identified primarily with an institutionalist approach, are indeed Odell and Rohrlich, whose core claims are that economic belief cultures (Rohrlich, 1987) and changes in reigning ideas (Odell, 1982) help define and change policy content.

Odell (1982) finds it necessary to bring in the role of ideas, of altered ways of perceiving the economic, in order to describe fully the shifts in US monetary policy during the 1960s and early 1970s, and rejects the idea that theories relying on interests, power dynamics and international market conditions alone are adequate for an explanation of US monetary policy. In asserting the role and political power of ideas in the modern course of US monetary policy,[17] he theorizes a conflict of ideas within the complex structures of state. This involves policy-makers typically disagreeing among themselves over the validity of particular ideas and often reassessing policy and interest in the face of new ones. Here, as recent attention to 'epistemic communities' by Haas (1992) has shown, the idea of policy entrepreneurs and experts as potentially important in shaping and reshaping the interpretations of decision-makers is stressed. Odell (1982) also argues that 'specific beliefs' (individuals' causal maps of the world and the immediate situation) and 'general beliefs' (theories or ideologies) appear as influential predispositions in the policy process.

The issue of 'beliefs' is given a new slant in Rohrlich's (1987) 'cognitive dynamics' approach, which demonstrates that not only are decision-makers' preferences and general beliefs of great importance in their definition of a situation, but that the entire policy-making community is subject to, and constrained by, an 'economic culture' which legitimates the methods and goals involved in the ordering of the state's economic life. It is Rohrlich's argument, well made in the limited context of the adoption of liberalism in nineteenth-century Britain, that: '[The] culture designates what will be perceived in the surrounding environment, how it will be interpreted, and which reactions will be considered appropriate ... [it] provides the litmus test that any economic policy must pass to be considered legitimate' (1987: 70).

Certainly, the conception of societal demands and their impact is rather flawed in this model, and the cognitive dynamics approach can only conceptualize the functioning of cognitions in the operational processes of state policy-making in a general fashion. The approach does nevertheless underscore the point that any explanation of the adoption of new policy or of policy preferences or options must include consideration of contextual ideology and the broader economic culture. Some support for this model is found in Thurrow's (1992) assertion of fundamental divergences in economic philosophy between 'individualistic' Anglo-Saxon economy (the US and UK) and the 'communitarian' philosophies of the Japanese and continental European economies. These philosophies are, as in Rohrlich's model, a product of historical experience.

FPA, public policy studies and the benefits of exchange

The form of integrative analysis suggested above has also been seen to work to good effect in analysis of public policy and foreign policy, where the ideas-institution nexus (in varying form) has evolved in recent collaborative study of beliefs, institutions and foreign policy change (Goldstein and Keohane, 1993) and in wide-reaching studies covering development policies, oil politics and technology (see, respectively, Sikkink, 1991; Alt, 1987; Adler, 1986). Foremost here too, Checkel's (1993) study of the Gorbachev foreign policy revolution centres on the diffusion of new policy ideas under transforming international conditions through domestic institutional structure. In a powerful multi-variate analysis, Checkel demonstrates that the concepts and intellectual frameworks of Soviet academic specialists 'mattered tremendously' in the development of the Gorbachev revolution, with a systematic explanation of how institutional and political variables constrained or enhanced their ability to influence policy.

Political economists are learning and should learn from such work, as analysts of comparative politics and proponents of foreign policy analysis (FPA) are doing from the literatures on ideas and institutions in IPE. This involves a reassessment of the merits and utility of cognitive analysis among political economists, partly reflecting a lack of theoretical rigour – sometimes a product of an ignorance of much of the referenced literature – and partly a result of the nature of popularized cognitive approaches in the International Relations of the 1960s and 1970s.[18] Much of this analysis focused only imprecisely on the political power and institutional contexts of ideas, and used cognitions and belief systems to explain abberations in foreign policy behaviour.

The value of a more systematic analysis of the interaction of ideas and institutions is then suggested by broader public and foreign policy analysis, as well as by the considered centrality of the idea-institution nexus to outcomes in US trade and import policy. How, though, does the importance of ideas and institutions in the shaping of state behaviour in the foreign economic realm appear if we look to the trade policies of other states? In particular, how important do these factors appear if we turn to the case of the European Union, where the application of FEP concepts is immediately troubled by a state-centricity (that is a prior focus on the nation state and an assumption of the state as pivotal actor) and the supranationality and unique complexity of the EU?

European Union trade policy and positive political economy analysis: challenge and opportunity

However complex the organization and however distinctive the European Union is as an interlocutor and policy-maker in international trade, the existence of an institutionalized and legally governed trade policy system and a fluid set of trade policy interests and objectives enables the contruction of an effectively institutionalist political economy approach to its case. This is in spite of the fact that such an approach has been previously developed and tested (like other FEP approaches) in relation to the state. The key here is the way in which the historically based institutionalist approach has re-theorized the state as an organizational structure consisting of institutions of governance and a set of rules, laws and ideas. The EU is not a state in terms of unitary government, absolute sovereignty and statehood, but in this domain, it enjoys the range of policy-making powers of state policy-makers such as the United States, Japan and Brazil, has exclusive power in the conduct of external trade relations on behalf of its member states, and operates a common commercial policy and an ordered variegated trade regime. If we observe as characteristic of an institutionalist-based approach the tracking and charting of complex policy processes over time and the management of international and social pressures by an identified set of institutional actors in a legally governed order, then such an approach is as theoretically achievable in the multi-levelled transnational EU domain as it is in the case of the United States. The issue thus becomes the suitability rather than the possibility of such a framework (open, as argued throughout, to the role of ideas and values) in the understanding of EU external trade strategy and policies.

The case for an analytical framework based principally on conceptualizing an interplay of domestic structures, values and policy ideas is actually compelling. When we analyse the construction or formulation of EC trade policy we confront a division of powers and responsibilities which is truly Byzantine; a multi-tiered policy process founded on a complex set of checks and balances; and a heterodoxy of ideas and beliefs internalized within that system.

The instititutional basis to this system is clearly complex, but we can easily identify relevant institutions and begin to characterize the relationships between them. The Commission enjoys a relatively wide latitude and there are real Commission 'powerbrokers' in the shape of the officials at the director-general and director level whose mandate it is to reconcile political and technical level considerations (Howell et al., 1992: 405). Ultimately, however, the Commission and its external affairs directorate (as the executive branch), must operate under the political direction of the Council of Ministers, which has the formal author-ity to make all important policy decisions. The latter institution also has mechanisms for overseeing Commission activity, for instance via consultative committees, and in the '113 committee' regional and national bureaucracy intersects. The European Court of Justice also has an impact on trade policy-making through its rulings, and the European Parliament, in addition to a general advisory role, must give assent to Association agreements and is em-powered to veto trade agreements that create new trade organizations such as the forthcoming World Trade Organization (WTO).[19]

Equally, within this complex structure there are cross-currents of contending liberal and mercantilist forces. One broad characterization of this interplay of ideas is an essentially liberal northern tier (the UK, Denmark, Holland and Germany) and an activist neo-mercantilist core of largely southern states, led by Italy and France. However one conceptualizes the balance of these forces, and we have already noted the concept of individualist and communitarian cultures within the EU, the ideological context is manifestly one of internal fracture with divisions widely influenced by the market in question. In agri-culture, for example, northern liberals demonstrate a clear relaxation of their broad commitment to free trade and limited government intervention.

The Community's current qualified liberal posture reflects in significant part the weighting of these forces within the decision-making process, not least in the trade stances of two of the larger powers (the UK and Germany) and in the philosophies of key Commissioners Brittan, Bangemann and Andriessen. However, the clear evidence of safeguards, mechanisms of market protection and anti-dumping action, etc. and the agonizing over the Uruguay Round of the GATT, designed to further liberalize world trade, demonstrate how communitarian principles and protectionist leanings continue to impart a clear influence on the Community's trade strategy and regime.

Further study of the political economy of EC commercial policy is clearly needed, but this limited analysis does strongly suggest the suitability of an integrated domestic-centred approach as proposed here. Competing ideas, values and ideological forces interplay within a multi-levelled process which brings into account twelve views at governmental level and which leaves decisions as the product of compromise (Presa, 1993: 190). This unquestion-ably gives rise to an inertia and conservatism in EC trade policy, and to a torturously bureaucratic process which deeply influences substance (Ostry, 1990; and Patterson, 1983).

It should be added that such investigation is extremely important in the simple broadening of the empirical focus of FEP study, which must also include wider analysis of developing economies and their foreign economic policies. This remains a particular need outside of neo-Marxian considerations of dependent foreign policies. One may interestingly note that Mares's (1990) valuable study of Colombian trade and development policy 1951–68, though indebted to public choice analysis, contends that policy shifts in this period are incomprehensible without addressing institutional dynamics.

UNDERSTANDING INTERNATIONAL TRADE POLICIES: A FINAL OVERVIEW

In the understanding of trade politics and the formulation of policies (and of foreign economic policies more generally), we confront a complexity and a multiplicity of influences that makes any single method of analysis inadequate on its own. What is demanded, and to some extent what is emerging, is a process of exchange and bridging between levels and forms, and a more eclectic use of theory. One immediately identifies Odell's (1990) prominent call for an integrated theory of trade policy formulation, and several examples of integrative political economy approaches have been highlighted here. This chapter has, however, argued for a particular new direction within this evolving path of political economy theory, namely a centralization of the influential role played in the shaping of trade and foreign economic policies by domestic structures and by ideas and values.

Societal demands and international pressures (centralized in society-centred and systems-level approaches), whilst influential on trade policy choices, are channelled through the organizational structures of states or policy-making agencies. Institutional structure is much more than a conduit for such forces, and political behaviour responds to the constraints and opportunities presented by institutions. The suggested emphasis on institutions must, however, be loose enough to address effective bureaucratic politics within the complex range of domestic structures constituting the state or policy-making agency, and must also advance and represent the fundamental point that ideas and values are important influences on policy. In complex institutional structures, ideas conflict and compete for ascendancy and values and beliefs appear as influential predispositions among those engaged in the policy process, all with consequences for policy debates and outcomes. This chapter has pointed to evidence of the above in the trade policy-making systems of both the United States and the European Union, and in wider international policy-making.

This leads then in the direction of a synergy of cognitive and institutionalist ideas that is as yet under-developed in the study of FEP and in other sub-disciplines of International Relations. An account of international forces – for instance the constraining effects of GATT codes and of international market pressures – is important in any analysis as such forces help to shape a universe of possible policy outcomes, but attention must be focused on domestic factors if we seek to understand how options were formulated, internal politics played out, and particular policy outcomes arrived at. This is the fundamental limitation of systemic approaches: political outcomes and policy choices have complex domestic roots and international forces are merely 'contextualizing' as opposed to 'determining' factors. They can only be understood through analysis of the interplay of unit and sub-unit level variables at the heart of the suggested framework.

The promotion of such an integrated domestic-centred approach stands in support of current trends towards a synthesis and bridging of disparate analytical frameworks in FEP in order to realize improved understandings of international trade policies. Given the importance of trade policies to contemporary international relations we must continue to make such progress; exchanges of ideas between oft-separated schools of thought and more eclectic uses of theory are important ways forward, which can be usefully combined with greater efforts to examine the political economy of a wider range of foreign economic policies.

Finally, the relevance and value of such enterprises to the study of foreign economic policy and to the development of IPE should not cloud the importance of these issues and departures for study in the wider International Relations field. Work on the political power of ideas and on the importance of domestic structures and forces to foreign policy behaviour is of general interest, as are debates over the relative merits of parsimonious 'single-factor' and complex 'integrative' frameworks in the understanding of state behaviour. This chapter has pursued a precise theme – the issue of international trade policy formulation and its understanding – but it concludes with the hope that it has not only been thought-provoking for specialists working the political economy terrain, but that it has raised wider issues and ideas relevant to all those engaged in the study of international relations.

NOTES

1. This is very much in line with Odell's (1990) call for a continuation of an establishing process of 'intellectual bridging' in this realm.
2. See, for example, Checkel, 1993; Sikkink, 1991; and Adler, 1986.
3. The principal exception here is Murphy (1990), who draws on a vast literature on EC policy-making *per se*. The political economy of anti-dumping undertakings have been more comprehensively treated; see, for example, Tharakan (1991). There remains, however, an overall lack of detailed study of EC trade policy and trade politics.
4. In the broadest terms, International Political Economy is the study of the effects of the pursuit of wealth, power and security at the international level. It encompasses the quest to explain the effects and the sources of governments' economic policies.
5. The 'descriptive' content is judged here as the identification of particular factors or endowments central to commercial patterns and policy choices.
6. Criticisms have centred on the idealized conditions of perfect competition and unrestricted exchange in the pure and neoclassical models, and follow from the evidence of trade patterns contradicting the classical doctrine of comparative advantage. The fundamental point here is that trade action is shaped by political imperatives, the political process and ideology, and not simply by efficiency calculations. For standard critiques of the descriptive relevence of orthodox liberal trade theory, see Barry-Jones (1982) and Kuttner (1983).

7. The principal work here is Krugman's (1986) edited volume on the new international economics. Stegemann (1989) and Richardson (1990) provide useful overviews of the strategic trade policy theory.

8. An 'exchange rate hypothesis', widely used in explanation of heightened US protectionism in the early eighties (Bergsten, 1982; Bergsten and Williamson, 1983), is troubled by the contradictory evidence of the European example and by patterns of protectionist sentiment in the US in the more recent times of a declining US dollar value.

9. Takasc (1981: 687) notes that, among economists: 'It is generally agreed that in a modern industrial economy the cyclical state of the economy and the country's competitive position internationally are the principal determinants of the degree of protectionist pressure. Low levels of economic activity, high unemployment, unused capacity, trade deficits, rapid increases in imports, and increases in import penetration all operate to increase the temptation to protect domestic industries from import competition.'

10. Odell (1982: 20) stresses: 'The central task of economics as a discipline is not to explain government behaviour, but rather to explain trade flows, the commodity composition of trade and production, financial flows, price movements, and so on.'

11. The division of subsequent analysis into systems-level, society- and state-centred approaches owes much to Ikenberry et al.'s (1988) survey of approaches to explaining American foreign economic policy. This chapter joins Odell (1990) in a seperate treatment of cognitive approaches. Concise overviews on the theory of the political economy of foreign economic policies also feature in Odell and Willett (1988), Cohen (1990) and Rohrlich (1987).

12. In the study of international politics, see the major contribution of Waltz (1979), and the debate in Keohane 1986.

13. Several historical episodes in American policy either confound or escape analysis under this theory. The essays by Goldstein, Mastanduno, Haggard and Frieden in a special edition of *International Organisation* (Vol. 42, Winter 1988) raise examples ranging from Smoot-Hawley in the 1930s to US trade policy in the 1970s and 1980s.

14. Lake's (1988) 'structural' analysis at least recognizes the fundamental need to examine domestic politics seriously and postulates a political contest between the foreign policy executive (seeking to adopt policies reflective of the national interest) and the legislature (seen as reflecting societally generated interests). International pressures remain the shapers of trade strategies, but the extent to which they permeate into actual policy depends on the relative power of the foreign policy executive in the domestic arena.

15. This is reflected in the differing categorizations of FEP theory in Ikenberry et al. (1988), and Odell (1990) and their degree of overlap. Ikenberry et al. (1988) identify three analytical and theoretical approaches to FEP: system-, society-, and state-centred, whilst Odell (1990) categorizes analysis of international trade policy (the principal field of FEP theorizing) along the themes of market conditions, political institutions, beliefs and values, and global political economic structures.

16. March and Olsen (1984) have described a renaissance in the institutionalist perspective in political theory as a whole and not merely in political economy studies. In this spirit these analyses are a part of a 'new institutionalism', restoring traditional political science interest in the role of organizational structure in the definition and management of public policy.

17. Odell (1982) concludes, for example, that the policy innovation of creating a new international reserve asset and a new basis to US monetary policy in the mid-1960s

could only be satisfactorily explained by the factor of intellectual innovation. And in another investigated phase of monetary policy, he illustrates how an oscillation away from traditional alliance diplomacy after 1968 and then back again in 1972 was driven in large part by changing sways in monetary theory and by the impact of new ideas through personnel changes.

18. See Jervis (1977) and the earlier work on images by Holsti (1967).
19. For fuller considerations of the trade policy process, see Murphy (1990) and Howell et al. (1992).

REFERENCES

Adler, E., 1986, 'Ideological Guerillas and the Quest for Technological Autonomy', *International Organisation*, 40, Summer.

Allison, G. and Halperin, M.H., 1974, 'Bureaucratic Politics and Foreign Policy', Washington, DC, Brookings Institution.

Alt, J.E., 1987, 'Crude Politics: Oil and the Political Economy of Unemployment in Britain and Norway, 1970–85', *British Journal of Political Science*, 17.

Baldwin, R.E., 1985, 'The Political Economy of U.S. Import Policy', Cambridge, MIT Press.

Barry-Jones, R.J., 1982, 'International Political Economy: Problems and Issues, Part II', *Review of International Studies*, 8.

Bergsten, C.F., 1982, 'What to Do About US–Japan Economic Conflict', *Foreign Affairs*, 60.

Bergsten, C.F. and Williamson, J., 1983, 'Exchange Rates and Trade Policy', in W. Cline, *Trade Policy in the 1980s*, Cambridge, MA, MIT Press.

Checkel, J., 1993, 'Ideas, Institutions and the Gorbachev Foreign Policy Revolution', *World Politics*, 45, January.

Cohen, B.J., 1990, 'The Political Economy of International Trade', *International Organisation*, 44, Spring.

Destler, I.M, 1986, 'American Trade Politics: System Under Stress', Washington, DC, IIE.

Frieden, J., 1988, 'Sectoral Conflict and Foreign Economic Policy, 1914–1940', *International Organisation*, 42, Winter.

Gallorati, M., 1985, 'Towards a Business Cycle Model of Tariffs', *International Organisation*, 39, Winter.

Goldstein, J., 1986 'The Political Economy of Trade: Institutions of Protection', *American Political Science Review*, 80(1).

Goldstein, J., 1988, 'Ideas, Institutions and American Trade Policy', *International Organisation*, 42, Winter.

Goldstein, J., 1989, 'The Impact of Ideas on Trade Policy', *International Organisation*, 43, Winter.

Goldstein, J. and Keohane, R.O., 1993, *Ideas and Foreign Policy: Beliefs, Institutions, and Political Change*, Ithaca, Cornell University Press.

Gourevitch, P., 1986, *Politics in Hard Times*, Ithaca, Cornell University Press.

Gowa, J., 1989, 'Rational Hegemons, Excludable Goods, and Small Groups', *World Politics*, 41(3).

Grilli, E., 1983, 'Macro-Economic Determinants of Trade Protection', *The World Economy*, 11(3).

Haas, P.M., 1992, 'Epistemic Communities and International Policy Co-ordination', *International Organisation*, 46, Winter.

Hall, P., 1986, *Governing the Economy: The Politics of State Intervention in Britain and France*, New York, Oxford University Press.

Holsti, O.R., 1967, 'Cognitive Dynamics and Images of the Enemy', in D. Finlay et al., *Enemies In Politics*, Chicago, Rand McNally.

Howell, T.R. et al., 1992, *Conflict Among Nations: Trade Policies in the 1990s*, Boulder, CO, Westview Press.

Ikenberry, G.J., 1988, 'Conclusion: An Institutional Approach to American Foreign Economic Policy', *International Organisation*, 42, Winter.

Ikenberry, G.J., Lake, D.A. and Mastanduno, M., 1988, 'Introduction: Approaches to Explaining American Foreign Economic Policy', *International Organisation*, 42, Winter.

James, A., 1993, 'System or Society?', *Review of International Studies*, 19(3).

Jervis, R. 1977, *Perception and Misperception in International Politics*, Princeton, Princeton University Press.

Katzenstein, P.J., 1978, *Between Power and Plenty: Foreign Economic Policies of Advanced Industrial States*, Madison, University of Wisconsin Press.

Keohane, R.O., ed., 1986, *Neorealism and its Critics*, New York, Columbia University Press.

Keohane, R.O. and Nye. J.S., 1977, Power And Interdependence, Boston, Little, Brown.

Kesselman, M., 1992, 'How Should One Study Economic Policy-making?', *World Politics*, July 1992.

Kindleberger, C., 1973, *The World in Depression*, Berkeley, CA, University of California Press.

Krasner, S., 1976, 'State Power and the Structure of International Trade', *World Politics*, 28, April.

Krasner, S., 1978, *Defending the National Interest*, Princeton, NJ, Princeton University Press.

Krasner, S., 1982, 'Structural Causes and Regime Consequences', *International Organisation*, 36, Spring.

Krugman, P.R. (ed.), 1986, *Strategic Trade Policy and the New International Economics*, Cambridge, MA, MIT Press.

Kuttner, R., 1983, 'The Free Trade Fallacy', *New Republic*, 28.

Lake, D.A., 1988, *Power, Protectionism, and Free Trade: International Sources of U.S. Commercial Strategy, 1887–1939*, Ithaca, NY, Cornell University Press.

Lavergne, R.P, 1983, *The Political Economy of U.S. Tariffs*, New York, Academic Press.

Magee, S.P. and Young, L., 1987, 'Endogenous Protection in the United States', in R.M.Stern (ed.) *U.S. Trade Policies in a Changing World Economy*, Cambridge, MA, MIT Press.

March, J.G. and Olsen, J.P., 1984, *Rediscovering Institutions: The Organisational Basis of Politics*, New York, Free Press.

Mares, D., 1990, 'Domestic Institutions and Shifts in Trade and Development Policy: Colombia 1951–68', in J.S. Odell and T.D.Willett, 1990.

Marks, S.V. and McArthur, J., 1990, 'Empirical Analyses of the Determinants of Protection: A Survey and Some Results', in J.S. Odell and T.D. Willett, 1990.

Mastanduno, M., 1988, 'Trade as a Strategic Weapon: American and Alliance Export Control Policy in the Early Post-War Period', *International Organisation*, 42(1), 121–50.

McKeown, T.J., 1986, 'The Limitations of "Structural" Theories of Commercial Policy', *International Organisation*, 40, Winter.

Milner, H.V., 1988, 'Trading Places: Industries for Free Trade', *World Politics*, 40(3).

Murphy, H.A., 1990, *The European Community and the International Trading System: Volume II*, Brussels, Centre for European Policy Studies.

Nowell, G., 1983, 'The French State and Developing World Oil Market', *Research in Political Economy*, 6.

Odell, J.S., 1982, *U.S. International Monetary Policy: Markets, Power, Ideas And Sources of Change*, New Jersey, Princeton University Press.

Odell, J.S., 1990, 'Understanding International Trade Policies: An Emerging Synthesis', *World Politics*, 43, October.

Odell, J.S. and Willett, T.D. (eds), 1990, *International Trade Policies: Gains from Exchange Between Economics and Political Science*, Michigan, University of Michigan Press.

Ostry, S., 1990, 'Europe 1992 and the Evolution of the Multilateral Trading System', *Case Western Reserve Journal of International Law*, 22(2).

Pastor, R., 1980, *Congress and the Politics of U.S. Foreign Economic Policy, 1929–1976*, Berkeley, CA, University of California Press.

Patterson, G., 1983, 'The European Community as a Threat to the System', in W. Cline (ed.) *Trade Policy in the 1980s*, Washington, DC, IIE.

Pincus, J.J., 1977, *Pressure Groups and Politics in Antebellum Tariffs*, New York, Columbia University Press.

Presa, S., 1993, 'A Concise Overview of E.C. Trade Policy', *European Economy*, 52.

Ray, E., 1981, 'Determinants of Tariff and Non-tariff Trade Restrictions in the U.S.', *Journal of Political Economy*, 81.

Richardson, J.D., 1990, 'The Political Economy of Strategic Trade Policy', *International Organisation*, 44, Winter.

Rohrlich, P.E., 1987, 'Economic Culture and Foreign Policy: The Cognitive Analysis of Economic Policy-making', *International Organisation*, 41, Winter.

Samuels, R., 1987, 'The Business of the Japanese State', Ithaca, NY, Cornell University Press.

Schattsneider, E.E., 1935, *Politics, Pressures and the Tariff*, New York, Prentice Hall.

Sikkink, K., 1991, *Ideas and Institutions: Developmentalism in Brazil and Argentina*, Ithaca, NY, Cornell University Press.

Stegemann, K., 1989, 'Policy Rivalry Among Industrial States: What Can We Learn from Models of Strategic Trade Policy', *International Organisation*, 43, Winter.

Strange, S., 1983, 'Cave! Hic Dragones: A Critique of Regime Analysis', in S. Krasner (ed.) *International Regimes*, (Ithaca, NY, Cornell University Press).

Takasc, W., 1981, 'Pressures for Protectionism: An Empirical Analysis', *Economic Inquiry*, 19.

Tharakan, P.M., 1991, 'The Political Economy of Anti-dumping Undertakings in the European Communities', *European Economic Review* (North Holland), 35.

Thurrow, L., 1992, *Head To Head: The Coming Economic Battles Among Japan, Europe and America*, New York, William Morrow.

Waltz, K.V., 1979, *Theory of International Politics*, Cambridge, MA, Addison-Wesley.

7

The international dimension of gender inequality and feminist politics: a 'new direction' for International Political Economy?

Jill Krause

INTRODUCTION

A collection of essays inspired by 'new directions' in the study of International Relations would be incomplete if it did not reflect the growing interest in gender issues and the contribution which feminist scholarship has begun to make to the field of study. Feminist interventions have taken place in the context of a greater degree of theoretical self-reflexivity within the discipline and share some common ground with other 'critical' approaches to the study of International Relations, while at the same time retaining a distinctive focus and agenda.[1] What many feminist approaches share with other critical approaches is a dissatisfaction with state-centric analysis, a critique of positivism and a concern with how power is implicated in 'claims to know'.

Feminist scholarship in the field has highlighted the problems of bias and distortion which occur when theory is written from the perspective of particular dominant groups. Feminist critiques of international theory have argued that the model of the state employed in much theory is built upon the model of 'sovereign man'.[2] This model of sovereign man, in much international theory, has been built upon male identified roles and reflects an 'abstract masculinity', based on a need for a singular identity, for separation and a denial of relatedness (Di Stefano, 1983). Feminist critiques share some common ground with those made by postmodern or poststructuralist writers. Richard Ashley, for example, has argued that the social practices involved in the production of a text must be explored in relation to the dominant social forces and practices of an age (1989). All critical theorists of International Relations reject the notion that theory and analysis can be 'value-free'. Theories of international relations, like all theories, are ideological. They can not be value-free because the reality that such theories claim to describe is made 'real' by the power of particular groups to impose definitions.

Problems of 'invisibility' in International Relations have also been highlighted. John Maclean claims that numerous issues and areas are rendered invisible in the study of International Relations as a consequence of the 'reductionism' of much international theory and of a 'methodological' individualism which seeks to explain social relations and social phenomenon in terms of 'facts' about reified sovereign states (1982: 118). The invisibility of gender issues might also be attributed to methodological individualism. By making the study of relations between reified sovereign states the central focus of International Relations, the scope of what is considered to be 'legitimate' inquiry is delimited to exclude the analysis of the international dimension of gender inequality.

Critiques have also centred on positivism as a dominant mode of analysis in International Relations. It has been suggested that positivism puts at a distance, objectifies and separates the 'knower' from the object of study. When applied to the study of the social world, positivism denies the role of social practice in the making and transformation of social orders (Maclean: 118). The work of Jurgen Habermas has influenced many critical theorists of international relations. Habermas (1971) claims that in class societies knowledge becomes an instrument for control, which restricts epistemological considerations to questions of internal methodology and loses sight of the epistemological subject and how her/his position and interests informs research. Epistemology is not transcendent, but a 'moment' of emancipation. As Cox argues: 'Theory is always for someone and for some purpose ... The world is seen from a standpoint definable in terms of nation, or social class, of the dominance or subordination of a rising or declining power (1981: 128).

Feminist critiques similarly claim that positivist epistemologies delimit the field of legitimate inquiry. The split between epistemology and ontology is granted the status of objective truth so that epistemology comes to be defined as excluding ontological considerations. Critical theory refuses to separate theory and theoretical understanding from practical activity and frames its research project with the explicit intention of furthering the aims of oppositional groups. Its expressed aim of furthering the self understanding of groups committed to transforming society has appealed, therefore, to feminists who wish to investigate the international dimension of gender inequalities and develop strategies to challenge and change the status of women.

A contribution of this kind cannot do justice to the many ways in which feminist scholarship is taking the discipline of International Relations in interesting and challenging new directions. Its purpose is rather to suggest ways in which the analysis of gender in international political economy might enrich our understanding of how international processes, both political and economic, serve to perpetuate particular kinds of power relations and of the role played by oppositional groups in challenging that same order. It also explores the links between feminist standpoint theory, feminist practice and other critical approaches. The first section explores gender in both the theory and practice of international political economy (IPE). The second section argues that the 'new IPE' represents a useful site from which to develop an analysis of the international dimensions of gender inequality. The third section suggests ways in which feminist standpoints can contribute to the development of a feminist international politics. In conclusion, it considers briefly the nature and role of the state; a central theme in many of the chapters in this book. It suggests that while critical approaches to IPE necessarily challenge the state-centric analysis characteristic of much 'orthodox' IPE, an understanding of the relationship between the state and counter-hegemonic movements should, nevertheless, be part of the feminist IPE project.

GENDER IN THE THEORY AND PRACTICE OF IPE

The study of international political economy has become a dynamic and expanding area of study within the discipline of International Relations in recent years. From an initial rather narrow focus on the relationship between state power and decision-making in the context of constraints imposed by the economic environment, IPE has expanded to include the activities of multi-national corporations, the influence on state policy of military industrial complexes, the role of international organizations in the international economy and the problems of world debt and development. IPE scholars have also explored the power of ideas and ideology in perpetuating particular kinds of power relationships. As yet, this has not been extended to aspects of gender relations. However, it is clear that an exploration of gender relations is needed because ideas about the 'naturalness' of forms of gender inequality are integral to understanding how the international economy functions. The gender-specific impact of global restructuring, structural adjustment, debt and the feminization of poverty have long been recognized, but not theorized in IPE. There is then both a need to understand why gender is missing from what is otherwise an expansive range of issues and concerns, and also to suggest ways in which, to paraphrase Cynthia Enloe, gender makes the world of international political economy go around.[3]

Gender relations are rendered invisible in IPE because of the way in which both 'economic' and 'political' activity has been defined. In capitalist economies the market is always viewed as the core of economic activity. Participation in the labour force and the inclusion of production in both national accounts and in the measurements of international economic activity has been defined in relation to the connection to the market, or to the performance of work for pay or profit. Unremunerated work is not, and the person performing it (usually a woman) is not included because the work is not part of the market of paid exchanges for goods or services and so is not viewed as economically significant. This is based on a 'common-sense' view of what constitutes 'economic' activity. IPE has also explored particular kinds of power relationships which underpin economic activity, but the measure of 'power' and what may be construed as 'political' has not been expanded to include areas outside of what is conventionally defined as the 'public sphere'. Much feminist analysis in International Relations is involved in working towards new definitions of the 'economic' and 'political' which will reunite what has conventionally been set off as separate. Gender relations have not been seriously considered, although, as Sarah Brown has argued: 'when gender is viewed as an inequality of power which is constructed as a socially relevant difference in order to keep that inequality in place, then gender itself can be seen as an outcome of social processes of subordination (1988: 471).

Christine Sylvester has argued that theories about IPE, like all theories, bear the collective mark of their collective and individual creators and these have been marked as to gender, race and class. Consequently, 'there is a hidden gender to the field which affects how we think about empirical international relations and political economy' (1991: 230). Neo-realism, which has been the dominant paradigm in IPE, is built upon the central concepts and categories of realism, but has been 'updated for the era of economic interdependence' (1991: 231). In neo-realist analysis, politics dominates economics. Hegemonic states are seen to create and maintain a particular form of order in the international economy. In this context transnational corporations and other significant 'actors' may be viewed as instruments of foreign policy or extensions of state power. By concentrating on impersonal structures of states and markets, it is not possible to see how women's activities have been demoted to the 'private' sphere (1991: 239). One might add that it is also impossible to see that women and men enter into the formal economy as 'gendered workers', that is as bearers of a gender identity. Neo-realist analysis contains another form of gender bias. Ann Tickner (1991: 193) has argued that one should be wary of the gender bias of the model of 'rational economic man' which underpins neo-realist analysis, while Sylvester claims that 'the rationality assumption prominent in neo-realism may also derive from a deep, unexamined cultural expectation that men are supposed to be motivated by calculations of instrumental interests' (1991: 237).

The neo-Marxist paradigm has offered an alternative analysis of international political economy which views the international system as a product of the historical expansion of capitalism as an economic and social system. In this model key 'actors' are social classes and economic relations are seen as structured for the benefit of dominant class interests. Antonio Gramsci produced important work in the 1920s which extended Marxist analysis to include the importance of culture and 'legitimising ideas' in perpetuating dominant orders (1978). Many contemporary Marxist theorists have developed this aspect of Marxist analysis to show the ways in which ideas and ideologies are used to advance the goals of global capital.

However, Marxism has also failed adequately to explore the gender dimension of inequality and failed to theorize forms of resistance which arise in response to the experience of gender subordination. Marx's emphasis on the importance of the economic position of the male worker overlooks the fact that the subject has a gender as well as a class identity. So while Marxist theory has been able to show how market theories represent the experience of the ruling group, it has had little to offer in terms of explaining why power is gendered (Hartsock, 1983: 145). Marxist critiques of private property have also failed to develop the significance of the fact that property is usually in male control. Contemporary Marxist analysis often assumes that conflicts are either directly or indirectly linked to class conflict. In consequence this gender-blind analysis produces an incomplete account of the life processes of human beings (Hartsock, 1983: 148).

This is not to suggest that Marxist analysis which makes gender central to an understanding of international political economy and which suggests some basis for a feminist oppositional politics has not been attempted elsewhere. Most notable, perhaps, has been the work of Maria Mies. Mies (1986) has drawn upon Wallerstein's world-systems theory to trace out the gender dimension of the emergence and evolution of two world systems, patriarchy and capitalism. Mies argues that capitalism can not function without patriarchy. The sixteenth-century capitalist revolution was itself a patriarchal revolution in which male control was asserted over women and violence was used to define women and colonial people as property.

An integral part of the expansion and development of capitalism, according to Mies, has been the move into the income-generating export production centres of the economy by Third World women. At the same time women involved in household production in both the West and the Third World have increasingly been encouraged to define themselves as 'consumers'. Mies suggests that the extension of the housewife ideology from the West to the Third World and from richer to poorer classes has helped to isolate and atomize women workers and mystify the process of labour control (1986: 110). Mies claims that there is a parallel between 'housewifization' and colonization, the coercion of women in the home and of 'under-developed' communities in the periphery. (1986: 219). She claims that patriarchal societies condition women to be primary care takers while capitalism devalues women's work and remunerates women less when they become paid labourers (1986: 180).

The role played by ideology historically in legitimizing colonialism has also been explored from a feminist perspective. Joanna de Groot (1991) has argued that the development of the international economy has been driven by misogyny as well as racism and exploitation based on class. In order to understand the growth of the world system, one needs to understand the cultural and ideological dimension of the process of expansion (1991: 107). European involvement in the expansion and intensification of the world system needed not just trade, investment and military aggression, but also involved the construction of new systematic interpretations of different societies in the system (1991: 111). The European sense of difference and superiority was expressed in a series of opposed definitions and images which reinforced negative conceptions of Asian and African societies by stressing what non-European societies were not. Within this context, discussions about women and gender issues were central to the intellectual and ideological construction of the non-European 'Other' (1991: 113). De Groot argues that: '"Inferiority" in the treatment of women was part of the definition of non-European "inferiority" in general, and debates or actions concerning women were thus a central part of European entrepreneurial, imperial or missionary strategies in general' (1991: 114). She suggests that the analysis by élite European men of the position of women in non-European societies was an expression of power relations. The position of élite European men in the world system was connected by patterns of gender and class power which sustained male authority over women and the control of the propertied over the labouring classes (1991: 115).

In the related field of development studies, there is now an extensive feminist literature which explores how both dominant theories of development and the impact of particular policies have been profoundly gendered. Historically, theories about the nature of economic activity have ignored the contribution which 'women's work' makes to the international economy. Writing in 1970, Ester Boserup argued that the under-representation of subsistence production made Third World countries appear poorer than they were and over-represented rates of growth. Today, the marginalization of women's contribution to the development process continues to cause serious distortions in measures to promote and measure development as well as having a devastating impact on Third World states generally and on women and children in particular.[4]

It is, perhaps, in the area of development that one can see most clearly the importance of gender in IPE, by exploring the gender-specific impact of development policies and examining the role played in this process by both international organizations and multinational corporations. The centre-piece of recent IMF strategies has been export-led growth and structural adjustment.[5] Indebted governments set aside territory specifically for the use of factories producing goods for international markets. The most important attraction for the transnational company is the availability of cheap female labour. It has been suggested that women make up, on average, 70 per cent of workers in Export Production Zones (Allison, Ashworth and Redclift, 1986: 12). Elson and Pearson claim that the provision of women into such jobs has been encouraged because it can be viewed as a way of involving women in the development process(1991: 18). World market factories producing components for the electronics industry are usually owned or partially owned by subsidiaries of Japanese, North American and European multinationals (1991: 20). These have been particularly important in the development of trade in consumer goods. A number of large US and European retailing firms are now placing large contracts with world market factories. When deciding where to locate a crucial factor is the availability of a suitable labour force, which is defined in terms of low cost and high productivity. It seems that women are the cheapest and most productive of all workers. Elson and Pearson claim that one cannot understand the characteristics of the international economy in terms of class and national struggles alone; gender must be incorporated into the analysis (1991: 31).

The rapid growth and expansion of Export Production Zones cannot be viewed solely in terms of IMF policy and the related problems of debt and under-development. They must also be viewed in the context of a wider process of restructuring, which is one of the most striking features of the contemporary international economy. This process is giving rise to profound challenges in how we think about IPE, as neither neo-realist nor Marxist models of North/ South structural inequalities nor dependency models seem to be able to fully capture this phenomenon. Feminist writers have identified a number of areas in which a comprehension of gender relations is essential for understanding capitalist relations. In both North and South restructuring is having a profound effect on the composition of the workforce. In the North, the pattern of restructuring is showing such marked similarities with many Third World states, with women ghettoized in assembly-line work with poor pay and prospects, that Mitter (1986) claims that a 'new proletariat' is emerging in both the North and South.

One aspect of global restructuring is the increasing numbers of part-time and home workers. The rise in home working in the west is a manifestation of more 'flexible manning' (Mitter and van Luijken, 1989: 4). In response to the 1970s oil crisis, big companies in the West resorted to international subcontracting to survive. Initially the knowledge-intensive parts of the production process went to the West, while transnational corporations shifted the labour-intensive parts of the production process to developing countries where cheap female labour was abundant. However, in more recent years as big business emphasizes the importance of managerial flexibility and decentralized production, corporate strategies in the West have sought a more flexible workforce to undermine the power of trade unions. Home-working in Europe is becoming the mirror image of Third World women working in the export production industry. Mitter and van Luijken claim that women constitute the majority of home-workers because everywhere women constitute the poorest sections of society (1989: 4). They claim that there is a marked similarity between home-work and housework; both are done by women and both remain invisible. To call home-working the 'informal sector' is to misrepresent the numbers involved. It is not outside or parallel to the formal sector. It is an integral part of the capitalist market economy (1989: 7).[6]

The net result of these trends is a gradual feminization of the workforce. Feminist scholars differ in their explanations of just why and how the workforce in some areas is becoming feminized, but clearly a complex array of factors contribute to this process.[7] As Enloe has argued, international political economy works in the way it does because of the decisions which are taken which cheapen the value of women's work, because home and workplace tasks become feminized and because the organization of factory rules, jobs and machinery are all designed to keep women's labour cheap and productive. Keeping women's labour cheap and productive requires daily effort, and this effort is integral to international political economy (1989: 160). Enloe suggests that with global restructuring feminized patterns of racial inequality are emerging which are interwoven with ideas about motherhood and 'feminine respectability'.[8] Employers in both the North and South are also able to exploit ideas about the 'natural dexterity' and 'nimble fingers' of women. Skills are thus defined in an ideologically biased way and women's skills are not rewarded. In addition, despite the fact that male unemployment is increasing, masculinity is still identified with the breadwinner status and this provides another justification for paying women less (1989: 162).

A further aspect of the international economy which has attracted the interest of feminist scholars in particular is the rapid growth of sex tourism, or prostitution which is linked to the expansion of the tourist industry. In a number of countries, tourism has also become an important earner of foreign currency. In Thailand, the Philippines, the Caribbean, and Brazil, the growing sex in-

dustry is linked closely with the expansion of tourism and is inextricably linked
to the problems of debt and development strategies (Umfreville, 1990: 41).

Sex tourism does not involve just women, although it is overwhelmingly
women who are drawn into this particular form of prostitution; frequently
women who have been displaced as a direct consequence of 'development'.
Nor can prostitution be viewed solely from the perspective of tourism, but it
is nevertheless conditioned by the demands of a stratified international market
and the impact of development policies which are themselves conditioned by
global economic processes (Thahn Dam, 1983: 549). Thahn Dam has suggested
that prostitution is becoming an internationally traded commodity. The growing integration of the tourist industry which links countries, hotel chains and
package holiday firms is a crucial enabling factor which allows spare capacity
in airline seats and hotel beds to be matched with the demand for esoteric
sexual services (1983: 334). With the growing internationalization of capital
one finds the spread of prostitution. It is, she claims, no accident that Bangkok
and Manila, both major cities which have experienced massive growth in
prostitution in recent years, are also both major centres for multinational
corporations and regional centres for international organizations (1983: 337).
Increasingly the issue of prostitution needs a global perspective. Enloe argues
that it is both a part of the international political system and the international
economy, and 'that it is not taken seriously says more about the ideological
construction of seriousness than the politics of tourism' (1989: 40).

THE 'NEW IPE' ...

Global restructuring, the increasingly complex international division of
labour, and the growing recognition of the many dimensions of interdependence and the relationship between debt, 'development' and environmental
degradation are all integral parts of the phenomenon of globalization. Globalization is changing our understanding of the world and giving rise to new
theories. The 'new International Political Economy' is a response to these
challenges (Tooze and Murphy, 1991). The new IPE recognizes that social
relations are becoming increasingly globalized and that it is necessary therefore
to get away from the state-centric models of the international economy in the
academic study of IPE and focus on a number of agents, both governmental
and non-governmental.

It also echoes many of the criticisms of orthodox approaches to the study of
the international found elsewhere. Tooze, for example, has argued that there is
in effect an 'unwritten preface' to IPE analysis. Most work in IPE is produced
within the mainstream theory of knowledge shared by most social sciences,
which combines positivism with empiricism and which posits the separation of
'facts' and 'values'. Tooze attributes this dominance in part to the influence of
American economics. He argues that:

> in the case of much contemporary IPE, the predominant but often implicit epistemo-
> logy tends to define the boundaries of legitimate enquiry so as to preclude or

discourage consideration of philosophical or epistemological questions both within and outside the mode of knowledge (1988: 287–8).

In Robert Gilpin's work, for example, there is an underlying assumption that ideologies can be tested against a separate and external 'reality' (1988: 291).[9] In fact, not only does liberal ideology provide specific explanations for particular developments and policies for agencies, but the definition of reality against which all other views and actions are judged (1988: 291). Richard Ashley (1984) has similarly critiqued neo-realism because it claims to offer a 'truly scientific' approach to the study of international relations when it in fact betrays both realism's commitment to political autonomy by reducing politics to economics, renders science a purely technical enterprise and subordinates practice to an interest in control.

In short, conventional IPE is limited in scope, non-reflexive and potentially harmful in the political functions which it serves (Tooze, 1988: 291). The new IPE grows out of a recognition of the subjectivity of the social sciences and encourages historical modes of analysis and explanation. It is also built upon a recognition of the intimate connection between theory and practice. For this reason a number of critical IPE scholars have also drawn upon the work of Gramsci (1978) which identified the rise of transnational ideologies and transnational class alliances and explored how they cemented or legitimized particular dominant economic projects. In this spirit it has been argued that there is a need to develop a counter-hegemonic set of concepts and concerns in order to deal with the problems of militarism, and economic and social inequalities (Gill and Law, 1988).

Undoubtedly critical IPE is a useful site from which to analyse the international dimension of gender inequalities and feminist politics. Theories which have arisen in response to the phenomenon of globalization recognize that international processes shape and transform economic activity so social and economic change can no longer be viewed as an entirely internal affair. It is necessary, therefore, to tease out the international dimension of social change, while recognizing the specificity of some areas. However, thus far critical approaches to IPE have not analysed the ways in which female subordination has been created and sustained both nationally and internationally (Whitworth, 1993).

While the agenda of IPE has expanded to include debt, the activities of Export Production Zones, international organizations and the role played by ideas and ideology in the reproduction of power relations, critical approaches to IPE have not really explored the gender dimension. Whitworth contends that IPE must also explore the assumptions about the role of women and men in all societies, how this informs the practices of particular men and women and how this, in turn, serves to reproduce gender relations in the context of the material and historical conditions of the age. She also points out that while empirical information about women in the international economy is valuable, analysis of structural inequalities between men and women is also needed (1993: 10). We also need to understand gender relations rather than simply 'add women' because it forces us to think about how men and women act as gendered agents and explores the ways in which ideas about 'masculinity' and 'femininity' work. Given the obvious importance of other forms of social inequality revolving around class and race in understanding international political economy, one might argue that what is needed is a feminist analysis which is sensitive to how other dimensions such as class and race cut across gender historically.

... AND FEMINIST STANDPOINTS

Whitworth has argued that in many respects feminist interventions in IPE parallel other critical approaches (1993: 1). The new IPE attempts to get beyond 'adding in' actors and issues to profound ontological and epistemological challenges to the discipline which will challenge the prevailing orthodoxy and provide spaces for the voices of the marginalized to be heard (1993: 4). A further challenge to IPE which emerges from the demand to take gender seriously is the need to address the question of whether 'our perception and understanding would be different, if knowledge was produced from different realities, different versions of the world-from women's experience?' (Zalewski, 1993: 18).

In this task, feminist standpoint is undoubtedly useful. Standpoint approaches argue that material life activity has important epistemological and ontological consequences for both understanding and constructing social relations. Furthermore, because material life is structured differently for different groups, the vision available to each represents an inversion of others in systems of domination (Harding, 1991: 150). By adopting a feminist standpoint the first aim is to reverse the usual understanding of events, and reveal hidden assumptions in dominant theories or 'common-sense' views of the world. A feminist standpoint must be struggled for. It represents an engaged position – that is why it is feminist – not 'feminine'. A standpoint is not natural to all women, but an achieved position (Harding 1990: 90). Standpoint suggests ways in which both theory and practice can be directed in a liberatory direction.

Clearly, attempts to theorize from the position of 'women's lives' are problematic and, while feminist scholars have a great deal to say about the issues and areas conventionally defined as IPE and have argued for the inclusion of areas which have been conventionally set off from the main/malestream, there has never been a single feminist theory or approach. The causes of gender inequality and oppression are complex, require careful understanding of how gender intersects with race and class to produce different experiences of oppression and require different strategies to change women's subordinate status. Similarly the importance of the cultural context in which being defined 'male' or 'female' takes place has been highlighted (Marchand, 1994). However, standpoint theorists do not attempt to reinstate the notion of an homogeneous women's experience to serve as the grounds for knowledge claims (Harding, 1990). While feminist epistemologies embody a strong commitment to legitimize women's 'ways of knowing' and a political commitment to challenge male dominance, because 'masculinity' and 'femininity' are always categories within every race, class and culture there can only be 'feminisms' and 'feminist standpoints'. Nor do feminist standpoint approaches preclude analysis by class or race or any other category; it welcomes analysis by excluded 'others' as complementary (Hirschmann, 1992: 30). While the social construction of gender is not opposed to or more important than class, or race or ethnicity, it needs to be viewed separately (1992: 30).

The notion of a standpoint suggests that there are some commonalities between women which are based specifically on their experience of gender subordination. These common experiences could be used to explore the possibilities for building alliances between feminist groups. While recognizing the importance of specificity and difference in some contexts, increasingly international processes affect the process of social and economic change and create the conditions for transnational political alliances. Gender relations are constantly amended by economic and social processes, by new technologies and ideas which increasingly have an international dimension. International processes can also create the conditions for feminist politics in the Third World. The dumping of the Dalkon Shield intra-uterine device, banned in the United States because of its harmful effects, on to Third World women is an oft-cited, but nevertheless important example. The operation of military institutions, sex tourism and even the implementation of energy schemes, which are integral parts of 'development', all profoundly affect the lives of women and encourage the growth of feminist movements.

Third World nationalist movements often present feminism as a product of decadent Western capitalism, based on a foreign culture and of no relevance to women in the Third World. However, while Western feminists have sometimes been guilty of misunderstanding the position, specific problems and concerns of non-Western women, it is an oversimplification to suggest that feminism is in itself a foreign ideology. Feminism is no more or less 'alien' than other ideologies, like socialism and, indeed, nationalism, which have influenced both the internal social and economic structure of states and their external politics. In a study of the impact of both feminism and nationalism in the Third World Jayawardena argued that feminism was not imposed on Third World women, but rather historical circumstances produced important national and ideological changes that affected women through the impact of imperialism (1986: 2). Historically Western thought has been a significant element in the development of feminism in many parts of Asia, but Jayawardena claims that movements for women's emancipation took place against a background of nationalist struggle in which the assertion of national and cultural identity was coupled with reforms which promoted education, scientific and cultural advance (1986: 4). Jayawardena's analysis suggests that resistance to imperialism and foreign domination was coupled with opposition to feudal structures and traditional forms of patriarchal authority(1986: 4). The growth of capitalism thus changed the social order and gave birth to new social movements and structures.

Feminists who challenge all forms of patriarchal domination and aim to improve the status of the worlds women are often accused of 'interfering with culture'. Attempts to use international organizations to improve the status of women are also often resisted on the same grounds.[10] However, this ignores the changes which are already being experienced by all countries both directly and indirectly and completely disregards the fact that development processes, for example, are already built upon all kinds of neo-colonialist assumptions about the status of women as dependants and men as 'bread-winners', and often serve to deprive women of traditional rights and access to resources (Ashworth and May, 1990: 5). At the same time, Western ideologies and values, technologies and commercialism intrinsically interfere with culture, collective traditions and value systems. The 'problem' is not the status of feminism in itself, but rather the danger inherent in falsely universalizing the conditions of women's oppression, and attempting to interpret and represent the experiences of others. Feminist theory must recognize other significant divisions besides gender and be able to allow the articulation of different experiences of gender oppression. Similarly a feminist politics must recognize the need for different strategies to challenge forms of gender inequality and build upon the many sites of feminist struggle.

A central theme in a number of chapters in this book has been the role of the state and the relationship between counter-hegemonic movements and the state. Critical approaches to IPE necessarily challenge both the territorial and conceptual boundaries of the state as the central unit of analysis. Gender is a relation characterized by inequalities of power. Power in IPE can no longer be viewed as something which is used by states, but which extends to social relations. Furthermore, as argued throughout this chapter, social relations, including gender relations, are increasingly shaped and transformed by international processes. Nevertheless, the question of the sites of feminist political struggle inevitably raises the question of the relationship between feminist oppositional movements and other counter-hegemonic movements. It also raises the question of whether or not the state can act as an agent for the realization of feminist goals. Feminists need to understand what social forces construct the political projects of the state and in what senses, if any, the state can be used as an instrument for change. Whilst it is beyond the scope of this chapter, the role played by dominant and oppositional forces in supporting and challenging the existing order and their relation to the state must be a part of the feminist IPE project. In this task IPE scholars can neither derive direct guidance from existing state theory nor draw upon any one feminist theory of the state.[11]

Feminist scholarship has repeatedly shown that whilst women take part in political struggles, most notably nationalist struggles, in no sense can these be seen as watersheds in the emancipation of women. Women are changed by the experience of participation, and while apparently recognizing common cause with men in nationalist struggle, they frequently express aspirations for changes in the social position of women (Ridd and Calloway, 1987). However, despite participating in struggle at all levels, women are often unable to consolidate the gains made during times of political upheaval and at a later stage are pushed back into 'traditional' roles and into subordinate social positions.

Feminist scholarship has also shown that women's integration into the state has historically followed a different trajectory from men's (Kandiyoti, 1991). This experience would strongly suggest that while feminist movements might sometimes find common cause with other oppositional groups, they do not necessarily have common interests. There are undoubtedly dangers inherent in generalizing about the degree to which the state supports the collective interests of men as a group. However, while gender relations are embedded in wider power relations, it is clear that men's power over women is in some senses institutionalized in both the state and in broader social structures. Liberal feminists who argue for the participation and inclusion of women in all institutions of the state as a route to 'first class citizenship' have been criticized precisely because they fail to address the degree to which state power is patriarchal (Connell, 1990). Certainly the state cannot be seen simply as a neutral arbiter which, empirically, has been 'seized' by men and which can be 'captured' by women in the interests of advancing feminist goals.

In recent years, a number of developments in state theory have broadened the conception of the state. The state is no longer seen as a 'managerial structure', or a body concerned solely with repression, coercion and social control. In the Gramscian tradition, the state is seen as incorporating a number of institutions whose role appears strictly 'private' or primarily ideological, including the church, family and school (Yuval-Davis, 1987: 4). Recent feminist analysis has looked at how gender is constituted by the structure of various social institutions and at how gender is tied into intricate patterns of domination. Feminists have also begun to view gender as a collective phenomenon, an aspect of both personal life and of social institutions (Connell, 1987). The state can, therefore, be seen as 'patriarchal', but patriarchy is embedded in its procedures and processes. Men's overall social supremacy is embedded not only in the formal institutions of the state but also in the family, workplace, the functioning of the economy, the media and the church. This broader conception of the state is undoubtedly useful to feminist scholars in starting to think about the complex linkages between women and the state and the problematic relationship between feminist movements and the state. It may well be that a feminist analysis will reveal a much more complex relationship between the international, the state and 'civil society' and cast doubt upon the degree to which the state can be viewed as an agent of change, from a feminist perspective. A feminist IPE will need to develop an approach which recognizes the complex links between knowledge, power and interests. It will also explore how all hegemonic structures are imbued with patriarchal ideology and practice and how feminist standpoints offer sites of resistance to hegemonic discourse and power and create spaces for women to be heard.

NOTES

1. I recognize that there are a number of 'feminisms'. However, feminist postmodern and poststructuralist approaches and feminist engagements with critical theory

have perhaps contributed the most to current debates in International Relations in both the US and Britain.

2. Sylvester, 1993: 164.
3. See Enloe, Bananas, Beaches and Bases, 1989: 1–18.
4. There is an extensive literature dealing with the gender-specific impact of development . See, for example, Elson, 1990.
5. See, for example, George, 1989: 45–57 for a discussion of IMF policy.
6. Mitter and Luijken point out that it is 'fiendishly difficult' to quantify the numbers involved in this type of production. The statistical problem gets compounded by the fact that workers are often not seen as 'employed' by either their families or even themselves. For this reason they frequently fail to register in workforce surveys. However, research by Mitter and Luijken would suggest that a substantial part of output from home-based units provides direct inputs into the consumption and production activities of the so called 'formal sector'.
7. See Mackintosh, in Young, Wolkowitz and McCullagh, 1991 and Mitter, 1986.
8. For a more detailed discussion of 'myths' of femininity and masculinity in this context see Enloe, 1989: 160–69.
9. Gilpin, 1976.
10. For example, the IMF takes the view that it should not be involved in questions of how the burden of debt is adjusted between various social groups in recipient states in apparent deference to indigenous culture and tradition.
11. A discussion of the state and gender politics which covers many of the debates in feminist theories can be found in Connell, 1990.

REFERENCES

Allison, Helen, Ashworth, Georgina and Redclift, Nanneke, 1986, *Hardcash: Man Made Development and its Consequences: A Feminist Perspective on Aid*, London, Change Publications.

Ashworth, Georgina and May, Nicky, 1990, *Of Conjuring and Caring*, London, Change Publications.

Ashley, Richard, 1984, 'The Poverty of Neo-realism' *International Organisation*, 38(2).

Ashley, Richard, 1989, 'Untying the Sovereign State: A Double Reading of the Anarchy Problematique', *Millennium Journal of International Studies*, 17(2).

Boserup, Ester, 1970, *Women's Role in Economic Development*, New York, St. Martin's Press.

Brown, Sarah, 1988, 'Feminism, International Theory and International Relations of Gender Inequality', *Millennium Journal of International Studies*, 17(3).

Connell, R.W., 1990, ' The State, Gender, and Sexual Politics: Theory and Appraisal', *Theory and Society*, 19: 507–44.

Cox, Robert, 1981, 'Social Forces, States and World Orders: Beyond International Relations Theory', *Millennium Journal of International Studies*, 10(2).

de Groot, Joanna, 1991, 'Conceptions and Misconceptions: The Historical and Cultural Context of Discussions of Women in Development', in Afshar, Haleh, *Women, Development and Survival in the Third World*, London, Longman.

Di Stefano, Christine, 1983, 'Masculinity as Ideology in Political Theory: The Case of Hobbesian Man Considered', *Women's Studies International Forum*, 6.

Elson, Diane, 1990, *Male Bias in the Development Process*, Manchester University Press.

Elson, Diane and Pearson, Ruth, 1991, 'The Situation of Women and the Internationalisation of Factory Production', in Young, Kate, Wolkowitz, Carol and McCullugh,

Roslyn, *Of Marriage and the Market: Women's Subordination Internationally and its Lessons*, London, Routledge.

Enloe, Cynthia, 1989, *Bananas, Beaches and Bases: Making Feminist Sense of International Politics*, London, Pandora.

Gill, Stephen and Law, David, 1988, *The Global Political Economy: Perspectives, Problems and Politics*, Brighton, Harvester Wheatsheaf.

Gilpin, Robert, 1976, *US Power and the Multinational Corporation*, London, Macmillan.

George, Susan, 1989, *A Fate Worse than Debt*, London, Penguin.

Gramsci, Antonio, 1978, *Selections from Political Writings*, Lawrence and Wishart.

Habermas, Jurgen, 1971, *Knowledge and Human Interests*, London, Heinemann.

Harding, Sandra, 1990, 'Feminism, Science and Anti-Enlightenment Critique', in Nicholson, Linda, *Feminism/Postmodernism*.

Harding, Sandra, 1991, *Whose Science? Whose Knowledge? Thinking From Women's Lives*, Milton Keynes, Open University Press.

Hartsock, Nancy, 1983, *Money, Sex and Power: Towards a Feminist Historical Materialism*, Boston, Northeastern University Press.

Hirschmann, Nancy, 1992, *Rethinking Obligation: A Feminist Method for Political Theory*, London, Cornell University Press.

Jayawardena, Kumari, 1986, *Feminism and Nationalism in the Third World*, London, Zed Books.

Maclean, John, 1982, 'Political Theory, International Theory and Problems of Ideology', *Millennium Journal of International Studies*, 10(2).

Mackintosh, Maureen, 1991, 'Gender and Economics: The Sexual Division of Labour and the Subordination of Women', in Young, Wolkowitz and McCullagh.

Marchand, Marianne, 1994, 'Latin American Voices of Resistance; Women's Movements and Development Debates', in Rostow, S., Rupert, M. and Samatur, A., *The Global Economy as Political Space: Essays in Critical Theory and International Political Economy*, forthcoming, Cambridge University Press.

Mies, Maria, 1986, *Patriarchy and Accumulation on a World Scale*, London, Zed Books.

Mitter, Swasti, 1986, *Common Fate, Common Bond*, London, Pluto Press.

Ridd, Rosemary and Calloway, Helen, 1987, *Caught up in Conflict*, New York University Press.

Sylvester, Christine, 1990, 'The Emperors' Theories and Transformations; Looking at the Field Through Feminist Lenses', in Sylvester, Christine and Pirages, Dennis (eds) *Transformations in the Global Political Economy*, London, Macmillan.

Sylvester, Christine, 1993, *Feminist Theory and International Relations in a Postmodern Era*, Cambridge, Cambridge University Press.

Thahn Dam, Thoung, 1983, 'The Dynamics of Sex Tourism; The Case of South East Asia', *Development and Change*, 14: 533–53.

Tickner, Ann, 1991, 'On the Fringes of the Global Economy', in Tooze, Roger and Murphy, Craig, *The New International Political Economy*, 1991.

Tooze, Roger, 1988, 'The Unwritten Preface: "International Political Economy" and Epistemology', *Millennium Journal of International Studies*, 17(2), Summer.

Tooze, Roger and Murphy, Craig, 1991, *The New International Political Economy*, Boulder, CO, Lynne Rienner Publications.

Umfreville, Mabel, 1990, *S£XONOMYC$: An Introduction to the Political Economy of Sex, Time and Gender*, London, Change Publications.

Van Luijken, Anneke and Mitter, Swasti, 1989, *Unseen Phenomenon: The Rise of Homeworking*, London, Change Publications.

Whitworth, Sandra, 1993, 'Theory As Exclusion: Gender and International Political Economy', in Stubbs, R. and Underhill, G., *Political Economy and the Changing Global Order*, Basingstoke, Macmillan.

Young, K., Wolkowitz, C. and McCullagh, R., 1991, *Of Marriage and the Market: Women's Subordination Internationally and its Lessons*, London, Routledge.

Yuval-Davis, Nira and Anthias, Floya, 1989, *Woman, Nation, State*, Basingstoke, Macmillan.

Zalewski, Marysia, 1993, 'Feminist Standpoint Theory Meets International Relations Theory: A Feminist Version of David and Goliath?', *The Fletcher Forum*, Summer.

8

A neo-Gramscian approach to international organization: an expanded analysis of current reforms to UN development activities

Kelley Lee

INTRODUCTION

Amidst historic changes in the global political economy (GPE) since the late 1980s, there has been a combination of renewed aspirations for, yet increasing disenchantment with, the role of the United Nations.[1] These changes have accelerated a recurrent debate on reforming the UN system to make it a more effective force in international relations. Since the mid-1980s this debate has led to the initiation of a number of expert groups, committees and studies, both within and outside the UN, to seek ways forward.

While the UN's role in peace and security has received the bulk of attention, it is widely recognized that development activities are also vital to future world order. Indeed, an estimated 70 per cent of the UN's resources is spent on economic and social development (Bertrand, 1985: 34).[2] Towards setting an 'agenda for development', Secretary-General Boutros-Ghali has set in motion a reform programme that will affect the key institutions concerned with development including the UN Development Programme (UNDP), special funds and specialized agencies. These reforms are in response to widespread criticisms, among both developed and developing countries, that the UN has performed disappointingly in narrowing the gap between rich and poor. Fundamental institutional and policy changes are envisaged.

It is argued in this chapter that recently proposed reforms, and analyses of them, have been confined too narrowly to the rationalization of existing structures and processes. Among policy-makers and scholars, it has been assumed that global interests are steadily converging, giving rise to the need for greater multilateral cooperation. This convergence is seen as part of an emerging neo-liberal world order. As part of the UN's response to these changes, proposed reforms of UN development activities have focused on rationalizing its functions, financing and procedures.

The analytical framework of this chapter puts forth a fuller analysis of UN reform. It is argued that the study and practice of international organization (IO) has lagged behind that of other aspects of International Relations, and that it continues to be dominated by a liberal–realist orthodoxy. Current reform debates have been firmly located within this orthodoxy. This has led to particular views of the problems that the UN faces and the solutions deemed appropriate to address them. Notably there have been increasing efforts to 'depoliticize' and technocratize the UN's development agenda.

Through the application of a Gramscian framework[2] to UN reform, this chapter locates current debates within shifting material, institutional and ideological forces in the GPE (Cox, 1987). Such a perspective reveals how proposed reforms have been affected by, and have contributed to, an emerging neo-liberal hegemonic order. This has been evident in the emphasis placed on 'fixing' institutional mechanisms. By recognizing that this is a particular and value-based problematic, and challenging the assumption that it is necessarily of universal interest, this chapter seeks to redefine the debate on UN reform. This redefinition places fundamentally normative and political issues at the centre of discussion – who should decide what the UN does, who should pay for UN development activities, and how should these activities be carried out? It is only by doing so that we can arrive at a more critical understanding of the UN's role in the emerging 'new world order'.

ORTHODOXY AND THE STUDY OF INTERNATIONAL ORGANIZATION

The study of IO has been the Cinderella of international relations, overshadowed by East–West tensions until a resurgence of faith in multilateralism followed the end of the Cold War. Yet, despite half a century having elapsed since the creation of the UN, the theory and practice of IO have remained rooted in post-war thinking. While recent debates in international theory have been lively, there have been little corresponding discussion in IO. Hence many questions remain unanswered regarding the nature of IO – why does it emerge, how does it work, and what role does it play in International Relations?

Conventional or orthodox thinking on IO has centred on liberal and, to a lesser extent, realist-based theories. Traditional liberal theories of IO focus on formal and informal institutions, established by member states to promote and pursue cooperative behaviour in functional, often sector-based, areas. It is believed that, through broadening the scope and authority of such institutions, an international community will develop built on technical, economic and social links between states (Mitrany, 1948: 350–63).

More recent work by liberal-institutionalists or neo-liberals, led by Robert Keohane, has broadened the scope of inquiry to include international regimes and conventions. Regimes are defined as concrete procedures, rules and institutions for certain kinds of activities. Conventions are informal institutions with implicit rules and understandings (Keohane, 1979). Both arise when there is a convergence of interests among states on a particular issue area where multilateral cooperation is required. This has shifted scholarly attention to the circumstances under which such cooperation takes place, what Cox (1992) calls the 'processes through which cooperative arrangements at the international level are constructed'. Liberal-institutionalism is a thriving theoretical approach which is currently being used to explain the end of the Cold War, revival of multilateralism, and strengthening of regional organizations (e.g. Martin, 1992).[2]

Realist and neo-realist theories of IO derive from traditional realist assumptions that states are the primary unit of analysis, states are driven by the pursuit of self-interest, and the international system is inherently conflictual. IO is thus understood as the institutional means by which militarily and economically powerful states seek to achieve their ends. As Gill writes, IO is 'simply reflecting a series of inter-state bargains and thus an underlying structure of power between states, rather than a series of structural changes which generate new conditions and promote changing conceptions of interests and identity' (1993: 6). The UN is seen not as an actor in its own right but as an arena in which state actors compete. This view has not essentially changed with the development of neo-realist theory. While greater attention has been paid to economic forces and the growth in number and scope of IO since 1945, neo-realists have continued to overlook it as a subject of particular interest (Archer, 1992).

The development of an expanded analytical framework for the study of IO begins with identifying three main inadequacies of liberal and realist-based theories: (a) state-centrism; (b) positivism; and (c) a limited concept of power. First, the liberal-realist orthodoxy focuses on the state as the primary unit of analysis, which leads to a reductionist understanding of IO. *Reductionism* concerns the belief that explanation in social and political theory should begin with the behaviour of individual actors rather than the structure of a society (Walker, 1989: 175). In orthodox IO theory, such 'methodological individualism' assumes that the actor exists and can be understood apart from any social arrangement. Social facts are facts about individual actors; the international system is thus seen as a construct of the states which compose it (Murphy and Tooze, 1991: 19). Thus despite recognition of links above and below the level of states, and the increased role of non-state actors, IO continues to be defined primarily in terms of formal and informal institutions established by member states to promote cooperative behaviour among themselves.

The problem with methodological individualism is that it offers a limited description and explanation of the interplay of ideas, material interests and institutions in the GPE (Cox, 1981). By giving primacy to actors, such analyses deny validity to what Murphy and Tooze call 'contextually bound explanations' and 'concrete social wholes' (1991: 19). As a result there is a failure to recognize non-actor variables which impact upon, but do not derive from, individual actors. This is evident in hegemonic liberal-realist economic theories which exclude the possibility that 'the economy is part of a transnational whole which produces important political effects independently of the agency of the state' (Rosenberg, 1990: 287). In the study of IO, it is argued that IO cannot be understood apart from the structural forces which shape world order. Rather there is a dialectical relationship between actor and structure (Gill, 1993: 5–8), of which IO is a part.

The second inadequacy of the liberal-realist orthodoxy is its essentially positivist view of IO. Briefly, *positivism* assumes the existence of an objective or external reality which is independent of how we observe and understand that reality. From this so-called 'real world' it is assumed that we can derive value-neutral 'facts'. Positivism thus separates what 'is' from what 'ought' to be, which leads to a distinction between empirical and normative inquiry. In social science (including International Relations), the generation of such 'facts' through empirical research is believed to lead to explanations of causation among them (i.e. theoretical statements), which in turn are tested against reality (Tooze, 1988). From empirically testable facts, it is argued, laws can be derived which are universally valid across time and space. In the pursuit of knowledge, therefore, the role of the scholar is to understand reality but remain objectively removed from it.

The quest for a positivist study of international relations is rooted in post-war efforts to develop a 'science' of foreign policy (Hoffman, 1977). While scholars seek facts about the international system, and may even use this knowledge to help policy-makers, the essential nature of the international system is believed to remain unchanged. This assumption has been especially prominent in the study and practice of IO. Liberal theory, for example, views UN specialized agencies as bodies of technical experts striving to reach agreement on apolitical matters (e.g. health, telecommunications, transport). Similarly, liberal-institutionalism assumes that human behaviour is rational, and that IO can be explained through empiricist methods such as rational-choice theory and micro-economic analysis (Keohane and Nye, 1977). Since the late 1980s efforts to build a 'new world order' have also sought to put aside value-based interests. This so-called 'end of ideology' has brought forth calls for 'practical' solutions to needs which are assumed universal to all people (e.g. human rights, democracy, environment).

The critique of positivism by many international relations scholars in recent years has derived from broader debates within the philosophy of science and socio-political theory. Such debates have raised fundamental issues concerning epistemology and ontology. *Epistemology* concerns 'how we come to have knowledge of the world, and how we can validate knowledge claims' (Maclean, 1981). It deals with the theory behind how we define knowledge, how we can produce it, and the criteria by which we judge knowledge as an accurate reflection of the world around us. Importantly, such questions are not merely of intellectual interest, but have practical implications. Post-positivists argue that how we think about the world affects how we act within and ultimately structure that world (Maclean, 1981: 49, 55). *Ontology* refers to 'what can be said to be real or to exist independently of the mind of the observer' (Maclean, 1981: 48). Or as Gill and Law (1988) write, it is what we believe to be 'the nature of reality and its underlying units, which form the starting point of theoretical explanation'. Realism's assumption, for example, that human nature and state units are competitive and self-seeking leads to a particular ontology of what are considered the important questions to be addressed in International Relations.

The main criticism of positivism has been its neglect of epistemological and ontological issues. By assuming that 'facts exist in their own right and are epistemologically prior to theory' (Tooze 1985), positivism sees 'reality' as independent of knowledge (observation and explanation) of it (Cox, 1981). But rather than putting this forth as a particular and philosophically contested view, these assumptions are taken as given. This has led to a failure to recognize the role of beliefs and values in all perspectives (Murphy and Tooze, 1991: 18), and to make its own normatively based assumptions explicit.

Post-positivism rejects this distinction between the factual and normative, arguing that 'perspectives are themselves one of the interacting social forces in the political economy, as well as a basis for theories which seek to explain it' (Gill and Law, 1988: xvii) This is because perspectives determine what knowledge should be sought, how it should be sought, how it should be judged as valid, and how it should be applied in practice. Hence the belief in 'knowledge for the sake of knowledge' ignores the schemata that scholars implicitly hold of what knowledge is for, what Habermas (1971) calls 'knowledge-constitutive interest'. This interest may or may not be intentional. Indeed, it is the un-intentional promotion of social purposes which positivism accepts as natural and which post-positivism seeks to expose. Thus International Relations has never been 'a strictly academic, independent, critical scholarly enterprise' (Krippendorf, 1987).

The third inadequacy of the liberal-realist orthodoxy is its limited concept of power, focusing on the competitive pursuit of national interests by states and, to a lesser extent, the exercise of control over decision-making and observable outcomes. As an extension of the state, power in IO is defined in material (i.e. military or economic) terms. Thus there are no power relations distinct from those of the state system. This is what Lukes (1974) calls 'one-dimensional' power, with hegemony defined as 'a preponderance of material resources' (Keohane, 1984: 32).

This is a limited view of power because it provides an incomplete understanding of how power arises from structural forces in the GPE. *Structural power* is defined by Isaac (1987) as an 'enduring capacity to act, which may or may not be exercised on any particular occasion', deriving from 'the way in which power is implicated in the constitution of the conditions of interaction'. Power, in other words, can be intrinsic to a social context rather than a unique characteristic of individuals. In this way, power relations can exist beyond the conscious intent of individuals, deriving from 'social identities as participants in enduring, socially structured relationships' (1987: 74–5).

Overall, the liberal-realist orthodoxy has proved to be a barrier to the theoretical development of the study of IO, both by failing to recognize its own embedded assumptions and by setting limited criteria to assess and ultimately reject alternative approaches. As Walker points out, this has meant that 'a positive assessment of the plurality of theoretical perspectives is quickly closed off by the preference given to a highly specific and philosophically-contested account of what a proper research programme should look like' (1989: 164). It has been this neglect of fundamental debate in the theory and practice of IO that accounts for the lack of critical thought. It is the purpose of the following sections to develop such an approach, and to apply it in an expanded analysis of current debates on the reform of UN development activities.

GRAMSCI AND THE STUDY OF INTERNATIONAL ORGANIZATION

The shortcomings of liberal and realist-based approaches to IO described above are addressed in this section through the development of an expanded analytical framework. This framework is based on the selected ideas of Antonio Gramsci and is located within the emerging school of post-positivist approaches. Initially the application of Gramscian ideas to IO may seem anomalous, for two reasons. First, his work focused largely on the national contexts of Germany and Italy of the 1920s rather than on international relations. Second, it may seem regressive to some to return to a Marxist writer with Marxism apparently discredited since the end of the Cold War. However, it should be emphasized that this framework does not derive from Gramsci's materialist and structuralist view of world order. Nor does it delve into detailed interpretation of his work, which has given rise to a rich body of writing on political and social theory (Femia, 1981; Simon, 1982). Rather this chapter limits itself to appropriating two key concepts – consensus and hegemony – to enrich the study of IO. For this purpose the work of Robert Cox, notably his adaptation of Gramscian ideas to International Relations, is particularly helpful.

Gill summarizes a neo-Gramscian or historical materialist approach to International Relations as having three main characteristics. First, it recognizes the importance of both agent and structure in historical development and its analysis. Eschewing methodological individualism and reductionism, it is held that social relations consist of historic structures. Since 1945 there has been a historically specific ensemble of social structures and forces producing the globalization of the international political economy. This emerging world order is increasingly characterized by a 'global system of production and exchange', and the universalization of aspects of social life (Gill, 1993: 31). It is within this *global political economy* (GPE) that analysis of the UN's role in development should be located.

Second, a neo-Gramscian approach critiques the positivism of liberal and realist theories. Post-positivists hold that social reality and knowledge production are interdependent. The latter, in turn, cannot be separated from how concrete material interests are defined and realized. In historical and social change, therefore, there is a mutual or dialectical interaction between thought and action, theory and practice, the cognitive and the concrete. As Gill writes, 'Gramsci was able to show how, at least in this sense, theory is always for someone and for some purpose' (1993: 24).

Third, and related to the above, this approach views ethical and normative considerations as an integral part of analysis. Acknowledging that the role of the scholar cannot be separated from the social context which he or she studies, Gramsci argues for an explicit use of scholarship to further debates on social justice, legitimacy and moral credibility. As Gill writes,

> the normative goal of the Gramscian approach is to move towards the solution of the fundamental problem of political philosophy: the nature of the good society and thus, politically, the construction of an 'ethical' state and a society (1993: 25).

Applied to the study of IO, this expanded analytical framework begins with Cox's broader notion of IO as 'a historical process rather than a set of institutions' (Cox, 1980). It is held that IO plays a dual role in the GPE, 'promoting specific class interests while acting to establish principles of international relations which can command the widest possible legitimacy' (Linklater, 1992). Specific international institutions are also amalgams of material and ideological forces. Or as Cox writes,

> International institutions can no longer be thought of as separate self-contained agencies with specific tasks and programmes; they have to be thought of primarily as aggregations of influence on issue-areas which far overflow their own institutional boundaries (1980: 393).

To understand how IO emerges, is maintained and reproduced, it is useful to draw on Gramsci's concepts of consensus and hegemony. Of particular importance is the distinction between coercive and consensual leadership. The use of coercion or force to assert leadership is what Gramsci calls domination. The mobilization of the active *consent* of peripheral groups to a given order, through intellectual, moral and political leadership, is more effective and sustainable than coercion. *Hegemony* is achieved by core interests (in the form of classes, states or transnational actors) through a combination of coercive and consensual means. The latter is built on a system of alliances which must be continually readjusted and renegotiated to prevent peripheral groups from forming a potentially counter-hegemonic movement. This is done by granting limited concessions which are, or are at least perceived to be, in the interests of the periphery. However, such concessions do not threaten or displace the core (Simon, 1982: 37). It is important to note that Gramsci's ideas should not be mistaken for simple 'conspiracy theories'. To do so would be to undervalue his contribution to critical thinking. Rather his approach is akin to Lukes' (1974) 'three-dimensional' view of power, which holds that power need not be wielded intentionally or with purpose in order to exist. As well as being vested in individual actors, power can be structurally embedded in social constructs. Thus unequal power relations and conflicting interests may exist where the consent of subordinate groups is achieved.

Taking Gramsci's concepts of hegemony and consensus, we can then ask what are the core interests in the GPE and how does IO fit within this framework? Eschewing economistic and structuralist views of world order, this chapter adopts Cox's notion of a 'transnational managerial class'. The emerging core consists of public servants and officials in national and international agencies involved in economic management (e.g. World Bank, GATT, Ministry of Finance, Department of Trade and Industry), senior managers of TNCs, and experts concerned with the maintenance of the world economy (e.g. economists, technical specialists) (Cox, 1987: 359–60). Peripheral groups, in contrast, are defined as individuals, groups or states whose interests are subordinate to the emerging neo-liberal world order. It is this transnational taxonomy of core-periphery interests that can be used to develop a fuller understanding of current debates on UN reform. This can be achieved by locating proposed reforms within particular historic structures, and within material, institutional and ideological shifts in the GPE. It is concluded that there is a clear need for fundamental reform of UN development activities, but not necessarily in the direction envisioned by core interests.

THE UN'S CHANGING ROLE IN DEVELOPMENT: FORM AND REFORM

The development activities of the UN were conceived in 1945 as an extension of its role in maintaining peace and security. The failure of the League of Nations, and the Great Depression of the 1930s, led to the conviction that peace could not be built on military considerations alone but required attention to socio-economic needs. Furthermore, building and strengthening the post-war system required the integration of national economies within a peaceful world order. Thus the UN mandate was broadened, as stated in Article 55a of the UN Charter, to the promotion of 'higher standards of living, full employment, and conditions of economic and social progress and development'.

While peace and security issues became the primary responsibility of the Security Council, the Economic and Social Council (Ecosoc) was created in 1946 to coordinate UN development activities, including those of the specialized agencies. Under the authority of the UN General Assembly, the initially eighteen-member Ecosoc (enlarged to fifty-four in 1974) was to play a quasi-executive role with recommendatory powers. Under Ecosoc a variety of committees and commissions were created spanning a wide range of issues, including population, science and technology, human rights, urban development, narcotics and the status of women. In addition, development activities were taken up by the functionally defined specialized agencies, which were encouraged to incorporate development into their mandates. Finally, special funds and conferences were established over time to deal with particular areas of concern. These include the UN Children's Fund (1948), UN Conference on Trade and Development (1964) and UN Population Fund (1969).

To help finance these activities two additional funds were established – the Expanded Programme of Technical Assistance and the UN Special Fund – to channel voluntary contributions through designated executing agencies. They were consolidated in 1965 as the UN Development Programme (UNDP). More significant, however, was the role of the Bretton Woods institutions which, with the economic reconstruction of Western Europe and Japan, became increasingly focused on the needs of less developed countries (LDCs). In 1960 the Bank's development arm, the International Development Association, was created to provide soft loans to low-income countries. To give these initiatives a coordinated launch, the 1960s were proclaimed as the UN's First Development Decade.

Importantly, the unifying force underlying these initiatives was a strong degree of consensus, among both developed and developing countries, towards a particular development paradigm. From 1945 to the early 1960s, efforts focused on integrating developing countries into the *pax Americana* or hegemonic framework of post-war liberalism, sustained by US material and intellectual leadership (Cox, 1987, ch. 7). This 'stages of growth' or modernization approach advocated rapid economic growth (measured by GNP) through the building of industrial and economic infrastructure, and foreign investment (Rostow, 1968). UN activities, in the form of sector-based assistance, and the transfer of resources, technology and technical expertise from North to South, were strongly informed by this model (UN General Assembly, 1950). In this way LDCs were expected to emulate the development pattern of industrialized economies.

By the mid-1960s this development model, and the role of the UN within it, began to be challenged. During the immediate post-war period, modernization theory was sustained by rapid growth in the world economy fuelled by American economic policies (Cox, 1987: 244). With recovery in Western Europe and Japan creating greater competition for world markets, this growth slowed. By the late 1960s strains were apparent in the institutional mechanisms of the international monetary system, culminating in the US dollar crisis of 1971 (Solomon, 1982, ch. 11). For development scholars and policy-makers, the adverse effects on LDCs of these structural shifts brought forth new ideas. These ideas challenged the assumption that LDCs could follow in the footsteps of industrialized countries within the existing world economy. It was argued that the post-war liberal economy was structurally biased and perpetuated the unequal position of LDCs. Thus the idea that the gap between rich and poor would eventually be closed was rejected in favour of a fundamental restructuring of international economic relations. This became known as *dependency theory* (Myrdal, 1970; Sears, 1972).

These ideas were taken up by policy-makers in LDCs, increasingly mobilized politically under the banners of the Group of 77 and Nonaligned Movement. In the UN, LDC interests were articulated with greater force, beginning with UNCTAD in 1964 and peaking in 1974 with demands in the UN General Assembly for a New International Economic Order (NIEO). This was followed by similar demands in the specialized agencies including the New World Information and Communication Order (UNESCO), Equity in Orbit (ITU) and Health for All (WHO). Even in the World Bank, under President Robert McNamara, there was a rethinking of lending policies towards poverty alleviation under a 'basic needs' approach (McNamara, 1981).

In essence this was an attempt by LDCs to initiate a counter-hegemonic movement by challenging the fundamental ideas and core interests which sustained the post-war order. While core groups continued to be materially dominant, broad consent to *pax Americana* had broken down. LDCs thus sought to renegotiate the terms by which they participated in the world economy. Demands to redefine the UN's development activities, through changes in mandate and institutional mechanisms, were an important part of this movement. In December 1974 a wide-ranging dialogue was launched that would enhance 'the ability of the United Nations system to work with the necessary degree of speed, efficiency, and cohesion towards the establishment of a new international economic order'.[3] This was followed in May 1975 by the report

A New United Nations Structure for Global Economic Cooperation (UNGA, 1975), and the appointment of an Ad Hoc Committee on the Restructuring of the Economic and Social Sectors of the United Nations System to prepare proposals for the UN General Assembly on institutional reform.[4] The Committee considered eight problem areas including the role of Ecosoc, inter-agency coordination and financial management.

With the majority of UN votes in the hands of LDCs, these initiatives were successfully launched. It soon became clear, however, that there were disagreements between core and peripheral groups on the appropriate role of the UN. For example, in the Committee's report (1976), LDCs supported a substantially strengthened UNGA as 'the principal forum for negotiation and policy-making' on 'international economic, social and related problems' (UNGA, 1976). Similarly, it was proposed that Ecosoc would be 'the central forum for the discussion of international economic and social issues of a global or inter-disciplinary nature', and that UNCTAD play 'a major role' similar to GATT (UNGA, 1976: 9, 11). All other UN bodies were to 'act in conformity with [their] responsibilities' and 'should give full and prompt effect to their policy recommendations' (UNGA, 1976: 9, 11). The overall aim of these reforms was to centralize within the UNGA the variety of activities which had evolved in piecemeal fashion since 1945.

For core state and private interests, there were a number of objections to proposed reforms. Materially the reforms could lead to large-scale transfer of resources to LDCs. As Meltzer (1978) points out, by the 1970s four out of every five dollars within the UN system were already being spent on development activities. This would be achieved through a shift in decision-making power over the management of the world economy, from more exclusive institutions (i.e. World Bank, Group of Seven, OECD) to the more universally representative UN General Assembly. The latter was seen by core states as a more politicized body which would interfere with the management of the world economy by economic experts. And ideologically the reforms posed a serious challenge to political and economic neo-liberalism. It was held that the way forward for LDCs was to embrace rather than reject integration into the GPE.

With these objections, the task for core interests was to renegotiate the consent of peripheral groups. Since the mid-1980s this has been achieved through a combination of coercive and consensual tactics. Current reforms to UN development activities have been an important part of this new consensus which, once achieved, has laid the foundations for an emerging neo-liberal hegemonic order. This consensus has centred on an essentially positivist problematic which seeks to de-politicize and technocratize the UN development agenda.

CURRENT REFORM OF UN DEVELOPMENT ACTIVITIES: AN EMERGING NEO-LIBERAL HEGEMONIC ORDER

The current phase of UN development activities, from the mid-1980s, can be described as both a product of, and a contributor to, the reassertion of core

interests in the GPE. In terms of material interests, the accelerated globalization of the world economy has undermined the capacity of peripheral groups
to pursue alternative development strategies. This has been accompanied by
the consolidation of neo-liberal ideas and policies, notably the way in which
problems of peripheral groups and the appropriate role of the UN in addressing
them are defined. Support for these ideas in turn has been provided through
core IOs led by the World Bank and IMF. It is in this context of an emerging
neo-liberal hegemonic order that proposed reforms to the UN's development
activities can be more fully understood.

By the mid-1980s the instabilities in the world economy of the previous
decade had brought forth a restructuring of material interests in the GPE.
The globalized nature of production and exchange relations had led to a
growing core of state and private interests whose activities centred on transnational links across both developed and developing countries. At the same
time there have been more peripheral players in this globalization process. For
most LDC governments, especially non oil-exporting countries, mounting
foreign debt, declining export markets, terms of trade and foreign aid have
halted the growth of previous decades (Griffith-Jones, 1987). The important
exceptions have been the newly industrializing countries (NICs) which have
embraced the global marketplace with enthusiasm. On the whole, however,
given this material decline, LDCs have been less able to bargain with developed
countries.

These structural shifts in the GPE since the 1980s have been accompanied
by corresponding changes in development thinking among scholars and policy-
makers. In broad terms there has been a return to a preoccupation with
domestic policies within a framework of neo-liberal ideology. In contrast to
dependency theory, which attributes underdevelopment to the structure of the
world economy, neo-liberalism locates the problem within LDCs themselves –
corruption, the misuse of funds and, most importantly, an overly large role of
government in the economy (e.g. central planning, state ownership, welfare
programmes). Assuming the need to separate value-based political processes
from fact-based economic mechanisms, neo-liberal development policies have
focused on reforming government, strengthening the role of the market and
integrating LDCs more fully into the world economy.

In Gramscian terms neo-liberal ideas have been hegemonic in that they
have been sustained by renewed consensus among core and peripheral interests.
While some policies, such as the World Bank's structural adjustment programmes, have been imposed, coercion does not adequately explain the extent
to which such ideas have been accepted. It is argued that core interests have
supported neo-liberalism not only for material gain but also because there has
been a genuine belief that it will lead to development. For peripheral interests
(LDCs as well as the 'emerging market economies' of Central and Eastern
Europe), consent has been given with conviction that participation in the global
marketplace will benefit them. The intellectual void left by the failure of
dependency theory and centrally planned economies, as well as the rapid
growth of NICs, has given further legitimacy to neo-liberalism. It is for these

reasons that, by the mid-1990s, there are few economies in the world outside this emerging hegemonic order.

The institutional basis of the emerging hegemony has centred on IOs that play a key role in the maintenance of the world economy – notably the World Bank, IMF, GATT, OECD and Group of Seven. In order to strengthen this core, a number of studies have been initiated to reform UN development activities. Within the UN, a 1985 report by the UN Joint Inspection Unit, *Some Reflections on Reform of the United Nations*[5] criticized the sector-based institutional structure of the UN which produced narrowly-defined and un-coordinated programmes. The report was followed by the appointment in 1986 of a High-Level Inter-governmental Experts (Committee of Eighteen) to review the efficiency, administration and financial functioning of the UN. The re-commendations of the Committee's report, *Review of the Efficiency of the Administrative and Financial Functioning of the United Nations* (UNGA, 1986), were adopted in Resolution 41/213 by the UN General Assembly in December 1986. More recently Secretary-General Boutros-Ghali appointed a High-Level Intergovernmental Panel of Experts in January 1992 to make recommendations about the reform of UN economic and social activities (UNGA, 1993a). The panel's findings, submitted to the UN General Assembly in September 1992, led Boutros-Ghali to appoint Kenneth Dadzie as Special Adviser and Delegate of the Secretary-General responsible for overseeing their implementation (UNGA, 1993a and 1993b).

Outside the UN a number of other studies have contributed to the reform debate. In 1988 the UN Association of the US published a collection of papers generated by its UN Management and Decision-Making Project (Fromuth, 1988). The Nordic UN Project, commissioned by Scandinavian governments in the early 1990s, included an analysis of the UNDP, specialized agencies and Bretton Woods Institutions (Kalderen, 1991). In 1992 a specially appointed committee of the US Senate issued its report on UN reform (US Commission on Improving the Effectiveness of the United Nations, 1993) and in 1993 the Academic Council of the UN (ACUNS) published its report (Dirks et al., 1993). Finally there has continued to be keen scholarly attention to the subject (Beigbeder, 1987; Saksena, 1993; Taylor, 1993).

This flurry of debate in recent years shows that there has been no shortage of commitment to improving UN development activities. However, the aim of this chapter is not to evaluate the *content* of proposed reforms (i.e. whether they will work), but to locate the *process* of this debate within the context of the emerging neo-liberal hegemonic order. It is argued that the above studies have sought changes in the UN system parallel with neo-liberal reforms at the state level. They have been strongly positivist in their efforts to 'fix' the UN system and make it more technically efficient. In this way, it is hoped that UN development activities will be integrated within the institutional framework of the GPE. This conceptualization of the problematic has arisen not only from internal shortfalls in the UN system, but from broader shifts in material, ideological and institutional forces. It is only by recognizing this that the reform debate can be broadened into a more critical understanding of UN development activities.

To this end, three related questions can be said to lie at the heart of any debate on UN reform: who should decide what the UN does; who should pay for UN development activities; and how should these activities be carried out? These questions are essentially normative in that their resolution cannot be achieved through technical knowledge or expertise. Rather they must be the subject of ongoing discussion and negotiation amongst a plurality of interests. Yet it has been a positivist search for a final 'right' answer that has characterized debate so far.

An identity crisis: who should decide what the UN does?

Perhaps the most fundamental question regarding UN reform is who should decide what the UN does in the development sphere. At the heart of this question lies the issue of power. Given so many interests to be represented, and changes in these interests over time, finding an acceptable formula for them to participate in decision-making is clearly a daunting task.

Rather than recognizing the invariably normative basis of this question, current debate has been strongly positivist in seeking to rationalize decision-making. It has been assumed that by improving institutional mechanisms or the quality of technical information, better decisions can be reached. For example the World Bank's *World Development Report* (1993) on the health sector advocates cost-effectiveness measures to allocate resources among different 'burdens of disease' (World Bank, 1993). Similarly the frequently criticized lack of coordination of UN development activities has led to recommendations to merge UNCTAD, UNICEF, UNDP, UNFPA and UNEP 'to improve their work' (UNGA, 1986), decentralize decision-making of UN organizations to regional and country offices (UNGA, 1992 and 1993), create an intergovernmental board to oversee the development programmes of central organs (Murphy, 1992: 64), and alter the size of the UNDP's governing council and format of meetings (Kalderen, 1991). Overall the failings of the UN to solve the problems of LDCs have been attributed to inadequate information, misunderstanding or faulty operational procedures. Fundamental conflicts in values, beliefs and interests have not been addressed.

These efforts to 'de-politicize' the UN, by relying on so-called technical methods of decision-making, have been an important part of the emerging hegemony. As Murphy describes, there is a consensus once again between peripheral and core interests:

> The texts agreed upon in [the 1992 UNCTAD meeting] in Cartagena included references to a host of principles that earlier had only been championed by the OECD: an unambiguous preference for free markets; disregard of any notion of withdrawal from the world economy; an equation of democratization and the protection of human rights with development; and all the rhetoric regarding the need to decrease corruption and increase efficiency of governments in the South (1992: 63–4).

Yet, analysed more critically, UN development activities have been far from value-neutral. Framed within a particular historic bloc, and focused within core IOs which sustain them, these activities have been directed at the creation and maintenance of a neo-liberal world economy. Since the mid-1980s development assistance given by specialized agencies, such as the WHO and ITU (Lee, forthcoming), have supported a stronger role for TNCs. These market-led policies have received financial support from the World Bank and IMF within their own neo-liberal policy agendas. Other UN institutions, which in the past have sought radical change, have been gradually incorporated into this new order. In UNCTAD a project to put 'computer power at the service of governments in poor countries', for example, is intended to speed customs transactions, improve debt management and facilitate trade relations (*The Economist*, 1992).

More detailed analysis of the process of decision-making, and its impact on the nature of development activities, is required than can be offered here. There is a need to understand more critically the nature of the emerging consensus in the UN and, in particular, whether it derives from a real convergence of core and peripheral interests or, as argued here, from a hegemony of core international institutions and ideas.

The financial crisis: who should pay for UN activities?

The question of who should pay the financial costs of UN development activities relates closely to control over decision-making. From the 1980s demands for greater financial economies by major contributors to the UN budget (Geneva Group) have been a key issue in the reform debate. Pressure for change has been exerted through threatened or actual withdrawal of membership, and the reduction, withholding or delayed payment of contributions.[6] In response the UN General Assembly has adopted several resolutions, as well as the appointment of the Committee of Eighteen, to improve budgetary procedures, financial management and accountability, and levels of expenditure (UNGA, 1985). A number of bodies have also been created to evaluate programmes for cost-effectiveness. These include the Programme Coordination and Evaluation Unit of the UNDP (1985); the Evaluation Unit, Bureau of Programming and Management of the ILO; and the Programme Evaluation Unit, later renamed the Central Evaluation Section, of the UNHCR (1990).

It is clear that finances have been used by the Geneva Group as a 'carrot and stick' to support particular UN activities and reforms. This has been so in the development sphere, which is increasingly dependent on voluntary contributions (e.g. UNDP, special funds). While assessed contributions have stagnated under the principle of zero budget growth, extra-budgetary funds have rapidly increased.[7] Changes to overall funding levels have been less dramatic than the reallocation of funds to selected institutions and the increased conditionality attached to their use. For example, multilateral funding to the health sector is expected to increase substantially in coming years. However, most of this money will be channelled through the World Bank in the form of loans to LDCs (Buse, 1993). Those institutions favoured by recent funding trends have been those in which core interests have a greater say over how resources are used.

Core institutions have also defined the financial problems of the UN in particular ways, and given legitimacy to selected forms of knowledge and expertise to resolve them. Consistent with the neo-liberal development paradigm, which blames weaknesses in financial management and expenditure for persistent underdevelopment, the UN's problems are seen to be the need to achieve 'value for money'. This view has led to the enhancement of economic analysis and expertise in development.

However, the key normative question of who should pay for UN development activities (i.e. redistributive issues) has been given little attention. Given a reluctance to address the sensitive area of national-level responsibility for development, the UNDP's *Human Development Report* (1994) makes a valiant attempt to propose alternative global-level sources of development financing. These include taxes on global foreign exchange movements and pollution generators (e.g. per barrel of crude oil purchased), payment for services to ensure global human security (e.g. protection of the environment), and compensation for violations of principles of free trade (UNDP, 1994). It is doubtful, however, whether the UNDP's proposals will make a substantive impact given its uncertain future and marginal status in the emerging neo-liberal order. As with decision-making issues, debate on financial reform in core institutions has continued to take place within a narrowly inscribed problematic.

How should UN development activities be carried out?

The third question that lies at the heart of UN reform is how UN development activities should be carried out. Like decision-making and financing, different development strategies can be located within particular historic structures. During the post-war period, modernization theory sought to integrate LDCs into the rapidly evolving liberal international economy. Dependency theory from the mid-1960s stemmed from the decline of post-war hegemony. Since the early 1980s, the failure of import substitution and planned economic models to redress persistent inequalities between rich and poor has created an intellectual void in development theory. Neo-liberalism has stepped in to fill this gap.

The ascendance of a neo-liberal development strategy has given core interests a defining role in setting and implementing the policy agenda. As Ecosoc and UNDP have proved to be ineffectual shadows of their intended roles, the World Bank has become a source of intellectual leadership beyond its role as a lending institution. Together with core states, private interests and other IOs, the World Bank has increasingly defined the form of aid given to LDCs, the conditions under which it is given, and the criteria by which to judge its effective use. Other UN development activities have become supplementary to this strategy. As stated by Secretary-General Boutros-Ghali in justifying the recent truncation of the UN Secretariat's economic divisions, there was no point in doing things that the World Bank does better (*The Economist*, 1993).

The most notable feature of the neo-liberal development strategy has been the emphasis placed on the role of the private sector. As an extension of the globalization of production and exchange relations, and the 'retreat of govern-ment' in core states, LDCs have followed suit by encouraging economic growth through the cultivation of private sector initiatives. This has led to the removal of barriers to trade in goods and services, direct foreign investment, joint ventures and foreign exchange. Since the mid-1980s UN development activities have become an important part of these policy reforms. The World Bank's structural adjustment programmes have served as the overall framework for private sector-driven development strategies. Policies and programmes of UN special funds and specialized agencies have added support. These include UNICEF's Bamako Initiative to recover drug costs through user fees; the ITU's Maitland Commission, which encourages private investment for tele-communications; the creation of the UNDP Office for Project Services, which is 'self-financing' and 'expands or shrinks with its business'; and WHO's IWC Initiative to explore, *inter alia*, private sector initiatives for the health sector (UN 1993; WHO, 1993; UNICEF, 1993; Lee, forthcoming; Schachner, 1993).

Again, the aim is not to evaluate the content of such a development strategy, but to locate it within the emerging neo-liberal hegemonic order. There is a need to question the consensus surrounding this strategy as due not necessarily to its proven effectiveness, but to the ascendance of core interests in the GPE. Indeed, there is growing evidence that World Bank-led development projects have had adverse social and environmental effects (Chaterjee, 1992). Rather than embracing a 'one size fits all' development model, with current reforms to UN development activities tied to it, it is argued that the reform debate must be broadened. A globalized world order does not mean a homogeneity of needs and interests. Therefore development strategies are needed which take into account, for example, local participation, social conditions, cultural values and environments. These must be evaluated not simply in terms of technical merit and economic viability, but normatively in relation to the diverse aspira-tions of local populations. It is only by raising such questions that true debate can take place.

CONCLUSION: DEVELOPMENT WITHIN A NEO-LIBERAL HEGEMONIC ORDER?

The current flurry of interest in UN reform presents an important op-portunity to strengthen the role of multilateralism in international relations. This chapter has argued that the reform debate so far has been narrowly conceived because of continued orthodoxy in the study of IO. This has been evident in the three main inadequacies of liberal-realist approaches: state-centrism, positivism and a limited concept of power. This theoretical narrow-ness has had practical implications by shaping how problems of the UN, and the solutions deemed appropriate to address them, have been defined.

The expanded analysis of this chapter seeks a more critical understanding of the current reform debate. This is achieved by locating it within an emerging neo-liberal hegemonic order characterized by core material interests, institu-tions and ideas. While there are clear problems with the operational aspects of

UN development activities, the emphasis on finding technical solutions belies the need to understand underlying power relations within the UN system and the GPE.

By placing power relations at the centre of analysis, the debate on UN reform can be significantly broadened. This requires three essentially normative questions to be addressed. First, who should decide what the UN does raises key issues of human rights, legitimacy and power in international relations. A broadened reform agenda would seek ways to widen, rather than narrow, participation in UN decision-making. Second, who should pay for UN development activities concerns the issue of responsibility for the global poor. The financing of the UN invariably involves redistributive issues which cannot be resolved by improved financial management. Third, the question of how UN development activities should be carried out must be answered through real debate between different development strategies. Such strategies would vary in their aims, the means put forth to achieve those aims, and the interests which benefit from them.

NOTES

1. The UN family here includes the UN system, its specialized agencies and special funds, as well as the World Bank, IMF and GATT.
2. See Gill, 1993, for how Gramscian thought has recently been applied to IR.
3. UN Doc.A/32/PV.109, p. 6.
4. UN General Assembly Resolution 3362, 16 September 1975.
5. Bertrand Report, 1985.
6. The US government has been the main initiator of this pressure as contained in the Kaussebaum Amendment to the US Foreign Relations Act of August 1985, and the Gramm-Rudman Balanced Budget Act of December 1985. In August 1993, Secretary-General Boutros-Ghali reported that the UN was owed US$2 billion, mainly by the US. See also Philps, A., 1993.
7. UN General Assembly Resolution 40/237, 18 December 1985.
8. For a discussion of WHO see Walt, 1993. See also Saksena, 1993.

REFERENCES

Archer, C., 1992, *International Organizations*, London, Routledge.
Beigbeder, Y., 1987, *Management Problems in United Nations Organizations: Reform or Decline?*, London, Pinter.
Bertrand, M., 1985, *Some Reflections on Reform of the United Nations*, Geneva, UN Joint Inspection Unit (UN Doc. JIU/REP/85/9).
Buse, K., 1993, *The World Bank and International Health Policy: Genesis, Evolution and Implications*, M.Sc. Dissertation, London, London School of Hygiene and Tropical Medicine.
Chatterjee, P., 1992, 'How to Waste $5 Billion a Year', *Guardian*, 7 August.
Cox, R., 1980, 'The Crisis of World Order and the Problem of International Organization in the 1980s', *International Journal*, 35(2): 370–85.
Cox, R., 1981, 'Social Forces, States, and World Orders: Beyond International Relations Theory', *Millennium*, 10(2): 126–550.

Cox, R., 1987, *Production, Power and World Order: Social Forces in the Making of History*, New York, Columbia University Press.

Cox, R., 1992, 'Multilateralism and World Order', *Review of International Studies*, 18(2): 162–80.

Dirks, G., Matthews, R., Rauf, T., Riddell-Dixon, E. and Sjlander, C., 1993, *The State of the United Nations, 1993: North–South Perspectives*, Providence, RI, Academic Council on the United Nations System.

The Economist, 1992, 'The Man from UNCTAD', 4 July: 76.

Femia, J., 1981, *Gramsci's Political Thought: Hegemony, Consciousness and the Revolutionary Process*, Oxford, Oxford University Press.

Fromuth, P. (ed.), *A Successor Vision: The United Nations Tomorrow*, Lanham, MD, UN Association of the US.

Gill, S., 1993, *Gramsci, Historical Materialism and International Relations*, Cambridge, Cambridge University Press.

Gill, S. and Law, D., 1988, *The Global Political Economy: Perspectives, Problems and Policies*, Brighton, Wheatsheaf.

Griffith-Jones, S., 1987, 'The International Debt Problem - Problems and Solutions', *WIDER Working Paper No. 2*, Helsinki.

Habermas, J., 1971, *Knowledge and Human Interests*, Boston, MA, Beacon.

Hoffman, S., 1977, 'An American Social Science: International Relations', *Daedalus*, 106(3): 41–60.

Isaac, J., 1987, *Power and Marxist Theory: A realist view*, Ithaca, NY, Cornell University Press.

Kalderen, L., 1991, 'The United Nations and the Bretton Woods Institutions', in Nordic UN Project, *The United Nations, Issues and Options*, Stockholm, Almqvist & Wiskell.

Keohane, R., 1984, *After Hegemony: Cooperation and Discord in the World Political Economy*, Princeton, NJ, Princeton University Press.

Keohane, R., 1989, *International Institutions and State Power: Essays in International Relations Theory*, Boulder, CO, Westview.

Keohane, R. and Nye, J., 1977, *Power and Independence*, Boston, Little, Brown.

Krippendorf, E., 1987, 'The Dominance of American Approaches in International Relations', *Millennium*, 16(2): 207–14.

Lee, K., forthcoming, *Global Telecommunications Regulation: A Political Economy Perspective*, London, Pinter.

Linklater, A., 1992, 'The Question of the Next Stage of International Relations Theory: A Critical-Theoretical Point of View', *Millennium*, 21(1): 77–98.

Lukes, S., 1974, *Power: A Radical View*, London, Macmillan.

Maclean, J., 1981, 'Marxist Epistemology, Explanation of "Change" and the Study of International Relations', in Buzan, B. and Jones, R.B.J. (eds), *Change and the Study of International Relations: The Evaded Dimension*, London, Pinter.

McNamara, R., 1981, *The McNamara Years at the World Bank: Major Policy Addresses of R.S. McNamara 1968–1981*, Washington, World Bank.

Martin, L., 1992, 'Interests, Power and Multilateralism', *International Organization*, 46(4).

Meltzer, R., 1978, 'Restructuring the United Nations System: Institutional Reform Efforts in the Context of North–South Relations', *International Organization*, 32(4): 993–1017.

Mitrany, D., 1948, 'The Functional Approach to World Organization', *International Affairs*, 24(3): 350–630.

Murphy, C., 1992, 'The United Nations' Capacity to Promote Sustainable Development:

The Lessons of a Year that "Eludes all Facile Judgement"', in *The State of the United Nations: 1992*, Providence, RI, ACUNS.

Murphy, C. and Tooze, R. (eds), 1991, *The New International Political Economy*, Boulder, CO, Lynne Rienner.

Myrdal, G., 1970, *The Challenge of World Poverty*, New York, Pantheon.

Philps, A., 1993, 'Lack of cash threatens UN peace troops', *Daily Telegraph*, 15 May: 12.

Rosenberg, J., 1990, 'What's the Matter with Realism?', *Review of International Studies*, 16(4).

Rostow, W., 1968, *The Stages of Economic Growth*, Cambridge, Cambridge University Press.

Saksena, K., 1993, *Reforming the United Nations: The Challenge of Relevance*, London, Sage.

Schachner, M., 1993, 'Office for Project Services (OPS): Organizational Reform in the Field of Development Cooperation', Paper presented to the ECPR Joint Sessions of Workshops, University of Leiden, April.

Seers, D., 1972, 'The Meaning of Development', in Bastor, N. (ed.), *Measuring Development*, London, Frank Cass.

Simon, R., 1982, *Gramsci's Political Thought: An introduction*, London, Lawrence & Wishart.

Solomon, R., 1982, *The International Monetary System, 1945–1981*, New York, Harper & Row.

Taylor, P., 1993, *International Organization in the Modern World*, London, Pinter.

Tooze, R., 1985, 'International Political Economy', in Smith, S. (ed.), *International Relations: British and American Perspectives*, London, Basil Blackwell.

Tooze, R., 1988, 'Liberal International Political Economy', in Jones, R.B.J. (ed.), *The Worlds of Political Economy: Alternative Approaches to the Study of Contemporary Political Economy*, London, Pinter.

United Nations, 1993, UN Doc. A/C.5/47/88, 4 March.

United Nations General Assembly, 1950, *Measures for the Economic Development of Underdeveloped Countries*, New York.

United Nations General Assembly, 1975, *A New United Nations Structure for Global Economic Cooperation*, Report of the Group of Experts on the Structure of the United Nations System (UN Doc.E./AC.62.9), New York.

United Nations General Assembly, 1986, *Report of the Group of High-Level Intergovernmental Experts to Review the Efficiency of the Administrative and Financial Functioning of the United Nations (Committee of Eighteen)*, UN Doc. A/41/49, New York.

United Nations General Assembly, 1993a, *Report of the Special Adviser and Delegate of the Secretary-General on the Reform of the Economic and Social Sectors*, 7 February, New York.

United Nations General Assembly, 1993b, *Review of the Efficiency of the Administrative and Financial Functioning of the United Nations* (UN Doc. A/C.5/47/88, 4 March), New York.

UNICEF, 1993, *The Bamako Initiative, Interim Progress Report*, New York, UNICEF Executive Board.

US Commission on Improving the Effectiveness of the United Nations, 1993, *Defining Purpose: The U.N. and the Health of Nations*, Washington, US Congress.

Walker, R.W., 1989, 'History and Structure in the Theory of International Relations', *Millennium*, 18(2).

World Health Organization, 1993, *IWC, Health Development in Countries in Greatest Need*, Geneva.

9

Conflict and cooperation in a context of change: a case study of the Senegal river basin

Anne Guest

INTRODUCTION

Water, like oil, is an essential and finite resource. Unlike oil, it cannot be replaced by a substitute commodity. Since a large proportion of the available freshwater resources of the world is found in international rivers – that is, rivers which are shared by more than one country – the potential for zero-sum conflict, or for a 'tragedy of the commons' (Hardin, 1987) would seem to be extremely large, especially in areas which rely on increasing supplies of water for development (Howlett and Thomas, 1993). The Jordan valley and the basin of the Euphrates are often cited as examples of a possible future conflict scenario.

An analysis of when and where conflict might occur, and with what degree of intensity has been offered by Robert Mandel (Mandel, 1991). He looked at disputes over fourteen international rivers in different parts of the world, and discovered two distinct patterns:

— that cases focusing on border definition issues involved more severe conflict than those dealing with pollution – i.e. that the issue at stake had a significant effect on the degree of conflict; and
— that cases triggered by human-initiated technological disruptions displayed more severe conflict than those triggered by natural disaster – i.e. that change caused conflict, and that the particular form of the agent of that change was a factor in determining the intensity of the conflict.

Mandel also concluded that conflict was more intense in situations of high mutual antagonism prior to the dispute over the river; that a combination of high scarcity and high inequality in access to the river's resources was likely to lead to greater conflict; that conflict levels were low when the countries sharing the river were equally balanced in terms of power; that developed nations were neither more nor less likely to be involved in conflict than developing countries; and that recent disputes had not differed in intensity from earlier ones.

The summary of his findings stated that conflict potential was greatest in basins with 'non-cooperative settings, environmental imbalances, and power asymmetries, perhaps particularly those involving boundary definition issues or human-initiated technological disruptions'. On the basis of these conclusions Mandel predicted that unless attention was focused on achieving integrated river basin development in areas of potential conflict, 'water war may well be just around the bend' (Mandel, 1991: 38).

My hunch was that this was not the case. Though Mandel's conclusions could not be disputed, he had explored conflict in a vacuum which had resulted in an unnecessarily gloomy picture. The international river basins which I had examined appeared to display an unusual level of cooperation. Even in the crucial area of the Middle East, none of the wars since 1948 could be directly attributed to water (Cooley, 1984).[1] Under the surface belligerency between Israel and its neighbours, signs of a will to cooperate had been increasing at a time when the shortage of water was becoming more acute. Israel had shared irrigation technology with Jordan;[2] Israeli farmers were being charged a far higher price for water in preparation for a reorientation of the economy away from irrigated agriculture. In 1991, Arnon Soffer of the Israeli Foreign Ministry was quoted as saying: 'Jordan is desperately short of water, despite having imported highly efficient irrigation technology. In my view we could give 50 mcm of water to Jordan without difficulty. The water is not worth fighting about' (Pearce, 1991).

Certain questions arose from discovering these instances of cooperation within international river basins:

— was the perception of more cooperation and less conflict than would be anticipated from Mandel's analysis a correct one?
— if so, how had this situation come about?
— was it the result of a factor specific to water as a resource, or to the international river basin as a regional unit, or to the case under study?
— what are the implications for the direction of international relations theory?

The aim of this chapter is to present some preliminary findings from a research project on cooperation and conflict in the particular context of the development of the Senegal river basin. The first section describes the methodology of the study, the middle section presents the findings from the case study, and the final section attempts to relate these findings to International Relations.

METHODOLOGY

The first problem in addressing such an extended range of questions was one of methodology. Originally the aim of the project was to establish a theoretical framework within which individual cases could be examined. This proved impossible. The number of issues arising from international river basins, and the range of concepts which were applicable to them, extended beyond the boundaries of any existing theory. Attempts to apply several theories simultaneously resulted in total confusion.

The project therefore changed its focus from the theoretical to the empirical. Ideally an empirically based study would have examined several river basins in order to make a positive identification of common factors. Unfortunately restrictions on the time and length of the study meant that only one basin could be examined in the necessary detail.

The international river basin which was chosen for immediate analysis was the Senegal. The Senegal river rises in the highlands of Guinea, flows through the western edge of Mali, and then forms the boundary between Senegal and Mauritania until it reaches the sea. The reasons for choosing this basin were:

— that the river crossed a semi-arid area;
— that the three riparian states[3] were all under-developed;
— that the legal agreement for the development of the Senegal basin was one of the most advanced in the world; and
— that despite continuous cooperation over the development of the basin, two of the riparian states – Mauritania and Senegal – had been involved in a dispute which was so serious that diplomatic relations had been severed for nearly three years (1989–92). The dispute had centred on the river.

The combination of a potentially conflictual environment with the fact of seventeen years of cooperation broken by a serious conflict seemed to offer a chance to understand some of the mechanisms of cooperation and conflict in international river basins. The methodology adopted for the study was foreign policy decision-making analysis. The resources used in the analysis were records in archives and government offices in Senegal; documentary and published material from French, English and other Senegalese sources; and interviews with diplomats, government officials, employees of the river basin organization, NGOs and experts in the fields of engineering, hydrology, economics, geography, development studies and anthropology. By a process of comparison and deduction from the facts obtained, an understanding of the causes of cooperation and conflict gradually emerged.

THE SENEGAL BASIN

Before attempting any explanations, the first step was to examine the situation as it appeared. Was cooperation a surface illusion or was it a reality reflected in day-to-day cooperative behaviour? What part did the 1989–92 conflict between Senegal and Mauritania play in the behaviour patterns focused on the valley? The following section looks at the reality of cooperation.

The reality of cooperation

The organization currently responsible for the development of the river – Organisation pour la mise en valeur du fleuve Sénégal (OMVS) – was the culmination of attempts to cooperate which began at independence. Founded in 1972, the OMVS is governed by two basic agreements (Godana, 1985; Parnall and Utton, 1976). The first – *Convention Relative au Statut du Fleuve Sénégal*, 11 March 1972 – established the international status of the river and made a declaration of intent for its development. The second – *Convention Relative au Statut Juridique des Ouvrages Communs*, 21 December 1978 – agreed on the common ownership of the major river projects: the Manantali dam in Mali, the Diama dam in the Delta, the improved river ports at St-Louis (Senegal) and Kayes (Mali), and all associated works.

The OMVS is a permanent body consisting of an annual meeting of heads of state at which the major decisions are taken, a biannual meeting of the Conseil des Ministres at which routine decisions are taken, and the Haut Commissariat, which oversees the execution of the decisions. The first task of the OMVS was to commission studies of the river, draw up plans and seek international financing for its projects. Its success in doing this was confirmed by its achievement in completing two large dams (opened in 1986 and 1987) in one of the poorest areas of the world.

One of the shadows over this story of successful cooperation was the failure to prepare land suitable for irrigation at the rate that had been anticipated. Of the 375,000 hectares earmarked for development, only 56,736 hectares had been prepared for use by 1988 (Seck, 1991). Though this failure could be attributed partly to the unexpectedly high costs of preparing the land, its main cause was that the élite involved in making the cooperation agreements had not demonstrated the relevance of cooperation to the farmers of the valley. The traditional style of cultivation in the valley – a combination of rain-fed and flood recession agriculture – was ideally suited to the high-risk conditions of the area. Irrigated agriculture appeared to involve greater immediate risks, which were not offset by the promise of increased returns in the long term (Adams, 1977 and 1985). Many of the people in the valley therefore proved resistant to the implications of cooperation. Cooperation, to them, had, and has, a very hollow ring.

Nevertheless, cooperation seemed to have real substance at the level of the élite, and the benefits of this cooperation should not be dismissed lightly. The conflict of 1989–92 gave a demonstration of its value. The conflict arose from a tribal clash between herders and farmers in the valley. Incidents between the two groups were common because, though their use of land could be complementary in good years, in years of drought it was inevitably competitive. The situation was aggravated by the increased value of land in Mauritania following the construction of the dams. Of the two racial groups in Mauritania, the Moors had always dominated the black Africans. The black Africans had farmed in the valley because the Moors had not wished to do so. Once irrigation opened up possibilities of higher returns, the Moors began to move into the valley, and the black African farmers were squeezed off their land. Their marginal existence became even more perilous: they could not afford to give any concession to the herders. In this sense – by raising the stakes in the perennial competition for land – cooperation had created conflict.

At the same time the impetus generated by cooperation within the OMVS was instrumental in solving the dispute. The Conseil des Ministres continued to meet from 1989 to 1992, and was attended by representatives of all three states.[4] The exact impact of this continuing contact on the course of the dispute is not known, but an informed guess would suggest that it was a constant reminder to the decision-makers in the two states of the advantages of cooperation. It is certain that strong influences were at work during the three years of the dispute to prevent a very tense situation spilling over into war.

What, then, could be concluded about the reality of cooperation in the Senegal basin? For the people of the valley, cooperation on the élite model appeared to have very little to offer. But for the decision-making élite, co-operation had become more than a signature on a piece of paper. It had become engrained in the decision-making habits of the states. Why was this so?

The basis of cooperation

The decision of the three riparian states to cooperate over the development of the river was a conscious choice. In order to explain this choice the case study focused on four areas:

1. Internal economic factors: how far was each state economically dependent on the river in the present, and for the future?
2. External economic factors: was financial aid a significant factor in the economy of the area and did this give the donors a chance to influence policy decisions?
3. External political factors: did the OMVS reflect an environment of regional cooperation?
4. Internal political factors: what was the role of the state leaders and how were they influenced by those whom they governed?

Internal economic factors   The extent to which each state depended on the river varied. Senegal's economy was based on the groundnut, which was grown in the central basin of the country. The development of the river basin was seen as a means of diversifying the economy into cereal crops, and at the same time attaining food self-sufficiency. The valley was thought to offer hope of economic independence in the future.

Mauritania had access to foreign exchange through its exports of iron ore and fish products, but it was reluctant to rely on these to buy all its food from abroad. The only area in the country where arable farming could be practised was the Senegal valley. Much of the rest of the country was desert. In past years the nomads living in the desert had made a significant contribution to the economy with their herds of camels and cattle, but repeated drought had made their traditional way of life untenable. The emphasis on the valley as the only source of food production had intensified, therefore.

Mali, unlike the other two countries, had access to arable land and adequate water in another river valley – that of the Niger. Mali viewed the Senegal river as a source of power for the development of the mineral deposits in the west of the country, and as a communication link to the ocean. (Mali is land-locked.) Though Mali's economic expectations of the valley related to industry and communication rather than agriculture, they were – as in the other two countries – part of the myth of future prosperity.

For all three countries there appeared to be significant future advantages to be gained from the development of the valley. Since development would be impossible without cooperation (because of the relative positions of the three countries on the river) there was a powerful economic incentive to cooperate.

External economic factors: aid   Aid has always been very important to the Senegal basin countries (World Bank, 1991: 242). The question to be addressed here is whether the high levels of assistance gave the donors any hold over decision-making processes. The conclusion seems to be that they did not. There are several reasons for this. The first is that there was no dominant donor. Though aid from France was the principal input to the area in the early 1960s, the desire for independence from the former colonial power led Mauritania and Mali to make conscious efforts to attract other sources of funding. In Mauritania French aid was balanced by Arab aid; in Mali it was balanced by aid from the Eastern bloc. Even in Senegal, where aid was still predominantly French, President Senghor was able to control French influence by playing on French guilt over the colonial past.

This general balancing of donors by recipients was not reflected in the funding for the OMVS projects. Here the finance was overwhelmingly Arab. There is some evidence that the Arabs had a cautionary effect on the formula-tion of the projects,[5] but despite this the OMVS was allowed to go ahead with its plans to build two dams which were known to be economically incompatible. The explanation for this lies in the donor environment of the early 1970s. Oil was creating an embarrassment of riches and any well-designed project – from the engineering point of view – was welcomed even if its economic potential was dubious.

The last point to be made is that not only did the donor community have very little influence on the decisions made by the riparian states, but that its preference – when it had one – was strongly in favour of regional cooperation. This applied to the USSR, the USA and the Arab world, as well as to France and the European Community.

External political factors: the environment of regional cooperation   There were strong historic and ethnic ties between the countries of the Senegal basin. They shared a common experience of colonization under France as units of French West Africa (AOF). Within the AOF they were treated as parts of the same economic entity, organized for the benefit of French trade. Though the river valley was not a significant part of the AOF economy, it had its own links in the shared ethnic origins of the population, and in a system of informal trading.

When political independence was granted in 1960, there was a conscious realization that true independence – which relied on economic viability – would not be possible without cooperation. Mali and Senegal tried to establish a formal unit for cooperation by joining together in the Mali Federation. The diverse views of the two leaders, Keita and Senghor, led to its rapid demise. But other regional organizations quickly followed: the UDAO, a customs union, which evolved into the UDEAO in 1965; the UAM, a group for economic harmonization, which became OCAM in 1965; river basin organizations for Lake Chad (1964) and the Niger (1963); and on a wider scale, the OAU. The leaders of post-independence French West Africa were regional cooperation addicts. A quotation from President Keita of Mali illustrates the philosophy of the leaders of the independent French West African states:

> We are convinced that the States of Africa will never be independent, in the full sense of the word, if they remain small States, more or less opposed to one another, each having its own policy, its own economy, each taking no account of the policy of the others (Keita, 1961).

It was generally accepted by these leaders that inter-state conflict was dysfunctional (Zartman, 1966). The threat to the independent existence of their state was seen to be the ex-colonial power, and the most potent weapon against this threat was cooperation. This was the milieu in which the OMVS functioned. It appears to have been a context peculiar to the African continent.

Internal political factors: leaders and decision-making processes The original leaders of the three states – Senghor (Senegal), Keita (Mali), Ould Daddah (Mauritania) – had a decisive effect on the course of regional cooperation. All three had received a French education, and were of a philosophical bent. They agreed on the necessity of cooperation for the peaceful development of their countries. They located their vision of true independence within a context of regional interdependence.[6]

Nor were they hampered by the need to explain and justify their decisions to their people. Political consciousness had not yet been aroused among the mass of the population. The valley population, which might have objected to the impact of the plans on its livelihood, was, in each of the three states, a long way from the centre of power. This meant that political consciousness was even more slow to develop than elsewhere, and that even if voices had been raised they would not have been heard. Among those who had been educated in each state there was a jostling for power in the early years, but the goal was personal advancement and not the resolution of any particular issue. The style of government was that of the 'princely ruler', an 'arbitrating, compromising tactical ruler who seeks power and authority, but not to the point of denying the political and ideological independence of others' (Jackson and Rosberg, 1982). Only when the ruler failed in his role as arbitrator could he be removed.[7]

CONCLUSIONS FROM THE CASE STUDY

Clearly the level of cooperation in the development of the Senegal river basin had been very high. Consideration of the four areas leading to the 1972 OMVS Agreements reveal interesting and possibly unexpected factors behind this cooperation. The river was seen as a source of economic expectation for the future. It was also seen as a focus for regional integration. This integration was not the result of economic pressure from donors: it came from a conscious decision taken by three particular and exceptional leaders – Senghor, Keita and Ould Daddah. Their decision was taken in the environment of post-independence Africa, where cooperation was seen as a means of combating weakness to achieve future strength and independence. It was also taken against a background of shared history and culture. But it was a decision that was not advantageous at all levels. Although the state might profit from the large-scale projects on the river, the people of the valley were exposed to higher risks in the day-to-day management of their resources. This was not a consideration that the three leaders were forced to acknowledge in 1972, because their style of 'princely rule' absolved them from direct responsibility to the people.

Since 1972, cooperation has continued to flourish and has resulted in the realization of some of the goals of the OMVS. The two large dams at Diama and Manantali were completed in 1986 and 1987. In all three countries some land has been prepared for irrigated agriculture. Nevertheless substantial goals remain unfulfilled: there are no turbines at Manantali, so there is no extra power supply for Bamako or Nouakchott, or for the development of the mineral resources in the west of Mali; the rate of development of irrigated farming has been disappointing and most farmers continue to rely on traditional agricultural practices; navigation down the river from Mali to the sea has remained nothing more than a dream.

In addition, from 1989 to 1992 Senegal and Mauritania were embroiled in a dispute which verged on open war. What had happened to the cooperative environment? What were the issues that had challenged it? Were they the issues that Mandel had identified – border definition issues, human-initiated technological disruption, high scarcity of resources and high inequality of access – pressures which related specifically to the regime of the river, or were they more generalized pressures resulting from events outside the region? In an attempt to answer these questions, the following section investigates the background against which the 1989–92 conflict took place.

From the particular to the universal?

In the world at large the period from 1989 to 1992 was dominated by the thawing of the Cold War. In many African countries the thaw was significant because the Cold War had been played out in surrogate conflicts on their territories.[8] The Senegal region had never been involved in the superpower conflict in this way. Geo-politically the region was insignificant. It had few resources and its territory was not strategically placed as a springboard to other areas. Only to France, as the old colonial power, was the region important.

Nevertheless, the issues which have arisen in the course of the development of the river reflect some of the most pressing global issues engaging the post-Cold War world. These issues lay at the root of the conflict in the area. It is not easy to separate out these issues since they were closely interrelated, but in order to facilitate awareness it is useful to consider them under the rubrics of 'nationalism', ethnicity and the state', 'development' and 'the environment'.

Nationalism, ethnicity and the state

Earlier in this chapter reference was made to the dispute between the Moors and black Africans in Mauritania for land in the Senegal valley. The origins of this dispute lie prior to independence, to when the French carved up their empire into administrative areas, one of which they chose to call Mauritania. Mauritania had no natural identity. It lumped together a desert land of nomadic Moors, and a river valley – at its southern extremity – peopled by black Africans. The Moors formed 80 per cent of the population and the black Africans 20 per cent. The Moors naturally looked to the Arabs of the north, and the black Africans to their ethnic relations in Senegal and Mali.

The first president of Mauritania – Ould Daddah – set about constructing a national identity, making a virtue of the fundamental division within his state. He presented Mauritania as a bridge between the Arab and African worlds. As long as each group was relatively satisfied by the division of economic and political spoils in the state, Mauritania could be envisaged as a bridge. But the droughts that drove the Moors out of the desert and onto the lands of the Senegal valley upset the balance to such an extent that coexistence no longer seemed possible. Fifty thousand black Africans were driven across the river into Senegal by the Moors during the 1989–92 dispute.[9] Their papers were taken from them, so that they had no proof of their identity as Mauritanians. At the time of writing, they are still in camps on the Senegalese bank of the river, refugees whose state refuses to acknowledge their right of citizenship.

This situation is an uncomfortable and dramatic illustration of the post-Cold War debate over the nature of the state, and of its value as the accepted unit of political and social organization. It highlights the discrepancy existing between the minimalist definition of the state – implicit in the United Nations recognition of states in terms of bounded territory[10] – and the more comprehensive definition of the state which adds to the idea of state as 'territory', not only 'legitimate institutional authority' and 'organisational capacity', but also 'popular recognition' (Jackson and Rosberg, 1984, 1986, 1990).[11]

Though many African states have suffered a weakness of institutional authority and organizational capacity, Mauritania has not been one of them. The question hanging over the statehood of Mauritania is the more fundamental question of popular recognition. Crawford Young (1988) suggests that popular recognition of the state depends on a common acceptance of the identity of the state: 'The state is an idea, deeply implanted in the minds of its citizens and officials, as something abstract yet personal which is much more than the simple sum of its institutions of governance'. To the people of Mauritania, the idea of Mauritania which Ould Daddah created has gone. Mauritania is no longer a bridge. It is the battleground for the competing economic and political claims of the two racial groups within its borders. At stake are the lives of fifty thousand refugees who are living in limbo on the Senegalese bank of the river.

Development

One of the issues at the heart of the battle taking place in Mauritania is the question of the nature of development. It is also an issue which has been taken up by the Senegalese farmers with their government.[12] In both Senegal and Mauritania the conflict is between the farmers who have cultivated the valley for many years, and the government, which has imposed large-scale plans for development in the area.

When the OMVS plans for the valley were drawn up, the needs of the resident population were ignored since it was assumed that they would ultimately benefit from the shift to a more reliable and productive form of agriculture. Socio-economic studies of the valley were not considered important. The people were not consulted.

This lack of consultation has had negative effects for both sides. From the governments' point of view the economic benefits of the dam schemes in terms of food self-sufficiency have not been realized because the farmers have not cooperated in the changes. They cannot afford the increased risks of capital outlay for seeds and tools when the government is offering no insurance against failure. They use irrigated land when conditions are good, but revert to their traditional methods – and mixed economy – at times of risk. This is not the way to reap the benefits of a multi-million pound dam development scheme.

In both countries, members of the wealthy élite have attempted to move into the valley to take advantage of the new capital-intensive production methods, and cut out the traditional farmers. In Senegal, the Mourides[13] tried to buy land, but were hounded out by the local farmers. In Mauritania, the black farmers were in no position to stand up to the Moorish élite. In 1983 the land law was changed, revoking the traditional land rights of the farmers, and allowing Moors to move onto the land.

A gulf exists between the governments of Senegal and Mauritania and the people of the valley. Governments think of development in terms of big schemes to generate foreign reserves, while farmers think of development in terms of improving what exists (Adams, 1992; Pearce, 1992; Scudder, 1989 and 1991). This is an old debate: is development about increasing GNP or increasing and equalizing the standard of living of each member of the population? But there is also a new debate here about the legitimacy of the state which chooses to ignore the needs of a large section of its population (Tordoff, 1993). How can it be said to have any popular recognition?

The environment

The final set of issues which directly contributed to the 1989–92 conflict are environmental. Concerns have been raised – especially in the developed world – that environmental degradation will lead to pressure which will result in wars over resources, or 'greenwars' (Bennett, 1991). The conflict between Senegal and Mauritania could be seen as a textbook illustration of this scenario. Pressure on the resources of the valley, because of past droughts and because of the increased value of the land following the completion of the dams, reached breaking-point. A minor incident between farmers and herders triggered off a conflict which took three years to resolve.

But was this simply a 'greenwar'? The 1989–92 dispute involved the racial conflict in Mauritania, which challenged the identity of the state and revived an old territorial dispute over the position of the boundary between Senegal and Mauritania along the river.[14] None of this would have occurred if the river valley had not been developed according to the vision of the three leaders in 1972, who had no concept of the necessity of allowing for a synthesis of economic, social and environmental considerations.[15] Cooperation – an admirable idea in theory – had actually led to conflict.

CONCLUSION

This study of cooperation and conflict in the Senegal river basin has revealed some of the unforeseen problems that can arise when the concept of cooperation is put into practice. Seventeen years of integrated river basin development ended – even if only temporarily – in three years of conflict between two of the riparian states.

The process of cooperation is not a simple one. The issues it raises are multi-faceted and intertwined at several levels. This has been illustrated by the three themes that have been selected for examination – nationalism, development and the environment. Nationalism was a stumbling block not only at the state level, where political and military concerns were paramount, but at the sub-state level, where the identity of the state was challenged by competing ethnic groups and by demands for social and economic security. Development proved to be not just about economic growth, but also about popular participation, administrative capacity and the ability to project state needs internationally. Common to both nationalism and development were the questions of citizenship and accountability. The environmental theme interweaved the other issues at every level. The Rio Summit emphasized the need for governments to involve the people if development is to work in partnership with the environment. In the Senegal valley the progress of these sub-state concerns was overtaken by the crisis caused by regional environmental pressures beyond the control of any one state.

Thus the case study of the Senegal river basin shows how the complexity of issue-linkages challenges the boundaries of established political processes, and calls into question any state-centric interpretation of international relations. In addition, it demonstrates that even in a geo-politically insignificant area of the world there is no corner where the current concerns of International Relations do not have an impact.

NOTES

1. Cooley attempted to prove otherwise, but in my view failed to do so.
2. Information given at a seminar in November 1992, by a Jordanian negotiator in the Middle East Peace talks.

3. There are four riparian states, but Guinea has not been involved in the development of the river in recent years. This situation may change in the near future.

4. Meetings were held in Bamako, on 19 February and 10 July 1991, and at Nouakchott on 16 and 17 July 1991. Accounts of these meetings can be found in OMVS records in Dakar under the heading of: *Compte Rendu de la ... session ordinaire du conseil des ministres de L'OMVS*.

5 This was the view of W.R. Rangeley, when interviewed in July 1993. Mr Rangeley was present at the fundraising meetings of the OMVS as an observer of the World Bank. He acted as mediator between the OMVS and Arab donors at some stages of the negotiations.

6. Succeeding leaders of the three states have been equally committed to regional cooperation.

7. As Keita was in 1968 for his refusal to compromise over his commitment to a strongly doctrinaire socialism.

8. Somalia and Angola are the most obvious examples of this.

9. There is some dispute about the numbers. In May 1991 UNHCR estimated that there were 150,000 Mauritanians in refugee camps in Senegal, but 50,000 is the number most usually quoted.

10. In the case of African states, the Organization of African Unity decided to accept the post-colonial state boundaries, however irrational they might be.

11. These categories are suggested by Jackson and Rosberg. Weber's classic definition of the state was: 'A differentiated set of institutions and personnel embodying centrality in the sense that political relations radiate outwards to cover a territorially demarcated area, over which it claims a monopoly of binding and permanent rule-making, backed up by physical violence.' Jackson and Rosberg felt that this definition was inadequate since it did not account for the weakness of African states. They introduced the idea of a distinction between *de jure* and *de facto* legitimacy. *De jure* recognition is the recognition given to all states in the international system by virtue of their acceptance by the United Nations. *De facto* legitimacy describes a functioning unit with institutional authority, organizational capacity and popular recognition. Jackson and Rosberg concluded that many African states had *de jure*, but not *de facto*, legitimacy. In other words, the African state was strong in juridical terms but in political and sociological terms it was weak.

12. The Senegalese farmers were slow to raise their voices. They have only recently begun to form a more coherent body of protest, and only then because of the input of NGOs such as the Institute of Development Anthropology, and individuals such as Adrian Adams (Adams, 1977, 1985, 1992).

13. The Mourides are one of the Muslim brotherhoods in Senegal. They play a dominant role in the politics, economics and social life of the state.

14. In 1933 France established the boundary between the two administrative areas of Senegal and Mauritania to the north of the river, i.e. on the Mauritanian side. Traditionally many Senegalese crossed the river to farm the north bank during the growing season. When the OMVS was set up, there was an agreement between Presidents Senghor and Ould Daddah that the boundary would be in the middle. The 1989–92 dispute gave Senegal the occasion to remind Mauritania that there had never been a formal agreement to change the boundary, and to demand that the farmers be allowed to continue to farm the north bank.

15. The synthesis of economic, social and environmental considerations was an important focus of the Dublin Conference on Water and the Environment (January 1992), which was one of the preparatory conferences leading up to the Rio Summit.

REFERENCES

Adams, A., 1977, *Le Long voyage des gens du fleuve*, Paris, Francois Maspero.

Adams, A., 1985, *La Terre et les gens du fleuve*, Paris, L'Harmattan.

Adams, W.M., 1992, *Wasting the Rain*, London, Earthscan.

Bennett, O. (ed.), 1991, *Greenwar*, London, Panos Institute.

Cooley, J.K., 1984, 'War over Water', *Foreign Policy*, 54.

Godana, B.A., 1985, *Africa's Shared Water Resources*, London, Frances Pinter.

Hardin, G., 1987, 'The Tragedy of the Commons', in S.W. Menard and E.W. Moen (eds), *Perspectives on Population*, Oxford, Oxford University Press.

Howlett, D. and Thomas, C. (eds), 1993, *Resource Politics*, Buckingham, Open University Press.

Human Development Report, Oxford, Oxford University Press.

Jackson, R., 1990, *Quasi-states; sovereignty, international relations and the Third World*, Cambridge, Cambridge University Press.

Jackson, R. and Rosberg, C.G., 1982, *Personal Rule in Black Africa*, Berkeley, University of California Press.

Jackson, R. and Rosberg, C.G., 1984, 'Popular Legitimacy in African Multi-Ethnic States', *Journal of Modern African Studies*, 22(2).

Jackson, R. and Rosberg, C.G., 1986, 'Sovereignty and Underdevelopment: Judicial Statehood in the African Crisis', *Journal of Modern African Studies*, 24(1).

Keita, M., 1961, 'The Foreign Policy of Mali', an address given at Chatham House, 7 June, *International Affairs*, 37(4).

Mandel, R., 1991, *Sources of International River Basin Disputes*, Paper prepared for presentation at the Annual meeting of the International Studies Association, Vancouver, British Columbia, March 1991.

Parnall, T. and Utton, A.E., 1976, 'Senegal Valley Authority: A Unique Experiment in International River Basin Planning', *Indiana Law Journal*, 51(2).

Pearce, F., 1991, 'Wells of Conflict on the West Bank', *New Scientist*, 1 June.

Pearch, F., 1992, *The Dammed*, London, Bodley Head.

Scudder, T., 1989, 'River Basin Projects in Africa', *Environment*, 31(2).

Scudder, T., 1991, 'The Need and Justification for Maintaining Transboundary Flood Regimes: The Africa case', *Natural Resources Journal*, 31(1).

Seck, S.M., 1991, 'Sur la dynamique de l'irrigation dans la vallée du fleuve', in *La vallée du fleuve Sénégal*, B. Crousse, P. Mathieu and S.M. Seck (eds), Paris, Karthala.

Tordoff, W., 1993, *Government and Politics in Africa*, Basingstoke, Macmillan.

World Bank, 1991, *World Development Report*, Oxford, Oxford University Press.

Young, C., 1988, 'The Colonial State and its Political Legacy', in D. Rothchild and N. Chazan (eds), *The Precarious Balance: State and Society in Africa*, Boulder, CO, Westview Press.

Zartman, I.W., 1966, *International Relations in the New Africa*, Englewood Cliffs, NJ, Prentice-Hall.

10
The West and the future of military intervention

Thomas G. Otte, Andrew M. Dorman
and Wyn Q. Bowen

'Out of timber so crooked as that man is made of nothing perfectly straight can be made.' *Immanuel Kant*[1]

INTRODUCTION: TERRITORIALITY, HUMAN RIGHTS AND INTERVENTION – A 'NEW' WORLD ORDER?

When the Cold War came to an end, for one short 'unipolar moment' (Krauthammer, 1992: 296ff.; see also Layne, 1993), a new world order seemed to emerge from the ruins of the order of Yalta. The events of 1989, it has been argued, signalled the triumph of the West in a world in which everything had become the West; democracy and freedom prevailed and with them international peace and harmony. History – with a capital (Hegelian) H – had, it seemed, come to an end (Fukuyama, 1989 and 1992: 6).

History, however, habitually mocks man's hopes, expectations and predictions. History has not come to an end, nor has a truly 'new' world order emerged. On the contrary, the violent eruption of so many conflicts all over the globe, often after having lain dormant for centuries, has led many to look back with nostalgia to the 'remarkably stable and predictable atmosphere of the Cold War'.[2] The 'great sea-change' (Pinto, 1991) is still under way, and the softened-up structure of the international system has not, as yet, hardened again into a new mould.

However, with the breakdown of the bipolar world order the cornerstone of the international system, i.e. the fact that the Westphalian international system consists of states, has become more clearly discernible again. After the end of the ideological conflict the state has again become the focus of international order and of concepts of order. Transnational erosion and international integration notwithstanding, the state remains what it always has been: an international actor in its own right and a sphere of internal and external protection of its citizens (Morgenthau, 1967a: 493ff; Weber, 1978: 54ff; Schmitt, 1988; Arendt, 1958; Kojeve, 1991: 170ff.). That protection can only be guaranteed within a given territorial framework; likewise, universal human rights can only be realized within the legal framework provided by the state (Dahrendorf, 1990: 4ff.).

The renewed importance of the quasi-archaic element of territoriality and sovereign statehood was clearly demonstrated in the Gulf War. Whilst economic considerations were undoubtedly a contributing factor in the West's decision to reverse Iraq's occupation of Kuwait, the war was mainly fought in defence of one of the fundamental principles of international politics: the inviolability of sovereign statehood. Iraq's attempted 'etatocide' of its small neighbour was a clear violation of that principle and a threat to regional stability, and, therefore, had to be averted (Kissinger, 1992: 238–48). Even more tellingly the war was halted once the aggressor's territoriality and stability were considered to be under threat.

While territoriality and regional stability seem to enjoy priority in international affairs, the growth of United Nations humanitarian missions, as in Somalia, and its increasing, though hesitant, involvement in Bosnia highlight a new, humanitarian dimension of post-Cold War international politics. In an international states system, more integrated than ever before, internationally sanctioned military intervention on 'humanitarian' grounds has therefore become an issue (Clarke and Beck, 1993: 112ff.; for an older discussion of this issue see Akehurst, 1984).

Military intervention is – and probably remains – a well-established instrument of statecraft and feature of the international system (Northedge, 1974; Howard, 1964; Bull, 1991; Young, 1968). Despite this fact the subject of intervention in general, and of humanitarian intervention in particular, is still surrounded by scholarly confusion. In traditional Realist thought intervention is regarded as an instrument of foreign policy for the safeguarding of whatever is perceived to be the national interest. Realist scholars acknowledge that:

> [a]ll nations will continue to be guided in their decisions to intervene and their choice of means of intervention by what they regard as their respective national interests. There is indeed an urgent need for the governments of the great powers to abide by certain rules according to which the game of intervention is played. But these rules must be deduced not from abstract principles which are incapable of controlling the actions of governments, but from the interests of the governments concerned and from their practice of foreign policy reflecting those interests (c.f. Morgenthau, 1967b: 430).

In this respect, traditional realism is primarily concerned with the concept of the 'national interest defined as power' (Morgenthau, 1967b: 7ff.) based on a 'narrow' concept of national security (Buzan, 1991: 34ff.; Gilpin, 1986: 306).

But, in light of the growing importance of the humanitarian dimension of post-Cold War international affairs and of the growing constraints placed upon governments, the question arises itself whether the contents of the concept of military intervention have changed, and whether humanitarian intervention is a mere variation of traditional military intervention or an entirely new phenomenon in international politics. Given the confusion surrounding the question of intervention it is essential to begin our discussion of the West and the future of military intervention in the international system with an explicit definition. For the purpose of this discussion military intervention will be defined thus:

Military intervention is the planned limited use of force for a transitory period by a state (or a group of states) superior in power against a weaker state in order to change the target state's domestic structure or its external policies; it is the continuation of politics with the limited addition of means of military force in order to re-establish the normal (pre-intervention) pattern of bilateral relations by forcing the target state into compliance.[3]

To examine the relationship of humanitarian intervention *vis-à-vis* military intervention and its affects upon realist interpretations two states have been selected as case studies: the United States and Britain. Both played prominent roles during the Cold War and in the post-Cold War period. Their status as permanent members of the United Nations Security Council and as members of NATO have given them both major roles to play within the international system. The case studies examine the factors that influence the decision whether to intervene militarily and how the new ideas of humanitarian intervention have affected this process.

THE UNITED STATES

The outcome of the 1992 American presidential election and the foreign policy approach pursued by the US in the first nine months of Bill Clinton's presidency have been dictated by two coincidental phenomena: the disappearance of the overwhelming threat once posed to US national interests by the former Soviet Union, and the emergence of a domestic social and economic agenda in dire need of government attention. The interaction of these two phenomena over the period since the Gulf War has resulted in the division of American society along familiar lines, similar, although far from identical, to those witnessed in the US following the momentous foreign policy successes of the First and Second World Wars.

This division is between those in the media, the public and Congress who favour a major retrenchment of the US at a time of a sharply reduced external threat and severe domestic hardship, and those favouring a limited retrenchment of the US. This second group recognize the need to concentrate resources on contemporary domestic problems, at the same time identifying the need to keep the US on an internationalist footing perceiving America to be inextricably involved in the world as the sole superpower. Although this portrait of the contemporary political environment in the US is a very general one it none the less illustrates diverging views pertaining to the national interest of the US beyond the basic consensus regarding the imperative of ensuring the 'physical survival and constitutional integrity' of the United States (c.f. Brown, 1984: 20). Consequently, the means by which the national interest should be protected and promoted are intensely debated in the US at the present moment.

Although President Clinton was elected to address domestic issues and has primarily been preoccupied with these issues since his inauguration in January 1993, he has simultaneously emphasized the need for the US to remain fundamentally involved at the international level, so that it can head the collective global effort to promote peace, freedom, democracy and free market economics around the globe. In doing so Bill Clinton clearly recognizes America's unprecedented power and influence in the post-Cold War world, and hence her inextricable involvement around the globe. These twin desires (that is, to remain globally involved but also to concentrate the application of American efforts and resources upon the domestic agenda) have driven the Clinton administration, over its first nine months in office, to favour an internationalist foreign policy coupled with an emphasis on multilateral deliberations regarding military intervention.

In concentrating on the need for and the desirability of a multilateral approach to international crises over this period the Clinton administration has failed in three respects: to develop a new rationale for the American national purpose beyond the water's edge; to identify American national interests in the post-Cold War world; and consequently, to identify how and why the US will intervene militarily in the future. These failings have contributed significantly to US foreign policy failures in Bosnia, Somalia and in Haiti and, in addition, they have resulted in significant public, media and Congressional pressure for the US to avoid becoming entangled overseas. As a result the Clinton administration has been under great pressure to formulate a foreign policy rationale explicitly dictating when, how and why the US will use military force overseas. This is imperative when the American domestic agenda demands immediate attention and effective action from the Clinton administration.

US success in the Cold War undermined the assumptions that had guided American national security policy for nearly half a century by removing from the strategic equation the perceived fundamental threat to US national interests (Hendrickson, 1992: 395). Consequently this left the country without the sense of purpose which had permeated American politics and society since the beginning of the Cold War (Smith, 1992: 180). In a recent article in *Foreign Affairs* Norman Ornstein (1992: 2) described this situation by quoting Oscar Wilde, who said that there were 'two great tragedies in human existence: one is never to get one's dearest desire, the other is to get it'. Here Ornstein was obviously referring to US success in the Cold War and the doctrinal void and lack of a concrete sense of purpose beyond the territorial US that this created in US national security policy-making.

Having lost this fundamental rationale, the US is still confronted with the problem of having to redefine the national interest at the level of its domestic, foreign and security policies. The New World Order (NWO) rhetoric of George Bush, which accompanied the swift, and hence popular, US-led victory in the Gulf War, initially brought to Bush's foreign policy Wilsonian hopes of creating an effective, collective, global security system 'administered by international institutions, and resting on the commitment of leading states to the maintenance of peaceful international relations' (Falk, 1992: 145). President Bush hoped this NWO would replace the Cold War order, and ultimately dictate US foreign and national security policy just as the Cold War had dictated the rationale of US foreign policy prior to December 1989.

The idealism of this proposed NWO disguised, however, the true nature of the post-Cold War, politico-strategic environment in which the removal of the superpower nuclear stalemate took the lid off 'long suppressed' ethnic, national-istic and other regional tensions (Falk,1992: 148). Thus the Cold War had the dual effect of containing the perceived Soviet threat to US national interests and keeping the lid on regional ethnic, nationalistic and religious tensions and conflicts around the world. The Gulf coalition and the successful collective security effort to remove Iraq from Kuwait, in the name of this NWO, papered over these problems and can therefore be regarded as the period of calm before the storm between the Cold War, or the era of the 'long peace' as John Lewis Gaddis depicted the Cold War (Falk, 1992: 148), and the post-Cold War era.

Although President Bush's NWO envisaged a 'new partnership of nations that transcended the Cold War', which was based upon 'consultation, co-operation, collective action' (Gardner, 1992: 272) and affirmed the principle that aggression against the territorial integrity of a state was not to be tolerated, President Bush failed to define America's role in an increasingly troubled and conflict-ridden world. He also failed to define exactly when, how, and why the US would resort to military intervention to protect which specific national interest. This failure coincided, in the spring of 1991, with the emergence of an increasingly pressing and problematical domestic economic and social agenda in the US. It was this coincidence of phenomena that President Clinton in-herited, with all its political and strategic connotations, in January 1993.

Prior to September 1993 the Clinton administration's policy towards military intervention paid inadequate attention to the necessity of tying acts of military intervention/non-intervention to the US national interest. However, through a trial-and-error foreign policy involving painful losses and humiliations abroad, US military intervention policy under the Clinton administration since mid-September 1993 has begun to show signs of being pulled more into line with the US national interest. This has been evident through a spate of adminis-tration foreign policy speeches and action on the ground in Somalia during September and October 1993.

The Clinton administration has consistently stated that the US must remain as world leader to 'build a world of security, freedom, democracy, free markets and growth' (Tonelson, 1993: 167). According to Bill Clinton, US leadership does not mean, however, that the US seeks to 'act alone', to 'act rashly' or to do things 'which could draw the US into a conflict not of her own making and not of her own ability to resolve, but simply to advise them of concerted action that the international community can and should take to deal with these issues'.[4] In pursuing these goals, the Clinton administration has stressed the need for other countries to take their fair share of the responsibilities. Thus Clinton's desire to limit the application of resources to world crises, in order to court the American public by concentrating US time, effort and resources on the pressing domestic agenda, interacted with his parallel desire to continue leading the world. This theme emerged in the 1992 election, and placed a marked multilateral emphasis on Clinton's foreign policy – for example, in Bosnia, where the US is involved with NATO and the UN and where the Western European Union and the EC are also involved; in Somalia with the

UN; and in Haiti with the UN and the Organization of American States (OAS).

This multilateral emphasis has been driven by the perceived need to reduce the nation's expenditure on global commitments and defence, but not to abandon them at a time of reduced threats to American interests and, more importantly, at a time when domestic problems demand concerted action.

It has been argued that multilateralism, and the related concept of collective security, theoretically assume that 'all nation's perceive international problems the same way and are prepared to run the same risks for vindicating their view' (Kissinger, 1993). This view conflicts with the post-Cold War world, however, with its resultant nationalistic and ethnic fragmentation. In such a world 'universal causes are hard to come by'.[5] This situation, and the Clinton administration's pursuit of a multilateral foreign policy, has complicated the US position over Bosnia, Somalia and Haiti and consequently resulted in criticism of Bill Clinton's handling of these affairs in relation to US national interests.

In pursuing a multilateral approach to US foreign policy, and in seeking coalitions and international consensus wherever possible when addressing international crises, Bill Clinton has risked removing from his calculations what should be the primary rationale for US foreign and national security policy, and hence for US military intervention: the national interest. For example: in November 1992 President Bush committed 20,000 troops to Somalia on a humanitarian operation on behalf of the UN in order to stave off the impending starvation of thousands of Somali people caught in that country's civil war. Since Clinton's inauguration, however, the rationale for this UN mission has altered dramatically from a humanitarian mission into an effort to 'disarm warring factions', to apprehend 'criminal elements' (notably General Aideed), and to establish a national police force, a prison system and a judicial system (Kirkpatrick, 1993). Furthermore, US involvement in Somalia has been over-personalized and politicized with the emphasis in UN policy on hunting down the Somali warlord General Aideed. In its eagerness to pursue a multilateral foreign policy, the Clinton administration recommitted US troops to this task at the request of the UN, but failed to explain to the American electorate why the US should become involved in an altered, non-humanitarian operation concerned with the internal politics of Somalia – a distant country with which Americans have no special ties (Kirkpatrick, 1993).

The Clinton administration's emphasis on multilateralism in its foreign policy and rationale for military intervention has resulted in the failure of the administration to formulate an all-purpose national vision to dictate how and why the US will militarily intervene in the affairs of other nations. In an age of US multilateralism there exists the risk, as in Somalia, that American lives and resources will be put in jeopardy when the US national interest is not clearly and precisely set within a national vision guiding US foreign policy. Prior to 1989 the Soviet threat provided this vision and hence justified the expense of American resources and lives on countering this threat.

The omission of such an all-embracing vision has potentially very damaging consequences for the US, none more serious than the loss of US standing and credibility on the world stage. Certain Clinton administration statements concerning the Bosnian conflict are a testament to this potentiality. In the absence of a coherent national vision, Secretary of State Warren Christopher has been consistently inconsistent in his description of the impact of the Bosnian conflict on American national interests. Prior to his failed attempts to develop a Western policy consensus over Bosnia and to promote the US preference for arming the Bosnian Muslims and using air strikes on Serbian artillery positions, Warren Christopher described the Bosnian situation as a 'conflagration that could envelop all of Southern Europe and perhaps rage beyond': implicitly recognizing a perception that the Bosnian war could threaten the stability of the European continent, which has been a vital interest of the US since the beginning of the Cold War. On other occasions since then Warren Christopher has stated that the Bosnian conflict does 'not affect American vital interests' (c.f. Cohen, 1993) and that it was a 'humanitarian crisis a long way from home in the middle of another continent'.[6]

Such inconsistency in identifying the US national interest in the UN operation in Somalia has resulted in the death of US servicemen and the televised image of their bodies being dragged through the streets of Mogadishu. This has inevitably generated Congressional and public pressure for the Clinton administration to limit its actions on the international stage, to bring US troops home for their own protection and hence to define the US national interest in narrow, domestic terms at a time of major economic and societal decay in America. To defuse such pressures and reduce criticism of his foreign policy Bill Clinton could act to define the American national purpose in line with redefined US national interests. If Bill Clinton does nothing, he risks the rise in influence of those in the US advocating major retrenchment and a limited definition of the US national interest. This would subsequently entail the jeopardizing of real US interests around the globe, such as oil supplies, markets for American goods and services, the provision of protection for allies, nonproliferation, and so forth.

BRITAIN

During the Cold War British foreign and defence policy was concentrated upon dealing with the perceived threat posed by the Soviet Union. This led successive governments to emphasize Britain's membership of NATO, to preserve the 'special relationship' with the United States and to retain a strategic nuclear deterrent (Croft and Williams, 1991: 147). The end of the Cold War and the collapse of the Soviet Union has found Britain with what has been described by William Wallace (1993) as: 'A Government which has no clear sense of its place in the world or its foreign policy priorities'. This position is primarily due to internal conflicts within the government. At a time when Willem van Eekelen (1992) has argued that defence policy will return to its position as the servant of foreign and economic policy, in Britain foreign and economic policy have become diametrically opposed. The British Foreign Secretary, Douglas Hurd has tended to adopt the van Eekelen line. *The Times* leader column noted:

Mr. Hurd is clear that Britain, which exports twice as much of its gross domestic product as Japan, cannot neglect its interest in 'a safer and more decent world': anarchy interferes with trade, generally involves appalling human rights abuse and unchecked, has a tendency to lead to wider conflict.

Douglas Hurd (1992) went as far as saying:

Some problems – state-sponsored terrorism, for example, or the proliferation of ballistic missiles – may prick our skin more than our consciences. But, if we really want a world that is more secure, more prosperous and more stable, then humanitarian problems can be just as threatening and must be seen not just as a moral issue, but as a potential security threat as well.

This speech, however, was rapidly countered by the Secretary of State for Defence, Malcolm Rifkind, who referred to the national interest along more traditional conservative lines (Rifkind, 1993).

Rifkind has found himself in a very difficult position. Britain's economic weakness and large public sector borrowing requirement has encouraged the Treasury to demand sweeping cuts in Britain's defence budget. In late 1993 reports in the press about the alleged top-heaviness of the Royal Air Force in comparison to other air forces such as Israel's highlighted the prominence being given to the need to make defence cuts (Bellamy, 1993a). This was confirmed by the chiefs of the defence staff, who are known to have used their right of access to the prime minister to ensure that their views were heard (Brown, 1993). The Chief of the Air Staff, Sir Michael Graydon, went as far as publicly airing his concern about the Royal Air Force's future before making a hasty retraction (Almond and Jones, 1993). Consequently, Malcolm Rifkind has been forced to make significant defence reductions beyond those announced in the 'Options for Change' review.[8] The cancellation of the tactical air-to-surface missile is an obvious example (Barrie, 1993).

The reorganization of defence policy has, however, left the Trident programme virtually untouched.[9] Not only has Trident been viewed by the Conservative Party as its 'sacred cow', but it has also traditionally been used as one of Britain's justifications for its permanent seat on the UN Security Council. Thus the bulk of Britain's defence cuts have fallen upon its conventional forces. With the advent of NATO's new Strategic Concept, a major reorganization of NATO's command structure has been undertaken.[10] This has resulted in Britain's loss of its one major command. It led the British government to pursue successfully command of the new Allied Command Europe Rapid Reaction Corps (ARRC) at Germany's expense, resulting in the commitment of a significant number of troops. This led to the observation that:

[t]he ARRC presents great potential for a crisis in Britain's ability to sustain its current level of commitments. Having fought to take a leading role in the ARRC, Britain finds itself committed to commanding that force and to providing two divisions. The corollary of this commitment is that whenever the ARRC is deployed, British troops will be first on call. However, as any discussion of army overstretch makes clear, units

allocated to the ARRC are likely to be committed to other roles. The first occasion on which the ARRC is called upon – which given a deteriorating security environment, could be in the near future – could also precipitate a crisis for the Government (George and Ryan, 1993).

To cover the high cost of the ARRC commitment Rifkind has had to achieve short-term savings by delaying a number of re-equipment programmes, including the replacement of the amphibious warfare ships, thereby reducing Britain's seaborne protection forces (House of Commons Defence Committee, 1993: xiv). As a result, the Ministry of Defence has been loath to undertake further overseas commitments. Amongst its West European allies Britain was noticeable in failing to send ground troops to Somalia when the United States called for assistance.[12]

This position has been heavily criticized by the House of Commons Select Committee on Defence, who concluded that:

> the United Kingdom's position in the world owes much to its defence expertise, and the level of national commitment to defence. *The maintenance of that position is at risk if the United Kingdom does not respond to the international peacekeeping requirement on a scale commensurate with membership of the Security Council, let alone the legitimate demands of UK public opinion* (House of Commons Defence Committee, 1993; original emphasis).

The threat to Britain's permanent seat on the UN Security Council is of real concern. Whilst for budgetary reasons the British government will attempt to minimize the level of future military deployments overseas, it is certain to continue to participate in the majority of UN- or European-sponsored actions in order to justify the retention of its permanent seat. This policy has been clear over Yugoslavia. It was noticeable that Britain was one of only two EU states to vote against the EU sending military forces as peacekeepers during the initial breakup of the Yugoslav Federation. Yet it later managed to pull together an infantry force for the escort of humanitarian aid in Bosnia (Schmidt, 1993: 29). Subsequently, this commitment has been reinforced following the ceasefire in Sarejevo (Pringle, 1994).

The problem of conflicting views on the future use of military intervention between the Foreign Office and the Treasury, assisted by the Ministry of Defence, is further confused by the Armed Services themselves. Whilst none appear to be particularly concerned about the relative merits of retaining this power-projection capability, all are attempting to play on the perceived link between Britain's participation in United Nations peacekeeping and peace-making missions and the preservation of its status as one of the permanent members.

Thus the army has managed to reduce the level of its cuts by focusing on the problems of providing suitable infantry forces for UN missions given the necessity of internal security operations in Northern Ireland and manning the ARRC. The Royal Air Force (RAF) has managed to protect its most important programme, the European Fighter Aircraft, by highlighting its role in providing air cover and support to any use of military force (Cook, 1992). However, the long-term retention of No. 2 Group within Germany appears doubtful. The relative success of both the army and RAF is clear from the recent defence estimates, whose cuts were primarily aimed at the Royal Navy.[14]

What is noticeably new within the Royal Navy is a move from a concern about destroyer and frigate numbers to one stressing the importance of core units. The Royal Navy appears to be returning to an emphasis on the big ships. Thus only two days after the announcement of the 1993 defence cuts the navy was reported to be considering the reintroduction of the large conventional carrier into its inventory (Elliott, 1993). Whilst exaggerated in nature, the only justification for this and the replacement of the amphibious fleet can be the preservation of a naval power projection capability beyond the range of UK bases.

The return of inter-service fighting for scarce defence resources will lead to an emphasis by the individual services upon their power projection capabilities in order to substantiate themselves. However, the pressure from the Treasury for still further cuts can only lead to a diminution of the capability of the armed forces. In retaining a limited power projection capability the British government will allow itself the potential to utilize such a capability.

With the ultimate decision remaining with the prime minister and his cabinet, the role of public opinion has an increasingly pro-active role to play. The inherent contradiction between the lack of public interest in Somalia, which allowed the British government to make only a relatively minor contribution, and Britain's leadership of 'Operation Irma' (Savill, 1993), the evacuation of wounded from Bosnia, indicates the responsiveness of the key decision-makers to public opinion. This responsiveness is further reinforced when other British interests are at stake. This was typified by Britain's recent reinforcement of its military commitment in Bosnia in support of the British army commander on the ground and as a means of preserving Britain's position within the United Nations (Bellamy and Brown, 1994).

CONCLUSION: THE WEST AND THE FUTURE OF INTERVENTION IN THE INTERNATIONAL SYSTEM – A 'NEW' GAME

With the end of the Cold War old certainties have disappeared and new uncertainties have arisen. The international system is passing through a period of systemic transition, a geo-political interlude, that will eventually lead to multipolarity (Layne, 1993: 35ff.; Waltz, 1993: 50ff.; Jervis, 1992). The collapse of the Soviet Union has created a 'power vacuum' (Vaclav Havel) into which other Great Powers or potential Great Powers will push. Moreover, the end of the East–West ideological conflict removed one of the structural constraints which kept the lid on numerous regional conflicts and rivalries which duly broke out in the open after 1989/90. Both developments have profound implications for the possible future interventionist behaviour of various governments and the future of intervention in the international system.

There has been a clearly discernible and continuous process of the rise and fall of Great Powers during the course of modern history (Dehio, 1963; Thompson, 1992; Kennedy, 1989: xviff.; Bull, 1977: 200ff.; Hinsley, 1982: 153ff.; Kaiser, 1990). Whether a state will attempt to attain Great Power status depends to a large extent on structural constraints pressing it to become a Great Power as much as on its capablities (Layne, 1993: 9; Waltz, 1979: 131ff.; Snyder, 1991: 19ff). The striving for Great Power status has to be underpinned by economic, technological and military capabilities; these capabilities are an indispensable precondition for any state to be able to provide for its own security in the anarchic international 'self-help system' (Waltz, 1979: 107, 131; Kennedy, 1989. For an alternative view see Mawil, 1990/1: 91–106). The current period of systemic change in international politics brought about by the collapse of the Soviet Union affords an opportunity for, and exerts structural pressure on, a number of eligible states to become Great Powers.

As was shown above, Great Power status is linked to the capability, if not to launch independently, at least to initiate and participate in a military intervention. This applies both to countries which have already attained Great Power status and are now trying to maintain it, and to those currently eligible for that status. In Europe, Germany, in many ways bound to lead because of its population strength, economic power and geographical position, is already beginning to exert its potential leadership in European security affairs. Germany's prominent role in providing economic aid to the former Soviet Union and Eastern Europe and in bringing about European recognition of Slovenia and Croatia would indicate that the extent of its geo-political interests is expanding. However, as its insufficient political and military support for the Gulf War allies has shown, without a credible military capability Germany will not succeed in its attempts to obtain a permanent seat on the UN Security Council, the ultimate recognition of its *de facto* Great Power status.[15] There is parallel development in the Far East where Japan is poised to take on a more prominent international role (e.g. Friedburg, 1993/4).

The rise of both these nations is widely held to be a threat to Britain's permanent membership of the UN Security Council. It is one of only two (the other being France) European states currently to have a comprehensive, though in comparison to the United States limited, capability to undertake and sustain military interventions and to project military force. Moreover, its position is unique in that it is not only a European nuclear power but also retains command of NATO's new Rapid Reaction Corps. For the foreseeable future the British government faces a difficult task. It has to match future military commitments with its strained economic position. It will continue to participate in UN or NATO/WEU sponsored military actions in order to justify Britain's permanent seat on the UN Security Council and also to satisfy the inconsistent moralistic demands of domestic public opinion.

The position of the United States in this period of change is a quite different one. Only the United States possesses imposing strength in all categories (economic, technological and military) of Great Power capabilities. For the time being, it enjoys unrivalled preeminence in international affairs. However, with the disappearance of a direct, manifest threat to US national security and with an ever more pressing domestic agenda, the American security outlook seems to be somewhat confused. As the Clinton administration's foreign policy doctrine is being developed and formulated, it appears more than likely that the United States will continue to employ the instrument of military intervention whenever its strategic but not necessarily humanitarian interests are threatened.[16]

Throughout the Cold War, under the auspices of the global ideological conflict, the United States and the Soviet Union were engaged in an elaborate game of intervention and proxy wars on the periphery. Since the end of the Cold War a 'new game' of intervention with potentially more participants has begun. Military intervention will remain an instrument of statecraft and thus a constant feature of international politics. The various powers may have different motivations for participating in this new game, but they are all linked to their perceived respective national interests. The national interest remains the main driving force behind the foreign policy actions of individual states. It is a wide enough concept to embrace the more traditional concern with national security and international power as well as humanitarian concerns (Morgenthau, 1967: 219ff.; Snyder, 1991: 19ff.). Humanitarian intervention, defined as a forcible action without the prior invitation or consent of the target state's government for the specific purpose of protecting fundamental human rights (Arend and Beck, 1993: 113), fulfils all the essential characteristics of 'traditional' military intervention: it is military intervention with a humanitarian objective. In conclusion, it may, therefore, be argued that the post-Cold War international system may see the beginning of a new game of intervention, perhaps over different issues, possibly with new actors, but that they will abide by the same old rules

NOTES

1. Cf. Emmanuel Kant, 1910, 'Idee zu einter allgemeinen Geschichte in Welt-buergerlicher Absicht', in Kant, E., *Gesammelte Schriften. Akademie Ausgabe*, Vol. 8, Berlin: 23.
2. Former US Secretary of State Lawrence Eagleburger, as quoted in Waltz, 1993: 44. See also Mearsheimer, 1990.
3. For a fuller discussion of the problems of defining military intervention, see Otte, forthcoming.
4. Cf. 'A Grave Disappointment to us all', *International Herald Tribune*, 7 May 1993.
5. Ibid.
6. Cf. 'Clinton's Washington is retrenching', *International Herald Tribune*, 9 June.
7. 'Hurd's troubled world', *The Times*, 29 January 1993.
8. The Chancellor of the Exchequer's autumn budget has resulted in further defence cuts of £1.8 bn over the next few years. See Bellamy, 1993b.
9. The recent announcements of cuts in Trident warhead numbers appear to have more to do with the problems at the Aldermaston plant than with a desire for arms control. See Fairhall, 1993.
10. Agreed at the NATO Heads of State and Government meeting in Rome, 7–8 November 1991, *NATO Press Communiqué S-1 (91) 85*, 7 November 1991.
11. Statement on the Defence Estimates 1993 - Defending our Future, *CM.2270*, London, HMSO: 10.

12. Britain's contribution consisted merely of providing Hercules aircraft to support the airlift of humanitarian aid to the more remote regions of Somalia. See ibid.: xxiii.

13. The army succeeded in having its strength increased by 3,000 men, resulting in the retention of two infantry battalions. Statement on the Defence Estimates 1993 - Defending Our Future, *CM.2270*, London, HMSO: 10. The army also succeeded in ordering a further 259 Challenger 2 main battle tanks. See Bellamy, 1993b.

14. The £1.05 bn reduction in the defence budget was primarily met by the decision to sell or mothball the 'Upholder' class conventional submarines. See Wood and Evans, 1993.

15. For a more detailed discussion see Dorman, forthcoming.

16. For a more detailed discussion see Bowen, forthcoming.

REFERENCES

Akehurst, Michael, 1984, 'Humanitarian Intervention', in Bull, Hedley (ed.), *Intervention in World Politics*, Oxford, Clarendon: 95-118.

Almond, Peter and Jones, George, 1993, 'RAF apologises to Rifkind', *Daily Telegraph*, 10 November: 1-2.

Arend, Anthony Clark and Beck, Robert J., 1993, *International Law and the Use of Force*, London and New York, Routledge.

Arendt, Hannah, 1958, *The Human Condition*, 2nd edn, Chicago, University of Chicago Press.

Barrie, Douglas, 1993, 'Nuclear conflicts', *Flight International*, 4(393), 27 October-2 November: 18.

Bellamy, Christopher, 1993a, 'Why the RAF has so many, and Israel so few', *The Independent*, 25 October: 6.

Bellamy, Christopher, 1993b, 'Extra front-line soldiers and tanks promised', *The Independent*, 2 December: 13.

Bellamy, Christopher and Brown, Colin, 1994, 'Extra British troops on standby for Bosnia', *The Independent*, 8 March: 1.

Bowen, Wyn Q., forthcoming, 'The United States and the Future of Military Intervention', in Thomas G. Otte and Andrew M. Dorman, *Military Intervention: From Gunboat Diplomacy to Humanitarian Intervention*, London, Dartmouth Press.

Brown, S., 1984, *On the Front Burner: Issues in US Foreign Policy*, Boston, MA, Little, Brown.

Brown, Colin, 1993, 'Chief of Staff protest to Major over cuts', *The Independent*, 25 October: 6.

Bull, Hedley, 1991, *The Anarchical Society: A Study of Order in International Politics*, London, Macmillan.

Buzan, Barry, 1991, 'Is international security possible?', in Ken Booth (ed.), *New Thinking about Strategy and International Security*, London, HarperCollins: 31-55.

Cohen, R., 1993, 'Confused, *ad hoc*, and unexplained', *International Herald Tribune*, 9 June.

Cook, Nick, 1992, 'The fight begins for the few', *Jane's Defence Weekly*, 18(10), 5 September: 49.

Croft, Stuart and Williams, Phil, 1991, 'The United Kingdom', in Karp, Regina Cowen, *Security with nuclear weapons? Different perspectives on national security*, Oxford, Oxford University Press for SIPRI.

Dahrendorf, Ralf, 1990, *Reflections on the Revolution in Europe*, London, Chatto & Windus.

Dehio, Ludwig, 1963, *The Precarious Balance: The Politics of Power in Europe, 1494-1945*, London, Chatto & Windus.

Dorman, Andrew M., forthcoming, 'Western Europe and the Future of Intervention', in Thomas G. Otte and Andrew M. Dorman (eds), *Military Intervention: From Gunboat Diplomacy to Humanitarian Intervention*, London, Dartmouth Press.

Eekelen, W. van, 1992, 'WEU on the way back to Brussels', speech given at Chatham House on 22 September, reprinted in *WEU Press Review*, 161, 24 September.

Elliott, Simon, 1993, 'UK plans for return of fast-jet carriers', *Flight International*, 144(4), 14-20 July: 5.

Fairhall, David, 1993, 'Aldermaston plant delay a factor in decision to scale down warheads', *Guardian*, 16 November: 2.

Falk, R., 1992, 'In Search of a New World Order', *Current History*, 92(573), April.

Friedberg, Aaron L., 1993/4, 'Ripe for Rivalry: Prospects for Peace in a Multipolar Asia', *International Security*, xviii(3): 5-33.

Fukuyama, Francis, 1989, 'The End of History?', in *National Interest*, 16: 3-18.

Fukuyama, Francis, 1992, *The End of History and the Last Man*, Harmondsworth, Penguin.

Gardner, R.N., 1992, 'Practical Internationalism', in Graham Allison and Gregory F. Treverton, *Rethinking America's Security: Beyond Cold War to New World Order*, New York and London, Norton.

George, Bruce and Ryan, Nick, 1993, 'Options for Change: a political critique', in *Brassey's Defence Yearbook 1993*, ed. Centre for Defence Studies, King's College, London, Brassey's (UK).

Gilpin, Robert, 1986, 'The Richness of the Tradition of Political Realism', in Robert O. Keohane (ed.), *Neorealism and its Critics*, New York, Columbia University Press: 301-21.

Hendrickson, D.C., 1992, 'The End of American History: American security and national purpose and the New World Order', in Graham Allison and Gregory F. Treverton, *Rethinking America's Security: Beyond Cold War to New World Order*, New York and London, Norton.

Hinsley, F.H., 1982, *Power and the Pursuit of Peace: Theory and Practice in the History of Relations between States*, Cambridge, Cambridge University Press.

House of Commons Defence Committee, 1993, Fourth Report: United Kingdom Peacekeeping and Intervention Forces: report together with the proceedings of the Committee relating to the report, Minutes of Evidence and Memoranda, *House of Commons Papers 1992-93 188*, London, HMSO.

Howard, M., 1964, 'Military Power and International Order', *International Affairs*, xi(2): 397-408.

Hurd, Douglas, 1992, 'Foreign policy and international security', *RUSI Journal*, 137(6), December.

Jervis, Robert, 1992, 'The Future of World Politics: Will it Resemble the Past?', in Sean M. Lynn-Jones and Steven E. Miller (eds), *America's Strategy in a Changing World*, Cambridge, MA and London, MIT Press: 3-37.

Kaiser, David, 1990, *Politics and War: European conflict from Philip II to Hitler*, Cambridge, MA, Harvard University Press.

Kennedy, Paul M., 1989, *The Rise and Fall of the Great Powers: Economic Change and Military Conflict from 1500 to 2000*, London, Fontana.

Kirkpatrick, Jeanne, 1993, 'Clinton does have a Foreign Policy Agenda: just ask Boutros Ghali', *International Herald Tribune*, 28-29 August.

Kissinger, Henry, 1992, 'Balance of Power Sustained', in Allison and Treverton: 238-48.

Kissinger, Henry, 1993, 'Foreign Policy is about the National Interest', *International Herald Tribune*, 25 October: 5.

Kojeve, Alexandre, 1991, 'Tyranny and Wisdom', in Leo Strauss, *On Tyranny, including the Strauss-Kojeve Correspondence*, ed. Victor Gourevitch and Michael S. Roth, rev. edn., New York, Free Press:135-76.

Maull, Hanns W., 1990/1, 'Germany and Japan: The New Civilian Powers', *Foreign Affairs*, lxix(5): 91-106.

Rifkind, Malcolm, 1993, 'Peacekeeping or peacemaking? Implications and prospects', *RUSI Journal*, 138(2), April: 1-6.

Krauthammer, Charles, 1992, 'The Unipolar Moment', in Graham Allison and Gregory F. Treverton (eds), *Rethinking America's Security: Beyond Cold War to New World Order*, New York and London, Norton: 295-306.

Layne, Christopher, 1993, 'The Unipolar Illusion: Why New Great Powers Will Rise', *International Security*, 5(4): 5-51.

Morgenthau, Hans J., 1967a, *Politics Among Nations: The Struggle for Power and Peace*, 4th edn, New York, Alfred A. Knopf.

Morgenthau, Hans J., 1967b, 'To Intervene or not to Intervene', *Foreign Affairs*, clx(3): 425-36.

Northedge, F.S., 1974, 'The Resort to Force', in Northedge, F.S., *The Use of Force in International Relations*, London: 11-35.

Ornstein, N., 1992, 'Foreign Policy and the 1992 Election', *Foreign Affairs*, 71(3), Summer.

Otte, Thomas G., forthcoming, 'On Intervention: Some Introductory Remarks', in Thomas G. Otte and Andrew M. Dorman (eds), *Military Intervention: From Gunboat Diplomacy to Humanitarian Intervention*, London, Dartmouth Press.

Pinto, Diana, 1991, 'The Great Sea Change', *Daedalus*, cxxi(4): 129-50.

Pringle, Peter, 1994, 'Turkish troops to join UN forces in Bosnia', *The Independent*, 10 March: 1.

Savill, Annika, 1993, 'Sarajevo's symbol of agony flies in', *The Independent*, 10 August: 1.

Schmidt, Peter, 1993, *The Special Franco-German relationship in the 1990s*, Chaillot Papers no. 8, Paris, Institute for Security Studies.

Schmitt, Carl, 1988, *Der Nomos der Erde im Volkerrecht des Ius Publicum Europaeum*, 3rd edn, Berlin, Duncker & Humblot.

Smith, G., 1992, 'What Role for America?', *Current History*, 92(573), April.

Snyder, Jack, 1991, *Myths of Empire: Domestic Politics and International Ambition*, Ithaca, NY and London, Cornell University Press.

Thompson, William R., 1992, 'Dehio, Long Cycles, and the Geohistorical Context of Structural Transition', *World Politics*, xlv(1): 127-52.

Wallace, William, 1993, 'Britain's search for a new role in the world', *Observer*, 15 August.

Waltz, Kenneth N., 1979, *Theory of International Politics*, Reading, MA, Addison-Wesley.

Weber, Max, 1978, *Economy and Society*, 2nd edn, Vol i, ed. Guenther Roth and Claus Wittich, Berkeley, CA and London, University of California Press.

Wood, Nicholas and Evans, Michael, 1993, 'Backbench Tories draw the line on defence cuts', *The Times*, 6 July: 1.

Young, Oran R., 1968, 'Intervention and International Systems', *Journal of International Affairs*, xxii(2): 177-87.

PART III
BOUNDARIES REDRAWN

11
Earth, power, knowledge: towards a critical global environmental politics[1]

Peter Doran

In the 1960s and 1970s a number of writers (Schmid, 1968; Carroll, 1972; Reid and Yanarella, 1976) raised important questions about the political orientation of peace research. They criticized scholars for uncritically adopting a 'systems perspective' aimed at controlling and integrating the international system, and thereby adopting the value orientation of the existing international institutions and their most powerful members. Peace research seemed to be in danger of becoming a factor supporting the status quo of the international power structures by formulating its problems exclusively in terms meaningful to supranational institutions. Implicit in the critique, according to James Skelly (1988) was the view that researchers had failed to be reflective about their production of knowledge – knowledge that was intended to be in the service of peace and often was not.

The argument set out in this chapter will show that a parallel intellectual challenge exists today for those who would address the questions raised by environmental degradation – questions addressed within the rapidly expanding International Relations sub-discipline of Global Environmental Politics (GEP). Within the GEP literature the academic agenda can also appear to be an unreflective and uncritical extension of the desire to control and integrate the international system, this time in the service of an ascendant ideology of global environmental management (Finger, 1992) or 'eco-cracy' (Sachs, 1992), reflecting the corresponding values and interests of existing international institutions and their most powerful members. The result is one of the discipline's 'distinctive silences' (Walker, 1993).

Global Environmental Politics has been rapidly colonized by students of international regimes and institutions, focusing on 'efforts to negotiate multi-lateral agreements for co-operation to protect the environment and natural resources' (Porter and Welsh Brown, 1991: 32). Hurrell and Kingsbury (1992) narrowly define the parameters for investigation as the processes by which inter-state agreements on the environment are negotiated, the rules and regimes established to facilitate cooperation, international institutions, and the conflicting political forces which intervene. Subsequently, in an early survey of the literature Barbara Jancar (1991/92: 30) notes an absence of 'depth analyses of the interconnection between science and technology, institutional structures and ideology'. Scholars, she observes, seem caught up in industrial categories of thought in their political and economic manifestations. The industrial paradigm remains the privileged domain for analysis where the national interest is uncritically defined in terms of human activities geared towards economic growth and military strategy, with the accompanying ideologies. The environment remains a marginal phenomenon. There is clearly a place for analyses of inter-state negotiation, regime formation, and the role of international organizations like the United Nations in responding to and helping to set the international agenda on environment and development issues. The strength of any perspective, however, is only revealed by our knowledge of its limitations and omissions. Just as feminist scholarship has begun to interrogate the gendered identities of international relations, so the questions raised by environmental politics will demand a new spirit of self-criticism and reflection. Timely signs of this spirit are already hovering over the academe, inspiring the arts of deconstruction, semiotics, genealogy and intertextualism. The politics of environmentalism and these recent philosophical interventions in International Relations are postmodern allies, with intersecting genealogies. Inevitably these interpretive approaches provide the cue for the development of a critical Global Environmental Politics, given their distinctive capacity to capture what Mark Neufield (1993: 53) has called the 'constitutive and potentially transformative nature of human consciousness in terms of the global order'.

The heart of a critical GEP can be sketched in three brief statements which underline the generative possibilities of the aforementioned alliance of interpretive approaches to International Relations and environmental politics:

1. Human understanding of nature, or the environment, is historical and cultural. As such it is implicated in the operations of power and knowledge (Foucault, 1979). With Roland Barthes (1972) we can understand constructions of nature as myths which can help to conceal the role of human agency. Rather than being seen as a 'factual system', nature must be viewed as part of a 'semiological system' – it belongs to the order of signs. Political ecology is a response to the construction of a nature myth sanctioned by a European scientific discourse that has represented nature as an unproblematic object, knowable via classification and experiment, and above all infinitely manipulable in the service of human purposes.[2] Critical interventions in the discourse of nature by political ecologists contribute to a process of demythologizing nature, placing it within history, and politicizing it in the process, thus exposing the origins of unsustainable human/nature relations and proposing alternative and transformative practices.

2. Nature is always experienced as an 'ideological construction' through the mediation of society (Wilson, 1992) interacting and playing off a number of other discursive themes (science, development, industrialism, capitalism, patriarchy) associated with modernity. The consequences for the environment have been devastating. As Julian Saurin (1993) has recently observed, modernization and global environmental degradation have historically coincided. Globalized modernity has generated particular modes of power/knowledge and as a historically specific construct nature has been constituted within the

associated social relations and cultural practices, including the nation state. If 'it is in the question of administrative form and organizational order (and the type of knowledge generated within), that modernity and environmental degradation are most closely bound' (Saurin, 1993) then the ideology of the state system itself (Alger, 1984–85), along with its formative security, military, economic, and political practices, must be placed at the centre of a critical GEP agenda. Matthias Finger (1991) has argued that nation states have become a major problem for the biosphere, both as harmful actors and promoters of unsustainable practices and as obstacles to learning our way out of the ecological crisis. The importance of this focus is indicated by David Campbell's (1992) work, which has demonstrated the pivotal role of US foreign policy discourse in enframing, limiting and domesticating a particular meaning of humanity within a particular form of domestic order, including the social relations of production. Campbell has recognized the implications, suggesting that environmental danger can be figured in a manner that challenges traditional forms of identity inscribed in the capitalist economy of the 'West'.

3. A critical GEP which seeks to investigate the links between environmental degradation, the ideology of the states system and the practices of modernity requires approaches that can generate insights 'into the very orders in which regulatory international institutions are embedded' (Neufield, 1993: 57), namely interpretive or post-structuralist. Interpretive social science maintains that all social and political orders, including regulating institutions like the state, are the products of social practices, the products of unstable intersubjective meanings. Deploying such tools of analysis, a critical GEP can participate in the re-evaluation of the formative social, cultural, economic and political practices of modernity associated with the historical emergence and contemporary role of the states system and identified today as contributors to the degradation of the habitat. Moreover, interpretive approaches can be deployed to demonstrate how these practices have been involved in the construction and legitimation of a representation of nature (e.g. as an economic resource) and the world system for modern human beings while effectively concealing and delimiting the possibilities for critical reflection on their consequences.

A key conceptual tool which can be applied here is Michel Foucault's 'discursive regime' (Foucault, 1986: 55), or set of rules which permit and order statements and understandings, providing the criteria for their status as true or false. Simon Dalby, a critical geo-politics scholar who has examined the notion of environmental security[3], has described how language and discourse play a key role in maintaining political arrangements by aiding and abetting the reproduction of social existence as human practice. Discourses mobilize rules, codes, procedures and legitimacy for particular institutional and political arrangements. Above all they embody power and may conceal relations of power, thereby serving an ideological function. In this latter capacity a discourse can not only express but repress or delimit that which is available for public discussion (Dalby, 1990). Aptly, in the context of a critical Global

Environmental Politics, we might describe this process as a form of linguistic enclosure which participates in the construction of a reserve of public unconsciousness by appropriating to itself the authority to determine the permissible boundaries of expression, critique and dissent: epistemological dispossession. As Finger (1992) has argued, only in the context of new cultural perspectives will epistemological alternatives to industrial development, to technological science and to nation-state power politics become 'thinkable' again.

MODERNITY, THE STATE AND THE POLITICS OF KNOWLEDGE

Two events in 1992 brought together a number of the most important themes in international environmental politics. These were the United Nations-sponsored 'Earth Summit'[4] on the environment and development, and the commemoration of the five hundredth anniversary of Christobal Colon's landing off the shores of the Bahamas – the 'Columbian Encounter'. For Turner and Butzer (1992) the 'Earth Summit' attested to our recognition that people have transformed and continue to transform the earth with serious implications for the physical well-being of the planet and its inhabitants. The scale and pace of environmental change associated with the 'Columbian Encounter' foreshadowed similar transformations associated with the colonization of other countries by Europeans during the sixteenth and seventeenth centuries and with the further escalation of human impacts following the Industrial Revolution. These processes of ecological transformation, colonization and industrialization are also bound up with the history of state formation and the rise of modernity. As Jeremy Rifkin has put it:

> The transition to the nation-state took place over five hundred years, the path of development paralleling the worldwide enclosure of the global commons ... Nature was enclosed and commodified and native people subdued and colonized. The great merchant trading companies also brought the Enlightenment worldview with them wherever they established a beachhead and regime ... Efficiency and material progress became the secular watchwords of the age (Rifkin, 1991: 95–100).

The year 1492, then, can be viewed as a watermark for both the beginning of the global change that the United Nations Conference on Environment and Development set out to address and the emergence of the modern world system. Anthony Giddens (1990) has identified the nation-state system as one of the four dimensions of the globalization process that have accompanied the rise of modernity. The others are the world capitalist economy, the world military order, and the international division of labour. Other important institutions are industrialism, the unprecedented surveillance capacities deployed by nation states to develop coordinated control over delimited territories, and the state's privileged control over the technologies of violence, which has been enhanced by the industrialization of war. This latter point is consistent with an observation by Shiv Visvanathan (1988), who has suggested that Thomas Hobbes must be counted along with Francis Bacon and Rene Déscartes as a major figure in the genealogy of modern science, with his conception of a society based on the scientific method. For Hobbes modernity demanded a movement from the 'state of nature' to civil society, a rational society constructed so that the sovereign or the state monopolized the 'legitimate' means of terror and man-made instruments of death:

> Modernity as society is inaugurated not merely through a contract; but as a theorem, a Euclidian list of propositions which makes society possible. Science, thus, colonizes society at the very moment of inauguration, by conceptualizing it and by policing it ... In fact it is the grammar of science that provides for the everyday fascism of modernity-as-technocracy (Visvanathan, 1988: 260–61).

The European West, then, provided and frequently forced on the rest of the world all that has become the basis of a depersonalized power, governing human conscience and speech: natural science, rationalism, scientism, the Industrial Revolution, and also revolution as such, as a fanatical abstraction. Visvanathan has argued that the contemporary rituals of this 'laboratory state' (1988) are most evident in the development project which has been pursued or imposed by the leading industrialized states. Since the Second World War development and science have merged with national security as reasons of state (Nandy, 1988: 1). Visvanathan and others thus view political environmental movements as responses to a totalitarian structure built into the global development project of the modern state, which is increasingly at the service of globalizing institutions.

As a primary institutional vehicle of modernity the state is inevitably embedded within particular modes of knowledge – a dominant knowledge which stands indicted of displacing, marginalizing and destroying the other knowledge systems it encounters. A critical Global Environmental Politics therefore begins here – with the politics of knowledge. By adopting an orientation which is reflective a critical GEP complements the emergence of a 'reflexive modernity' – the essential response to the creation of a world 'risk society' (Beck, 1992).[5]

THE LIMITS OF MODERNITY

> As philosophers, we offer resistance to those ecological experts who preach respect for science, but foster neglect for historical tradition, local flair and the earthly virtue, *self-limitation* [original emphasis].[6]

The globalizing processes accomplished through the institutions of modernity have given rise to a particular sense of the 'global', as the eco-feminist Vandana Shiva (Mies and Shiva, 1993) has described. The 'global' in the dominant political discourse is the political space in which a particular dominant local seeks global control, and frees itself of local, national and international restraints. The global does not represent the universal human interest, it represents a particular local and parochial interest which has been globalized through the scope of its reach.

Shiva believes that the planet's 'security' has been invoked by the rapacious institutions of the 'North' to destroy and kill the very cultures which employ a planetary consciousness to guide their concrete daily actions. The ordinary Indian woman who worships the tulsi plant and the peasant who treats seeds as sacred are employing reflexive categories which ensure that their actions are informed by an awareness of the links between the great and the small, from planets to plants and people. This is the kind of knowledge that ensures that limits, restraints and responsibilities are always transparent and cannot be externalized or denied. Recognition that the great exists in the small and that every act therefore has not only global but cosmic implications fosters a consciousness in which demands are made on the self, not on others. Shiva has argued that the moral framework of the globalizing reach of modernity, with its dominating knowledge system, is quite the opposite. Reflexive relationships have been absent.

Wolfgang Sachs (1988) has observed the abundance of reports about the state of the planet as the curtain has finally been pulled away from the global survival crisis, and the evidence, for the most part, is undeniable.[7] The proposed policies of resource management, however, ignore the option of intelligent self-limitation. For André Gorz (1993) the technocratic response of the states system and its experts is anti-political and inevitably antithetical to the radical-democratic project of the political ecology movement, which has self-limitation at the heart of its social project. It seeks to restore areas of self-supervision and autonomy to resist and undo the colonization of the 'life world' by the rule of experts, quantification, monetary evaluation and dependency. Self-limitation, he adds, remains the only non-authoritarian, democratic way towards an eco-compatible industrial post-capitalist civilization. Capitalism has abolished everything in tradition, in the mode of life, in everyday civilization, that might serve as anchorage for a common norm of sufficiency; and has abolished at the same time the prospect that choosing to work and consume less might give access to a better, freer life.

Paradoxically it is the unprecedented production of risks[8], hazards and modern insecurities which has opened up the possibility of a radicalized reflexive modernization, according to Ulrich Beck (1992). In his influential *Risk Society: Towards a New Modernity*, Beck argues that the dangerous consequences of scientific and industrial development can no longer be limited in time, as the lives of future generations will be affected, and spatial consequences are equally unamenable to limitation. The '*effets pervers*' of modernization will have to be dealt with through the radicalization of modernity – the evolution of a reflexive modernity more amenable to self-limitation.

Beck acknowledges that the process of reflexive modernization is already under way, manifest in the critique of science developing in the environmental movement and among the lay masses. These dissidents of actually existing modernity are breaking free from the new culturally imposed constraints of a scientism which has demanded their identification with particular social institutions and their ideologies. Visvanathan believes that: 'This insurrection of the local knowledges which demands a return to the sacred is providing the crystal seed around which the challenge to the laboratory states of modernity has begun' (1988: 286).

Beck's work is built around a three-stage periodization of social change:

1. pre-modernity;
2. simple modernity – co-extensive with industrial society; and
3. reflexive modernity – co-extensive with risk society.

The axial principle of industrial society is the distribution of goods, while that of the risk society is the distribution of 'bads'. Industrial society is structured through social classes, while the risk society is individualized. The two coexist alongside each other today, as the industrialized world and science continue to generate risk. Echoing Gorz's scepticism about the capacity of the institutional responses to environmental degradation, Beck cites the observations of a number of sociologists and anthropologists on risk:

1. Physical risks are always created and effected in social systems, for example by the organizations and institutions which are supposed to manage and control the risky activity.
2. The magnitude of the physical risks is therefore a direct function of the quality of social relations and processes, e.g. transparency, accountability, democratization.
3. The primary risk is therefore that of social dependency upon institutions and actors who may well be alien, obscure and inaccessible to most people affected by the risks in question.

Just as some environmentalists[9] have observed in the wake of the emergence of global environmental management[10], Beck argues that the most common response by those who have been responsible for generating and managing risks has been an attempt to 'adapt procedures and self-presentation in order to secure or repair credibility, without fundamentally questioning the forms of power or social control involved' (1992: 4). Like Shiva, Beck identifies an absence of reflexivity in the social and political interactions between experts and social groups over modern risk production because of the systematic assumption of realism in science. A reflexive approach would be characterized by learning processes which recognize the conditions underpinning scientific conclusions, draw out questions of social situation, and examine these with an openness to different forms of knowledge. Negotiation would take place between different epistemologies and subcultural forms, amongst different discourses and involve the development of the social and moral identities of the actors involved (Beck, 1992: 5).

Beck draws a parallel between the nineteenth century – when modernization demystified privileges of rank and religious world views – and today, as reflexive modernity launches another process of demystification directed at received understandings of science and technology. He sees an antagonism opening up between industrial society and modernity. No longer should we seek to conceive of modernity within the categories of industrial society, for 'we are witnessing not the end but the beginning of a modernity – that is, of a modernity beyond its classical design' (Beck, 1992: 10).

For Beck, perhaps somewhat optimistically, the key to the establishment of a modernity which might free itself from the interest in mastery in favour of 'self-control' and 'self-limitation' is modernity's encounter with itself.[11] What he seeks is a pedagogy of scientific rationality which will conceive of that rationality as changeable by discussion of self-produced threats. This would mean a transfer of the substantive abilities for criticism and learning to the foundations of knowledge and the application of it – what Beck has called an elevation of the actually latent reflexivity of the modernization process into scientific consciousness. What the rise of the green parties across the world has shown is that this pedagogical project will involve an intensely political struggle.

SYSTEMS OF KNOWLEDGE AND THE ENVIRONMENT

We have noted Saurin's (1993) observation that it is in the question of administrative form and organizational order – together with the type of knowledge generated within – that modernity and environmental degradation are most clearly bound up. The dominant source of the dynamism behind modernity as described by Giddens (1990) is the separation of time and space,[12] which permits time-space distanciation of indefinite scope and provides the conditions for the development of disembedding mechanisms responsible for lifting out social activity from localized contexts.

Saurin (1993) has made a number of observations which begin to demonstrate the significance of these dynamics for the environment and the type of knowledge system associated with them. Followings Giddens's observation that modernity increasingly tears space away from place by fostering relations between absent others who are locationally distant from any given situation of face-to-face interaction, Saurin argues that the fundamental break between the processes of production and consumption also involves the removal and abstraction of knowledge about that self-same relationship: '... neither a perfunctory knowledge of the technical procedures of production nor the environmental circumstances and costs of production are visible to the distanced consumer (Saurin, 1993: 4).

Distanciation and mediation of action thus raise a central dilemma – namely an undermining of the relationship between intention, action and outcome, or a confusion of our comprehension of causality. Here we have one argument which illustrates Giddens' (1990) view that ecological threats are the outcome of socially organized knowledge, mediated by the impact of industrialism on the material environment. As the nation-state system is one of the most important dimensions of the globalization process that has accompanied and constituted the rise of modernity, the politics of the knowledge systems that have been integral to the process take centre stage in a critical Global Environmental Politics. It is to a brief examination of the question of knowledge systems that we now turn.

A number of authors at the United Nations University's World Institute for Development Economics Research Institute[13] have begun to explore how modernity, understood as a dominating system of knowledge, has marginalized and disenfranchised the knowledge of rural non-industrial communities. Tariq Banuri and Frederique Apffel Marglin write:

> The modern system of knowledge, along with its associated set of values, has been elevated to the highest status, while alternatives are at best viewed as inferior forms of knowledge and, at worst, as non knowledge ... The deterioration of forestry resources and the environmental crisis in general must be viewed from the angle of the politics of knowledge and a critical approach to the dominant, modern system of knowledge (1993: 2).

Banuri and Apffel Marglin understand all cultures as knowledge systems composed of systems of epistemology, transmission, innovation and power. They note the cultural specificity of exclusive binary oppositions – overlaid with a series of hierarchies – in the West. For Banuri the binary opposition that is most distinctive in Western culture is the subordination of the personal to the impersonal. He believes this view forms a foundational element of various Western theories, indeed the entire sensibility which is described as 'Western' (Banuri, 1990: 83). While it once provided for a tremendous increase in human ability to control and manipulate nature it is now to be found at the root of a myriad of problems, including a loss of meaning, alienation, an unprecedented rationalization of violence and destruction of the environment.

For the WIDER authors the central problem is the imperialistic pretension of universality made on behalf of Western episteme and the total inability of its adherents to regard competing systems with anything but contempt – indeed, an inability even to contemplate their existence. Exposure of the radical shortcomings of modern responses such as the paradigmatic example of 'scientific forestry',[14] the authors suggest, has given rise to a resurgence of interest in local or subjugated knowledge in order to look for answers to the environmental crisis in general, by incorporating the rationale behind non-modern technologies and practices into modern systems. A 'systems of knowledge' framework of analysis makes this approach possible as it is based on the view that there are multiple ways of defining reality. There are diverse and competent communities of knowledge which embrace numerous ways of understanding, perceiving, experiencing and defining reality, including relations between people and between people and their environment. The dominant modern or scientific knowledge system, though not exclusively Western in origin, is said to enjoy its privileged position because of a number of background assumptions deeply rooted in Western civilization.

The importance of the encounter with alternative knowledge systems lies in the subsequent exposure of these foundational assumptions, which permits scholars and actors to proceed to critical reflection. Enrique Dussel's use of the concept of exteriority in his *Philosophy of Liberation* (1985) expresses the critical function of looking beyond a dominant knowledge system to perceive other realities. This process corresponds to interior transcendentality. While critique may be intrinsic to the human sciences' approaches to politics and technology, Dussel points out that it can only and at most affirm the *proyecto*[15] of the system if the dialectical totality of a given system is taken as the ultimate horizon. If, on the contrary, one begins with the demand for justice from exteriority, the same functional totality is placed in question by the exigencies implicit in the construction of a new, future order, one that is already an incipient *proyecto* of the people (Dussel, 1985: 169).

A central element among the invisible assumptions that inform the dominant knowledge system of modernity is an instrumental view of nature which contrasts, for example, with indigenous knowledge systems that imbue nature with sacred meaning. Banuri and Apffel Marglin make the far-reaching claim that such alternative perspectives exist everywhere:

> albeit in somewhat circumscribed, degraded and disregarded forms. They are exhibited in a variety of ways, most prominently in protest efforts such as those of the Chipko volunteers in Uttarakhand or of the forest villagers of Sivakka in Finland. The alternative systems of knowledge do not have to be created from a whole cloth; what needs to be done is to allow them to exist and to accord them the respect and legitimacy they deserve (1993: 11).

Discussing some of the chief characteristics of the dominant modern knowledge system, the authors suggest that individualism directly implies an instrumental attitude towards the environment as it participates in the construction of nature as either a source of gratification or a constraint on that gratification. Either way it must be manipulated and controlled, and protection of the environment becomes no more than a mere strategy. The other dimensions of the modern knowledge system reinforce this trajectory. The subject/object dichotomy, for example, leads to what James Hillman (1975) has described as the 'de-souling' of nature, licensing modern science to discover/construct a silent world.

THE RISE OF GLOBAL ENVIRONMENTAL MANAGEMENT

The staging of the 'Earth Summit' in Rio de Janeiro marked the ascendance of 'global environmental management' – a top-down approach to problems first raised by the grassroots-oriented political ecology movement of the 1970s. Matthias Finger (1992) and others believe not only that this approach is likely to be largely ineffective but that it will demand a price in the form of a new global technocracy with serious implications for democracy. The technocratic response, then, amounts to an antithesis of the programme advocated by political ecologists, who view the extension of participation, democracy and autonomy as the preconditions for sustainable societies and the decolonization of the life-world by the totalitarian rationality of the modern economic and industrial system (Bookchin, 1986; Gorz, 1993; Eckersley, 1992).

Signs of what was to follow were present in the text of the Brundtland Report[16] (1987) according to Wolfgang Sachs, who believes the publication announced the fulfilment of a long-held aspiration on the part of the world's modernizing élite – the marriage of popular concern for the environment with their own 'craving for development'. The development discourse has been rehabilitated and transformed into a discourse for survival:

> Today 'survival of the planet' is well on its way to becoming the wholesale justi-fication for a new wave of state interventions in people's lives all over the world ... the experts who used to look after economic growth now claim to be presiding over survival itself (Sachs, 1992: 33).

This emergent global discourse of technocratic management is said to dis-regard intelligent self-restraint while inventing new procedures, institutions and grammars to keep the present system afloat and defer the day of judge-ment. Capital, bureaucracy and science, the venerable trinity of Western modernization, writes Sachs, declare themselves indispensable in the new crisis, promising to prevent the worst through better engineering, integrated planning and more sophisticated models. Calls for securing the survival of the planet turn out to be little more than calls for the survival of the existing industrial system.

The association of the emergent discourse of global environmental manage-ment with a largely discredited development project imposed on the Third World establishes the discourse within a lineage of conceptual trapping, or the enclosure of language and cultures (*The Ecologist*, 1992). Ivan Illich once observed that enclosure inaugurates a 'new ecological order'. It defines power and redefines meaning in a process which has been compared to translation. Within the new order enclosure redefines how the environment is managed, by whom and for whose benefit. This is the process that gathered pace throughout the eras of state-formation, colonialism and economic development, and which proceeds today through the discursive prism of global environmental manage-ment. A consistent characteristic of the process is a failure to tolerate other approaches, to demonstrate any degree of tolerance towards the thousands of other, more or less independent, languages which make up the social universe. Enclosure claims that its own social frame, its language, is a universal norm, an all-embracing matrix which can assimilate all others (*The Ecologist*, 1992: 154).

Illich's critique is echoed in Shiv Visvanathan's incisive reading of *Mrs Brundtland's Disenchanted Cosmos* in the *Brundtland Report* (WCED, 1987). He discerns in the report a narrative that mimics modern violence – 'bloodless and antiseptic' – and advocates new styles of control and surveillance akin to Bentham's panopticon vision of vigilance:

> The new epidemic of reports uses the style of concern to control: it re-states certain problems to erase people's memory of them ... It is killing through concepts, through coding, by creating grammars that decide which sentence can be spoken and which cannot (Visvanathan, 1992: 378).

If fears about the direction of the emerging discourse of global environmental management have any foundation, a critical Global Environmental Politics must begin to account for its dynamic by investigating the epistemological, cultural and power practices embedded in and reproduced by the states system. Clearly there are implications for the system's adaptive capacities in the wake of global environmental change if it can be shown that it is implicated in the very practices which have come under scrutiny for their contribution to the creation of the environmental crises in the first place. Two primary objectives for a critical GEP are:

1. To identify, describe and account for the origins and dynamics of the emergent discourse of global environmental management in international relations.
2. To locate the dominant discourse within the spectrum of approaches to the environmental problematic identified by political ecologists, and critically evaluate its underlying cultural and political assumptions and problem defining/solving capacities. In the process a space is opened up within the discipline for the rehabilitation and recognition of marginalized and subjugated local knowledge systems in international politics.

ONE APPROACH TO A CRITICAL GLOBAL ENVIRONMENTAL POLITICS

The approach to a critical GEP advocated here would extend to the environment the kind of questions already raised by post-structuralist or interpretive scholars working in areas like critical geo-politics (Ashley, 1987; Der Derian and Shapiro, 1989; Shapiro, 1988; Walker, 1986; Agnew and O'Tuathail, 1987). Central to the critical geo-politics school is the view that geographical space is produced and not 'given' naturally. Geo-politics thus comes to be understood as practice and as discourse involved in the production of geo-political scripts, texts and procedures that create ways of describing and acting in the world political scene. This innovative approach to our understanding of geographical space and the operation of power offers an ideal methodological cue to follow in the investigation of the emerging and competing environmental discourses. Following Simon Dalby (1992) it can be argued that just as security discourse has been trapped within the metaphysics and structures of Western philosophy and the will to dominate and control, so it is with the dominant environmental discourse of the states system. This discourse engages in a social creation of nature – a creation myth – as a resource to be administered by a technologically sophisticated states system constituted by and instrumental in the reproduction of the patterns of knowledge, practices and power which continue to inform the emerging institutions of global environmental management.

More specifically, a critical GEP could be built on the Diremptive/Redemptive model advocated by Bradley Klein (1988) and Alastair Pennycook (1990) for a post-modern politics of peace. Drawing on the work of Michel Foucault and others, Klein and Pennycook envisage a model for examining international relations which is capable of conceptualizing the interrelationship of culture, power and knowledge. It aims to:

challenge the hegemonizing character of the prevailing discursive practices (the

Diremptive) and to validate the subjugated knowledges and identities that have been submerged beneath or marginalized by the predominant discursive practices and power/knowledge relationships (the Redemptive) (Pennycook, 1990: 57).

The concept of culture plays a central role in Pennycook's model. His interpretation holds that culture is not merely reflective of a social system and not merely an informing spirit that conditions the behaviour of its adherents, but is both reflective and productive of the system. The Diremptive/Redemptive project is based on a view that the transfer of knowledge around the world at unprecedented and accelerating speeds through a diverse range of media and institutions demands a more rigorous conceptualization of knowledge than has been the case in studies of international politics until now. Knowledge circulation and transfers raise important questions: how is knowledge constituted by, and constitutive of, different socio-cultural systems? Who defines, regulates and legitimates forms of knowledge, and who is given and who is denied access to that knowledge? The reductionist view of knowledge held by the liberal-humanist has been linked to the massive transfer of science and technology from the powerful to the powerless or dependent, with all the accompanying implications. Pennycook adds:

> The most fundamental problem with this concept of a one-way flow of a fixed body of knowledge lies in its relation to the massive export of science and technology from Europe, North America and Japan to the poorer nations of the world. Scientific thought, and its subsequent nineteenth-century colonization of the humanities to form the social sciences, has been intimately associated with the concepts of development and modernization. As Wallerstein suggests, 'the concept of development is not merely one of the central components of the ideology both of Western civilization and of world social science, but is in fact the central organizing concept on which all else is hinged'. [Immanuel Wallerstein, 1984: 173] The technological advance of the West, then, has served to legitimate Western culture's normative assumptions about development and knowledge. Thus within unequal relations of power and the discourse of development, a positivist, instrumental concept of knowledge that stresses efficiency and articulates an unquestioning, objectivist relationship between knowledge and truth has become the predominant paradigm (Pennycook, 1990: 64).

For Pennycook the most complete conceptualization of the relations between power, knowledge and culture has come from the French philosopher, Michel Foucault, for whom power is the means by which reality is produced. In Foucault's view people are vehicles of power, not its point of application. Further, it is not possible for power to be exercised without knowledge, or for knowledge but to engender power. Criticism performs its work by facilitating the re-emergence or insurrection of subjugated, popular, or 'unqualified' knowledges. Drawing on this approach a critical GEP begins with the question of whether the language of global environmental management reproduces its own system of referents, possibly creating that to which it purports to be responding. In doing so the space is cleared for a consideration of the knowledge systems and practices which occupy the place of exteriority. Criticism commences with a breaching of the enclosure of epistemology which protects the networks of power which enmesh the environment, production, distribution, politics and the law.

The 'discursive regime' is a central concept in Foucault's analyses of historical transformation. These regimes or sets of rules permit and order statements and allow their identification as true or false, right or wrong. Citing Philp (1985), Matless (1992) adds that these rules are not laid down and consciously followed, do not form a methodology or paradigm, but

> provide the necessary preconditions for the formation of statements, and as such they operate 'behind the backs' of speakers of a discourse. Indeed, the place, function and character of the 'knowers', authors and audiences of a discourse are also a function of these discursive rules (Philp, 1985: 69).

CONCLUSION

Just as the critical study of geo-politics in discursive terms is the study of the socio-cultural resources and rules by which geographs (earth writing) of international politics get written, so a discursive or interpretive approach to Global Environmental Politics could facilitate a critical investigation of the socio-cultural resources and rules by which the environmental strategies of international politics and institutions are formulated.

Post-structuralists hold that structures are not complete, stationary and universal. Rather, they are virtual or exist as instanciations only, shifting, incomplete and strategic. Structures hold down a certain world, patrol understandings about it and ward off alternative worlds. Our social practices, theories, actions and institutions, including the states system, are all informed by and rely upon a discursive knowledge that gives us a world. Gearoid O'Tuathail (1989) concludes that rather than seeking to define how the world really is, the social scientist needs to study how worlds are made by social practices. To overlook this task is to become implicated in an assumption that phenomena are natural or universal – an assumption which has conferred upon a particular science, scientists and scientific knowledge an authoritarian power to construct what is seen/true. This attitude has served as a device for epistemological and physical domination relying on an assumption that the relationship between language and reality is innocent, unmediated and transparent. With Roland Barthes, however, a critical GEP begins with the knowledge that language is always inhabited by power.

The power which inhabits the language of 'intellectuals of statecraft' has been instrumental in the naturalization of formal geopolitical reasoning and its institutions. O'Tuathail and Agnew (1992) have suggested that this reasoning has been framed by the ideological and political limitations of particular forms of knowledge. The discourse speaking behind the backs of realists and neo-realists in International Relations shores up the 'Old Politics' of economic growth, strong military defence and conventional political style. The 'New Politics' of the political ecologists demands that ecological imperatives guide economic decisions, that rights to participation and the freedom to realize alternative lifestyles should be extended, and that disarmament be promoted in order to reduce international tension (Poguntke, 1993). Traditional sources of economic and political security are reinterpreted and re-articulated as systematic sources of multiple and mutually reinforcing insecurities and risk profiles, including the destruction of the habitat.

A critical Global Environmental Politics provides a space for some of these new questions and interpretations by extending the exploration of the links between the spatial politics of the state, the economy and modernity to generate new understandings of the environmental crises. Simon Dalby (1993) has noted the persistence of geo-political thinking in both policy-making and academic circles in the wake of the Cold War, with portrayals of security as a spatial practice of protecting internal political identities against external threats. It is the task of a critical discipline to question the 'taken for grantedness' of such understandings (Der Derian and Shapiro, 1989). Drawing on Jacques Lacan's work on aggression in spatial dynamics, Teresa Brennan (1993) has suggested that the state should be understood as centrally involved in the dynamics of centralization, providing the general conditions of production. Spatial control and spatial expansion, executed through the development of means of transportation and domination or means of war, have been the conditions of the invisible hand extending its global grasp. In a sense, Brennan adds, *they are the state*. The state has provided the spatio-temporal conditions of production from the beginning. The states system occupies a central mediating role in the productive processes and accompanying ideologies facing a radical challenge from the advocates of a New Politics, a transformative project which seeks to build something new upon a culture which turns its back on the cult of accumulation and self-aggrandizement in favour of self-limitation.

NOTES

1. Global environmental politics is the term used by a number of scholars to describe the emerging International Relations sub-discipline which addresses questions relating to the environment.
2. For a history of the impact of industrialization and colonialism on the meaning attached to the term 'resource' see Vandana Shiva, 'Resources', in Wolfgang Sachs (ed), 1992, *The Development Dictionary: A Guide to Knowledge as Power*, London, Zed Books. She plots the passage from an understanding of the regenerative capacity of nature based on a need for human restraint to the modern view of nature as dead and without value until destiny is bestowed by the needs of industrial capitalism – a view sanctioned by science.
3. See Dalby, 1990, 1992, 1993.
4. The United Nations Conference on Environment and Development took place in Rio de Janeiro, Brazil, from 3 to 14 June 1992. Representatives of over 140 nations took part.
5. Reflexivity refers to the sociological and political process in modern societies whereby 'modernisation itself is becoming its own theme for critical reflection. An important driving force behind this process is the set of problems resulting from technological and economic development itself. In other words the creation of a 'risk society'. See Giddens (1990) for the clearest introduction to these themes.

6. The 'Declaration on Soil' by Sigmar Groeneveld, Lee Hoinacki, Ivan Illich and friends appeared in *IFDA Dossier* 81, April/June 1991: 57–8.
7. In his *Traditions, Tyranny and Utopias* (1992) Ashis Nandy points to a powerful mechanism which suggests that no easy assumptions about confronting denial in the 'North' can be made. Nandy has suggested that an isomorphism exists in the internal structures of knowledge, persons and cultures (i.e. what we do to others we do not only to ourselves but also to our cognitive ventures) and that power has become the legitimate modern means of denying this to ourselves and forcing this denial upon others.
8. The concept of risk, according to Ulrich Beck (1992) is directly bound to the concept of reflexive modernization. Risk may be defined as a systematic way of dealing with hazards and insecurities induced and introduced by modernization itself.
9. Matthias Finger has described nation states as 'industrial development agencies' striving for material wealth and independence from environmental constraints. Putting nation states in charge of the global ecological crisis, as the UNCED process has sanctioned, will lead only to attempts to sustain industrial development in an age of ecologically imposed limitations and constraints (*Eco-currents*, 1991, 1 (4), September).
10. See, for example, Doran, P., 1993, 'The Earth Summit (UNCED): Ecology as Spectacle', in *Paradigms: Kent Journal of International Relations*, 7(1) Summer: 55–65.
11. A characteristic of modernity is the presumption of wholesale reflexivity, including reflection upon the nature of reflection itself, according to Anthony Giddens (1990: 39).
12. The introduction of clock time and the later standardization of international time zones finally ended the need to refer to socio-spatial markers in order to tell the time. Uniformity of time measurement has been matched by uniformity in social organization of time. This 'emptying of time', according to Giddens (1990) is in large part the precondition for the 'emptying of space'. Coordination across time has been the basis of the control of space.
13. The World Institute for Development Economics Research (UNU/WIDER), Katajanokanlaituri 6, SF-00160 Helsinki, Finland.
14. Banuri and Apffel Marglin (1993) identify three major problems with 'scientific forestry'. These are the harmful effects brought about by its claim to a privileged status for its mode of knowing, which legitimizes colonization and exploitation of the object of its knowledge, a problem inherent in an instrumentalist view of the world; the 'scientific' justification of short-term commercial practices; and direct state control compounds these problems due to corruption, inefficiency and waste.
15. Dussel uses the Spanish word *proyecto* to convey a Heideggerian sense of self projection into the future. The nearest English word is project.
16. The World Commission on Environment and Development, 1987, *Our Common Future*, Oxford, Oxford University Press.

REFERENCES

Agnew, J.A. and O'Tuathail, G., 1987, 'The historiography of American geopolitics', *International Studies Association*, Washington.
Alger, C., 1984/85, 'Bridging the Micro and Macro in International Relations', *Alternatives*, X (3), Winter.

Ashley, R.K., 1987, 'The Geopolitics of Geopolitical Space: toward a critical social theory of international politics', *Alternatives*, 12(4): 403–34.

Banuri, T., 1990, 'Modernisation and its discontents: a cultural perspective on theories of development', in F.A. Marglin and S.A. Marglin (eds), *Dominating Knowledge: Development, Culture and Resistance*, Oxford, Clarendon Press.

Banuri, T. and Apffel Marglin, F., 1993, *Who Will Save the Forests?*, London, Zed Books.

Barthes, R., 1972, *Mythologies*, London, J. Cape.

Baumann, Z., 1989, *Modernity and the Holocaust*, Cambridge, Polity.

Baurque, C., 1993, *The End of Economics?*, London, Zed Books.

Beck, U., 1992, *Risk Society: Towards a New Modernity*, London, Sage Publications.

Bookchin, M., 1986, *Toward an Ecological Society*, Montreal-Buffalo, Black Rose Books.

Brennan, T., 1993, *History After Lacan*, London, Routledge.

Campbell, D., 1992, *Writing Security: United States Foreign Policy and the Politics of Identity*, Manchester, Manchester University Press.

Carroll, B., 1972, 'Peace Research: The Cult of Power', *Journal of Conflict Resolution*, xvi: 587–616.

Dalby, S., 1990, *Creating the Second Cold War: The Discourse of Politics*, London, Pinter Publishers.

Dalby, S., 1992, 'Security, Modernity, Ecology: The Dilemmas of Post Cold War Security Discourse', *Alternatives*, 17(1): 95–134.

Dalby, S., 1993, 'Dilemmas of Environmental Security: Geopolitical Discourse or Ecospheric Integrity?', *Carleton Geography Discussion Papers, Discussion Paper no. 11*, Carleton University, Ottawa, Canada.

Der Derian, J. and Shapiro, M., 1989, *International/Intertextual Relations: Postmodern Readings of World Politics*, New York, Lexington Books.

Dussel, E., 1985, *Philosophy of Liberation*, New York, Maryknoll.

Eckersley, R., 1992, *Environmentalism and Political Theory: Toward an Ecocentric Approach*, New York, State University of New York.

Ecologist, 1992, 'Whose Common Future?', special issue, 22(4).

Finger, M., 1991, 'The Role of the Nation-State in Today's Global Ecological Crisis', *Eco-Currents*, 1(4), September.

Finger, M., 1991, 'The Military, the Nation State and the Environment', *The Ecologist*, 21(5), September/October: 220–5.

Finger, M., 1992, 'How to read the UNCED Process', *Eco-Currents*, 2(2), May.

Finger, M., 1993, 'Politics of the UNCED Process', in Sachs, W., *Global Ecology: A New Arena of Political Conflict*, London, Zed Books.

Foucault, M., 1979, Discipline and Punish: *The Birth of the Prison*, Harmondsworth, Middx., Penguin Books.

Foucault, M., 1980, *Power/Knowledge*, Brighton, Sussex, Harvester.

Foucault, M., 1986, 'Truth and Power', in Rabinow, P., *The Foucault Reader*, Harmondsworth, Middx., Penguin Books.

Giddens, A., 1990, *The Consequences of Modernity*, Cambridge, Polity Press.

Gorz, A., 1993, 'Ecology and Experts', *New Left Review*, 202: 55–67.

Havel, V., 1990, *Living in Truth*, London, Faber and Faber.

Hebdige, D., 'Postmodernism and "The Other Side"', *Journal of Communication Inquiry*, 10(2): 78–99.

Hillman, J., 1975, *Re-visioning Psychology*, New York, Harper and Row.

Hurrell, A. and Kingsbury B., 1992, *The International Politics of the Environment*, Oxford, Clarendon Press.

Illich, I. et al., 1991, 'Declaration on Soil', *IFDA Dossier*, 81, April/June: 57–8.

Illich, I., 1993, 'Health As One's Own Responsibility: No, Thankyou!', *The Aisling Magazine*, Uimhir 11: 50–55.

Jancar, Barbara, 1991/2, 'Environmental Studies: State of the Discipline', *International Studies Notes of the International Studies Association*, 16(3), Fall 1991, and 17(1), Winter 1992: 25–31.

Kakonen, J. (ed.), 1992, *Perspectives on Environmental Conflict and International Politics*, Tampere, Finland, Tampere Peace Research Institute.

Kim, H.P., 1990, 'The Green Politics of Peace', *IFDA Dossier*, 75/76, January/April: 3–18.

Klein, B., 1988, 'After Strategy: The Search for a Post-Modern Politics of Peace', *Alternatives*, 13: 293–318.

Kothari, R., 1987, 'On Humane Governance', *Alternatives*, 12(93): 277–90.

Kovel, J., 1991, *History and Spirit: An Inquiry into the Philosophy of Liberation*, Boston, MA, Beacon Press.

Marglin, F.A. and Apffel Marglin, S. (eds), 1990, *Dominating Knowledge: Development, Culture and Resistance*, Oxford, Clarendon Press.

Matless, D., 1992, 'An Occasion for Geography: Landscape, Representation, and Foucault's Corpus', *Society and Space*, 10: 41–56.

Mies, M., and Shiva, V., 1993, *Ecofeminism*, London, Zed Books.

Naess, A., 1973, 'The Shallow and the Deep, Long Range Ecology Movement', *Inquiry*, 16: 95–100.

Nandy, A., 1983, *The Intimate Enemy: Loss and Recovery of Self under Colonialism*, Delhi, Oxford University Press.

Nandy, A., 1988, 'Introduction: Science as a Reason of State', in Nandy, A. (ed.), *Science, Hegemony and Violence*, Oxford University Press/ United Nations University.

Nandy, A., 1992, *Traditions, Tyranny, and Utopias: Essays in the Politics of Awareness*, Delhi, Oxford University Press.

Neufield, M., 1993, 'Interpretation and the "Science" of International Relations', *Review of International Studies*, 19(1), January: 39–61.

O'Tuathail, Gearoid, 1989, *Critical Geopolitics: The Social Construction of Space and Place in the Practice of Statecraft*, Doctoral Dissertation, Graduate School of Syracuse.

Pennycook, A., 1990, 'The Diremptive/Redemptive Project: Postmodern Reflections on Culture and Knowledge in International Academic Relations', *Alternatives*, 15: 53–81.

Philp, M., 1985, 'Michel Foucault', in Skinner, Q. (ed.), *The Return of Grand Theory in the Human Sciences*, Cambridge, Cambridge University Press: 65–81.

Plumwood, V., 1993, *Feminism and the Mastery of Nature*, London, Routledge.

Poguntke, T., 1993, *Alternative Politics: The German Green Party*, Edinburgh, Edinburgh University Press.

Porter, G., and Welsh Brown, J., 1991, *Global Environmental Politics*, Oxford, Westview Press.

Reid G.R. and Yanarella, E.J., 1976, 'Toward a Critical Theory of Peace Research in the United States: the Search for an "Intelligible Core"', *Journal of Peace Research*, xiii: 315–41.

Rifkin, J., 1991, *Biosphere Politics*, London, HarperCollins.

Sachs, W., 1988, '*The Gospel of Global Efficiency*', IFDA Dossier, 68, November/ December: 33–9.

Sachs, W. (ed.), 1992, The Development Dictionary: A Guide to Knowledge as Power, London, Zed Books.

Saurin, J., 1993, 'Global Environmental Degradation, Modernity and Environmental Knowledge', *Environmental Politics*.

Schmid, H., 1968, 'Peace Research and Politics', *Journal of Peace Research*, V: 217–32.

Seager, J., 1993, *Earth Follies: Feminism, Politics and the Environment*, London, Earthscan Publications.

Shapiro, M., 1988, *The Politics of Representation*, Madison, University of Wisconsin Press.

Skelly, J.M., 1988, 'Power/Knowledge: The Problems of Peace Research and the Peace Movement', in Alger, C. and Stohl, M. (eds), *A Just Peace Through Transformation: Cultural, Economic and Political Foundations for Change*, Boulder, CO, Westview Press, 21–36.

Turner, B.L., and Butzer, K.W., 1992, 'The Columbian Encounter and Land-Use Change', *Environment*, 34(8), October: 16–20, 37–43.

Visvanathan, S., 1988, 'On the Annals of the Laboratory State', in Nandy, A. (ed.), *Science, Hegemony and Violence: A Requiem for Modernity*, Oxford University Press/United Nations University.

Visvanathan, S., 1992, 'Mrs. Brundtland's Disenchanted Cosmos', *Alternatives*, 16: 377–84.

Walker, R.B.J., 1986, 'Culture, Discourse and Insecurity', *Alternatives*, 11(4): 485–504.

Walker, R.B.J., 1993, *Inside/Outside: International Relations as Political Theory*, Cambridge, Cambridge University Press.

Wallerstein, I., 1984, *The Politics of the World Economy: the States, the Movements, and the Civilizations*, Cambridge, Cambridge University Press.

World Commission on Environment and Development, 1987, *Our Common Future*, Oxford, Oxford University Press.

Wilson, A., 1992, *The Culture of Nature: North American Landscape from Disney to Exxon Valdez*, Oxford, Blackwell.

12
Radicalizing regimes? Ecology and the critique of IR theory

Matthew Paterson

I smoke 'cos I'm hoping for an early death,
And I need to cling to something. (The Smiths, 'What She Said')

The motivation behind this chapter is a desire to explore some of the inadequacies of the ways in which much mainstream IR theory has been 'applied'
to environmental problems, and to find more adequate frameworks within
which to examine them.[1] The analyses of many IR scholars writing currently
about international environmental politics are still predominantly formed by
their particular understandings of IR in general. When viewed from a perspective that starts from environmental problems as the major focus of attention,
these are inappropriate. I shall start therefore by focusing on how analyses of
environmental problems based in mainstream IR theory (by which I take still
to be the neo-realism of Waltz or Gilpin and the neo-liberal institutionalism
associated with Robert Keohane in particular) depoliticize these problems –
they try to reduce them to problems of a predominantly technical nature.
Second, I will highlight some of the underlying ideological assumptions that
produce such analyses. Within this, I will suggest throughout that an adequate
analysis of international environmental problems necessarily involves a challenge to prevailing power relationships, between states, within states, within
capitalist economies, and within patriarchal forms of power.

I will then conclude by arguing that one way to move forward in our
understandings of these problems may be to use Green political thought and
the related academic literature. While as yet there is little specifically on the
questions with which IR scholars are familiar, this literature is clearly global
in implication, and does start with a focus on the environmental crisis rather
than on, for example, inter-state relations. I do not presume to have this
position fully worked out, but it does provide a more adequate basis on which
future research might be based.

THE ENVIRONMENT AND CONVENTIONAL THEORY: 'IT'S LIFE JIM, BUT NOT AS WE KNOW IT.'

Global environmental problems have mainly been analysed within the general terms set by the developing 'regimes' literature of the 1980s. Although

some, reflecting a realist tradition, do focus on conflict and national interests, a certain intellectual hegemony has arisen regarding basic assumptions about the international politics of these problems around Robert Keohane's 'neoliberal institutionalism'.[2]

The literature on international regimes and/or institutions[3] can be characterized as largely 'problem-solving theory', which Cox defines thus:

> It takes the world as it finds it, with the prevailing social and power relationships and the institutions into which they are organized, as the given framework for action. The general aim of problem-solving is to make these relationships and institutions work more smoothly by dealing effectively with particular sources of trouble (1981: 208).

In other words, the subtext of most writing on regimes is to try to establish the 'effectiveness' of a regime in its given issue-area. However, this presumes a notion of effectiveness that is supposed to be taken as unproblematic. We are supposed to take a leap of faith that, in the case of environmental questions, natural scientists from the relevant disciplines have established scientific criteria by which a regime can be judged 'effective' in terms of improving environmental conditions. Alternatively, regimes are simply judged to be effective if they can be shown to have altered state behaviour.

An ideal example appears in the recent volume edited by Peter Haas, Robert Keohane and Marc Levy (1993). There, the writers analyse the effectiveness of international institutions in particular fields in terms of three processes through which institutions affect outcomes:

> (1) They can contribute to more appropriate agendas, reflecting the convergence of political and technical consensus about the nature of environmental threats; (2) they can contribute to more comprehensive and specific international policies ... and (3) they can contribute to national policy responses (Keohane, Haas and Levy 1993: 8).

Throughout, the writers suggest that a successful regime is one which provides 'concrete mechanisms by which international institutions can alter the behavior of state actors, and in turn improve environmental quality' (1993: 19), without indicating that these assertions might have any problematic aspects. On the one hand, they assume that what constitutes an improvement in environmental quality is reasonably clear. On the other, they assume that state-centrism as an operational assumption (that either state actors are either the only ones which can significantly affect 'environmental quality', or that no other focus for IR is reasonable since the state remains the only fully legitimate international actor), is a valid starting point.

The criterion that regimes are judged to be effective if they affect state behaviour assumes that the contents of any particular regime (its 'principles, norms, rules and decision-making procedures') are desirable. In the environmental field, this usually means accepting the criteria set by natural scientists. However, these criteria can easily be shown to be largely political: whether they be critical loads for acid rain, chlorine loading in the stratosphere, or CO_2 limits, the decision to limit emissions at a given level is always ultimately political. This point gets routinely ignored by analysts of all sorts of regimes, but is especially important regarding environmental questions. Arguably a more reasonable assumption is that a basic consensus exists over goals (even if these consensuses have been hegemonically constructed and maintained). Such a consensus does not exist for environmental problems – hence a fallback position (by both politicians and analysts) has been to rely on the intellectual dominance of the natural sciences for 'objective' guidance. It is, however, by no means universally accepted that delegating effective decision-making to natural scientists is either desirable or necessary; this process constitutes what Habermas has called the 'scientization of politics' and necessarily a reduction in democracy (1968; see also Marcuse, 1964 for similar arguments).

Conventional approaches to regimes 'depoliticize' international environmental problems by providing criteria by which responses can be judged in a supposedly neutral manner - for environmental questions this becomes reductions in emissions, resources spent on the clean-up of particular ecosystems, and so on. Yet these cannot be isolated from other criteria. Environmental questions cannot be neatly boxed off from other political questions. The regimes established to resolve transnational environmental problems always benefit some social groups more than others, whether or not they are successful from a purely environmental point of view (and even if such a point of view were possible), and they also preclude the broader question of whether the existing political social and economic orders may themselves generate environmental crises.

Second, of course, when we look seriously not only at the regimes that have been established to address environmental problems, but also at the ways regime analysts have written about them, we see very clearly that they are simply not capable of producing an effective response, defined even by their own criteria. The volume by Haas, Keohane and Levy already mentioned (1993) is a prime example of this. They are concerned to show how international institutions have been important in influencing the outcomes of a number of environmental problems, a concern which appears largely motivated by Keohane's ongoing theoretical 'battle' with neo-realism.[4] In this they largely succeed, but only on the basis that they demonstrate that regimes affect state behaviour, which doesn't necessarily improve environmental quality; their theoretical concerns have skewed (from an environmental point of view) their normative questions and criteria of 'success'. They also reveal, possibly inadvertently, how peripheral the purely formal 'international level' is to the resolution of these problems, especially the international level in the formal environmental sphere.[5] As they point out, apparently without realizing its importance, 'if there is one key variable accounting for policy change, it is the degree of domestic environmentalist pressure in major industrialized democracies, not the decision-making rules of the relevant international institution' (Keohane, Haas and Levy, 1993: 14).

The most commonly cited examples of regimes which have been successful in addressing international environmental problems are the regime that addresses ozone depletion and the Mediterranean Action Plan.[6] However, analysis of many other regimes shows the limitations of what can be achieved at that level. The chapters on oil pollution and on international fisheries management in the Haas, Keohane and Levy book report that the institutions have been largely ineffective in altering trends in pollution (Mitchell, 1993; Peterson, 1993). This is true even while they have been 'successful' regimes in terms of altering state behaviour. In the case of global warming, while the international institutions have helped raise the issue on to the political agenda (Paterson, 1992), they have not substantially affected state policies on emissions paths. Even if one takes all the scientistic pronouncements on the environmental challenges (such as the Club of Rome's most recent volume, *Beyond the Limits* (Meadows et al., 1992)) with a pinch of salt, it is clear that the response to the environmental crisis to date is inadequate.

The point, then, is that so long as we think about regimes or inter-state relations more generally within frameworks that refuse to question underlying power structures or the ontological givens of IR, such as the state or the domestic/international split, we will be unable even to *think* responses which have any significant impact on environmental problems. Even if the responses can be shown to be effective in reducing individual pollutants, or managing particular resources, then it is highly probable that these achievements will only be offset by deteriorations elsewhere in the overall ecological system, and are limited precisely by their focus only on one pollutant.

UNDERLYING ASSUMPTIONS

The two problems identified above, that conventional thinking about regimes presumes what a regime is for, and that it is inadequate regarding environmental problems, can in turn be associated with three underlying problems in the way we often think about IR: a narrow vision of what IR entails, liberalism, and positivism.

Much of the limitation in how IR scholars tend to think about environmental problems derives from the origins of IR as an academic discipline, trying to produce an IR identity, which, as is generally the case with identity, was constructed in opposition to something, in this case the 'domestic'. The domestic/international dichotomy still largely informs what questions are considered permissible if you wish to call yourself a student of specifically International Relations. Even though it is often accepted that IR as a 'bounded subject matter' may leak through into other areas, there are limits. Thus, for those who have written on global environmental problems, the question 'why have these problems arisen in the first place?' does not usually get asked – this is presumably left to political economists, geographers, or someone else. This question is left to others, as it is supposedly not an 'international' question, even though, if you reverse the lens, and start from an environmental perspective, it is of course of supreme importance. Thus the established academic disciplinary boundaries impede our overall understanding of environmental politics, and are one source of why the analyses of environmental regimes are so limited.

IR writers on the environment have started with IR as the privileged vantage point, presuming its logics.[7] But starting from the other end, the environment, might suggest an entirely different logic to our enquiries. Rather than starting with our familiar assumptions of anarchy, the state-as-actor, etc., which necessarily generate questions such as 'How can nation states cooperate on environmental problems?', we start with other questions, such as 'Who are the important agents of environmental degradation?' This question, of course, often leads us away from state-centric analyses. For example, with regard to global warming, if we started by asking the latter question, the former question would only be one among many secondary questions we would ask. It would figure, since the state is clearly important in affecting energy use (sometimes even owning the industry) and general economic development paths on which energy demand depends.[8] Further, at the inter-state level some form of collective action is clearly necessary, but a myriad of other actors and subsequent interrelated questions would be more important. For example, 'What is people's relationship to energy use?' 'What are the dynamics behind increasing transport demand?' And, when international questions come to the fore, as they necessarily do with a problem such as global warming, 'What are the implications of such huge disparities of CO_2 emissions across the globe?'

This also helps to show how thinking purely in terms of the disciplinary parameters set by conventional IR is inadequate. It privileges the state not only as a unitary actor, but as the focus of our attention, and thereby presumes the answer to the question of who the relevant actors are. For global warming, these are more than simply state-actors or ones which the state can influence in any straightforward fashion. They would include local authorities, energy companies, individuals, environmental pressure groups, corporate decision-makers.[9] But because for conventional IR theory the state is a black box, the question of political struggles within the state's boundaries is usually ignored; where counted, these come in as 'measures of domestic political support' for what the *state* can or should do. This will necessarily lead to inadequate proposals for response, since it ignores many of the relevant agents of change.[10]

A second source of inadequacy is the (neo)liberalism implicit or explicit in much writing on these problems.[11] The hegemony of neo-liberal economic assumptions has of course been massive in environmental economics, and this has coloured the intellectual environment regarding thinking about the politics of global environmental questions. This has occurred to the extent that even many concerned with North/South aspects of environmental problems have regarded the 'convergence' of views on the global political economy between North and South in the 1980s in favour of neo-classical models as a necessary condition for solving environmental questions (see, for example, Lunde, 1991: 27–8).

The logic of this position is that state/economy relations at the domestic level can be presumed to be more or less liberal,[12] so that when states make contracts at the international level, they can be presumed to be able to implement them through the appropriate forms of regulation at the domestic level. No problems are perceived in this dynamic. However, serious analysis of the political economy of problems such as global warming can only serve to destabilize such comforting assumptions.

In particular, the level of lobbying by the oil and coal lobbies, and in Europe also by heavy industry generally, and the clear influence that they have had on climate policies in those countries, shows how unrealistic liberal assumptions about the political economy of global warming are. Of course, the main economic activity associated with global warming is fossil fuel use, ubiquitous in industrial economies. Energy markets and industries in all countries are notoriously illiberal. They are extremely heavily capitalized (destroying notions that producers and consumers make decisions on a comparable basis); they are frequently monopolies or tightly controlled oligopolies; they are often state-owned; they form some of the most intensive lobbies in Western democracies, in some cases to the extent that many observers fail to be able to distinguish where, for example, in the UK the energy lobby stops and the Department of Energy and now the Department of Trade and Industry starts. And of course they largely constitute a set of states (OPEC), some of which – it would be worth appropriating a well-worn phrase about the former USSR – do not have oil industries because they *are* oil industries![13]

It is relatively simple to show that positions adopted by states have been altered greatly by the effects of these industrial lobbies. For example, European heavy industry engaged in what *The Economist* states was their heaviest lobbying of the EC Commission ever (*The Economist*, 19 May 1992: 91) against the EC's proposed community-wide carbon/energy tax.[14] This lobbying was clearly successful in securing significant exemptions for some of heavy industry, especially that engaged in exporting, and in making sure that the tax would not be implemented until similar measures (i.e. ones with equivalent financial costs) were adopted in other industrialized countries. Oil and coal lobbies are also widely held to have been particularly influential in preventing the US following other industrialized countries in setting targets to limit CO_2 emissions. Even after the election of the less environmentally hostile Clinton,[15] the energy tax he proposed, in part to reduce CO_2 emissions, was watered down in Congress, in particular by Senator David Boren, a Southern Democrat highly dependent on energy interests (*Guardian*, 19 February 1993: 22).

The assumption of much mainstream theory is that these factors do not matter, and that we can therefore proceed on the basis that if we can design institutional arrangements through which states come to sign agreements, presumably progressively more stringent, we have done all we can do at the international level to address a problem. This strikes me as both inadequate and politically naïve.

The form of internationalism taken by much of these writings also reflects this liberal background and presumption in favour of the status quo. Since the underlying order is not to be challenged, the form of international cooperation analysed and espoused can be interpreted as one which simply shores up that order. It is reminiscent of Carr's criticism of internationalism: 'pleas for international solidarity and world union come from those dominant nations which may hope to exercise control over a unified world' (1946: 86). This is mirrored in perceptions by many in developing countries about the motives of Northern states in climate and other global environmental negotiations: 'In the South, some individuals also question the motive of those in the North. These individuals believe that the Climate Convention, whatever its stated objectives, represents a clever plan by the north to exercise control over the development plans, strategies and projects of the South' (Hyder, 1992: 327). In other words, the negotiations were interpreted as coming about at a point at which the North realized that it had used up its 'share' of the atmospheric resource (such a conception is common among statements by Southern diplomats and NGOs) but wished to keep up its profligate consumption patterns by restricting growth in the South.

The third source of the inadequacy of much conventional regime theory is in its positivist epistemological position, and in particular in the assumption of social-scientific neutrality. The assumption is that, even if 'value-free' analysis cannot be fully achieved, such an analysis should be attempted. This is also a factor which precludes expanding out the areas of possible enquiry, and criteria to be included for 'successful' regimes, as it limits the ability to bring in normative questions at each point of the investigation. This is the case because of the separation of facts from values in positivist epistemology, which results in a position that, even if values allow you to decide what you wish to analyse (as Keohane, for example, is explicit about (1989: 21)), they must be excluded from the manner in which you go about your analysis. When combined with the narrow focus of much IR mentioned above, this means that, for many analysts, analyses of environmental problems need to 'stick to the point', and concentrate on those environmental problems – concerns about social justice,[16] the legitimacy of the state, etc., are not considered relevant. Fortunately, the emergence of feminist, critical and post-structuralist approaches to IR have begun to loosen the stranglehold which positivism has had on IR for a number of decades.

If one rejects the notions of value-free science, then theorizing and analysis is always for someone. Academic work is always of benefit to some social group or other, and this should be made explicit. The implications of the unavoidability of partiality are particularly acute in relation to global environmental politics, where the disparities in the wealth and power of differing social groups involved in conflicts over those problems, whether considered by class, gender, race or simple geography, are extremely acute. This viewpoint makes it starkly clear that when one is analysing the global warming regime which is currently emerging, it is of extreme importance whether that regime is of benefit primarily to the global oil and coal industries, or to subsistence farmers and women travelling progressively further to collect water in the Sahel.[17]

Clearly, not everyone benefits equally from any particular regime, and this is not something that can simply be resolved through some mechanism derived from game theory such as side-payments. The inequalities go to the heart of how problems get defined in the first place, and to which particular problems get on to the political agenda. Thus during UNCED negotiations, consistent criticism was made that the dominant agenda was that which concerned Northern policy-makers and environmentalists – problems of climate change, ozone depletion, biodiversity, deforestation (but only that in Brazil or Malaysia, not in Canada or the ex-Soviet Union), and so on. Those in developing countries had other problems, such as desertification, soil erosion, water shortages, and so on, but were largely unsuccessful in forcing them to the top of the agenda. Their main success was negative – preventing a global convention on forests (Humphreys, 1993).

The problem is that questions such as 'Who benefits from international environmental institutions?' and 'Why should they be supported?' cannot be presumed to be unproblematic, as they largely are in most writings on environmental regimes, such as the Haas, Keohane and Levy volume. We must actively justify the operation of those institutions on explicitly political principles.

The assumptions underlying many analyses of regimes, particularly environmental ones – the narrow scope of enquiry, liberalism, positivism – are inadequate. First and foremost, they fail to give any guidance about how to go about addressing environmental problems in other than a piecemeal, after-the-fact ameliorative fashion at a purely formalized international level.

A point made succinctly by Peter Doran is worth emphasizing here, that 'they [conventional institutional and regime analysts] are unlikely to consider the possibility that the Earth Summit was no more than the latest chapter in a whole story of denial' (1993: 55). By starting regime analyses from the assumptions of the status quo, many writers make it impossible to envisage solutions to the political questions posed by the severity of environmental problems, and are thus led into practices of denial. Hence the optimism of the Haas, Keohane and Levy volume (1993), or of Peter Haas's *Saving the Mediterranean* (1990), or of Oran Young's *International Cooperation* (1989). As Doran points out, 'this is not an outright denial but one that asserts that things could be worse, one that is to be found in the assurance that actions are already being taken, including the action of announcing and reporting' (1993: 63). This last point is particularly telling. Indeed, in some studies, especially the more legalistic ones such as the mammoth study undertaken for UNCED by Peter Sand and others, the fact that states report on time on measures they have undertaken is regarded not simply as one measure of success among several, but as the primary measure of success of an agreement (Sand et al., 1992).

It is crucial to understand the politics of this denial. It means that responses to global environmental problems can only get progressively more authoritarian, based as they will have to be in technocratic monitoring of emissions, of actions undertaken, and ultimately of people's lives. This tendency is inevitable within a framework that accepts the underlying legitimacy of the status quo, since the only response to global environmental problems in the context of continued global economic growth and inter-state competition is for more and more 'global environmental management', which necessitates such technologies of control and surveillance (Doran, 1993: 60–61).

Underlying the analyses of most writers on the IR of environmental problems is a presumption in favour of the existing economic and political order. Since environmental problems are still regarded as relatively unimportant, compared for example to major economic questions, they are not allowed to question central organizing principles. This is most clearly reflected in the 'problem-solving' type thinking of Keohane, Haas or Oran Young. The point is to construct regimes to address the problems as best as is possible within the confines of the existing set of international political structures. Institutional tinkering is the only appropriate response within that framework. But what happens if that is insufficient? My guess is, that for these writers, assumptions concerning state sovereignty, economic growth, the legitimacy of relatively unfettered 'free' markets, would prevail. Of course, this could simply be a 'nouveau realpolitik', but if underlying ecological contradictions of the present order exist, then this form of thinking, which privileges one reality over another, is even more problematic.

In other words, it may be more appropriate to view environmental problems as arising from what Julian Saurin terms '*the normal and mundane practices of modernity*' (1993: 62).[18] Thus existing power structures, including the states system, capitalism and patriarchy, are unable to deal with them since they are themselves part of the origins of these problems.

GREEN POLITICS AND INTERNATIONAL RELATIONS

Since Green political thought both fundamentally questions these power structures and is rooted in an analysis of the nature of the environmental crisis, it may therefore be useful to conclude with a discussion of that literature, and what it might have to say about international relations and global environmental problems. There is as yet within the academic literature on Green political thought little focus specifically on international relations, despite a recognition of the global claims of Green politics (see for example Dobson, 1990; Eckersley, 1992).

For Dobson, Green political thought revolves around two central themes.[19] The first is the notion of 'limits to growth'; that because of the finitude of the planet, 'continuous and unlimited growth is *prima facie* impossible' (1990: 15). And second, Green politics rejects the anthropocentric assumptions of most Western thought, that human beings should be regarded as the only things we can place value on (Dobson, 1990: 63–72; also Eckersley, 1992: *passim*). It is the former that is most important here, since it leads most directly to arguments which challenge the existing organization of states. Specifically, it is argued by Greens that limits to growth mean that the organization of economic and political practices should be radically decentralized. The source of environmental problems and unsustainable practices is seen as rooted in the sheer scale of modern industrial production, and in the fact that the modern state is too large a political unit to deal effectively with these problems.

This argument concerning decentralization clearly engages some of the concerns outlined above. In particular it enables us to focus on the question of the state; on the ways in which this particular form of political power and organization can or should be challenged and transcended. Within Green political theory, the debate on this question has evolved over time. In response to the emergence of the global environmental crisis in the late 1960s and early 1970s, there was a tendency within Green literature to see the state system as something which needs transcending by moving to larger-scale forms of political organization, echoing earlier Idealist thought in IR which hankered after world government (e.g. Ophuls, 1977; Falk, 1972). There was, however, also a strand which suggested that the relationship between the state and environmental crisis is one where the scale of the state is too large to respond adequately to environmental problems, and forms of political and social organization should be scaled down (e.g. Goldsmith, 1972; Schumacher, 1976).

The tendency within Green thought since then has been to move in favour of the latter argument. The environmental crisis is seen as in part an effect of the scale of modern political organization; the institutions of the state are too remote effectively to respond to environmental problems, as those making state decisions are often not affected by the outcome of those decisions. Significant decentralization is therefore advocated.[20] This, however, is one which involves a decentralization of both political and economic power; linked here to the 'limits to growth' argument in Green thought, the argument is that forms of community which are more 'human-scale' and self-reliant need to be developed.[21]

There are, however, tensions within Green thought on this question. For some, it leads to an ecoanarchist position, whereby the state should be completely dismantled. This is a position common to the social ecology of Murray Bookchin and to the bioregionalism associated with, among others, Kirkpatrick Sale.[22] For others within the Green movement, however, this position is inadequate. Anarchism in particular comes under attack for providing no institutional basis for organizing transfers between rich and poor areas of the world, widely seen as essential to solving global environmental problems,[23] and for being unable to prevent the emergence of 'survivalist' responses to the environmental crisis where some communities practise environmental 'triage' on others.

An alternative within Green thought, as represented for example by Eckersley, as well as by eco-socialists (e.g. Gorz, 1980; Ryle, 1988), is still however highly critical of the centralized form of power in the state. The state is seen by these writers as something which has to be stripped of its capitalist character, decentralized considerably, and significantly democratized to make it more responsive to popular demands regarding environmental problems, but which would then be able to fulfil useful functions in relation to global environmental problems. The importance of this argument is to show how the state, and the interstate cooperation focused on by conventional IR theory, could be a useful part of a response to global environmental problems, but *only under certain conditions.*[24]

The question of strategy comes up again here, however, in how to create these conditions. And it is possibly a weak point in the present state of Green literature, at least as represented by Eckersley. She advocates, for example, 'government intervention ... to break down excessive concentrations of market power' (1992: 178). However, her formulation of this argument is weak, especially considering the arguments above which demonstrated the structural power of capital, for example in the power of energy companies to get the EC's carbon/energy tax proposal scrapped.[25] Green strategy is problematic here precisely because Greens are as critical of state power as they are of the power of large corporations, and reluctant to use the state in this situation.

One way out of this from within the Green literature therefore highlights how strategies which accept and use the state need to be complemented by more direct forms of political action, and by the construction of alternative economic forms. Ted Trainer highlights this, when he suggests that 'The fact that General Motors may have a larger intelligence organisation than Australia will yield it no power when most of us choose to cycle or walk to work' (1985: 279). The Green movement already has a variety of components of such a strategy. Derek Wall highlights several of these and refers to them as a matter of 'how to smash capitalism gently' (1990: 82–9). He includes more radical forms of 'Green consumerism' (such as represented by Trainer above): alternative investment, workers cooperatives and Local Exchange and Trading Schemes (LETS) (on these see Dauncey, 1988).

CONCLUSIONS

This brief survey of Green political thought inevitably fails to do justice to the arguments involved. However, it is possible to see how it might be able to improve both our understandings of global environmental politics, and normative proposals we might make about responses to global environmental problems. Two basic themes of use for IR scholars and practitioners can be highlighted in conclusion. One is that there are specific conditions which need fulfilling before the traditional focus on international cooperation is viable. These conditions, fairly stringent ones, involve a decentralization and democratization of the state, and a disentangling of the state from the power of capital. Second, and following in part from this last point, proposals to respond to global environmental problems need to incorporate strategies whose focus is not the state, but the direct combating of the power of capital (and the state), and the creation of alternative, sustainable economic forms.

NOTES

1. I should state at this point that while the intention is to argue in favour of rethinking IR in the light of the environmental crisis as a whole, global warming provides most of the specific material. This is not meant to imply that this constitutes the whole of the ecological crisis.
2. Even a cursory reading of the literature on international environmental politics would suggest this. It seems to be widely regarded that realism's emphasis on the importance of anarchy as an organizing principle, relative-gains maximizing as a model of state behaviour, and on the distribution of capabilities as the generator of outcomes, provides inadequate accounts of the politics of these problems. In particular, focus on the importance of institutions, in Keohane's sense, has been

prevalent. The literature which illustrates this (even where the debate is not specifically engaged with) is wide. See for a selection Haas (1990); Haas, Keohane and Levy (1993); Young (1989); Porter and Brown (1991); Hurrell and Kingsbury (1992). For an outline of neo-liberal institutionalist theory, see Keohane (1989).

3. I deliberately use these terms interchangeably. While it is rather tangential to the main aim here, it does seem to me that the usage of the two terms has become synonymous. Consider the definition of 'regime' given by Krasner which is now in common use: regimes are 'sets of implicit or explicit principles, norms, rules, and decision-making procedures around which actors' expectations converge in a given area of international relations' (1983: 2). Now compare this with the definition of institutions given in a recent work using this terminology: 'persistent and connected sets of rules and practices that prescribe behavioral roles, constrain activity, and shape expectations' (Keohane, Haas and Levy, 1993: 4–5). While differences between regimes and institutions can obviously be identified (see for example Young (1989)), these are of marginal importance.

4. A 'battle' which appears rather petty given the inadequacy of both concerning the scale of problems faced by contemporary world politics.

5. That is, international level institutions elsewhere in the system, such as the World Bank, may be extremely important, but these are left out of the analyses, presumably because they are not 'environmental' institutions. The World Bank has been often analysed/lambasted with regard to the environment, but primarily by environmental NGOs or Southern activists – which has not greatly penetrated theoretical analysis of environmental problems within Western IR (Caroline Thomas provides a valuable corrective to this, although she remains largely unconcerned with theoretical questions (1992: 78–95)).

6. The literature extolling the virtues and achievements of the Montreal Protocol on Substances which Deplete the Ozone Layer is immense. See for a selection Haas (1990a); Benedick (1991); Thomas (1992, chapter 6); or Parson (1993). On the latter, Peter Haas provides much of the material. See Haas (1989) and (1990).

7. What these logics precisely are depend on the theoretical position within IR which one takes.

8. The focus here is on energy since energy use is the primary human activity responsible for global warming, accounting for approximately 50 per cent of all greenhouse gas emissions. The Intergovernmental Panel on Climate Change (the main scientific review body on climate science) in 1990 gave a figure of 46 per cent (Houghton et al., 1990). However, the estimated proportion accounted for by energy has grown since then, as in the IPCC 1992 Update the contribution of CFCs is reduced following discoveries of ozone depletion-global warming interactions. See Houghton et al. (1992).

9. This is also assuming the status-quo organization of society around private enterprise and the nuclear family. Should such a system begin to change (as most Green political advocates suggest it must to cope with environmental problems), the relevant agents would also change.

10. Of course the state will interact with these agents. But many of their possible means of improving environmental conditions do not depend on the state.

11. I accept that the identification of liberalism here with the free market ideology of the New Right does violence to many writers within the liberal tradition. Many within that tradition have clear ethical positions which would contradict the position outlined here – in IR see for example Shue (1980) and Beitz (1979). However, there is no adequate title for the present hegemonic position on political

economy other than neo-liberal, and it certainly is in common usage, which is why I use it here. I am grateful to John MacMillan for this point.

12. By this I mean that state and the economy are presumed to be discrete entities; that the interaction is relatively small; and that since the state is the arena of authority, markets can be presumed to react without much fuss to political interventions in markets designed to meet policy goals such as emissions reductions – of course, the corollary is that such interventions will be 'reasonable'.

13. For example, Saudi Arabia derives 87 per cent of its foreign exchange from oil exports (IEA, 1992: 148).

14. The Commission announced a proposal on 25 September to tax energy to reduce emissions. The tax would be 50 per cent on the carbon content of a fuel, and 50 per cent on the energy content. It would be set US$3 per barrel of oil equivalent rising to $10 in the year 2000. However, despite the qualifications now contained, it still has to be finally approved by the Council. See Paterson (1993) or Grubb and Hope (1992) for an outline of some of the problems facing the Community in implementing the tax.

15. See Cockburn (1993) for evidence of Clinton's deficiencies on environmental questions, despite promising election pledges.

16. Distributive concerns are of course widespread within international environmental politics. However, the point here is that only very rarely do they go as far as to question the underlying sources of inequality. The analyses focus on how to respond to the environmental problems *within the context* of huge inequalities across the globe; hence the focus on North–South transfers to help developing countries address global environmental problems. This is consistent with Cox's notion of 'problem-solving theory'.

17. Women are held responsible in many countries for collecting basic goods, particularly water and woodfuel (see Sontheimer (1991) for examples of this), both of which are expected in many areas to become more scarce as a result of global warming. The gendered division of labour and patriarchal power which enables men to insulate themselves (more or less effectively) from these impacts constitutes an example of how existing power structures inhibit an effective response to environmental problems.

18. While Saurin focuses on modernity, this observation applies equally to the focus here on existing structures of power.

19. It should be noted that others place the focus elsewhere. Eckersley (1992), for example, focuses purely on the ecocentric ethics of Green Politics, while Goodin (1992), refers to a 'green theory of value' as being at the root of Green positions.

20. For a detailed outline of this argument, see for example Dryzek's *Rational Ecology* (1987).

21. It should be noted that self-reliance and self-sufficiency are seen as distinct in Green thought. Self-reliance, while indicating that in general communities will rely on their own resources, exchange of goods between communities is still envisaged. Self-sufficiency implies no economic exchange between communities. This intended both to mean that regions which are resource poor will not necessarily be starved, and that parochialism is less likely to be produced by the communitarianism in Green thought.

22. The list of Bookchin's publications is huge. His most full statement is in *The Ecology of Freedom* (1982); the simplest introduction is *Remaking Society* (1990). Kirkpatrick Sale's main work on bioregionalism is *Dwellers in the Land: The Bioregional Vision* (1985).

23. On anarchism's deficiencies in this regard, see for example Eckersley (1992: 170–9) or Barry (1994). On the necessity of resources transfers for environmental problems, see for example Grubb (1990: 287) or Flavin (1989: 70–71), and for a critique, see McCully (1991).

24. A third alternative currently emerging within Green thought is a renewed focus on the notion of the commons. In early literature, the commons were seen as the origin of many environmental problems (Hardin, 1968). However, recent literature both within Green thought (*Ecologist*, 1993; Wall, 1994) and in academic literature on common property resources (Berkes, 1989; Ostrom, 1990) has rehabilitated the notion, suggesting it often provides a form of political economy which is the most likely to produce sustainable practices. In political terms it neither involves the libertarianism of anarchism, nor the centralisation and authoritarianism (in the eyes of many Greens) of the State.

25. As represented in this quote, it is also underspecified as to what constitutes 'excessive'. It could arguably be compatible with existing US anti-trust legislation, which most Greens would regard as woefully inadequate.

REFERENCES

Barry, John, 1994, 'Discursive Sustainability: The State (and Citizen) of Green Political Theory', in Patrick Dunleavy and Jeff Stanyer (eds), *Contemporary Political Studies: Proceedings of the Annual Conference*, Belfast, Political Studies Association (UK): 1–12.

Beitz, Charles, 1979, *Political Theory and International Relations*, Princeton, NJ, Princeton University Press.

Benedick, Richard Elliot, 1991, *Ozone Diplomacy: New Directions in Safeguarding the Planet*, Cambridge, MA, Harvard University Press.

Berkes, Fikrit, (ed.), 1989, *Common Property Resources: Ecology and Community-Based Sustainable Development*, London, Belhaven.

Bookchin, Murray, 1982, *The Ecology of Freedom: The Emergence and Dissolution of Hierarchy*, Palo Alto, CA, Cheshire Books.

Bookchin, Murray, 1990, *Remaking Society: Pathways to a Green Future*, Boston, MA, South End Press.

Carr, E.H., 1946, *The Twenty Years' Crisis 1919–1939*, London, Macmillan.

Cockburn, Alexander, 1993, 'Win-win with Bruce Babbitt: The Clinton Administration Meets the Environment', *New Left Review*, 201: 46–59.

Cox, Robert W., 1981, 'Social Forces, States and World Orders: Beyond International Relations Theory', in Robert Keohane, 1986, *Neorealism and its Critics*, New York, Columbia University Press: 204–54.

Dauncey, Guy, 1988, *After the Crash*, London, Green Print.

Dobson, Andrew, 1990, *Green Political Thought*, London, Unwin Hyman.

Doran, Peter, 1993 'The Earth Summit (UNCED): Ecology as Spectacle', *Paradigms: Kent Journal of International Relations*, 7(1): 55–65.

Dryzek, John, 1987, *Rational Ecology: Environment and Political Economy*, Oxford, Blackwell.

Eckersley, Robyn, 1992, *Environmentalism and political theory: Towards an ecocentric approach*, London, UCL Press.

The Ecologist, 1993, *Whose Common Future? Reclaiming the Commons*, London, Earthscan.

Falk, Richard, 1972, *This Endangered Planet: Prospects and Proposals for Human Survival*, New York, Vintage.

Flavin, Christopher, 1989, *Slowing Global Warming: A Worldwide Strategy*, Worldwatch Paper 91, Washington DC, Worldwatch Institute.

Goldsmith, Edward, 1972, *A Blueprint for Survival*, London, Tom Stacey.

Goodin, Robert, 1992, *Green Political Theory*, Cambridge, Polity.

Gorz, André, 1980, *Ecology as Politics*, London, Pluto.

Grubb, Michael, 1990, *Energy Policies and the Greenhouse Effect: Volume One: Policy Appraisal*, London, Royal Institute of International Affairs.

Grubb, Michael and Hope, Chris, 1992, 'EC climate policy: where there's a will ...', *Energy Policy*, November.

Haas, Peter M., 1989, 'Do regimes matter? Epistemic communities and Mediterranean pollution control', *International Organization*, 43(3): 377–403.

Haas, Peter M., 1990, *Saving the Mediterranean: The Politics of International Environmental Cooperation*, New York, Columbia University Press.

Haas, Peter M., 1990a, 'Obtaining International Environmental Protection through Epistemic Consensus', *Millennium*, 19(3): 347–64.

Haas, P.M., Keohane, R.O. and Levy, M.A., 1993, *Institutions for the Earth: Sources of Effective Environmental Protection*, Cambridge, MA, MIT Press.

Habermas, Jürgen, 1968, *Toward A Rational Society*, London, Heinemann.

Hardin, Garrett, 1968, 'The Tragedy of the Commons', *Science*, 162: 1243–8.

Houghton, J.T., Jenkins, G.J. and Ephraums, J.J., 1990, *Climate Change: The IPCC Scientific Assessment*, Cambridge, Cambridge University Press for the Intergovernmental Panel on Climate Change.

Houghton J.T., Callander B.A. and Varney, S.A. (eds), 1992, *Climate Change 1992: The Supplementary Report to the IPCC Scientific Assessment*, Cambridge, Cambridge University Press.

Humphreys, David, 1993, 'The forests Debate of the UNCED Process', *Paradigms: Kent Journal of International Relations*, 7(1): 43–54.

Hurrell, Andrew and Kingsbury, Benedict, 1992, *The international politics of the environment*, Oxford, Oxford University Press.

Hyder, Tariq Osman, 1992, 'Climate Negotiations: The North/South Perspective', in Irving Mintzer (ed.), 1992, *Confronting Climate Change: Risks, Implications and Responses*, Cambridge, Cambridge University Press: 323–36.

IEA, 1992b, *Climate Change Policy Initiatives*, International Energy Agency, Paris.

Keohane, Robert O., 1989, *International Institutions and State Power: Essays in International Relations Theory*, Boulder, CO, Westview Press.

Keohane, Robert, Haas, Peter and Levy, Marc, 1993, 'The Effectiveness of International Environmental Institutions', in Haas, Keohane and Levy, 1993: 3–24.

Krasner, Stephen D., 1983, 'Structural causes and regime consequences: Regimes as intervening variables', in Stephen D. Krasner, 1983, *International Regimes*, Ithaca, NY, Cornell University Press: 1–22.

Lunde, Leiv, 1991, *The North/South Dimension in Global Greenhouse Politics*, paper presented to the European Consortium for Political Research Joint Sessions, Essex University, March.

Marcuse, Herbert, 1964, *One Dimensional Man*, London, Sphere.

McCully, Patrick, 1991, 'The case against climate aid', *The Ecologist*, 21(6): 246–51.

Meadows, Donella, Meadows, Dennis and Randers, Jorgen, 1992, *Beyond the Limits: Global Collapse or a Sustainable Future*, London, Earthscan.

Mitchell, Ronald, 1993, 'Intentional Oil Pollution of the Oceans', in Haas, Keohane and Levy, 1993: 183–248.

Ophuls, William, 1977, *Ecology and the Politics of Scarcity*, San Francisco, Freeman.

Ostrom, Elinor, 1990, *Governing the commons: The evolution of institutions for collective action*, Cambridge, Cambridge University Press.

Parson, Edward A., 1993, 'Protecting the Ozone Layer', in Haas, Keohane and Levy, 1993: 27–74.

Paterson, Matthew, 1992, 'Global Warming', in Thomas, 1992: 155–98.

Paterson, Matthew, 1993, 'The politics of global warming after the Earth Summit', *Environmental Politics*, 2(4): 174–90.

Peterson, M.J., 1993, 'International Fisheries Management', in Haas, Keohane and Levy, 1993: 249–307.

Porter, Gareth and Brown, Janet Welsh, 1991, *Global Environmental Politics*, Boulder, CO, Westview.

Ryle, Martin, 1988, *Ecology and Socialism*, London, Radius.

Sale, Kirkpatrick, 1985, *Dwellers in the Land: The Bioregional Vision*, San Francisco, Sierra Club Books.

Sand, Peter H., 1992, *The Effectiveness of International Environmental Agreements: A Survey of Existing Legal Instruments*, Cambridge, Grotius.

Saurin, Julian, 1993, 'Global Environmental Degradation, Modernity and Environmental Knowledge', *Environmental Politics*, 2(4): 46–64.

Schumacher, E.F., 1976, *Small Is Beautiful*, London, Sphere.

Shue, Henry, 1980, *Basic Rights*, Princeton, NJ, Princeton University Press.

Sontheimer, Sally (ed.), 1991, *Women and the Environment: A Reader, Crisis and Development in the Third World*, London, Earthscan.

Thomas, Caroline, 1992, *The Environment in International Relations*, London, Royal Institute of International Affairs.

Trainer, F.E., 1985, *Abandon Affluence!*, London, Zed Books,.

Wall, Derek, 1990, *Getting There: Steps to a Green Society*, London, Green Print.

Wall, Derek, 1994, 'Towards a Green Political Theory – In Defence of the Commons?' in Patrick Dunleavy and Jeff Stanyer (eds), 1994, *Contemporary Political Studies: Proceedings of the Annual Conference*, Political Studies Association (UK), Belfast: 13–28.

Young, Oran R, 1989, *International Cooperation: Building Regimes for Natural Resources and the Environment*, Ithaca, NY, Cornell University Press.

13
Rethinking International Political Economy

Simon Bromley

INTRODUCTION

[I]nsofar as modern social and political thought is a genuine attempt to understand what occurs and what may occur – insofar as it is not simply a form of persiflage – it has no option but to adopt a general strategy of understanding. And since modern social and political experience occurs in a determinate historical setting, under conditions directly encountered, any general strategy of understanding that is to stand the least chance of grasping it validly must be designed to insert itself, and be *capable* of inserting itself, into this determinate setting with some precision. It must, that is to say, be able to take due account of the highly specific historicity of modern social and political life. In this sense it has no option, however prudent and becoming its avowals of intellectual modesty, but to be a theory of the intelligibility, the susceptibility to explanation, of at least aspects of modern history as such. ... To put the point more forensically, it is only because of its capacity to refer determinately to the world that any modern system of political, social or economic thinking can be anything more than a complex system of tautologies (Dunn, 1990: 18–19).

The renewal of interest in the discipline of International Political Economy (IPE) owes much to its claim to be able to provide a general strategy of understanding appropriate to the modern international system.[1] Indeed, perhaps the greatest attraction of IPE and the strongest case for its cogency are to be located in its two central claims: that it seeks to provide a coherent account of the interaction of 'politics' and 'economics', of 'states' and 'markets', of 'authority' and 'allocation'; and that, by so doing, it can integrate a theory of the 'domestic' and the 'international', the 'local' and the 'global'. Now, were IPE able to meet these criteria, it would indeed offer a coherent basis from which to address questions concerning the historicity of, and the transformations in, the international system as a whole. How we formulate the discipline of IPE is, therefore, a question of some considerable intellectual importance.

In what follows I seek to address this question both critically and constructively. Perhaps somewhat recklessly, I argue that the discipline of IPE, as presently constituted, has failed to deliver on its central claims and, moreover, that it is incapable of doing so. In a more positive light, I then present an alternative prospectus for IPE which might meet these criteria and begin to outline what this would amount to as an agenda for future research. The argument is divided into four parts. In the first, the theoretical basis of IPE is critically examined and found wanting as a specification of the historical structure of the modern international system. The founding categories of IPE, in its many different variants, are seen to be incapable of providing determinate accounts of social structure. The second part shows that the modern definitions of IPE mark a consistent, but arbitrary, narrowing of the promise of earlier formulations of political economy. This restriction of the explanatory compass of IPE derives in large measure from the later emergence of the separate disciplines of economics and political science. The third part seeks to develop the insights of those earlier formulations which predate the emergence of IPE in its contemporary form. It seeks to show that the potential explanatory purchase, and thus the substantive research agenda, of IPE is much deeper and broader than is currently recognized. The concluding part begins to suggest what might be involved in exploring this agenda from the standpoint of Marx's analysis of capitalism as a global system.

THE CONTOURS OF INTERNATIONAL POLITICAL ECONOMY

Political economy is generally understood to involve the examination of the relationship between politics and economics. That much is clear. But as such titles as *Theories of Political Economy* (Caporaso and Levine, 1992) and *What Is Political Economy?* (Staniland, 1985) attest, it is by no means simple to define, with any degree of accuracy, 'political economy'. The difficulties are conventionally presented as of two kinds, relating both to the nature of politics and economics and to the character of the relationship between them. Beyond these problems, there lies a further difficulty in the definition of *international* political economy: what is it, if anything, about the international which demarcates the field of IPE from that of political economy? In much of the literature this question is never posed, save in a limited descriptive form. When it is directly addressed, a realist answer is generally given.

How, then, is the discipline of political economy constituted? In the modern disciplines of political and economic science, politics and economics have been defined either in terms of specific kinds of action, types of agency, or by reference to distinct organizations, or institutions. Thus politics has been defined either as command-based allocation, the collective domain of authority, or as the sites of policy determination and coercive sanctioning, that of the government and the state, respectively. Equally, economics can be regarded either as rational, exchange-oriented conduct, the maximizing use of resources in conditions of scarcity, or in terms of the means by which resources can be most rationally organized and allocated, especially the firm and the market. Most approaches in effect collapse the definition in terms of agency into the organizational or institutional form which typically expresses it: authority is, surely, the province of government and the state, just as exchange and allocation appear to be the business of firms and markets.

Given that 'politics' and 'economics', now understood as alternative modes of organizing agency, form the starting point of the argument, and given also the desire for causal accounts of the relations between these, then the relationship between politics and economics is generally taken to be either one of determination or one of interaction. It is, therefore, easy to see how three schools of political economy can be readily constructed on this basis: first, statist approaches emphasize the determining role of the state over market outcomes; second, liberal theories argue that the decentralized functioning of markets imposes significant constraints over the sphere of government; and third, pluralist or interactionist accounts argue that both statist and liberal schools capture important aspects of reality, but that the specific institutional characteristics of governments and firms are also important.

As noted above, no specific problems are held to arise from transposing these arguments directly into the field of International Political Economy. And if this is done, then we arrive at the familiar distinctions between those perspectives which dominate the academic literature: the state-centred approach of neo-realism and mercantilism; the focus on markets in the liberal school of international economics; and the institutional modelling of complex interdependence and of international regimes by transnationalism.

More recently, however, an alternative route has been taken in the development of both political economy and IPE. Since there is no logical reason to assume that a particular kind of agency is the sole province of a given institutional domain, one can assume 'behaviourial continuity' (Staniland, 1985) of action, of a given kind of agency across different organizations and institutions. In practice, this involves theorizing one institutional realm in terms of action typically assigned to the other. Two further approaches can then be derived, known generally as the 'economics of politics' and the 'politics of economics' (see Longstreth, 1990). On the one hand, rational (or public) choice theorists take assumptions from neo-classical economics, relating to atomistic, exchange-oriented, rational maximizing conduct and apply them to the political sphere. This provides the basis for constructing the micro-foundations of the liberal position. In the international domain, the procedures of rational choice theory have found their most congenial applications in providing the foundations for liberal economics in general, and for the analysis of international regimes in particular. On the other hand, power-centred theorists employ concepts taken from political analysis, and concerned with the collective, interest-based pursuit of power and influence by social forces, in order to analyse both states *and* markets, governments *and* firms. This kind of analysis is held to provide the means to understand the inherently collective processes of politics. Drawing extensively on Lindblom's analysis of *Politics and Markets* (1977), and especially on his account of the 'privileged position of business', as well as on the critical analysis of ideology, this strand is expressed in IPE in the analyses of 'structural power' and in the *soi-disant* neo-Gramscian school.

Theoretically speaking, this more or less defines the range of positions within both the discipline of contemporary political economy in general, and in IPE in particular. (What has generally passed for Marxian analysis in IPE draws on one of these variants for methodological sustenance whilst seeking to employ alternative substantive concepts to the mainstream literature.) It is how the discipline conducts its business, through refinements and applications of the different approaches, and by contestation between them; and it is how political economy and IPE are, for the most part, taught, as is demonstrated by the perspective-oriented focus of nearly all textbooks in the field. Surveying this diversity of competing approaches, many of the most thoughtful exponents of IPE have argued for an eclectic, if consistent, reconciliation of differing perspectives (e.g. Keohane, 1990). Another response is to call for an increase in historical sensitivity, using the term political economy 'to denote any and every attempt to understand just how the workings of a global system of production and exchange has affected, and does and could affect, the historically possible organization of collective human life' (Dunn, 1990: 19). That this latter approach is no more than the course of prudence for Dunn is shown by the failure of any and every attempt to specify a *single* analytical and methodological programme, not because of a series of 'contingent intellectual mishaps' but because of the irreducible causal plurality of the social world.

Now a plea for reconciliation, for refusing to erect explanatory procedures and methodological techniques into unbridgeable barriers in the way of integration, is always to be respected. We are, after all, trying to make sense of the same world. Moreover, Dunn's identification of political economy as a field to be explored historically is a salutary caution against overly abstract theorizing. The problem with these suggestions, however, is that calls for openness and for prudence do not, by themselves, meet Dunn's own injunction concerning the need 'to take due account of the highly specific historicity of modern social and political life': they do not, in short, enable us 'to refer determinately to the world'. Let us explore why this is the case and, more importantly, why it matters.

Robert Keohane's argument for an integration of realism, Marxism and liberalism rests on the claim that Marxism and realism are correct to argue that 'states are constrained by capitalism and by the state system' and on the observation that 'these explanations are incomplete' because 'they fail to pay sufficient attention to the institutions and patterns of interaction created by human beings that help to shape perceptions and expectations, and therefore alter the patterns of behaviour that take place within a given structure' (1990: 171, 175). Leaving aside the rather quaint suggestion that it is only the liberal tradition that recognizes that 'people really do make their own history', Keohane's proposal is strictly a methodological one. It is indeed necessary to study questions of institutional development and agency, and it might be argued that both realism and Marxism have been insufficiently attentive to these dimensions, but to call for a non-deterministic analysis of structural reproduction and transformation does not get us beyond the structural categories of realism and Marxism, it merely refines the scope of our analysis within them.

Turning now to calls for greater historical sensibility, it is perhaps the neo-Gramscian school which has gone furthest in this direction. Stephen Gill's articulation of the neo-Gramscian approach fits Dunn's definition of political economy as a field of historical inquiry seeking to reckon the historicity of the modern international system, and his account begins appropriately enough with some methodological considerations relating to the ontological contingency of the social (Gill, 1993a and 1993b). For while this tradition is concerned to analyse social structures, social reality is not reified into self-reproducing entities but analysed in terms of social forces, seen as combinations of ideas, institutions and material capabilities. In turn, social forces are analysed at the level of production, in relation to state-society complexes, and at the level of the world order. By comparison with Keohane's agenda, this approach certainly facilitates a much more radical interest in the development of the international system as *history*. Indeed its obsession with the ontological contingency of the international system, itself something of a strained overreaction to Kenneth Waltz's (1979) insistence on structural continuity, suggests an empirically open, historical study of differently constituted world orders. It is all the more curious, then, that the neo-Gramscians have singularly failed to develop a *theoretical*, as opposed to a descriptive, specification of the principal structures of the international system. For no amount of discussion of such themes as 'hegemony', 'historic blocs' and 'transnational capital' adds up to a theory of the modern states system or of the world market.

POLITICAL ECONOMY BEFORE 'POLITICS' AND 'ECONOMICS'

These recent articulations of IPE do not in fact depart from the contours of the discipline sketched above. As with the other schools of IPE, they start from the separation of politics and economics, of states and markets. The extent to which this separation is interrogated is empirical and historical. The separation is not posed as a theoretical problem. The historicity of states and markets can thus be recognized and described but it cannot be explained.[2] If analysis starts with this separation, then the reasons for it, the explanation of why ever greater aspects of the material production and reproduction of social life are commodified, and of why the collective organization of rule has increasingly come to be expressed largely through sovereign forms of political power, will always remain opaque. Moreover, if this is so, then the central narratives of what the history of the modern international system has been about, i.e. the progressive expansion of a capitalist world market and a sovereign states system, simply disappear from view.[3] And, then, what kind of explanation of the international system is it which denies itself the possibility of reference to the very processes which account for the ongoing separation and subsequent interaction of states and markets in the first place? Is it really credible that an account of the modern international political economy, of the development of the world market and the states system, is to be gained precisely by abstracting from the concrete processes which are its history?

In order to get a sense of the problems created by this overall disposition of IPE, we need to probe a little further into the meaning of the historical constitution and social reproduction of the separation of politics and economics, of states and markets in early modern Europe. Considered as a historiographical question, this subject is riven by controversy and we cannot hope to adjudicate on this here. By the same token, the interpretation of the social thought of this formative period is hotly contested. Notwithstanding these debates, it is clear that the connected processes of state-building and the spread of capitalist forms of economic production gave rise to a new set of arrangements which the distinctive discourse of 'civil society' sought to theorize in the seventeenth and eighteenth centuries. And whatever the precise timing and location of its arrival, and however uneven the facts of its historical constitution, in marked contrast with the fusion of rule and appropriation in pre-capitalist societies, the birth of 'civil society' registered simultaneously the privatization of production and the depersonalization of state authority.

In this context, Jurgen Habermas's still unsurpassed analysis of the resulting bourgeois public sphere notes that:

> Civil society came into existence as the corollary of a depersonalized state authority. ... The economic activity that had become private had to be oriented toward a commodity market that had expanded under public direction and supervision; the economic conditions under which this activity now took place lay outside the confines of the single household; for the first time they were of general interest. ... Significantly, in eighteenth-century cameralism ... this forerunner of political economy was part of 'police science', that is, of administrative science proper, together with the science of finance on the one hand and with agricultural technology on the other (which was becoming differentiated from traditional economics). This shows how closely connected the private sphere of civil society was to the organs of the public authority (1989: 19–20).

Especially in the eighteenth century, therefore, 'economics' came to refer not to the management of the patriarchal household but to the complex of state practices and regulations which served to constitute the national economy, and 'politics' no longer signified merely relations between the propertied but came to connote the separate institutions of governance and the gamut of their relations with an increasingly individuated 'people'. The discourse of political economy before 'economics', understood as a distinct realm of private property and markets, and before 'politics', understood as the field of power and the state, was precisely an attempt to make sense of these linked historical processes.

Indeed, one might read the history of modern social thought (including what is anachronistically now referred to as economic thought), from its beginnings with the social contract theorists, through the Scottish moralists and the reactionary critique of the French Revolution, to Hegel and Marx and to the founders of mainstream sociology, Durkheim and Weber, as a sustained examination of just what kind of *society* was produced with the inauguration of civil society in the West (see Frisby and Sayer, 1986). It was the formalization of economic thought in the marginalist revolution and the systematization of sociology in the later work of Max Weber which laid the basis for the naturalization of these questions in the twentieth century (Clarke, 1982).

For it was only with the full-fledged transition to industrial capitalism, which generalized capitalist economic forms throughout the national market, and with the consolidation of the liberal form of the separation of political power, based on the constitutional-representative state, that the modern social sciences of economics, politics and sociology could separate out from one another and emerge in their modern form. But, as Habermas pointed out, although 'we have become accustomed to deriving the essence of all capitalism from the competitive capitalism of this specific form' we should not forget that 'this phase lasted only for one blissful moment in the long history of capitalist development' (1989: 78, 79). In fact, the coincidence of developing theoretical formalization and the inauguration of the liberal epoch has had a number of adverse consequences. In the first place, substantively, there has been a pro- nounced tendency to take liberal forms of the market and the state as the norm and to write other histories as departures from this which need to be explained. These explanations, secondly, have been generally fashioned in terms of categories which serve to naturalize those liberal forms, indiscriminately deploy- ing concepts of agency specific to determinate social relations to any context whatsoever. (Rational choice theory is the logical terminus of this process.) Finally, and most importantly, because the liberal form of capitalism has been assumed to be the norm, and because methodologies have been elaborated which take this for granted, the development of a theory of capitalism which could uncover these processes of reification has been, by and large, ignored.

It is important to see that this is not simply a historical question. The separation of politics and economics, and hence the changing forms of the political and the economic, was not just a historical accomplishment, a finished process, which once completed gave rise to states on the one side, and to markets on the other. If the process had been a historical episode, involving a combination of primitive accumulation and state-building, then it would indeed matter little for the analysis of contemporary capitalist societies. However, there are several reasons why this kind of formulation is unhelpful in the case of IPE. To begin with, if our focus is the development of the international system, of the states system and the world market, then the processes of primitive accumulation and state-formation have been continuing features of its develop- ment to date. The geographical expansion of commodity relations and sovereign forms of rule have far from run their course in terms of world history. Equally, even in those societies where the direct producers have been dispossessed, the deepening and widening of commodity relations into new areas within and between societies, together with the accompanying transformations in the ar- ticulation of state power both domestically and internationally, are ongoing processes throughout the capitalist world.

These considerations already begin to suggest a research agenda for IPE far wider than its current concerns. But more importantly, in order to make sense of these processes we need to grasp the fact that these new forms of the political and the economic are not merely historical products, contingently related to capitalism; 'they are the means through which [capitalism] was historically constructed and has ever been regulated' (Corrigan and Sayer, 1985: 205). For this reason, to analyse the evolution of states and markets, historically and theoretically, outside of a more general specification of capitalist development is to take their reproduction for granted and, therefore, to render oneself silent as to the sources of their transformation. In turn, this implies that political economy cannot but be a determinate theory of the nature of modern capitalist society as such, a theory of the active, ongoing constitution of capitalist social forms, which is precisely what it had generally been before the second half of the nineteenth century.

THE PROMISE OF POLITICAL ECONOMY

In sum, then, the contemporary study of IPE represents a drastic narrowing of the promise of political economy. By taking the reproduction of capitalist social forms for granted, IPE has ignored large swathes of the historical creation of the sovereign states system and the world market, as well as their continuing social reproduction. Given this, how can the original promise of political economy be recovered? The problems begin, as we have seen, with the founding definitions of 'economics' and 'politics', since these presuppose, rather than explain, the relations which underpin generalized commodity production and sovereign forms of rule. Put succinctly, the distinction between politics and economics, between states and markets 'is one *internal* to the capitalist mode of production' (Sayer, 1985, original emphasis). If our categories assume this separation, then we both misread the history of capitalist society, as large parts of its reproduction are simply assumed, and falsely apply historically specific categories to non-capitalist societies. To get beyond this starting point, therefore, we must develop an account of the basic relations of this kind of society. In turn, this involves a historical and theoretical specification of the central structures of capitalist society considered as an increasingly global system. We shall argue that this should be accomplished in three stages: by the specification of structural contrasts; through the construction of historical narratives; and by the articulation of theoretical understandings. What follows is intended as no more than some suggestions for an agenda for future research.

On several occasions we have concluded that an account of the reproduction of the separation of the political and the economic *as separate* is called for, given that outside of capitalist societies, such an institutional development does not exist. This suggests that a starting point for a reinvigorated political economy should be the elucidation of the specificity of capitalist forms of social structure by means of comparison. For example, it is clear that feudal, capitalist and state-socialist systems have recognizably distinct patterns of state-economy relations, both internally and externally. Another way of formulating these issues is to note that the form taken by 'economics' and 'politics' under feudalism, capitalism and state socialism differed in systematic ways (see Therborn, 1978).

Internally, feudal states did not claim a monopoly of coercion or of political power (at least until the consolidation of Absolutist forms); they were territorially fragmented, and their relation to the feudal economy was largely extractive. Generalized commodity markets did not exist under feudalism, and market exchange was largely confined to the sphere of luxury goods and the limited amounts of production which were not directly consumed. That is to say, feudal markets were confined to the sphere of circulation. Capitalist states, by contrast, have claimed a monopoly of both coercion and binding authority, have been territorially unified, and have been concerned to secure the general conditions for commodity production and to effect a limited redistribution of the surplus. The market is fully generalized in capitalist economies, as the commodification of labour means that both producers and consumers must service many of their needs through exchange. State socialist polities appear to have claimed a monopoly of coercion and authority, to have been territorially unified, and to have been oriented towards the collective organization of production. Markets played a limited role in state socialist economies, serving to allocate labour to jobs and to distribute final consumption, though even in these cases prices were politically regulated. However, as the pattern of their collapse made clear, it was *party* control that organized these societies. Once party control was breached, a rapid disintegration of state power and of economic organization ensued.

These basic differences of political and economic organization under feudalism, capitalism and state socialism also imply certain basic differences in patterns of external interaction. Feudal relations were largely characterized by disputes over territorial jurisdiction and by questions of legitimate descent. This reflected the fact that rule and command over surplus labour were directly connected, access to political power demanded control over land and peasants and vice versa. Developed capitalist relations have centred on competition over trade shares and access to investment capital, arising from the mobility of capital in the spheres of commerce, production and money. The privatization of command over surplus labour, together with the market mediation of productive activity, mean that territorial rivalry plays an insignificant role. Relations between state socialist societies have usually focused on politico-ideological issues rather than on either economic or territorial disputes. Where power was extended across the border, it operated largely through party cadres overseeing control. A systematic survey of these forms, setting out their similarities and differences, would seem to be a necessary moment of a discipline which aims to identify the distinctive characteristics of the capitalist international system.

If the first task of IPE is the comparison of distinct types of historical society and a specification of the particular forms taken by their political and economic aspects, internally and externally, then the next must be a properly historical account of their development, of how they originated and how they were and are instantiated over time. Moreover, once our optic shifts from structural contrast to historical narrative, it is apparent that all development in the global system has been mixed development (see Halliday, 1993 and Hobsbawm, 1984). The change, conflict, rivalry and violence associated with this was not, and is not, something that is external to the creation of a capitalist world. It ought, therefore, to be centre-stage in the substantive historical narratives of IPE.

In the case of the capitalist world, this would involve elaborating the

development of the world market and the establishment and subsequent consolidation of the nation-state system. Broadly speaking, beyond accounting for
the transition to capitalism and the emergence of the nation state in Europe,
there are at least four processes that require sustained attention here, which
we might summarize under the headings of expansion and invasion, imperialism
and transformation, imitation and development and revolution and opposition:
the European expansion of people, commodities, institutions and capital into
the non-European world; the deliberate refashioning of social relations in the
non-capitalist regions of the world to render them congruent with those of the
capitalist heartlands; the (rare) projects of capitalist development and state-
formation launched by indigenous élites in areas which eluded or escaped direct
European control; and the revolutionary attempts to develop against the system
and to constitute an alternative to it.

If we consider the global spread of capitalist society from its origins in
Europe, then it is clear that this, in turn, set in train a process of uneven
development. The resulting penetration of modern capitalism into backward
formations, together with state-sponsored attempts to compete with the most
advanced metropoles (including the state socialist alternative), gave to subsequent development a combined character. In contrast to the liberal form,
involving the general public character of the state and the private nature of
command over surplus labour, this combined and uneven development of
capitalism on a global scale has often involved somewhat different patterns.
Historically, it has often been the case that the centralization of the location of
rule came before the narrowing of its content by the privatization of rights of
appropriation. In fact, in many cases neither process has been fully accomplished. The centralization of rule may face formidable obstacles in the form
of unyielding local sites of authority, especially when these have an independent
material base. And even where these sites are destroyed or incorporated, the
production and acquisition of the surplus need not take a private, economic
form, in which case the state acts as the dominant appropriator. In both cases,
either pre-capitalist forms or the state (or both) remain directly involved in
organizing the material reproduction of society and the appropriation of sur-
pluses. In these instances liberal forms of polity and economy do not emerge.

On the other hand, even in those regions where capitalism did develop
along liberal lines, subsequent departures from this have been common. The
rise of the interventionist state, whether under democratic or authoritarian
auspices, has attenuated the separation of the economic and the political,
qualifying the private command over surplus labour with public regulation
and undermining the general character of political power with particularistic
policies. In practice, significant institutional departures can occur in societies
whose structure remains capitalist, where production is carried out on the
basis of the private ownership of the means of production, the commodification of labour power and the market exchange of commodities. Pressed beyond
a certain point, however, developments of this kind compromise both the
reproduction of capital and the general authority of the state, thereby pre-
cipitating crises.

But, as we have argued in general above, comparison and history cannot alone define the ambit of IPE, since they do not explain either the systematic differences in the forms of society revealed by comparative and historical analysis or the social reproduction of the separation of the political and the economic under capitalism.[4] Thus the third moment of a new IPE needs to be theoretical, and it needs to be able to show (a) why such systematic differences between societies exist and (b) why the economic and the political are reproduced as separate under capitalism. It is in the exploration of these issues that the core concerns of IPE must surely be located if they are to be even remotely adequate to the historical reality of an increasingly global capitalism.

CAPITALISM AS A GLOBAL SYSTEM

Now, it is of course an open question as to just what kind of determinate specification and theorization of the international system can answer these questions. In my view, historical materialism continues to provide the necessary starting point for developing the agenda sketched above. Let us briefly review what might be involved in such an attempt. Marx placed the analysis of capitalist society at the centre of his work, giving specific attention to the emergence and character of such new social forms as the capitalist market and the sovereign, or purely political, state. Marx's method involved asking what kinds of social relations among people make possible the specific forms of a given kind of society. In answer, he reasoned that the dominance of a particular set of social relations, or social structure, in a given historical society could not be explained by the general characteristics of those relations, properties possessed in different contexts, but must rather involve some aspect of their functioning specific to each case where they are, in fact, dominant. If we could discover what this aspect was, then we could *explain*, rather than merely *describe*, the dominance of the phenomenon concerned. The hypothesis on which Marx fixed was that in each case the specific functioning of dominant social relations concerned their ability to organize the production of society's material infrastructure. As Godelier has put it: 'social relations dominate the overall functioning of a society and organize its long-term reproduction *if – and only if – they function at the same time as relations of production, if they constitute the social armature of that society's material base*' (1986: 208, original emphasis).

Let us emphasize that this is merely a hypothesis, whose validity can only be established empirically and historically. (Other hypotheses can and should be formulated, and can and should be tested against historical materialist arguments in terms of their ability to account for the real history of the modern international system.) It was never intended by Marx to be used as a suprahistorical theory. The crucial difference between this perspective and the paradigms of political economy sketched above, which begin with the separation of the economic and the political, is that it does not begin by privileging capitalist societies and then move on to explain other forms as a deviation. Rather, it applies a common methodology of explanation to all social orders.

Applying this methodology to capitalism, we can make a start in this if we examine more closely the changing forms of the political and the economic consequent upon the emergence of 'civil society'. What, precisely, is involved in the privatization of economic activity and the depersonalization of state authority that Habermas described as the essence of civil society? Contrary to the routine construal of Marx's thought within IPE (and IR more generally), Marx conceived of capitalism not as a type of economy but as a form of *society*, based upon novel forms of social relations and hence of the social itself. Derek Sayer, who has done so much to make plain this theme in Marx's work, notes that:

> These forms of modern sociality include what is, for the first time in human history, conceivable as 'the economy', and its essential counterpart, 'the state'. Both rest on a radical transformation of the character of social relationships and the nature of social power, in brief, from what Marx called relations of personal dependency to relations which are 'impersonal' and mediated by 'things': money, bureaucracy (1991: 2).

According to Marx, the 'abstraction of the political state' from particularistic communal forms of regulation comes into being only with the establishment or constitution of a modern civil society based on bourgeois forms of property. In this *burgerliche Gesellschaft* the social forms of both private and public power involve the ordering of society by relations among the impersonal forms of 'money' and 'law', private property and the bureaucratic state. Jurisdiction, administration and coercion become separated from the personal power of a possessing class and centralized in a universal, public power – the 'purely political' state. Thus the social forms of the 'market' and the 'sovereign' state *both* take on specific characteristics in capitalist societies. And for this reason, the emergence and reproduction of the specific relations of this kind of society is prior to both the constitution and separation of the economic and the political and the domestic and the international. Marx further emphasizes that it is only the generalized separation of the direct producers from the means of production, together with the constitution of these means as 'private property', which enable the bourgeoisie to constitute its class rule through the possession of 'things'; all earlier ruling classes required some form of direct 'political' domination over subordinate classes.

These issues have been well summarized by Simon Clarke:

> The separation of the [capitalist] state from civil society, and the formal and abstract character of state power, is the means by which the bourgeoisie secures its dominion over both civil society and the state. ... The class character of the capitalist state is not a matter of the subordination of the state to the power of a particular class, but is inherent in the very form of capitalist state power. The historical process through which the capitalist state emerged was not, therefore, simply a matter of the transfer of power from one class to another, but more fundamentally represented a change in the form of the state, underlying which was a change in the social relations of production (1988: 128, 130).

And this was not a transformation whose origins and effects can neatly be demarcated as 'domestic' or 'internal'. For '[i]n securing the uniform rule of the national currency and the national legal system these developments simultaneously defined the national sovereignty of the state against all particularistic powers within its boundaries, on the one hand, and against the sovereignty of other nations beyond its boundaries, on the other' (Clarke, 1988: 177).

In sum, the differentiation of both the 'economy' and the 'state', and with them the world market and the system of states, as distinct institutional orders are accounted for by the emergence and consolidation of capitalist relations of production on an increasingly global basis. It is, therefore, both the historical spread and the social reproduction of these new types of social relations which form the organizing theme of Marx's account of capitalism.

Viewed thus, the distinctive feature of capitalist society is the mediation of social power by direct control over things rather than over persons. As compared to non-capitalist societies, power takes the form of a generalized subjection of all individuals to such abstract features as the rule of law, money and bureaucracy. Thus the privatization of the economic refers to the process whereby command over surplus labour is transferred to a form of absolute private property shorn of all communal functions. It is, therefore, simultaneously a privatization of the political, of command over others. At the same time, the economic now becomes public as never before, both in the sense that it is oriented to a generalized market, rather than to the patriarchal household, the lord's domain or the king's estate, and to the extent that the exercise of the power of private property relates to legally defined roles rather than to personal status. The depersonalization of state authority refers both to the separation of rule from local fragmented sites and its constitution as centralized and to the separation of the office of rule and of law from the personal status of office-holders and law-makers. Politics is now constituted in terms of abstract authority and its role takes on a generalized character. Thus both the economic and the political undergo a dual redefinition of form with the arrival of capitalist civil society.

Understood dynamically, however, we must not take literally Marx's claim that the creation of a civil society based on capitalist property relations and the modern state was 'one and the same act'. Historically, this was rarely, if ever, the case. Marx's formulation is better understood as referring to the internal nature of the relation between an abstract public power, on the one hand, and the purely private command over surplus labour, on the other. Put differently, the maintenance of this characteristic separation of politics and economics under capitalist relations of production, both domestically and internationally, depends on their historical reproduction in a more or less *liberal* form.

This is so because the separation of the direct producers from the means of production must itself be actively reproduced through the exclusion of the working class from access to the means of production and subsistence, by compelling workers to labour beyond the necessary labour-time, and through the capitalist's continued control over the product. Equally, in the political sphere, the sovereign form of polity must be actively maintained by the subordination of state activities to the rule of law and money and through the bureaucratic exclusion of the people from the means of administration. Developments in these spheres are internally connected, since the social struggles of those without property in the means of production and administration often imply, both in their content and their form, an end to the division between the economic and the political in their capitalist form.

Thus, as Simon Clarke has again pointed out:

> The separation of the economic and the political is not an objective feature of a structure imposed by the logic of capital, it is an institutional framework which is only imposed on capitalist relations of production through a permanent class struggle, a framework which is accordingly a constant object of class struggle, which is only reproduced and transformed through that struggle (1991: 46).

These general theoretical considerations apply just as much to the reproduction of capitalism as a global system, as a states system and as a world market, as they do internally, and they too can be explored historically. Indeed, what is immediately apparent is the intimate connection between the formation of nationally unified sovereign states and the creation of the national markets of industrial capitalism, on the one hand, and the expansion of the nation-state system and the construction of a truly world market in the international economy, on the other (see Hobsbawm, 1975 and 1979). This is to be expected. For, as we have seen, the emergence and reproduction of capitalist relations of production, and hence the capitalist forms of the economic and the political, gave rise to a type of market that is not directly constrained by politically constituted communities and to a kind of polity which defines its rule in equally exclusive terms internally and externally. Equally, the conjoint consolidation of the nation-state system and the world market meant that capital mobility was not confined within national borders. On the contrary, precisely because of the redefinition of the forms of political and economic power described above, the birth of the national market was *coincident* with the internationalization of capital. Underpinning both was the expanding spread, albeit uneven, of capitalist relations of production. Finally, the fact that the reproduction of capitalist social relations is effected through a states system reinforces the mobility of capital *vis-à-vis* any particular state. Thus the political regulation of material reproduction, and the constitution of state power in forms other than the abstract rule of law and bureaucracy subordinated to money, are rendered doubly problematic: first, by the limits imposed on domestic intervention by the crisis tendencies of capital accumulation; and second, by the operation of capitalist competition upon individual nation states.

CONCLUSIONS

This brief and merely indicative sketch of the outlines of a historical materialist approach to the theorization of global capitalism is not intended to suggest that it is the only research programme capable of delivering on the promise of international political economy. Other frameworks can and should be explored. But it is increasingly clear that the *historical and only contingently reproduced* separation of distinct institutional orders within capitalist societies has never provided a logical basis for distinct *explanatory* frameworks; that the separate theorization of economics and politics constructed on this basis has always entailed a large amount of selective inattention to determinate features of our modern social and political condition; and that an adequate understanding of the modern world has from the *outset* demanded that we either explain it in the round, or not at all. It is, I submit, on this terrain that fruitful debate between historical materialism and other approaches should be conducted.

NOTES

1. Many thanks to Chris Boyle, Paul Cammack, Gregory Elliott, Luis Fernandes, Fred Halliday and Justin Rosenberg for helpful comments on an earlier draft.
2. Thus it is not surprising that Karl Polanyi has come to figure as a resource for IPE, since exactly similar problems beset his work. See Maurice Godelier's (1986, ch.5) excellent critique.
3. In some cases this is taken as a strength. For example Robert Gilpin asserts that 'state and market, whatever their respective origins, have independent existences, have logics of their own, and interact with one another' (1987: 10 n.1). Gilpin, who nonchalantly employed an ahistorical conception of the market across several millennia in an earlier work (1981), buttresses this view by the quite extraordinary assertion that 'capitalism' is 'too ambiguous a label to be used as an analytical category'. The reader must decide whether this is science or ideology.
4. It is at this point that we reach the limits of otherwise valuable historical studies such as Karl Polanyi (1944) and of the kind of comparative analysis developed by Lindblom (1977).

REFERENCES

Caporaso, J. and Levine, D., 1992, *Theories of Political Economy*, Cambridge, Cambridge University Press.
Clarke, S., 1982, *Marx, Marginalism and Modern Sociology*, London, Macmillan.
Clarke, S., 1988, *Keynesianism, Monetarism and the Crisis of the State*, Aldershot, Edward Elgar.
Clarke, S., 1991, 'The State Debate', in Clarke, S. (ed.), *The State Debate*, London, Macmillan.
Corrigan, P. and Sayer, D., 1985, *The Great Arch*, Oxford, Basil Blackwell.
Dunn, J., 1990, 'The Economic Limits to Modern Politics', in Dunn, J. (ed.), *The Economic Limits to Modern Politics*, Cambridge, Cambridge University Press.
Frisby, D. and Sayer, D., 1986, *Society*, London, Ellis Horwood.
Gill, S., 1993a, 'Gramsci and Global Politics', in Gill, S.(ed.), *Gramsci, Historical Materialism and International Relations*, Cambridge, Cambridge University Press.
Gill, S., 1993b, 'Epistemology, Ontology, and the "Italian School"', in Gill, S. (ed.), *Gramsci, Historical Materialism and International Relations*, Cambridge, Cambridge University Press.

Gilpin, R., 1981, *War and Change in World Politics*, Cambridge, Cambridge University Press.

Gilpin, R., 1987, *The Political Economy of International Relations*, Princeton, Princeton University Press.

Godelier, M., 1986, *The Mental and the Material*, London, Verso.

Habermas, J., 1989, *The Structural Transformation of the Public Sphere*, Cambridge, Polity Press.

Halliday, F., 1993, 'Cold War as Inter-Systemic Conflict', in Bowker, M. and Brown, R. (eds), *From Cold War to Collapse*, Cambridge, Cambridge University Press.

Hobsbawm, E., 1975, *The Age of Capital, 1848–1875*, London, Weidenfeld and Nicolson.

Hobsbawm, E., 1979, 'The Development of the World Economy', in *Cambridge Journal of Economics*, 3.

Hobsbawm, E., 1984, 'Marx and History', in *New Left Review*, 143.

Keohane, R., 1990, 'International Liberalism Reconsidered', in Dunn, J. (ed.), *The Economic Limits to Modern Politics*, Cambridge, Cambridge University Press.

Lindblom, C., 1977, *Politics and Markets*, New York, Basic Books.

Longstreth, F., 1990, 'Historical Political Economy and Liberal Democratic Capitalism', in *Economy and Society*, 19(1).

Polanyi, K., 1944, *The Great Transformation*, Boston, MA, Beacon Press.

Sayer, D., 1985, 'The Critique of Politics and Political Economy', in *Sociological Review*, 33.

Sayer, D., 1991, *Capitalism and Modernity*, London, Routledge.

Staniland, M., 1985, *What is Political Economy?*, New Haven, Yale University Press.

Therborn, G., 1978, *What Does The Ruling Class Do When It Rules?*, London, Verso.

Waltz, K., 1979, *Theory of International Politics*, Reading, MA, Addison-Wesley.

14

The end of International Relations? The state and international theory in the age of globalization[1]

Julian Saurin

This chapter, advocating new directions in International Relations, is moved in part by the spirit of Richard Rorty's proposition that 'Interesting philosophy is rarely an examination of the pros and cons of a thesis. Usually it is, implicitly or explicitly, a contest between an entrenched vocabulary which has become a nuisance and a half-formed new vocabulary which vaguely promises great things' (1989: 9). Criticism of the old by the new is, by definition, likely to appear relatively insecure, perhaps even presumptuous. Any debate regarding the direction in which International Relations (IR) should be moving must be informed from the outset by a discussion of the general purposes of IR as a discipline, and this should be considered by placing IR in the context of the other social sciences. As part of this, the historical-ideological status of IR needs to be identified clearly, namely, a project of intellectual nationalism which buttresses nationalism and a system of sovereign states. In these respects IR has been particularly susceptible to the conceit of scholars 'who will have it that "what they know is as old as the world" and which consists in taking a form of thought derived from a particular phase of history (and thus from a particular structure of social relations) and assuming it to be universally valid' (Cox, 1981: 133). The general contention of this chapter is that the conceit of IR has been the obsession with an assumed, imaginary and hence ideological form of social authority, i.e. the sovereign state, derived from the West European and transatlantic experience.[2] This 'assumed state' has been taken as a model and in turn has become the constitutive unit of the international system. The ontological primacy ascribed to the assumed state has effectively foreclosed alternative accounts of global social change and order that derive from the actual historical experiences of people across the world.

My central criticism then, is that the principal unit for explanation in orthodox IR is actually a mythic state, which bears little relationship to actual social history. This contention holds firm not just for 'Third World' states, but for all states. Out of this contention two major arguments are advanced: first, that the global historical record fails to confirm the strength of sovereignty as the irreducible determinant of global social order and the fixity of the assumed state form; and second, that the obsessive state-centrism of IR in particular, and the intellectual nationalism of the social sciences in general, have resulted in a pervasive blindness to fundamental forces of social change. In both cases inattention to the critical processes of globalization has been the major casualty of this theoretical nationalism.

The study of IR hitherto can be narrowly or broadly conceived. On the one hand, the IR orthodoxy delimits the subject of enquiry as the constitution of states and their interrelationships within the states system. On the other hand, IR may be more broadly characterized as seeking to incorporate consideration of economics, environmental change or religious forces or – to fill the tokenistic list – gender, as well as the more usual concerns with diplomatic relations, security and military power associated with the narrow conception of IR. Yet the so-called broader enquiries are entered into only to the extent that they seem to contribute to a greater understanding of the state and the workings of the states system. These newly found externalities 'are ad hoc corrections introduced as needed to save appearances like the epicycles of Ptolemaic astronomy.' Just as Herman Daly and John Cobb (1989: 37) have said of orthodox economics, so in IR such externalities 'do represent a recognition of neglected aspects of concrete experience but in such a way as to minimise restructuring of basic theory.' In both conceptions of IR - in the narrow conception explicitly, and in the broad conception more or less implicitly - the state is regarded as the irreducible locus of power, the ultimate arbiter of social conflict and, hence, the proper and authentic site of enquiry. Trapped by this *idée fixe*, permanently self-referential and chronically insular, International Relations has become normatively and politically irrelevant. It is a basic mistake to believe that explanations of state activity can be found solely through reference to that self-same state activity.

In this chapter, I want to argue that both the narrow and broad conceptions of IR are misguided theoretically and, as a consequence, practically misleading. Rather than regarding IR as a discipline in itself, constituted *sui generis* by the state, and concerned with the generation and manifestation of state power, I want to relocate IR as a part of social theory as a whole. Social theory is concerned with explaining the forms, distribution, articulation and consequences of social power. In the sense that I wish to use the term social theory, then I wish not to presuppose any irreducible or primordial expression of power. This means that I do not make an *a priori* assumption as is customary in IR, that either state or society (meaning 'national' society) are the points of analytical departure and return.

As part of social theory, IR has typically taken a particular spatial unit of analysis – the territorial state – as its analytical point of departure. However, the historical spatial dispersion of social, economic and cultural activity has not been bounded by the territorialist imperative. The debate that requires opening up can be indicated by three principal points. First, territorialism, the mark of the sovereign state, has had an extremely equivocal historical record. That is to say, the historical record of territorial integrity and authority has been much weaker than typically supposed. If this is indeed the case, then it is incumbent upon the student of social change to analyse the reasons for this and to examine the nature and basis of successful challenges to territorialism. Second, the focus on territorialism in orthodox IR has contributed to the ascendancy of a comparative method in which the sub-text of IR is one of the study of the rise and decline of the capacity of different states to enforce and maintain the organizing principle of territorialism and sovereignty. This has typically involved the disaggregation of global development into a parallel series of national narratives of separate and discrete development, which only come together in some contrived domain known as the international. The corollary of this focus is the displacement of analyses of the *global reconfiguration of social authority* which is not territorially based and which, indeed, transcends any spatial division of the world. One could go further, and argue that this global reconfiguration is unavailable to, or *explicable* in terms of, spatial units of analysis (as is assumed by the common division of analysis into local, regional, national, international processes). Third, the comparative method implied in much IR militates against an understanding of globalization. Globalization refers not to a 'comparative territorialism across the world', but to an analysis of the redefining and recomposition of all forms of social authority, including the principles of resource allocation and distribution, as well as principles of identity and representation.

THE FALLACY OF MISPLACED CONCRETENESS: SOVEREIGNTY AND INTERNATIONAL RELATIONS

Speaking of the modern scientific method and its dehumanising consequences, A. N. Whitehead in 1925 wrote 'that its methodological procedure is exclusive and intolerant ... It fixes attention on a definite group of abstractions, [and] neglects everything else' (1925: 200). The act of abstracting led, according to Whitehead, to the committal of the fallacy of misplaced concreteness, defined by him as 'neglecting the degree of abstraction involved when an actual entity is considered merely so far as it exemplifies certain categories of thought' (1929: 11). For IR, this has meant setting up the discipline in such a way as to use an idealized and ahistorical definition of a specific form of social authority – the territorially based and sovereign state – as the mean and measure of 'real' international relations. The intellectual nationalism which underlies state-centrism 'presupposes the image of the nation as a manifest, latent or desired form of collective identity and relates it to the nation state as a co-evolving or anticipated form of political organization' (Arnason, 1990: 209). Across most writing in the social sciences in general, but in IR in particular, 'the unit of analysis is usually merely implicit. It is not specified, and virtually never justified. It thereby becomes a highly questionable a priori assumption' (Wallerstein, 1991: 259). Once one has noted that to qualify as a state the two criteria of sovereignty and territoriality have to be fulfilled, it is difficult if not impossible to say what other characteristics all states share. Are the juridical definitions of statehood sufficiently strong to found a discipline upon?

The privileging of the juridical criterion of sovereignty in International Relations simultaneously involves the subordination or marginalization of

Table 14.1 Number of 'internal' and inter-state wars over the period 1500–1990

	1500–1800	1801–1900	1901–1945	1946–1990	Total
North America	1 : 2	1 : 6	0 : 2	0 : 0	2 : 10
Latin America	0 : 2	30 : 14	9 : 2	21 : 5	60 : 23
Europe	26 : 91	22 : 30	16 : 44	3 : 1	67 : 166
Middle East	0 : 4	5 : 10	3 : 2	9 : 7	17 : 23
South Asia	2 : 15	4 : 15	5 : 3	5 : 8	16 : 41
Far East	5 : 3	10 : 19	22 : 16	20 : 9	57 : 47
Oceania	–	1 : 0	0 : 2	–	1 : 2
Sub-Saharan Africa	–	7 : 19	0 : 6	24 : 6	31 : 31
Other Africa	0 : 2	10 : 20	5 : 9	19 : 2	34 : 33
Total	34 : 119	90 : 13	60 : 86	101 : 38	285 : 376

Note: Figures on the left of each column refer to 'internal' wars, those on the right to inter-state wars.

sociological accounts of the state. It is tempting to be guided by neat legal reductionism implied by the concept of sovereignty rather than the messy ambivalence and complex contingencies of sociological appreciations of labyrinthine and often unknown societies. Thus the prevailing discourse on the state has been one in which attempts are made at accounting for the 'failure' of communities to meet the abstract and juridical criteria of statehood. 'All of us have a number of different dimensions to our social identity', writes David Beetham (1984: 221); 'What the nation-state does is to single out one of these identities, and assign it sole political validity, [and] making it the exclusive basis of political allegiance.' What IR does is to take the *claim* upon that single identity and allegiance and cast it as the irreducible building bloc of world politics and hence, world order. It is precisely the refusal by numerous social groups to accept the claims made by state authorities of sovereignty and the corresponding singular allegiance and identity, combined with the impossibility of the modernist project of ultimate control to contain the myriad of social processes, that subverts the analytical centrality of the state in IR.

A number of key global historical developments need to be noted. There has been an increase in the incidence of the state using instrumental violence against domestic populations, relative to the incidence of war against external enemies. In other words, as inter-state warfare has declined, so internal suppression has increased. Table 14.1 shows the number of 'internal' and inter-state wars by region between 1500 and 1990.[3]

Briefly, over the period of almost five centuries the incidence of internal suppression has increased dramatically, as against the relative decline of inter-state warfare. This trend is only less clearly emphatic, though still noticeable, for Europe and North America. Contrary to the received interpretation that it is inter-state rivalry that fortifies the state and sovereignty and hence the states system, the record particularly since 1945 is that it is as a consequence of the turning in of the apparatuses of state violence that the state has attempted to consolidate itself. Thus, the war-making capacity of states – which has been the staple concern of much IR – has developed in the vast majority of states not for external use, but for internal control. The phrase favoured by historians of the state is that of 'state formation', but which may often be used as a synonym for genocide. The cost of state formation or 'modernization' needs to be measured in terms of systematic massacre of tens, indeed hundreds of millions of people.[4] The suggestion here is that the social consolidation of the state has been permanently frustrated, and continues to be frustrated by the constant challenges to the territorially centred claims of authority implied by sovereignty.

Quite contrary to Krasner's assertion that '[t]here are still no entities other than states that can make final authoritative decisions – the litmus test of organized political life,' (1993: 301) I want to argue that it is precisely the contest over the terms and criteria of decision-making, and, more importantly, the identity and composition of the authority-wielding community, which should be at the heart of our investigation. Krasner's assertion should not be taken as a point of departure as is assumed in orthodox IR, rather, it requires empirical verification. Krasner makes organized political life synonymous with the state. Indeed, his construction of the problem is tautologous: how do we know when there is organized political life? When we can identify a state. What are the criteria by which we would recognize a state? When we can see organized political life. His use of 'political' is typically narrow, treating politics as the stuff which occurs in the arena defined by the state, as opposed to a historical process which has thrown up states as a particular form of political organization amongst many other contending rule-making or authority-wielding organizations. Paraphrasing Bagehot (1953: 157), orthodox IR is informed by the belief that whilst one thinks that one is considering actual international relations in actual circumstances, one is privileging the analysis of fictitious relations in fictitious circumstances. The essentialist view of history and the state which Krasner reveals is one in which core characteristics are attributed to institutions or relationships which results in the assertion that those characteristics have a permanent historical presence. The assumption of intrinsic quality is not just a methodological convenience but expresses an ideological position. Criticizing the common tendency of *a priori* theorization in liberal political (state) theory, Callinicos writes, 'the methods it uses are those of conceptual analysis and a priori reflection on first principles.' An example of a first principle is that, to be a state, a state must be sovereign. 'The underlying assumption is that there is a set of political problems so universal as to be common to every form of society, which political theory can resolve without empirical investigations of the specific features of any particular society. Notoriously, this has led political thinkers again and again to treat the peculiar problem of their own time and place as problems for any society.' (Callinicos, 1984: 125) One may refer to this theoretical conclusion as the 'assumed state' i.e, it is assumed that all states derive from this ideal type.

The 'assumed state' is provided with its greatest anchorage in International

Relations by this concept of sovereignty. Consider Martin Wight's depiction of international relations being constituted by a state system whose 'internal marks, which have become progressively clear ... are first, sovereign states; second, their mutual recognition; third, their accepted hierarchy; fourth, their means of regular communication; fifth, their framework of law; sixth, their means of defending common interests.' (Wight, 1977: 129) Analysis can only flow from these first principles if accepted on the premiss that there is empirically a single and unrivalled public power within the territory to fit into the hierarchy, to engage in communications, etc. In short, sovereignty signifies that there is a power with exclusive jurisdiction internally and independence externally. But as Stankiewitz (1976: 77) remarks, 'Sovereignty makes a logical statement – a statement which depends on its logic and *not on the accuracy with which it describes political conditions*. It is a declaration that if order is to have certain characteristics then an ordering body or sovereign having certain qualities must exist' (emphasis added).

In certain crucial respects most states have not been able to maintain territorial integrity, or not had full control of their territory, or have been riven by civil war (which if halted does not necessarily mean that central authority has been effectively re-established): sovereign in international law they may claim to be, but empirically they are most definitely not sovereign. Table 14.2 indicates the incidence of these crises and in so doing shows that the state, far from being a well established and secure social institution, has been in chronic crisis.

Table 14.2 does not include the post-1989 fragmentation of the Soviet Union or Eastern Europe, but in any case approximately one-third of the world's states are represented in the table. In short, 'Because of the widespread dissatisfaction with the extrapolation of international relations with its state-centrism ... there is', using Zolberg's phrase, 'a necessity to re-examine the ontological mould within which [the state and world society] was formed' (1980/81: 253).

The fallacy of misplaced concreteness has occurred largely because of the strength of the grand narrative which has, more often implicitly than explicitly, guided social scientific research. In this respect it is not enough to look solely at IR, but rather to examine the metahistory of modernization and modernity of which IR is a part. As suggested at the outset, IR and International Theory must be located within the social scientific tradition of modernity. IR provides a central strand in the grand narrative of modernity wherein history is portrayed as sequential, progressive and emancipatory.[6] The project of enlightenment and new social order was, in the shadow of Hobbes and Hegel, to be contained within the territorially defined state, with the state acting as 'history's principal spiritual vehicle' (Soja 1989: 46). The state was posited as both the quintessential expression of modernity – rationally constituted, instrumentally directed, omnipresent and universally competent – and the *sine qua non* of progress. In Richard Norgaard's words, 'Modernity promised control over nature through science, material abundance through superior technology, and effective government through rational social organization ... Modernity ...

Table 14.2 Indications of chronic state crisis of sovereignty and territoriality, 1945–1990.[5]

States chronically unable to exercise full control over all all territory, 1945–1990	Regime not in full control of state territory – end 1990	General civil war 1945–1990	Foreign forces in occupation to sustain regime, 1980–1990
Afghanistan	Afghanistan	Afghanistan	Afghanistan
Angola	Angola	Angola	Angola
Chad	Burundi	Benin	Chad
Colombia	Chad	Chad	Cyprus
El Salvador	Colombia	Central African Rep	El Salvador
Ethiopia	El Salvador	Colombia	Ethiopia
Honduras	Ethiopia	Congo	Grenada
Kampuchea	India	Comoros	Honduras
Mozambique	Indonesia	Cyprus	Kampuchea
Namibia	Iraq	Djibouti	Lebanon
Peru	Kampuchea	Dominica	Namibia
Philippines	Laos	El Salvador	Panama
Sudan	Liberia	Ethiopia	Philippines
Thailand	Mozambique	Gambia	Sri Lanka
	Myanmar	Grenada	Western Sahara
	Namibia	Guatemala	
	Nicaragua	Honduras	
	Pakistan	India	
	Peru	Indonesia	
	Philippines	Iran	
	Rwanda	Iraq	
	Somalia	Kampuchea	
	Sudan	Laos	
	Surinam	Lebanon	
	Lebanon	Malaysia	
	Turkey	Mozambique	
	Western Sahara	Myanmar	
		Nicaragua	
		Nigeria	
		Pakistan	
		Peru	
		Philippines	
		Seychelles	
		South Africa	
		Sri Lanka	
		Surinam	
		Tanzania	
		Turkey	
		Uruguay	
		Uganda	
		Vietnam	

promised to transform the hithertofore slow and precarious course of human progress onto the fast track' (1994: 1). The inadequacies of the method and analysis of modernity lie in being seduced and led by the *promises* of modernity rather than being guided by the actual processes historically characterizing modernity, nor the contradictions and unpredictability generated by modernity.

THE INADEQUACY OF IR: MODERNIST CATEGORIES IN POSTMODERN CONDITIONS

The underlying contention so far is that the state-centrism characteristic of orthodox IR obscures – or more accurately, renders quite invisible – agents and processes which may be fundamental to more adequate explanations of social change and global order. A brief discursive on why this has come to pass is in order.

In a compelling series of essays, Wallerstein[7] has argued that 'It is our metahistory which determines our collection of data (or to put it more strongly, our creation of data). It is our metahistory which channels our formulation of hypotheses which fail to be disproved. It is our grand interpretation of history which renders our smaller interpretations credible' (1991: 60). Meta-history refers to the overarching historical vision, indeed even cosmology, that we have assumed or internalized, and from which all our categories of thought and modes of interpretation of the world derive. Clearly fundamental ontological characterizations arise from these meta-histories, as do associated epistemological certainties. Contesting meta-histories may be likened, in some senses to Kuhnian scientific paradigms in which paradigmatic incommensurability marked out pre-Copernican from Copernican science, or Newtonian science from Einsteinian science. Similarly meta-histories of, say, messianist Christianity, or Mayan world cycles, or French revolutionary modernist nationalism, or Marxist class struggle comprise incommensurable meta-histories characterized by wholly different notions of political community, notions of agency and teleology. Thus, the modernist and statist meta-history is one that portrays the particularist and territorially based political community as the principal bearer of historical progress.

Of course, there is considerable historical evidence to support this narrative. It appears that the state has been especially capable of large-scale social engineering, of establishing a permanent war economy, and of shaping the social division of labour to name just a few areas. The key historical claim emanating from the Enlightenment and infusing the project of modernity was the rational organization of society, whereby following agreement upon a development strategy[8] public authorities could mobilize and shape the future of society. The assumption that instrumental rationality could overcome the resistances of society to state-led 'progress', or ultimately resolve the contradictions thrown up by modernity and modernization, remains axiomatic to our meta-history. Not only did the historical development of the state (at least in north-west Europe) seem to confirm the state's claims to comprehensive competence, the concept of sovereignty – 'the idea that there is a final and absolute authority in the political community' (Hinsley, 1986: 1) – constituted an ideological buttress to that claim.

In the meta-history of modernization the story of the modern world goes something like this: some time in the seventeenth century, some people say in 1648 at the Treaty of Westphalia, the state system came into being. This system was composed of bounded social systems whose political definition was given by sovereign territoriality. Each territorial state was concerned[9] with survival in a fiercely competitive system. Some states were strong and expanded through territorial conquest or otherwise. Other states were weak and conceded to the stronger in an essentially zero-sum contest. One could narrate a story of rise and fall to which we could place the label 'British development' just as one could tell a story known as 'French development'. For each state, so a different tale could be told: this became known as national history. Though the tales varied, '[i]n the analysis of the drama of the modern world there is a very wide consensus on the basic plot ... and the basic cast of characters ... [And] that this play is performed in numerous (but countable) variants - one for each country (or state, or people) ... The primordiality of these units of analysis - the countries - has been mostly unquestioned' (Wallerstein, 1991: 54).

Wallerstein's main claim is that 'by the back door, and unanalyzed, a whole historiography and a whole theory of the modern world crept in as a substratum of history and social science. We live in states. There is a society underlying each state. States have histories and therefore traditions ... They have boundaries inside of which factors are "internal" and outside of which they are "external". They are "logically" independent entities such that for statistical purposes, they can be "compared" (1991: 246). Thus, following Wallerstein, I want to argue that IR has contributed to the pervasive organizing myth in which the fundamental constitution of the world is made up of states, with separate histories, and about which one can speak of two distinct and separate realms of activity, the domestic and the foreign or international.

This organizing myth sustains an intellectual agenda and mode of enquiry across all the social sciences: First, how do we 'account for the varying national itineraries of development'? Deploy the techniques of sociology, macro-economics, comparative politics. Second, 'how did countries cope with the disarray caused by their "modernization"?' Call in the sociologists, anthropologists and the economists. Third, 'and the one by which historical social sciences proved to the policy-makers the utility of answering the other two questions: how does a backward nation catch up?' (Wallerstein, 1991: 54–5). Each social science has fulfilled its part of the intellectual division of labour through adherence to the nationally constituted and territorially based state as the basic and irreducible unit of analysis. The problems of modernization – be they 'political', 'social' or 'economic' - are characterized as essentially sequential, indeed neo-Darwinian in nature. Thus the common hierarchical depiction of 'advanced industrialized', 'developed', 'developing', 'less developed', 'underdeveloped' and even 'undeveloped' is unequivocal in its assumption of an atomized system of states. Wallerstein mockingly answers his own rhetorical question by arguing that, 'Since the answers to questions one and two have been asserted to lie largely in the particular, endogenous history of those primordial entities - the countries - the answer to question number three has essentially been: replicate!' (1991: 54-5)

World development, of which international relations is a part, is then depicted as the aggregation of the progressive logics of all states. Typically one finds a process of sequential accounting or assemblage of building blocks, for example: the combination of individual activities becomes local activities, local activities in turn become national activities, and the aggregation of national activities becomes known as the 'international'. This process of aggregation leads to a comparative analysis between allegedly analogous units. The most common expression of this comparative method is the publication of league tables based on *national* statistics, which in turn are used as the basis of policy-making and policy appraisal.[10] Such comparisons and statistics and policies are only valid if, and only if, the primary and overwhelming logics of development are nationally (i.e. state) organized. The instanciation of criteria of organization, resource transfer and highly differentiated authority patterns invalidates to a large extent such inter-state comparisons. To quote Wallerstein again:

> It is futile to analyse the processes of the societal development of our multiple (national) societies as if they were autonomous, internally evolving structures, when they are and have been in fact primarily structures created by, and taking form in response to world scale processes. It is the world-scale structure and the processes of its development that provide the true subject of our collective enquiry (1991: 77).

Commenting on the principle of self-determination which lay at the heart of President Wilson's post-war dream, Robertson (1992: 19) rightly observes that 'Wilson sought a universal entitlement to particularism.' The establishment of this universal entitlement is normally portrayed as the consolidation, if not finalization, of the state system. This state system, through the fallacy of misplaced concreteness, in turn is transformed into the basis of international order (meaning *world* order). Of course, system integration does not necessarily imply anything about world social integration, and it is the possibility that the two may act in contradiction to each other which allows for the chronic weakness of the former, and its permanent subversion by the latter. The intellectual division of labour characteristic of modernity assigned the explanation of state and inter-state behaviour to IR as if the state and progress were unproblematically constituted. The task of IR has been to tell the story of the relationship between these territorially constituted national histories. Thus the intellectual injunction issued by Martin Wight (1966: 17) that '[b]y international theory is meant a tradition of speculation about relations between states, a tradition imagined as the twin of speculation about the state to which the name political theory is appropriated' still defines the discipline. My sympathy lies, however, with Wallerstein when he demands that '[t]he crucial issue is that [of] defining and explicating the units of analysis – the historical systems – [which then] become [the] central object of the scientific enterprise' (1991: 248). Rather than assume the state to be secure and self-evident – such that the task of IR scholars is reduced to being the chroniclers of the state –

our analysis needs to begin with 'mak[ing] the unit of analysis a subject of debate' (Wallerstein, 1991: 246).

Why, one might reasonably ask, should we not start with the state ? Isn't it to unnecessarily complicate matters to go 'beyond the state'? Surely, if you seek a sociology of the state one should ask a sociologist, or if you want an economic analysis of the state you should question an economist? Why not concede that IR is concerned with the analysis of inter-state relations, and accept our lot in the intellectual division of labour? Indeed, the intellectual border guards are unequivocal regarding the visa requirements. Alan James demands that 'the task of an academic studying the subject with that name [International Relations] is to gather and disseminate knowledge about it. It is not for such a person, least of all one paid for from public funds, to go off on his or her own tack, defining international on some other basis. Close regard must be paid to the relevant practitioner usage' (James, 1993: 269). Fortunately, the patrols are ineffective precisely because the territory is both poorly mapped and, more significantly, because the very activity of cartography – what communities the maps should show, what descriptions of the relationships between different communities should be, and by what authority the maps are drawn – is essentially contested.[11]

The inability to discipline the discipline of IR is significant in at least three respects: first, because the familiar inadequacies of empiricism and positivism apply. The IR orthodoxy, of which James is justly representative, pursues the line that

> Theories should not be changed unless there are pressing reasons to do so. The only pressing reason for changing a theory is disagreement with the fact. Discussion of incompatible facts will therefore lead to progress. Discussion of incompatible hypotheses will not. Hence, it is sound procedure to increase the number of facts. It is not sound procedure to increase the number of factually adequate, but incompatible, alternatives (Feyerabend, 1993: 26).

And, to continue with Paul Feyerabend's eloquent description of traditional enquiry, 'once these improvements have been carried out, the collection of facts for the purposes of tests seem indeed to be the only thing left to the scientists.' The fallaciousness with fact-finding and problem-solving that such a methodology entails arises because, 'Not only is the description of every fact dependent on *some* theory ... but there *also exist facts which cannot be unearthed except with the help of alternatives* to the theory to be tested, and which become unavailable as soon as such alternatives are excluded' (Feyerabend, 1993: 27; emphasis added) Second, as William Connolly (1983: 3) has observed:

> Those who simply use established concepts to get to the facts of political life, actually have the perceptions and modes of conduct available to them in limited and subtle and undetected ways. Such conceptual blinkers impede the work of any student of politics, but they are particularly corrosive of efforts to explore radical perspectives on politics. For to adopt without revision the concepts prevailing in a polity is to accept the terms of discourse loaded in favour of established practices.

Third, it is difficult to see how, if at all, orthodox IR and the social sciences wedded to the modernist project can give an account of the subversion of the modernist project by the forces of modernity themselves.[12]

The primary significance for IR of rejecting the *a priori* privileging of the state lies in not prejudging the origins of change of world order, as well as the constituent units of world order. The recent work of John Ruggie is instructive in this respect, for he identifies the limitations of IR as lying in the attachment to explaining postmodern processes and patterns through distinctly modernist political conceptual language. Thus he writes, 'The long and short of it is, then, that we are not very good as a discipline at studying the possibility of fundamental discontinuity in the international system; that is, at addressing the question of whether the modern system of states may be yielding in some instances to postmodern forms of configuring political space' (Ruggie, 1993: 144). As soon as we allow the possibility that the prime determinants of world order may not be found in the state system, but may be discerned in the mode of production, the rationalization of bureaucracies, the allegiance to God, or the breaching of ecological tolerances, then we need to concede that the *a priori* privileging of the state is unwarranted.

Notwithstanding the promises of the project of enlightenment with the state as the principal instrument of transformation, the historical record has been one of extraordinary failure. For example, according to a recent Human Development Report (UNDP: 1992) the richest fifth of the world receives 82.7 per cent of total world income, whilst the poorest fifth receives a meagre 1.4 per cent of total world income. Allied to the ever-widening income gap between rich and poor are a multitude of nutritional, health and educational inequalities which the state is either unable to offset, or actively contributes to. 'It is,' as Wallerstein (1991: 60) suggests, 'in fact precisely the reality of the ever-increasing historical disparities of development that has called into question the old organizing myths which have not been able to account adequately for these disparities, and which have therefore been pushing world scholarship to the construction of an alternative metahistory.'

Quite apart from the chronic failure in the promises of development which have undermined the legitimacy of the state, and exposed its modernizing pretensions, inadequate attention has been paid to the processes whereby social authority has been reconfigured, nor to the agents which contribute to the dynamic reconfiguration of social authority globally.

GLOBALIZATION AND DE-TERRITORIALIZATION : RECONFIGURING GLOBAL AUTHORITY

Any theory of International Relations which regards the state as an end in itself has failed to contend with a fundamental purpose of social theory, namely that of accounting for social change. The claim developed here is that the state is one amongst a multitude of competing principles for social organization. By 'organizing principle' I mean the criteria and terms by which society is constituted, including the criteria of resource allocation and distribution, the standards of authority, the status and terms of social identity, inclusion and exclusion.

The concept of sovereign statehood is intimately bound up with the control of a clearly demarcated territory. As indicated earlier the ability to enforce the boundaries is central to the security of both the concept and practice of sovereignty. Territorialism is, however, a particular expression of spatial authority: it is neither the only expression of spatial authority as the exclusivist tradition of sovereignty demands, nor is it the final and ultimate expression of spatial authority as the 'end of history' theorists imply. Territorialism is about being able to divide space into territory, and in particular, to ascribe jurisdictional competence to bounded physical areas. Space can also be divided by time, class, property, gender or any other social category. Indeed, these categories are not only social categories, but they are simultaneously spatial categories: they tell us about the social composition of space. The territorial appeal inherent in sovereignty is an attempt to thoroughly subsume contending socio-spatial authority patterns to that of the control of physical space.

That the theorization of globalization has grown out of cultural studies and communication studies is no accident. Culture avoids being located and tied down to any definable physical space. In cultural studies, the primary purpose of investigation is the examination of shifting relationships and identities – of patterns of authority and representation – and not the success or failure of people/societies to fulfil an *a priori* essence. It is precisely the ambivalence of their concerns that inhibits both their categorization, and crucially, their availability for control. Physical barriers to culture and communication are antipathetic. It is not as if the territorial boundaries of the state are given, and within which the historical content – culture – can be poured. 'We do not live inside a void that could be coloured with diverse shades of light,' writes Michel Foucault, 'we live inside a set of relations that delineates sites which are irreducible to one another and absolutely not superimposable on one another' (1986: 23). In other words, the territorial configuration of authority upon which 'statism' rests, is not an irreducible and primordial essence of social relations; rather, it is open to theoretical and historical enquiry to ascertain what configurations of authority obtain most forcefully at any given time. The configurations may be global in spread, and quite impossible to locate physically as originating in any 'country'. From the global factory to the electronically generated hyperspace, it has now become impossible to attach the particularistic label of sovereign territorial identity.

If territorialism is not the irreducible foundation of world order as is claimed here, then, what is? The general response of postmodernism to this question would be twofold: first, nothing is irreducible, there is no Archimedean point to be found and therefore, the second response would be, 'it depends'. It is the claimed absolute contingency of the contemporary condition which unnerves and unsettles the modernist scholar. Certainty, for example, in the progressive direction of history is replaced by ambivalence and doubt. It should not however be taken as paradoxical that modernity – the age of certainty, conviction and direction – should generate ambivalence, doubt and disorientation.[13]

In advocating that globalization should be the central concern of IR, it is vital to outline what is meant by this term, and equally, what this term should not be confused or conflated with. As argued above orthodox IR has concerned itself with the territorially defined authority. In this respect international relations can be seen as the interrelationship between authorities making similar claims. Following on from this, the concept of internationalization refers to the multiplication and intensification of exchanges or relationships between those similarly constituted units. The 'international' and 'internationalization' refer to an attempt to say that social order is a state bounded order, and constitute world order on the basis of statehood, but they are *not* synonymous with world order *per se*. Both the concepts of 'international' and 'internationalization' rest upon particularist claims to exclusive authority. 'Globalization' by contrast, admits of the fact that exclusivity is neither an actuality nor a historical possibility. Removing the error of making internationalization and globalization synonymous is a vital first step in theorizing the distinctiveness of contemporary 'globology' (sociology on a world scale). (Arnason, 1990: 24). Although anything approaching a proper portrayal of globalization studies is not possible here, a few indicative markers are appropriate.[14]

Whilst Robertson's general view is that 'Globalization as a concept refers both to the compression of the world and the intensification of consciousness of the world as a whole', it his specific formulation which demands attention, namely: 'Globalization is ... best understood as indicating the problem of *the form* in terms of which the world becomes "united" ...' (Robertson, 1992: 8 and 51, original emphasis). This formulation does not prejudge the form or unit by which the world becomes united, and indeed allows for the possibility of numerous forms. Thus the constitution of world order here does not assume that the order is composed of states, nor that states are the principal determinants of that order. Furthermore it does not presume that order need be territorially based – an attribute that remains implicit in many reassessments of world order. Ruggie has provocatively and accurately argued that 'There is an extraordinarily impoverished mind-set at work ... one that is able to visualize long-term challenges to the system of state only in terms of entities that are substitutable for the state' (1993: 143).

> We are still left with a common problem or question which unites the old and the new. [T]he crucial question remains as to the basic form or structure in terms of which that shift [in order] has occurred. That form has been imposed upon certain areas of the world is, of course, a crucial issue - but until the matter of form (more elaborately structuration) is adequately thematised our ability to comprehend the dynamics of the world-as-a-whole will be severely limited (Robertson, 1992: 25).

Crucially, the mind-set to which Ruggie refers has been most effectively challenged and undermined by scholars outside IR, principally historical sociologists, cultural theorists, critical geographers, communications theorists, ecological economists and anthropologists. What is evident across a myriad of social processes and conditions is that the strictures of the state are ignored, its authority flouted, and its legitimacy rejected. Furthermore, there are significant social processes which state authorities have been singularly unable either to comprehend or contain. In short, the argument of the globologists is that structuration or the form of order, is categorically not limited to the state and states system. The standard response of IR to apparently new challenges to the state and states system is to describe them as new 'issues' which the state, and hence IR scholars, need to address. This has certainly been the reaction to environment and gender, such that no self-respecting student of IR will fail to refer to these 'issues' in passing. Curiously, though, the vexity of the issue remains until it has been successfully incorporated into the prevailing orthodoxy, whence it will join the other issues on the dusty shelves of the academy. The ideological quality of this programme can be appreciated when one recognizes that the multiple subjects of history – which are the agents of environmental change, gendered relations, poverty, identity, class – become subordinated to the singular historical trajectory of the state. It is here that the concern with globalization and critical theory converge: a new meta-history is being proposed. As Edward Soja (1989: 25) has suggested:

> The development of critical social theory has revolved around the assertion of a mutable history against perspectives and practices that mystify the changeability of the world. The critical historical discourse thus sets itself against abstract and trans-historical universalisation (including notions of general ‘human nature’ which explain everything and nothing at the same time); against naturalism, empiricisms, and positivisms which proclaim the physical determinations of history apart from social origins; against religious and ideological fatalisms which project spiritual determinations and teleologies ... against any and all conceptualisations of the world which freeze the frangibility of time, the possibility of ‘breaking’ and remaking history (1989: 14).

The primary aim of this chapter was to develop a criticism of orthodox IR on the basis that the statism, which is foundational to the contending traditions to international relations, prevents the search for global sociological explanation of global order. What I labelled 'intellectual nationalism', and which is endemic to the social sciences founded on the nineteenth century intellectual division of labour, has historically maintained the illegitimate methodological separation of 'domestic' and 'foreign', 'internal' and 'international'. This separation only permits accounts of change to be measured in terms of the relative rise and fall of ahistorically constituted states. What we can be sure of is that sovereign states have not always existed; and, one day, they will cease to exist. To make this claim, and to account for such a dramatic historical change demands a much broader field of enquiry than IR currently cultivates. Only by rejecting the *a priori* analytical primacy accredited to the state can one begin to approximate a credible explanation of global social change. This then represents only the first, but critical step, in an innovatory as well as emancipatory reconceptualization of 'international relations'. Although intimations of a methodological shift were made in the final part of the chapter, no pretensions have been made regarding the complexity of the specific theorization of globalization. Throughout, however, the clear point has been made that the key innovatory and critical work has occurred, thus far, outside of IR. The mark of good philosophers, as opposed to loyal disciplinarians, is the willingness to engage with the nuisances from outside, to explore the half-formed vocabulary and to solicit progress from the vague promise of great things.

NOTES

1. I would like to thank Dr Jan Aart Scholte, Angus Cameron and Stefanie Lay for a number of useful discussions during the preparation of this chapter. I am of course responsible for the idiosyncrasies which follow.

2. This contention does not in any way imply that the state is an empty shell or devoid of power. It is reminiscent, though not identical with, Benedict Anderson's argument about the real power of imagined communities. See B. Anderson, 1991, *Imagined Communities: reflections on the origins and spread of nationalism* (revised edn), London, Verso.

3. The purpose in indicating the numbers and distribution of wars in Table 14.1 and the state crises where sovereignty and territorial integrity are fractured in Table 14.2 is not to provide a rigid typology since, for example, the internal/inter-state distinction is itself questionable. Rather it is to illustrate the epochal and conjunctural change of states. Table 14.1 is abstracted from R.L. Sivard (ed.), *World military and social expenditures, 1991* (14th edn), World Priorities Inc. Washington DC: 22–5.

4. As well as R.L. Sivard (various editions) see L. Kuper, 1981, *Genocide: its political use in the twentieth century*, Harmondsworth, Pelican, 1981.

5. The table was initially abstracted from M. Kidron and R. Segal, 1987, *New State of the World Atlas* (revised edn), London, Pan. A number of modifications and additions have been made.

6. The tradition of Realism is more ambivalent in terms of its interpretations of history. The cyclical views of history associated with, say, Machiavelli, clearly pre-date modernity and have few adherents in any case. The strong tradition of Realism which asserts an inherently anarchical and conflictual human condition from which emancipation is ultimately impossible, nevertheless assert that the sovereign state embodies the most effective means of containing that anarchy. In this sense, Realism falls within the terms of the modernist project.

7. The resort to Wallerstein's work here should not be seen as uncritical approval of his work or world-systems analysis in general. The turn to Wallerstein is provoked, however, in the words of Robertson, by the stimulus that 'World systems analysis is not a theory about the world. It is a protest against the ways in which social scientific enquiry was structured for all of us at its inception in the middle of the nineteenth century.' R. Robertson 'Mapping the global condition: globalization as the central concept', in Featherstone, 1990: 16.

8. The very idea that one could have a *development strategy* is revolutionary and quintessentially modern.

9. The unspoken assumption of the narrative is that states have personality and are agents.

10. See amongst many others, the work of Giddens on reflexivity, e.g. *The constitution of society*, Cambridge, Polity, 1984 and *The nation-state and violence: Volume two: A contemporary critique of historical materialism*, Cambridge, Polity, 1985. See also Schrijvers, 1993.

11. See the work in critical social geography, most especially Gregory, 1994; Soja, 1989; Sassen, 1991.
12. Reasons of space (what irony) prevent an elaboration of this crucial point, but see for example, Bauman, 1991; Bauman, 1989; Giddens, 1992; Norgaard, 1994; Beck, 1993; Nandy, 1988; Saurin, 1993.
13. See here, especially, Bauman, 1991. For a good review of debates on post-modernism see P. Rosenau, 1992, *Post-modernism and the social sciences: insights, inroads and intrusions*, Princeton, NJ, Princeton University Press.
14. In addition to the literature already cited, I would refer readers to further works by Dickens, Dunning, Giddens, Lefebre, Sassen, Gregory, O'Brien, Scholte and Sklair; full details are given in the references section.

REFERENCES

Anderson, B., 1991, *Imagined Communities: Reflections on the origins and spread of national-ism* (revised edn), London, Verso.

Arnason, J., 1990, 'Nationalism, globalization and modernity', in M. Featherstone (ed.), *Global Culture: Nationalism, Globalisation and Modernity*, London, Sage.

Bagehot, W., 1953, *Economic Studies*, Stanford, CA, Academic Reprints.

Bauman, Z., 1989, *Modernity and the Holocaust*, Cambridge, Polity.

Bauman, Z., 1991, *Modernity and Ambivalence*, Cambridge, Polity.

Beck, U., 1993, *Risk society*, London, Sage.

Beetham, D., 1984, 'The future of the nation-state', in G. McLennan, D. Held & S. Hall (eds), *The Idea of the State*, Oxford, Oxford University Press.

Callinicos, A., 1984, 'Marxism and politics', in A. Leftwich (ed.), *What is Politics?*, Oxford, Blackwell.

Connolly, W., 1983, *The Terms of Political Discourse*, Oxford, Martin Robertson.

Cox, R., 1981,'Social forces, states and world order: beyond international relations theory', *Millennium*, 10(2).

Daly, H. and Cobb, J., 1989, *For the Common Good: Redirecting the Economy Towards Community, the Environment and Sustainable Development*, London, Green Print.

Dickens, P., *Global Shift: The Internationalisation of Economic Activity*, (2nd edn), London, Paul Chapman.

Dunning, J., 1994, *The Globalisation of Business*, London, Routledge.

Featherstone, M. (ed.), 1990, *Global Culture: Nationalism, Globalisation and Modernity*, London, Sage.

Feyerabend, P., 1993 (3rd edn), *Against Method*, London.

Foucault, M., 1986, 'Of other spaces', *Diacritics*, 16.

Hinsley, F., 1986, *Sovereignty* (2nd edn.), Cambridge, Cambridge University Press.

Giddens, A., 1984, *The Constitution of Society*, Cambridge, Polity.

Giddens, A., 1985, *The Nation-state and Violence: Volume two: A Contemporary Critique of Historical Materialism*, Cambridge, Polity.

Giddens, A., 1990, *The Consequences of Modernity*, Cambridge, Polity.

Gregory, D., 1994, *Geographical Imaginations*, Oxford, Blackwell.

Jackson, R. and James, A. (eds), 1993, *States in a Changing World*, Oxford, Oxford University Press.

James, A., 1993, 'System or society?', *Review of International Studies* 19(3).

Kidron, M. and Segal, R., 1987, *New State of the World Atlas* (revised edn), London, Pan.

Krasner, S., 1993, 'Economic interdependence and independent statehood', in R. Jackson and A. James (eds), *States in a Changing World*, Oxford, Oxford University Press.

Lefebvre, H., 1991, *The Production of Space*, Oxford, Blackwell.

Leftwich, A. (ed.), 1984, *What is Politics?*, Oxford, Blackwell.

McLennan, G., Held, D. and Hall, S. (eds), 1984, *The Idea of the State*, Oxford, Oxford University Press.

Nandy, A. (ed.), 1988, *Science, Hegemony and Violence*, Delhi, Oxford University Press.

Norgaard, R., 1994, *Development Betrayed: the end of progress and a coevolutionary revisioning of the future*, London, Routledge.

O'Brien, R., 1992, *Global Financial Integration: The End of Geography?*, London, RIIA/Pinter.

Robertson, R., 1990, 'Mapping the global condition: globalisation as the central concept', in M. Featherstone (ed.), *Global Culture: Nationalism, Globalisation and Modernity*, London, Sage.

Robertson, R., 1992, *Globalisation: Social Theory and Global Culture*, London, Sage.

Rorty, R., 1989, *Contingency, Irony and Solidarity*, Cambridge, Cambridge University Press.

Ruggie, J.G., 1993, 'Territoriality and beyond: problematising modernity in international relations', *International Organisation*, 47(1).

Sassen, S., 1991, *The Global City*, Princeton, NJ, Princeton University Press.

Saurin, J., 1993, 'Global environmental degradation, modernity and environmental knowledge', *Environmental Politics* 2(4).

Scholte. J.A., 1993, *The International Relations of Social Change*, Buckingham, Open University Press.

Schrijvers, J., 1993, *The Violence of Development*, Utrecht/New Delhi, International Books/Kali for Women.

Sivard, R.L. (ed.), 1991, *World Military and Social Expenditures, 1991* (14th edn), Washington DC, World Priorities Inc.

Sklair, L., 1991, *The Sociology of the World System*, Hemel Hempstead, Harvester Wheatsheaf.

Soja, E., 1989, *Postmodern Geographies: the reassertion of space in critical social theory*, London, Verso.

Stankiewitz, W., 1976, *Aspects of Political Theory: Classical concepts in an age of relativism*, London, Collier Macmillan.

Wallerstein, I., 1991, *Unthinking Social Science: The Limits of Nineteenth Century Paradigms*, Cambridge, Polity.

UNDP, 1992, *Human Development Report, 1992*, Oxford, Oxford University Press.

Whitehead, A.N., 1925, *Science and the Modern World*, London, Macmillan.

Whitehead, A.N., 1929, *Process and Reality*, New York, Harper.

Wight, M. 1966, 'Why is there no international relations theory?', in H. Butterfield and M. Wight (eds), *Diplomatic Investigations*, London, George Allen & Unwin.

Wight, M., 1977, *Systems of States*, Leicester, Leicester University Press.

Zolberg, A., 1980/81, 'Origins of the modern world system: a missing link', *World Politics*, 33(2).

Index

Note: Abbreviations are used as in the text
Page numbers in **bold** type refer to **figures**
Page numbers in *italic* type refer to *tables*
Page numbers followed by 'n' refer to notes e.g. 123n